Mathematics
FOR CHILDREN

2nd Edition

JANETTE BOBIS + JOANNE MULLIGAN + TOM LOWRIE

Mathematics
FOR CHILDREN

*Challenging children to think
mathematically*

PEARSON

Prentice
Hall

Copyright © Pearson Education Australia (a division of Pearson Australia Group Pty Ltd) 2004

Pearson Education Australia
Unit 4, Level 2
14 Aquatic Drive
Frenchs Forest NSW 2086

www.pearsoned.com.au

Senior Acquisitions Editor: Nicole Meehan
Project Editor: Rebecca Pomponio
Editorial Coordinator: Jill Gillies
Copy Editor: Valerie Marlborough
Proofreader: Sonnet Editorial
Permissions Coordinator: Liz de Rome
Cover and internal design by Antart
Cover photograph from PhotoLibrary
Typeset by Midland Typesetters, Maryborough, Vic.

Printed in Malaysia, PP

3 4 5 08 07 06 05

Bobis, Janette Maree.
    Mathematics for children : challenging children to think
    mathematically.

    2nd ed.
    Includes index.
    ISBN 1 74103 224 5.

    1. Mathematics—Study and teaching (Primary).
    2. Mathematical ability. 3. Cognition in children. I. Bobis,
    Janette Maree. II. Mulligan, Joanne Therese. III. Lowrie,
    Tom. IV. Title.

    372.7044

An imprint of Pearson Education Australia
(a division of Pearson Australia Group Pty Ltd)

Contents

Preface xiii

Acknowledgements xvi

PART 1 CHILDREN LEARNING MATHEMATICS 1

Chapter 1: Understanding children's understandings of mathematics: insights from research and practice 2

Chapter overview 2

Chapter focus questions 3

Our conceptions of mathematics and numeracy 3

Memories of mathematics 3

What is numeracy? 5

How children learn mathematics 5

Constructivism 7

Three basic tenets of constructivism 7

Reflection on a classroom scenario 8

Constructivism and teacher education 13

Children's informal mathematics—a crucial step towards understanding mathematics 13

Play and learning mathematics 15

Language and learning mathematics 16

Children's understandings of mathematics 17

Snapshots of learning: lesson planning and assessment 18

The teacher's role in understanding children's understandings 25

Summary and implications for classroom practice 26

Action and reflection 26

References 26

Chapter 2: Challenging children to think mathematically: concepts and processes 29

Chapter overview 29

Chapter focus questions 31

Thinking mathematically 31

Investigating 32

Using technology—the Internet as a starting point for an investigation 34

Conjecturing and proposing 'what-if' situations 36

Reflection and application 36

Symbolising 39

What is problem solving? 40

Different types of problems 41

Problem solving and mathematical thinking 43

Representing the problem 44

Knowledge and problem-solving strategies 45

Affective factors 47

Mathematical thinking across a range of problem-solving activities 48

Co-operative tasks 48

Problem posing 49

Reflection on a classroom scenario A 49

Reflection on a classroom scenario B 53

Summary and implications for classroom practice 55

Action and reflection 55

References 55

PART 2 THE GROWTH OF MATHEMATICAL CONCEPTS AND PROCESSES 59

Chapter 3: Using real data to generate mathematical thinking 60

Chapter overview 60

Chapter focus questions 61

Reflection on a classroom scenario 61

Contents

The growth of mathematical understanding 64

Encouraging young children to visualise and organise data 64

Integrating number concepts and processes through children's representations of data 65

Counting, ordering, matching, grouping and partitioning processes 65

Allowing children to experiment with organising and displaying data 65

Questioning the meaning of approximations 66

Describing and comparing the shape of data 66

Understanding differences between continuous and discrete data 66

Classifying and categorising information 66

Collecting and handling data 68

Representing and interpreting data 69

Interpreting and reporting findings 72

Snapshots of learning: lesson planning and assessment 74

Summary and implications for classroom practice 85

Action and reflection 85

References 85

Chapter 4: Finding connections in space: shape, structure, location and transformations 87

Chapter overview 87

Visual thinking processes in space 89

Chapter focus questions 89

Reflection on a classroom scenario 90

The growth of mathematical understanding 93

Snapshots of learning: lesson planning and assessment 95

Shape and structure 96

Transformation and symmetry 101

Location and arrangement 105

Using computers to promote spatial awareness and geometric reasoning 111

Summary and implications for classroom practice 114

Action and reflection 114

References 115

Chapter 5: Constructing early number concepts and relationships 117

Chapter overview 117

Chapter focus questions 119

Reflection on a classroom scenario 119

Research on number learning 121

Using models and materials 122

The growth of mathematical understanding 123

Emergent numerical processes: classifying, matching, ordering, notating 123

Patterning, estimating and subitising 125

Intuitive notions of numbers 125

Base ten strategies and equal grouping 127

Developing mental computation strategies 129

Grouping and partitioning: using interrelationships 130

Arithmetical strategies and procedures 132

Learning Frameworks in Number 135

Assessing key aspects of number 137

Problem-based number learning 137

Snapshots of learning: lesson planning and assessment 143

Summary and implications for classroom practice 151

Action and reflection 152

References 152

Chapter 6: Promoting number sense: beyond computation 155

Chapter overview 155

Chapter focus questions 156

The growth of mathematical understanding: number and sense and computational fluency 157

Developing number sense through approximation and reasonableness of answers 158

Reflection on a classroom scenario 158

Mental, written and calculator-based strategies for solving computations 159

Strategies for effective mental computation and number fact knowledge 160

Moving from non-standard to standard written algorithms 170

Contents

Snapshots of learning: lesson planning and assessment 178

Promoting number sense in the classroom 184

Summary and implications for classroom practice 185

Action and reflection 186

References 186

Chapter 7: Integrating fractions, ratio and proportional reasoning 189

Chapter overview 189

Chapter focus questions 190

Reflection on a classroom scenario 191

The growth of mathematical understanding 192

Developing simple ratio 193

Developing early fraction ideas through data exploration 193

Establishing fair shares 194

Partitioning 194

Developing understanding of decimals 196

Snapshots of learning: lesson planning and assessment 200

Summary and implications for classroom practice 213

Action and reflection 214

References 214

Chapter 8: Using measurement to make links 216

Chapter overview 216

Chapter focus questions 218

Reflection on a classroom scenario 219

The growth of mathematical understanding 221

Snapshots of learning: lesson planning and assessment 222

The concept of time 222

Temperature 225

Linking time and temperature 227

Developing standard units 228

Identifying relationships between measurement concepts and attributes 233

Using relationships—length, perimeter and area 235

Using relationships—an application of volume and capacity 239

Making additional measurement links—science, technology and mathematics 240

Summary and implications for classroom practice 243

Action and reflection 244

References 244

Chapter 9: Exploring chance and probability 245

Chapter overview 245

Chapter focus questions 246

Reflection on a classroom scenario 246

The growth of mathematical understanding 249

Snapshots of learning: lesson planning and assessment 251

Summary and implications for classroom practice 267

Action and reflection 268

References 268

PART 3 FACILITATING MATHEMATICS LEARNING 271

Chapter 10: Linking assessment and instruction 272

Chapter overview 272

Chapter focus questions 273

Reflection on a classroom scenario 273

Where are they now? 274

Gathering the evidence 274

Assessment and evaluation 274

The process of assessment and instruction 275

Outcomes-based education 276

Observation 277

Questioning 277

Worksamples 282

Written tests 282

Portfolios 285

Individual interviews 287

Reporting 289

Reporting to parents and children 289

Reporting to others 290

Where to next? 290

Using developmental frameworks 290

How will they get there? Programming for learning 293

Planning at different levels 293

Summary and implications for classroom practice 298

Action and reflection 298

References 301

Chapter 11: Managing the learning environment 303

Chapter overview 303

Chapter focus questions 304

The learning environment 304

Factors that determine the nature of the learning environment 304

Determining the existing environment 305

Physically constructed learning environments 308

Setting up the learning environment—in the classroom 308

Learning environments—outside the classroom 311

Socially and emotionally constructed learning environments 312

Inquiry-based environments 312

Reflection on a classroom scenario A 313

Reflection on a classroom scenario B 316

Technology-rich learning environments 317

Reflection on a classroom scenario C 317

Instructional strategies for enhancing the learning environment 320

Grouping for instruction 320

The use of games in the mathematics classroom 324

Summary and implications for classroom practice 326

Action and reflection 327

References 328

Index 331

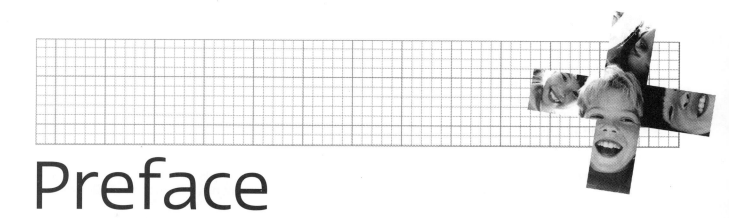

Preface

Mathematics for Children has been written with a focus on challenging children to 'think mathematically'. To achieve this, teachers must not only have a sound grasp of mathematics content, they need to understand how children learn mathematics and develop extensive pedagogical knowledge. A major aim of this book is to support educators developing this understanding and knowledge by encouraging them to reflect on children's learning and their own teaching of mathematics. For this reason, elements of theory, research and practice are blended in each chapter. While essentially written for preservice primary teachers, *Mathematics for Children* is also useful for practising teachers, early childhood educators, researchers, numeracy consultants and learning support staff.

This is the second edition of *Mathematics for Children*. It has been revised in recognition of the many advances in the field of mathematics education since the first edition was published in 1999 and in response to feedback from preservice teachers, teachers and researchers. We are active in preservice and continuing education programs for early childhood and primary teachers, and constantly reflect upon our own research and that of our colleagues to inform our teaching in these areas. Changes to our own knowledge and practices are now reflected in this book.

While the links between assessment and instruction were strongly emphasised in the first edition, we have now gone a step further and combined assessment and planning for instruction into one new chapter—Chapter 10. The result is a more seamless transition between assessment and instruction and affirms the trend in current curriculum documents.

In response to feedback from preservice teachers and practitioners, and recent changes in curriculum documents, a number of chapters have been significantly expanded. Chapter 5 retains the focus on the fundamental aspects of early number learning that encourages the growth of a rich variety of arithmetical strategies, number concepts and relationships. Mental computation and number sense are described as integral to this growth with aspects of developing written computations included. The development of number sense and mental computation also involves skills in estimation, judging the reasonableness of results and using numbers and patterns flexibly. Grouping and partitioning, and seeing interrelationships between these, demonstrates how base ten strategies can be used to assist the child to combine and extend existing grouping and partitioning strategies. Learning frameworks in number are described in terms of developments in some state initiatives such as the 'Count Me In Too Program' in NSW and the 'Early Years Numeracy Program' in Victoria.

Chapter 6 extends the focus on mental computation and the development of arithmetical strategies to include mental and written algorithms. It focuses on the transition from semi-formal computational methods and number relationships, to the development of more formal mathematical processes in the upper primary years.

Chapter 7 acknowledges the renewed importance of developing early fraction concepts with aspects of working with decimals included. It retains the integrated approach to experiences with fractions with updated views from current research and curricula.

The book, as with the first edition, is based on a constructivist approach to learning where children develop their own mathematical ideas, individually and within social contexts. In line with current emphases in curriculum documents regarding assessment practices, we maintain the successful and highly acclaimed emphasis on student worksamples.

The book is divided into three sections:

+ Part 1 focuses on how children learn mathematics and raises issues from theory, research and practice. It provides some exploratory activities designed to challenge the reader's current conceptions of mathematics and highlights the important shift in emphasis towards challenging children to *think mathematically* rather than just teaching them the *content* of mathematics.

+ Part 2 comprises the main part of the book. It focuses on the development of key mathematical concepts and processes within specific content areas such as number, data handling, space, measurement, and chance.

+ Part 3 examines more general aspects of facilitating mathematics learning, such as managing the learning environment, assessment and planning for instruction.

Each chapter contains a 'chapter overview' which introduces the reader to the main focus of each chapter and raises questions about the focus area for the reader to consider.

A 'scenario' from a real-life situation exemplifying some aspect of children's learning of mathematics is featured in each chapter. A purpose of the scenarios is to present a practical situation that highlights the focus of the chapter. Examples are drawn from a range of sources such as samples of children's mathematics, teachers' and researchers' reflective comments, comments from parents, or excerpts from transcripts. Each scenario is discussed in light of current theory and research about mathematics learning and the social context in which learning takes place. Thus, mathematics education theory and research is drawn from educational practice in order to relate issues arising from research to teachers' experiences.

Another major feature of the book is the way it attempts to 'map' the growth of key mathematical concepts and processes from informal to formal thinking. This is accomplished in the 'The growth of mathematical understanding' section of each chapter. This section is based on examples of how individual children develop knowledge and understanding of particular mathematical concepts and processes, based on research and practice. The process of acquiring particular mathematical concepts, processes and strategies are shown via a range of 'snapshots of learning' where individuals may show understanding, where they *reach* for understanding, or where they show misconceptions or difficulties. Children's progressions, or sometimes haphazard growth, that range from informal to formal mathematical ideas are presented. Accompanying many snapshots is a range of questions to assess learning, including anecdotal comments from children about their learning experiences.

While Chapter 10 focuses more closely on issues of assessment and reporting pupil progress, the main mathematical processes and key questions are highlighted in each snapshot. The intention is to assist educators in formulating questions to assess children's mathematics, and to provide clues as to *what to look for* as indicators of mathematical development. It is therefore highly recommended that readers examine these closely when formulating questions and tasks to assess children's learning. The approach advocated here lends itself well to catering for children from a range of abilities and linguistically and culturally diverse backgrounds. Because visual representation and interpretation is an ideal medium for learning generally, students can develop a wealth of language and mathematical skills. Specific reference to mathematical terms and contexts can provide opportunities for students from non-English speaking backgrounds to enhance language skills through integrated experiences. Additional investigations are posed to challenge more able children to extend their skills and understandings across many aspects of the curriculum.

Finally, a distinctive feature of the book is its interactive approach. Reflective questions, activities and ideas for action research are intended to encourage the cyclical process of reflection followed by practice and more reflection. It is our view that for professionals to continue their growth in understanding the mathematics of children they must be reflective practitioners and active researchers.

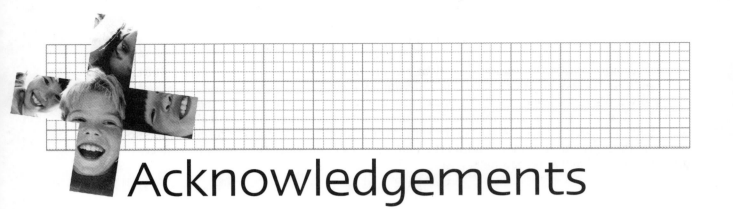

Acknowledgements

The authors wish to acknowledge all who have worked with us and contributed to the writing of this book. In particular, we would like to thank:

+ Anna Dickinson from Harbord Public School, Joanne Peters from Innisfail Primary School, Robyn Lowrie from St Joseph's at Wagga Wagga and their students who assisted with the collection of work samples;

+ Bob Dengate from Charles Sturt University, Bathurst, for his valuable help in selecting Internet sites;

+ colleagues who read and provided valuable feedback on the first edition and drafts of chapters—Tracey Smith, Bruce Wells, Peter Grootenboer, and Jane Watson;

+ colleagues from the Mathematics Education Research Group of Australasia and the Australian Association of Mathematics Teachers, for their support and direction; and

+ our families—for their patience and support.

Janette Bobis, Joanne Mulligan and Tom Lowrie

Children Learning
Mathematics

Chapter 1

Understanding children's understandings of mathematics: insights from research and practice

CHAPTER OVERVIEW

The understanding of *how* children learn mathematics and *what* they know at various stages of their development has been a driving force behind the lifelong work of many educational researchers and practitioners (e.g. Bruner, 1986; Carpenter & Moser, 1984; Cobb, Wood & Yackel, 1990; Dienes, 1960; Hughes, 1986; Skemp, 1989; Steffe, 1990; von Glasersfeld, 1991; Vygotsky, 1978). Their aims have been to describe, understand and document the mathematical development and thinking of children so as to inform research, teaching and curricula decisions of others working in the field. While our understanding of children's mathematical thinking is now quite extensive, it is by no means complete. To become better teachers of mathematics, it is crucial that we continue to broaden our knowledge of how children come to understand mathematical concepts. Such knowledge is necessary to ensure that we can challenge children sufficiently so that further learning will occur. Learning is about building on existing intuitive and informal experiences by providing challenges that require children to reach beyond their current level of understanding.

In the past, instruction in mathematics has been guided not by our knowledge of how children learn best, but by convention and personal experiences of traditional practices. A focus of this chapter, and this book, is the crucial role of *paying attention* to the details of children's mathematical ideas and strategies to gain a better understanding of what it is that *they* understand so as to inform our teaching.

> *Paying attention to the mathematical thinking of students engaged in active mathematical constructions, and trying to make sense of what students are doing and why they are doing it, is prerequisite, we believe, to gaining insight into the nature of the development of children's representations.*
>
> **(Maher & Davis, 1990, p. 89)**

A major premise of this book is that instructional practice which builds on children's initial understandings is more meaningful to children and will therefore foster their mathematical development more effectively. We believe that the development of mathematical understanding is a dynamic process that is not only influenced by contextual factors such as the gender, ethnicity, aboriginality and socioeconomic background of an individual, but also determined by the social interactions occurring throughout this process. For this reason we rely heavily on samples of work from individuals and groups of children from diverse backgrounds and have not provided a separate section dealing with issues such as aboriginality or special education.

This chapter provides insights into children's mathematical understandings by drawing upon significant theories and research of the past, and traces their development to more current interpretations of how children learn mathematics. It also offers practical examples of ways in which you can learn about how children construct their mathematical knowledge through explicit task-based challenges. Hence, a major focus of the chapter is the interactive relationship between theory, research and practice and how combined knowledge of the three can benefit us as teachers.

The challenge that faces us as teachers is how we can use young children's initial ideas about mathematics to facilitate a continual growth in their understandings. We, like other educators and researchers before us, cannot possibly provide all the answers to the questions presented here. However, it is hoped that this book will provide you with a head start to answering them and motivate you to want to explore further the mathematics of children.

Chapter focus questions

This chapter considers important questions that have been addressed in the past by many prominent mathematics educators (e.g. Bruner, 1986; Dienes, 1960; Hughes, 1986; Skemp, 1989) — 'How do children learn mathematics?' and 'What is mathematical understanding?'. We will be returning to these questions shortly. First, it is more important that you take time to think about the following questions:

1. Why is it important for teachers to comprehend children's understandings of mathematics? Why is the informal mathematical knowledge children acquire out of school important?

2. Why does there appear to be a failure to link the informal mathematics that children acquire and the formal mathematics taught at school?

If possible, share your thoughts with your peers.

OUR CONCEPTIONS OF MATHEMATICS AND NUMERACY

Memories of mathematics

Before we can begin to develop an understanding of children's mathematical knowledge, it is essential that we start with an understanding of our *own* experiences of learning mathematics. Our personal theories of how children learn mathematics and conceptions of what mathematics is are usually shaped by our own experiences. Such 'theories' and 'conceptions' may determine ultimately the way we teach mathematics to children.

Think back to your own experiences of learning mathematics at primary school. What teachers do you recall? What do you remember learning about in mathematics? How were you 'taught' mathematics? Can you recall specific episodes? What feelings do you associate with these memories?

Commonly, preservice teachers express the desire to teach differently from the way they were taught. This is due mostly to their lack of understanding of mathematics, even as adults, and the fact that they usually disliked the subject and the way it was taught. Yet our memories of primary and secondary mathematics teachers are often the only models we have on which to base our own practices. This has serious implications for the way mathematics continues to be taught in our schools because teachers often revert to teaching in the manner by which they were taught.

ACTIVITY 1.1

What is mathematics?

When the word 'mathematics' is mentioned, what do you think of? Make a list of words or phrases that you associate with mathematics. They may include feelings, 'topics', or the names of people or events. Alternatively, write a definition for mathematics—not from a dictionary, but your own definition.

Compare your responses with those of another person or a group of your peers. What similarities and differences do you notice? Were most people's responses associated with positive or negative feelings? Why do you think this was the case?

Consider the following definitions of mathematics provided by some primary school children and the definition appearing in a mathematics syllabus:

Maths is just numbers and doing 'sums' like 5 plus 3.
(*Caitlin, aged 7 years*)

Mathematics is addition, that's when you put things together. It's also subtraction, that's when you take things away . . . and division, when you break things up and the opposite of division is multiplication. That's when you make groups of things to see how many altogether.
(*Tom, aged 11 years*)

Mathematics is a reasoning and creative activity employing abstraction and generalisation to identify, describe and apply patterns and relationships. It . . .

■ is a powerful, precise and concise means of communication . . .
■ incorporates the processes of questioning, reflecting, reasoning and proof . . .
■ is a powerful tool for solving familiar and unfamiliar problems . . .
■ is integral to scientific and technological advances . . .

(*Board of Studies*, NSW, 2002, p. 7)

How do your responses compare with those of children and with that appearing in your own state's syllabus?

When presented with a definition of mathematics similar to that appearing in most curriculum documents, preservice teachers are often surprised by the lack of similarity between it and their own conceptions of mathematics. In particular, the notion of mathematics being a 'creative' activity is very foreign to most people. Research confirms that preservice teachers generally perceive mathematics to refer to 'numbers' or 'problems' and to consist of rules and procedures to memorise (Bobis & Cusworth, 1995). Even people who enjoyed mathematics at school report that they often did not understand what they were doing in mathematics, but because they had learnt the rules they considered themselves (and were considered by others) to be 'good' at mathematics. It is generally acknowledged that few people leave school with the realisation that mathematics is supposed to make sense—most leave school with a general feeling of anxiety where mathematics is concerned.

The restricted perception many teachers have of mathematics is usually a direct result of *what* they learnt in mathematics at school and *how* they learnt it. Do your present conceptions of mathematics need challenging? We hope that, by reading, discussing and reflecting on the contents of this book and similar materials, you might be able to clarify your own conceptions and understandings of mathematics and, in so doing, come to a greater understanding of what it is children understand about mathematics.

What is numeracy?

Issues surrounding numeracy, as distinct from mathematics, have come to the fore of education in the past decade. Since its emergence as an issue, the concept of numeracy has evolved, resulting in varying definitions of the term (Australian Association of Mathematics Teachers, 2003). This is partly due to the increasingly complex demands placed on numeracy levels of people in everyday life. As demands on our levels of numeracy change, so will the meaning of what constitutes numeracy. This has serious implications for the educational community as it will affect the degree to which practitioners and policy makers can engage in meaningful discussions of the issues surrounding numeracy.

Numeracy, a priority for all (Department of Education, Training and Youth Affairs, 2000) currently sets the Commonwealth's policy on numeracy in line with its National Literacy and Numeracy Plan, namely that 'every child should be numerate, able to read, write, spell and communicate at an appropriate level' (Australian Association of Mathematics Teachers, 1997, p. 3).

Definitions of numeracy differ widely and it is advisable to check the relevant syllabus for your state or territory. However, it is generally accepted that numeracy:

+ involves the effective use of mathematics to meet the general demands of everyday life;
+ requires a sound understanding of mathematics;
+ is the responsibility of every teacher, parent and community at all levels of education and in all disciplines;
+ varies in its level and kind according to each person's needs and the context in which it is applied.

(Australian Association of Mathematics Teachers, 2003)

HOW CHILDREN LEARN MATHEMATICS

Most theories concerned with the learning of mathematics address the question: How do children learn mathematics? In this section, we shall consider theories of learning constructed by prominent theorists whose research has influenced the direction of current curricula and classroom practice and contributed greatly to our understanding of how children learn mathematics. Included in this discussion will be the crucial role of play and language in the development of mathematical understanding. Throughout the rest of this book, individual chapters will deal with research and theoretical frameworks relating directly to their specific content areas. For example, Chapter 5 will consider research findings and their implications for practice in regard to number. Here, however, we will deal with more general theories of development such as that espoused by Piaget from whom the origins of constructivism, the philosophical perspective underpinning the framework of this book, can be traced.

5

ACTIVITY 1.2

How do children learn mathematics?

With a partner or small group of your peers, discuss and record your views concerning how children learn mathematics.

Share these views with another group of your peers. How do they compare?

When a class of first-year student teachers was asked to complete Activity 1.2, they came up with the following list:

How we think children learn mathematics

+ exploration, experimentation;
+ visual images—visualisation;
+ rote learning of rules and formulae, practice and repetition;
+ explanation, modelling;
+ physically—handling of materials;
+ from their culture, their environment and their interests;
+ discussions with other children and adults.

Each of the elements listed by these student teachers reflects part of their personal theories regarding how children learn mathematics. Table 1.1 shows how a group of students tried to match their personal theories with the developmental frameworks constructed by prominent learning theorists. It is interesting to see that many elements listed by the student teachers are also contained in the more intricate theories of Piaget and Dienes. How do these theories of learning fit with your view of how children learn mathematics?

TABLE 1.1 Learning frameworks of Piaget, Dienes and first-year student teachers

Piaget (1963)	Dienes (1960)	Preservice teachers
Pre-operational: Actions represented through thought and from language, but prelogical.	*Free play:* Manipulates and investigates materials for their own sake.	*Exploration:* Physical handling of materials. Learning about the environment.
	Generalisation: Manipulates materials to build, discover patterns and abstract commonalities.	*Experimentation:* Uses materials to discover things.
Concrete operational: Growing application of logic to physical situations.		
	Representation: Images and pictures are used as representations.	*Visualisation:* Visual images are formed.
		Symbols: Discussion.
Formal operational: Able to argue from abstract hypothesis and to make deductions based solely on logic	*Symbolisation:* Uses language symbols to describe representations.	*Culture:* Use of rules and formulae used in our culture.
	Formalisation: Rules and properties of mathematics are recognised.	

Despite Piaget's undoubted influence on mathematics education, he was in fact more interested in how knowledge in general was constructed rather than in mathematics specifically. Insights into the growth of mathematical thinking came as a result of his more general theory that described the development of thinking and understanding from birth to adulthood. Evidence for his theory was provided by numerous experiments—many of which dealt with mathematical concepts such as number, volume and probability.

Basically, Piaget claimed that cognitive development took place in an invariant sequence of stages. Each stage was characterised by the mode of learning for that period. For example, during the sensorimotor stage, a child's mode of acquiring knowledge is through the senses and direct action on objects. Progression through these stages was said to be purely a biological process. This meant that no amount of teaching could accelerate the rate at which a child could progress through the stages. Alternatively, Bruner (1986) saw learning as a developing process that could be influenced by teaching. Similarly, Vygotsky (1978) criticised Piaget's view of learning and emphasised the influence of learning on development. In particular, he viewed social interaction as a crucial source of opportunities to learn mathematics.

While many aspects of Piaget's theory have been challenged since its conception, his central message about the way children learn has changed our very conception of how children learn mathematics. In short, Piaget emphasised the active role of the learners in the construction of their own knowledge. The role of the teacher was no longer seen to be the transmitter of knowledge and the role of the learner was no longer simply to practise that which had been transmitted.

This central message has not only become the major tenet of constructivism, the philosophical position of many prominent mathematics researchers and educators of today (e.g. Cobb, 1994; Jaworski, 1998; Steffe, 1990; von Glasersfeld, 1991; 1995; Wood, 2002), but also underpins major recommendations for teaching in curriculum documents from around the world (Australian Education Council [AEC], 1991; National Council of Teachers of Mathematics, 2000).

CONSTRUCTIVISM

Three basic tenets of constructivism

While there are some differences in current constructivist views, they generally agree on the first major tenet of constructivism, which is:

> *Knowledge is not passively received, but actively constructed by the learner.*

Many student teachers when introduced to this statement focus on the word 'actively' and take it to mean simply that children learn by 'physically manipulating materials'. Teachers who use constructivist principles will undoubtedly provide many experiences that require the manipulation of materials—this is perhaps an implication of the statement for teaching methods. However, as advocated by Piaget, the emphasis is intended to fall on the term 'constructed'. By 'constructed' we mean that students use their prior knowledge to construct new meaning. According to Piaget (1963), children filter and interpret new information in terms of what they already understand. Mathematics learnt in this manner, then, should make sense.

A second major tenet of constructivism draws its influence from the work of Dienes (1960). He emphasised the development of abstract concepts and generalisations derived from students' *reflections* upon existing knowledge:

> *Students can construct new knowledge through reflection upon their physical and mental actions.*

A third major tenet derives its origins from the work of sociocultural theorists such as Vygotsky (1978) and their emphasis on the role played by social interaction in the learning process (see, for example, the work of Renshaw and Brown, 1997):

Learning is a social process.

This statement suggests that children learn through interaction with others. This view is in direct contrast to Piaget's beliefs about learning and cognitive development, but is the view held by many proponents of social constructivism today (Cobb, Wood & Yackel, 1990; Jaworski, 1998). For example, Cobb, Wood and Yackel (1990) believe that learning is both an *interactive* and *constructive* activity. Opportunities for children to construct mathematical knowledge arise through interaction with other children and with adults. Knowledge constructed in this way, according to Cobb, Wood and Yackel (1990, p. 137), is then constrained by 'an obligation to develop interpretations that fit with those' understood by the rest of society, that is, conventional knowledge. The practical implications of this statement are for teachers to encourage classroom discussion and provide opportunities for the sharing of ideas, explanations and opinions so that some common understanding might be reached by all involved.

More recently, there has been an increasing emphasis on the sociocultural aspects of mathematics education and their impact on school performance (Lerman, 2001; Zevenbergen, 2001). This has arisen from concerns of equity in education, particularly for under-represented and underachieving sections of the school population. From a sociocultural perspective, the classroom is viewed as a social context comprising individuals from different cultural and social backgrounds, with varying beliefs and expectations of education. The implications of these concerns for teachers lie in the inherent culture of the mathematics classroom and how this affects students from varying backgrounds as learners of mathematics.

ACTIVITY 1.3

Comparing principles of learning

1. How do the three tenets of constructivism fit with your personal view of how children learn mathematics?

2. Refer to *A national statement on mathematics for Australian schools* (Australian Education Council, 1991, pp. 16–17) or your state's syllabus, and locate statements that detail the underlying philosophical position regarding how children learn mathematics.

3. How do these statements compare with the three basic tenets of constructivism described above?

REFLECTION ON A CLASSROOM SCENARIO

Developing an understanding of scale 1

Children in Year 4 were about to start a mathematics and science and technology unit of work on temperature. Unaware of the children's previous experiences with temperature and its measurement, the teacher used the first session to gain information about the children's prior knowledge. After referring to her mathematics syllabus she searched the school's resource room for some unscaled thermometers. Unfortunately, the only thermometers available were marked in Celsius, made of glass and filled with mercury. The decision was made not to use these as they were considered inappropriate for the task and too dangerous for use with young children. The teacher decided that she could still achieve the desired outcome even without real thermometers.

She improvised by drawing an unscaled thermometer in the middle of a large sheet of paper and started her first lesson on temperature by asking the class to tell her everything they could about the strange object she had drawn. It was obvious to the children that it was a thermometer. They knew that a reading from the bottom of the thermometer would indicate cooler temperatures than a reading from the top half of the thermometer. However, they seemed to have only limited knowledge relating to the everyday use of thermometers, namely that they are used to measure 'our temperatures when we are sick' and 'the weather'. The use of numbers to indicate degrees of temperature was mentioned by a few children but they were unsure of what numbers should be used. The teacher suggested that they make up their own scales and asked for a few ideas to start everyone thinking. The first suggestions included the use of colours and words to indicate degrees of heat. Before specific examples could be given in very much detail, the teacher suggested that those who had some ideas could start work on their own scales and those who would like more help could stay on the floor and talk with her. Two boys stayed behind to clarify their ideas with each other, but the rest of the class dispersed to various points in the room and a nearby corridor. Most worked with a partner collaboratively, but a few groups of three were formed and a couple of children worked with a friend but produced individual scales. Figures 1.1, 1.2 and 1.3 are examples of the scales produced and Figure 1.4 is an example of what one child wrote about her temperature scale after she had completed it.

After the children had completed their informal scales, a sharing time was provided. The children sat in small groups on the floor or at their desks and they took it in turns to

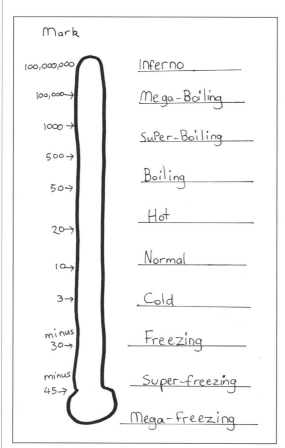

Figure 1.1 Mark used numbers and words to create his informal temperature scale

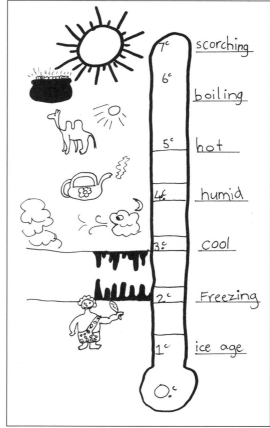

Figure 1.2 Wade combined numbers, words and pictures to create his temperature scale

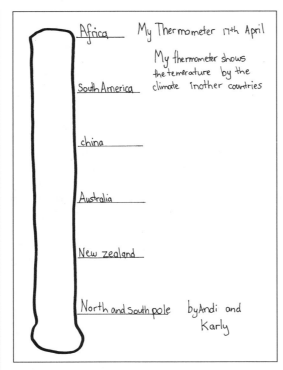

Africa _____

My Thermometer 17th April

My thermometer shows
the temerature by the
climate inother countries

South America _____

china _____

Australia _____

New zealand _____

North and South pole   by Andi and
                              Karly

Figure 1.3 Andi and Karly consulted an atlas and used the names of countries to show variation of temperature on their scale

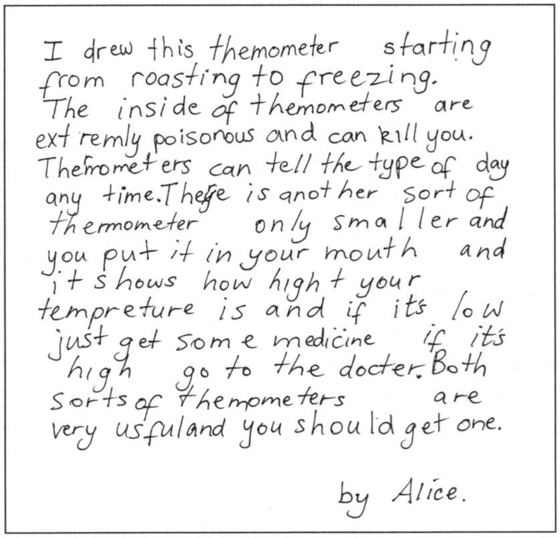

I drew this themometer starting from roasting to freezing. The inside of themometers are extremly poisonous and can kill you. Theromet ers can tell the type of day any time. There is another sort of themometer only smaller and you put it in your mouth and it shows how hight your tempreture is and if its low just get some medicine if its high go to the docter. Both Sorts of themometers are very usful and you should get one.

by Alice.

Figure 1.4 Alice's understanding of thermometers and temperature are revealed through her written comments about the activity

talk about their scales. At the end of the sharing time, the teacher asked each group if they could identify the similarities and differences between the scales they had just seen. A couple of them noted that children had used similar words, colours and pictures to represent variations in temperature, but that those who used numbers had huge differences in what they chose (compare the numerical scales used in Figures 1.1 and 1.2, for example). The teacher questioned the children further on this point and asked them to think of problems that might arise in real life if each person used his or her own scale to communicate temperature. Karly then suggested that, while it was fun to make up their own scales, there was a need to have just *one* scale that everyone knew about. The whole class agreed with her point.

Reflecting on the outcomes of this experience, the teacher made several comments:

I felt that this experience was a great lead-in to the unit of work on temperature. I learnt that the children had a lot of informal knowledge about temperature, but very little formal understanding of degrees. However, all but one child made their informal calibrations equal distance apart, roughly. This is good to know, as it indicates that they have some understanding of how scales of this type operate. The activity was open enough so that my weaker children could work at their own levels—most of these children used colours or pictures to represent their scale. My little group of non-English-speaking background children used Chinese words and we all had fun helping them to guess what an equivalent word in English might be. I was very pleased that I did not use the thermometers from the resource room, as I now know that the numerical values would have been meaningless to the majority of the children. I also realise that I have to build up their understandings of what zero degrees Celsius 'feels' like or what the approximate temperature of a sunny summer's day is in degrees Celsius. I'll have to do this before I get them to do any formal recording of temperatures; otherwise, they won't really make any connections between the numbers on a thermometer and what it actually 'feels' like temperature-wise.

Developing an understanding of scale 2

Some Year 4 children were about to start a mathematics unit of work on temperature. Unaware of the children's previous experiences with temperature, the teacher spoke to the teacher who had taught the class last year. From this she learnt that the class had 'done' some work on reading temperature with unmarked scales. After searching the school's resource room, she found some thermometers that were already marked in Celsius, made of glass and filled with mercury. The teacher was aware of the danger associated with mercury and decided not to let the children use them. Instead, she set up three containers at the front of the class. Each container held a quantity of water—one with ice cubes added, one with water straight from the tap and another with water that had been boiled recently but had been left to cool slightly. With the children sitting at their desks, the teacher asked for volunteers to come and feel the outside of each container and then report their observations to the rest of the class. Once the relative temperature of each container had been established, she placed a thermometer marked in degrees Celsius into each one and announced that they now had to wait for few minutes for the thermometers to react. While they were waiting, the teacher placed a picture of a thermometer on the overhead projector and asked the children to copy it into their workbooks. Figures 1.5 and 1.6 are examples of two children's drawings.

After three or four minutes, the teacher interrupted the children's drawing so that they could check the temperature on each of the thermometers. Children raised their hands

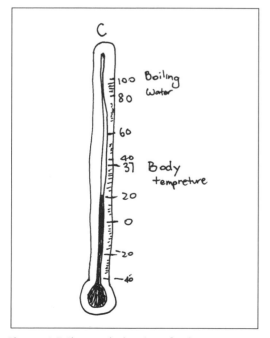

Figure 1.5 Shannon's drawing of a thermometer

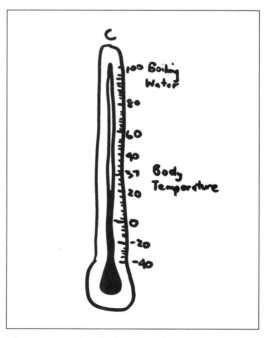

Figure 1.6 Melissa's drawing of a thermometer

eagerly in the hope of being chosen. Two boys and a girl were allowed to check the thermometers. The first boy looked at the thermometer in the water containing ice cubes, but didn't know what to look for. The teacher demonstrated by pointing to the mark where the mercury had risen and to the corresponding number. Hesitantly, the boy said '2'. The next two children had a little difficulty reading the numbers on the thermometers also, but managed without help from the teacher. The class was then instructed to record the temperature of each container in their workbooks.

On reflection of the lesson, the teacher commented:

> *The children were very excited about this activity and were all eager to come up and check the readings on the thermometers. We'll have to have more practice of reading the numbers though, because it seemed that a few of them are not sure of how to do this.*

ACTIVITY 1.4

Comparing the two settings

Before reading further, consider the two scenarios and samples of children's work just presented.

In which setting is the philosophical framework of constructivism more evident? In which setting has the teacher learnt more about the children's prior understandings in regard to temperature? What do you think each teacher will do next?

Share your responses with a peer or a group of other students.

Constructivist principles seem to be operating more in the first setting than the second. From the outset, the teacher is concerned with finding out what the children already know and what they can do rather than trying to teach them what she feels they should know. Hence, their prior knowledge, including their misconceptions, was to form the basis for the experiences to follow and the construction of new knowledge—the need for a standard scale.

The opportunity for children to 'construct' their own informal scales provided room for individual creativity and experimentation, and catered for varying abilities and ethnic backgrounds. While each scale was unique, each was meaningful to the creator. Such a discovery-like process was emphasised by both Piaget (1963) and Bruner (1986) as being important for mathematical understanding to occur as it ensured that the knowledge was meaningful. Liebeck (1984) made the same point more succinctly: 'If we "tell" children that they can multiply any number by 10 by adding a zero, they have gained nothing but mystery. But if they discover this fact for themselves, they have gained insight into the structure of our number system' (p. 239).

Another distinguishing feature of the first scenario that fits with constructivist principles is the emphasis placed on social interaction. Social interaction, particularly between children and significant adults, was considered by Vygotsky (1978) to be crucial in the learning process. A great deal of discussion not only occurs within the whole class, but children are also encouraged to share ideas and knowledge with their peers. Children in the first scenario were encouraged to reflect on their experiences through careful questioning by the teacher, through more discussion and by inviting the children to write about their experiences.

The most significant outcome from this experience is that the teacher now has better knowledge in regard to the range of understanding in which her students are operating. Such a range is determined by their prior learning at one end, and the tasks that they could complete successfully with support from a more knowledgeable person at the other end. This range was termed by Vygotsky as the 'zone of proximal development'. The zone in which a child might move, in learning, depends partly on the teacher's ability to recognise and understand the child's prior knowledge.

The second scenario provides us with little information regarding the children's prior knowledge. The experience is controlled by the teacher with little physical or mental involvement required by the children. The act of reading the temperature from the thermometers seemed to be meaningless to the children with no opportunities for them to reflect on the experience. The children's drawings shown in Figures 1.5 and 1.6 reveal little about their understanding of temperature. It would appear to someone passing the classroom that everyone was working quietly and learning by watching the demonstration. In reality, it is unlikely that anyone knows what these children understood from the lesson or already knew before it—not even their teacher.

Constructivism and teacher education

In response to the growing support for constructivist philosophies of learning in education (Australian Education Council, 1991; National Council of Teachers of Mathematics, 2000), a number of teacher-education programs adopted a constructivist approach in the way their courses were delivered (e.g. Aldridge & Bobis, 2003; Frid, 2000; Klein, 1999). According to constructivist principles, this usually translated into establishing a learning environment in which students construct their own knowledge by linking prior experiences to new knowledge, creating 'learning communities' in which prospective teachers would engage in rich discourse about important ideas (Putnam & Borko, 2000) and using reflection as a vehicle for reconceptualising knowledge and beliefs. It was anticipated that such modelling of a constructivist approach within teacher-education programs would translate into classroom practice. However, evidence as to the degree constructivist approaches have been translated into classroom practice is disappointing and often conflicting (Frid, 2000). To explore the extent to which constructivist approaches were translated into the classroom practices of their graduates, Aldridge and Bobis (2003) found that some beginning teachers' beliefs and practices were quite resilient to the reality of the classroom and teachers were able to enact their beliefs, albeit with some compromises. Other researchers (Smith, 2003) continue to explore possible strategies to strengthen the resilience of beginning teachers' beliefs and practices in preparation for the challenges they may face.

Children's informal mathematics—a crucial step towards understanding mathematics

A significant concern for the teacher in the first setting was her ability to help the children make connections between what they already knew and the conventional knowledge associated with temperature that she wanted them to come to understand. In the past, researchers and educators alike have tended to characterise the academic ability of young children in terms of what they *cannot* do. It is now clear from research that children, through such things as play and social interaction, develop their own (informal) mathematics long before entering school. For example, Gelman and Gelistel (1978) noted the extensive knowledge preschool children have of our number system with respect to counting, while Carpenter and Moser (1984) and Hughes (1986) investigated the ability of young children to use informal knowledge to solve simple addition and subtraction problems. More recently, Wright (1991), Wright, Steward, Stafford & Cain, (1998) and Young-Loveridge (1991) documented the development of arithmetical strategies in young children, while Mulligan and Mitchelmore (1997) reported the developments in children's use of strategies for multiplication and division. Hence, over the past few decades researchers have made significant leaps in understanding young

13

children's mathematical thinking. The realisation that children already possess a great deal of knowledge before formal instruction occurs has caused many educators to reconsider their beliefs about how children learn mathematics and about the ability of children to individually construct their own knowledge.

Throughout this chapter and the rest of this book, we use the terms 'informal' and 'formal' frequently. So what do we mean when we say a child has 'informal' mathematical knowledge or 'formal' knowledge? Informal mathematics develops because it is personally useful and meaningful. It is the result of active construction on the part of the learner—not just the absorption of transmitted information. Informal mathematics 'is the crucial middle-step between children's limited and imprecise intuitive knowledge based on direct perception and the powerful and precise mathematics based on abstract symbols taught in schools' (Baroody, 1987, p. 35). Formal mathematics, on the other hand, is that taught in schools. It involves the use of conventional symbols in a very precise form of communication. When understood, formal mathematics can increase greatly a child's efficiency in dealing with mathematical situations.

While informal mathematics is potentially powerful, it has its limitations. For example, a child's invented strategy for calculating subtraction involving small numbers might be cumbersome and too cognitively demanding when applied to larger numbers and therefore inappropriate to use in all instances. Hence, there is a need for children to understand more efficient or formal methods eventually. However, the extent to which children benefit from formal instruction in mathematics depends on how well it *blends* with their informal ideas. If a gap exists between what a child already knows and the formal instruction provided, learning difficulties may develop. For learners to take on new information that may require some effort to understand, it must make sense to them. Such an understanding cannot be imposed upon children; it must develop gradually as they actively try to make sense of the new knowledge. It is the role of the teacher to challenge existing knowledge so as to encourage the learner to 'reach' for a more sophisticated level of understanding. For example, consider the work-sample in Figure 1.7 and the discussion that ensued between Sanja, a 10-year-old girl, and her teacher.

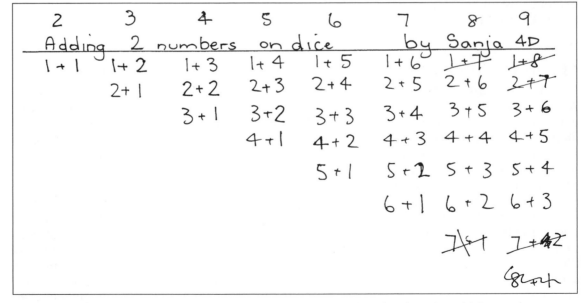

Figure 1.7 Sanja's list of sums for combinations of numbers on two dice after discussion with her teacher

Teacher:	(Stops to talk with Sanja about her recording.) Sanja, can you explain how you got these combinations? (Pointing to combinations in the last two columns.)
Sanja:	That's how you can make 8 and 9 with the numbers on two dice.
Teacher:	How did you make this one, 1 plus 7?
Sanja:	You can make 7, from 6 and 1, and 1 more is 7.
Teacher:	Show me what you mean with the dice.
Sanja:	(Turns dice over to show 6 dots on one die and 1 dot on the other.) See here's the 7 . . . Oh! (looking confused, and then looks at her teacher with a smile) I'm wrong. You can't do it. (Silence for a moment, and then rolls the dice over to show a 6 and a 2). Here is 8. Oh! But it's 6 and 2, not 7 and 1. So (pause) . . . my combinations have to stop at 6 and 6 . . . of course!

At first, Sanja thought her combinations (1 + 7, 7 + 1, 1 + 8, 8 + 1, 2 + 7 and 7 + 2) were correct and was even ready to 'prove' it to her teacher with the dice. To have 'told' Sanja which combinations were wrong might not have had the same impact as it did when the teacher let her detect the mistakes herself. Simply correcting children's errors may be quick and successful in the short term, but it is rarely successful in the long term because the children do not really understand what it is that they have done wrong. It is often more successful when a teacher tries to understand the error first and then provide opportunities for the child to see his or her own faulty reasoning, as in the case of Sanja. To avoid the development of learning difficulties and promote meaningful learning, teachers must know how to tailor instruction so that it blends with children's existing knowledge.

How do children develop their existing knowledge of mathematics before formal instruction? Two important media for learning before, during and after formal instruction are play and language.

Play and learning mathematics

While play remains important throughout the development of children, it is perhaps the most significant medium by which very young children acquire basic informal mathematical knowledge (Griffiths, 1994). It is through playing with blocks that they utilise shape-and-size relationships to construct towers; through water-and-sand play that they develop an awareness of capacity; and through sociodramatic play that they develop numeration skills as they count teddy bears and ensure there are enough cups for all toys to participate in a tea party.

The importance of play for the development of children's understanding was recognised by a number of the early learning theorists. For example, Vygotsky considered play to be 'itself a major source of development' (1978, p. 102). Through play, he believed children engaged in higher order mental processes as the constraints of the real world no longer existed. Piaget (1963) also considered play to be the medium by which children could develop cognitively and Dienes (1960) actually considered *learning* to be a process of increasingly intricate play. He saw it developing from 'primary play', or the simple handling and investigation of materials for their own sake, to what he termed 'secondary play', which involved children building with materials, discovering patterns and eventually forming abstract 'rules' concerning their constructions and patterns.

Today, the crucial role of play for the development of understanding in young children is recognised through teaching and curriculum documents that advocate its importance to teachers and provide practical classroom support (see Dockett & Lambert, 1996). Through play children can develop their understanding of many mathematical concepts 'by forming links and associations between the known and the new or unfamiliar . . . They have to make sense of their new information in some way in order to understand the situation' (Dockett & Lambert, 1996, p. 6).

As children approach and move beyond the formal school age, the role of *structured* play can be increased. The use of playing card games, bingo and games that utilise dice, such as Snakes and Ladders, will familiarise children with numeral names and encourage the automatic recall of number names for special arrangements of dots.

Language and learning mathematics

Language plays a crucial role in the process of children making sense of mathematics. It is language that communicates ideas, not only to other people but also to ourselves by helping us refine and clarify them in our minds. However, language is more than just spoken and written communication: it can include pictorial representations (diagrams, pictures and graphs), 'active' representations (performing and demonstrating) and imagery (Pirie & Kieren, 1994). Del Campo and Clements (1987) referred to each of these modes of communication as being either *receptive* (processing someone else's communication) or *expressive* (using your own language). Table 1.2 summarises Del Campo and Clement's four modes of communication and includes a fifth mode—imagining, added by Ellerton and Clements (1991). They included imagining, as they considered it a form of communication with oneself. The importance of mental imagery and visualisation strategies is now recognised by many researchers as important avenues for children to represent and communicate their mathematical ideas (Mulligan et al., 1996).

TABLE 1.2   Receptive and expressive modes of communication

Language mode	Receptive language (processing someone else's communication)	Expressive language (your own language)
spoken	listening	speaking
written	reading	writing
pictorial	interpreting diagrams, pictures	drawing
active	interpreting others' actions	performing, demonstrating
imagined	—	imagining

Source: Ellerton & Clements, 1991, p. 109

The Cockcroft Report (Cockcroft, 1982, p. 3) urged teachers to encourage children as early as possible to discuss and explain their mathematics so that 'they can share their ideas and develop and refine their understanding'. While this might sound like commonsense and good practice, in reality many mathematics classrooms have emphasised only receptive language such as listening to the teacher, reading 'sums' from the board and copying from texts. Griffiths and Clyne (1994) argued that by ignoring the expressive modes of communication we have 'denied children opportunities to investigate mathematics and to assimilate knowledge into meaningful contexts' and that such an approach has 'resulted in a narrowing of the mathematical concepts to those demonstrated or modelled by the teacher or the textbook' (p. 5).

Children who invent their own notation for communicating ideas about mathematics are taking crucial steps towards developing their understanding of mathematical concepts. Children will make more sense of mathematics if they are allowed to record and represent their mathematical information in their own way.

It is through long informal statements, often combining words, symbols and drawings, that children make sense of their ideas. These informal statements can eventually help children use more formal and succinct expressions.

Consider Figure 1.8. What does this child's work tell you about his understanding of addition?

While working with concrete materials, Timmy (aged 7 years) 'discovered' the commutative property of addition: that regardless of the order in which numbers are added, the answer will always be the same, so 6 plus 4 is the same as 4 plus 6. Understanding this property of addition (and multiplication) assists students in learning their basic facts—essentially cutting the number of basic facts to be learnt by half. His teacher encouraged him to record his discovery. Unable or unsatisfied with his ability to communicate his discovery solely in words or symbolic notation, he included drawings. From this piece of work, the teacher can see clearly that Timmy understands the commutative property but will need assistance in refining and clarifying his ideas to aid the communication of his thinking.

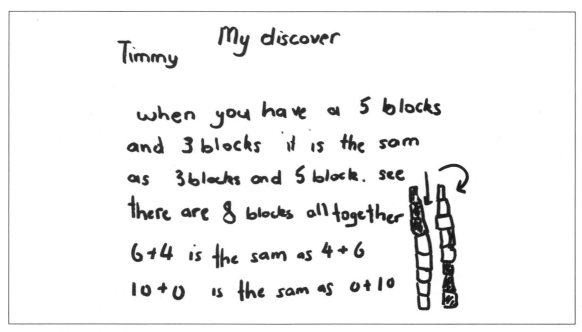

Figure 1.8 Timmy (aged 7 years) records his discovery in words, symbols and pictures

CHILDREN'S UNDERSTANDINGS OF MATHEMATICS

The question 'What is mathematical understanding?' has been addressed from a variety of approaches in recent decades. For instance, *categories* of understanding such as relational and instrumental (Skemp, 1989) and procedural and conceptual (Hiebert, 1990) have been proposed, where procedural or instrumental aspects focus on routine manipulation of either concrete materials, spoken words, written symbols or mental images. Such knowledge is relatively quick and easy to teach and assess but is often inflexible when applied to a new situation and easily forgotten if not practised. Alternatively, conceptual or relational aspects are taken to be rich in relationships, where concepts are linked to other concepts via an elaborate interconnected web of knowledge. Such knowledge is more difficult to assess but allows the learners to be flexible in their thinking and therefore more able to solve unfamiliar problems.

From a constructivist perspective, understanding is now being conceived as a *dynamic process* of organising one's knowledge structures (Serpinska, 1994). For example, Gray and Tall (1994) suggested the term 'proceptual' to indicate when conceptual and procedural thinking combine—as when a young child gradually learns to associate the symbol '3', originally used only to complete the procedural task of counting, to an array of conceptual relationships: $2 + 1$; $1 + 1 + 1$; and $4 - 1$. Pirie and Kieren (1994) proposed an alternative theory of understanding based on the notion that understanding is a dynamic, non-linear process of growth through eight levels, ranging from prior knowledge to the making and having of images, to the formalisation of images. Reflection is seen to be responsible for the consistent reorganisation of knowledge, and growth in understanding is characterised by continuous tracing back and forth through the various levels. Such perspectives are contrary to the dichotomy between procedures and concepts proposed by earlier views.

SNAPSHOTS OF LEARNING: LESSON PLANNING AND ASSESSMENT

If we accept the notion that understanding is a dynamic process from the informal to a more formal level, it is imperative that we as teachers learn to recognise what it is children understand about mathematics at any point along this continuum of growth. Returning to an earlier point made in this chapter, we must *make* time to *pay attention* to the details of children's mathematical ideas so as to gain a better understanding of what it is that they understand.

In this section we present 'snapshots' of children's mathematical thinking via work-samples and interview transcripts, and invite you to interpret the understandings evident in them. The samples are drawn from the research and practical experiences of one of the authors of this book and from the vast body of research literature pertaining to children's mathematical understandings.

1. The box task

In his book *Children and number* Martin Hughes described his use of a task which he referred to as the 'box task' (1986, p. 25). The box task was used to investigate the ability of preschool children to add and subtract with the aid of ten toy bricks and a box with a lid. In this interview, Hughes removes or adds a number of the bricks to the box in full view of the child (Gordon) being interviewed, but the child cannot see how many bricks are left before the lid is shut.

MH: I've taken three out. How many are left?
Gordon: I don't know. Five?
MH: Have a look and see. (Opens box.)
Gordon: (Counts bricks.) Seven!
MH: (Removes one brick and closes lid again.) I've taken another one out. How many are left now?
Gordon: I don't know. (Opens box and counts.) Six!

At this point, Hughes allows Gordon to watch as he empties all the bricks from the box and then puts two bricks back and shuts the lid.

MH: How many in the box now?

Gordon: Two.

MH: (Adds one brick in such a way that Gordon sees it going in but cannot see into the box.) How many now?

Gordon: Three.

MH: I'm putting one more in. (Adds one more, the same way.)

Gordon: Four. Four!

MH: And now I'm putting in two more. (Does so.)

Gordon: Six! Six!

MH: (Takes one brick out.) How many now?

Gordon: (Pause.) Five. Five!

Later in the interview, Hughes removed the box and asked Gordon the same questions that he had previously answered successfully. However, he was unable to solve any of them correctly.

Record or discuss your responses to this interview with a friend. What does this interview tell you about Gordon's ability to count, add and subtract?

Gordon seems to be a good counter when he can *see* the objects he is counting. He is said to be a *perceptual* counter (see Chapter 5 for an explanation of the framework in number). This ability helps him answer some of the interviewer's initial questions. While he had trouble solving the problems involving more than three bricks at one time, he could easily handle addition and subtraction problems with small numbers—those less than three. Without the box of bricks to refer to, however, questions such as 'three and one more' were meaningless to Gordon and he could not solve even the simple problems involving small numbers. Hence, we can see that Gordon is able to use his informal knowledge of mathematics to solve addition and subtraction problems involving numbers less than three, but seems to understand what to do only when the situation is *real* to him—that is, when concrete materials are involved. The ability to add and subtract small numbers, particularly when concrete materials are present, is quite typical for young children who have not had formal mathematical instruction.

2. Caitlin's clock

A well-known task used to gain knowledge about a young child's understanding of time is to simply ask the child to draw a clock face and write about it (Pengelly, 1985).

What do you make of Caitlin's clock face? How does her understanding compare with what you thought a typical 6-year-old should understand?

Caitlin's response was not a result of instruction, but a spontaneous reaction to the unexpected task, and is therefore quite informative in regard to what she understands about telling the time on an analogue clock. Her intention to show 8 o'clock is obvious, given her positioning of a long and a short arm in her drawing. Even though the numbers are not placed around the clock face correctly, they are properly sequenced and she has tried to indicate where the numbers should be by indicating which numbers should be at the 'top' and which ones *should* be on the 'bottom'. The fact that she wrote '21' for twelve is of no

The twelve is like a twenty-one. It is 8 o'clock.

This is the bottom

1 2 3 4 5 6 7 8 9 10 11 12

This is the top

Caitlin 6

Figure 1.9 Caitlin's (aged 6 years) clock face

great concern since it would not interfere with her ability to indicate a time on the clock face. However, she is already aware that there is something wrong with the way she has written it, indicating that this error could probably be self-corrected quite easily if she was questioned about it by a peer or an adult.

3. Symmetry

A preservice teacher interviewed her 11-year-old sister about her understanding of symmetry. The following transcript is an excerpt from the interview.

Student Teacher (ST): Do you know what 'symmetry' is?
Sister (S): You mean where they bury people?
ST: No! Symmetry not cemetery.
S: Oh! (laughs) Yeah. I know what it is. That's when you fold paper.
ST: Can you show me?
S: Yeah. (Takes a sheet of paper from her workbook and carefully starts to fold it in half.) You have to be careful and make sure you fold it exactly down the middle.
ST: Why is that?
S: (Looking at ST and sounding astonished.) Because then it wouldn't be symmetry. (Completes the fold and then opens the paper.)
ST: So where is the symmetry?
S: Here. (Running her finger down the fold.)

ST: Oh I see. Does this table have symmetry? (Indicates the table they are sitting at.)

S: No. You can't fold it. Only paper has symmetry.

Record what you make of this discussion. What is happening in terms of the sister's understanding of symmetry? Why do you think her understanding of symmetry has developed the way it has?

The sister's understanding of symmetry is extremely limited and shows how misconceptions can develop if children are exposed to just one type of experience to illustrate a mathematical concept. This Year 6 girl's idea of symmetry is that it must involve folding paper 'exactly down the middle'. At first glance, she seems to show an understanding of symmetry, but more thorough questioning requiring her to explain what and why she was doing things reveals her misunderstanding. It appears that she thinks symmetry is the actual *fold* in the paper. This misconception has probably been reinforced over the years by teachers who 'teach' symmetry solely through paper-folding tasks. To broaden children's concepts and to help stop misconceptions persisting beyond primary school, we must provide them with opportunities to grapple with concepts in a variety of situations. In the case of symmetry, children should experience not only paper-folding tasks, but also tasks involving the use of mirrors (e.g. mira mirrors) and they should be encouraged to discover other types of symmetry, such as rotational symmetry, in the natural and made environments.

While many people laugh at the girl's mistaken term 'cemetery', it is in fact an important issue to address—making sure that mathematical terms are not confused with everyday language terms. Children often say 'intercept' for 'intersect' or 'angel' for 'angle'. This problem can be overcome if teachers make sure they explicitly teach new terms when they arise and deal promptly with the misuse of terms.

4. Decimal dilemmas

A Year 6 teacher wanted to find out what her students understood about decimals, in particular when a decimal was multiplied by a single-digit whole number. She presented two computations orally to the class and asked them to solve the problems any way they liked, to write about how they solved them and to write a word problem to go with each one. Figures 1.10 and 1.11 on the next page are samples of work from two different students.

Compare the two samples of work. What does each child understand about decimals and about the multiplication of decimals?

If we were just concerned with getting the computations correct, we would consider the second student to be more successful. However, a closer look at their language (written and pictorial) indicates that the first student (Figure 1.10) actually understands decimal numbers to a far greater level than the second. This child's writing indicates that he was capable of actually 'solving' the problem mentally by rounding to the nearest whole number and then compensating for the nine-tenths later. This indicates that while he may have written the numbers in a standard vertical format, he used an invented strategy to solve it. This invented strategy makes great sense, but unfortunately some confusion exists over whether it should be 71.02 or 71.2. Further questioning of the child may shed some light as to where the confusion is.

His drawing and word problem also add to our understanding of what it is he understands about decimals and multiplication. For example, he is able to relate the '8.9' to a

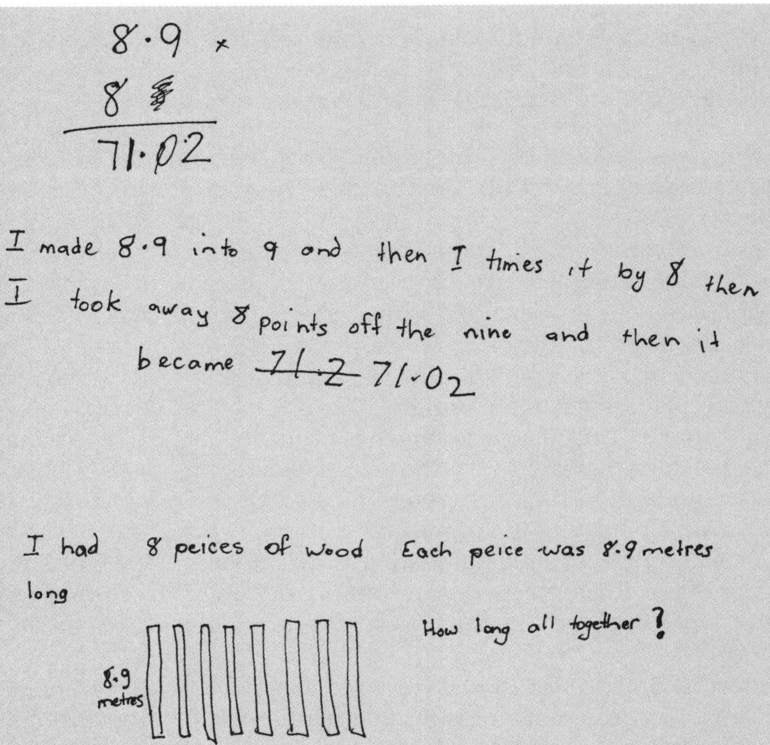

$$8 \cdot 9 \times$$
$$8 \quad \cancel{8}$$
$$\overline{71 \cdot 02}$$

I made 8·9 into 9 and then I times it by 8 then
I took away 8 points off the nine and then it
became ~~71·2~~ 71·0₂

I had 8 peices of wood Each peice was 8·9 metres
long

8·9
metres

How long all together ?

Figure 1.10 A student's worksample for 'eight point nine times eight'

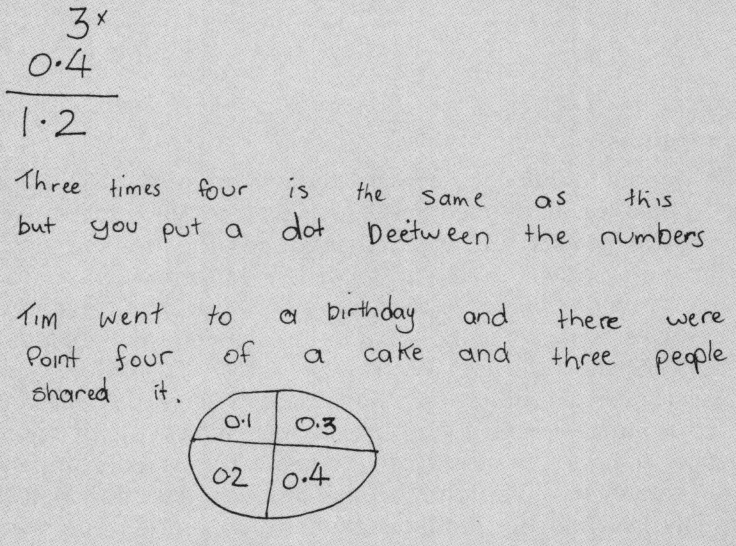

$$3 \times$$
$$0 \cdot 4$$
$$\overline{1 \cdot 2}$$

Three times four is the same as this
but you put a dot beetween the numbers

Tim went to a birthday and there were
Point four of a cake and three people
shared it .

Figure 1.11 A student's worksample for 'zero point four times three'

real-life situation quite successfully. Although it may be unrealistic to buy wood 8.9 metres long, it is significant to note that he knows that decimals are used in measurement situations like this one. His understanding of multiplication as '8 lots of 8.9' is revealed by his drawing and his word problem. It is unfortunate to think that, given a traditional pencil-and-paper test, this child would appear not to understand the multiplication of decimals.

Alternatively, the second child (Figure 1.11) successfully completes the formal algorithm and, given a traditional testing situation, would be considered quite good at multiplication involving a decimal. This is far from the truth. His written language reveals that he has no understanding of decimals—in fact, he thinks that decimals and whole numbers are the same thing except that one has a 'dot' for some reason. His drawing indicates that there may be some confusion between '0.4' and the fraction term 'quarters'. Such a confusion is quite common in children who have not been instructed in decimal fractions meaningfully. His word problem also reveals little understanding of decimals in a realistic situation—we do not normally talk about 'point four of a cake'. Also, the wording of his problem means that division, and not multiplication, is required for a correct solution.

5. Computer-enhanced learning

During a recent Smarties® competition to guess the flavour of the new green-coloured Smartie, a Year 5 class decided to investigate how many of each colour were in a mini pack. Small groups of children investigated the contents of their packs and were asked to record their findings using a graphing software package. Figures 1.12 and 1.13 are samples of work from two groups of students.

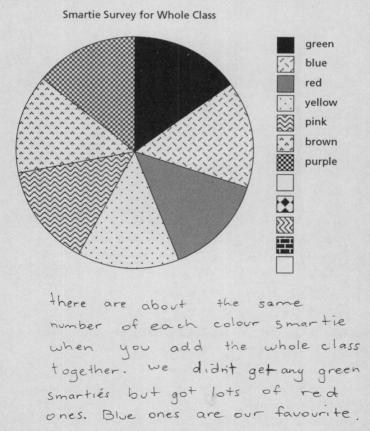

Smartie Survey for Whole Class

green
blue
red
yellow
pink
brown
purple

there are about the same number of each colour smartie when you add the whole class together. we didn't get any green smarties but got lots of red ones. Blue ones are our favourite.

Figure 1.12 A group of students use a pie graph to represent the number of each colour in their Smarties mini pack

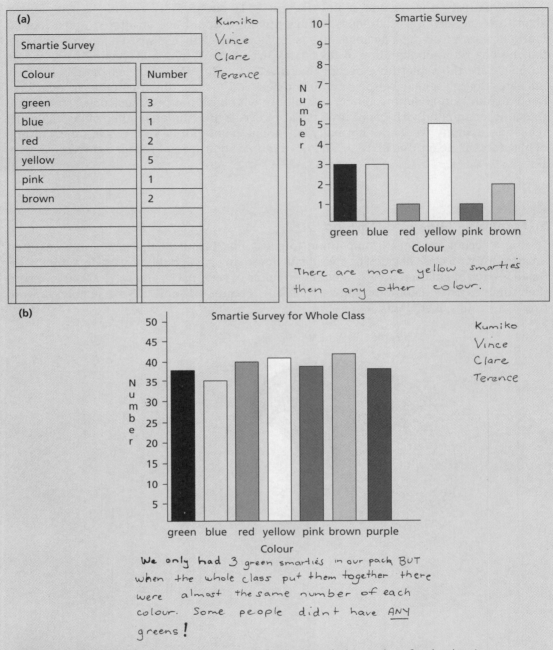

(a)

Smartie Survey	
Colour	Number
green	3
blue	1
red	2
yellow	5
pink	1
brown	2

Kumiko
Vince
Clare
Terence

Smartie Survey

There are more yellow smarties then any other colour.

(b)

Smartie Survey for Whole Class

Kumiko
Vince
Clare
Terence

We only had 3 green smarties in our pack BUT when the whole class put them together there were almost the same number of each colour. Some people didn't have ANY greens!

Figure 1.13 (a) and (b) A group of students tabulate and graph the number of each colour in their Smarties mini pack and graph the results for the whole class

How does the use of a computer-graphing program help to enhance the children's understanding of the investigation?

The use of a computer graphing program has allowed these children to construct multiple representations of the information they collected in a short period of time. The visual image of the graph is a very powerful source of information for the children, particularly in Figure 1.13 where the difference between the number of each colour Smartie for individual groups and for the whole class is obvious immediately when you compare the two column graphs. The writing accompanying each graph reveals that the children have interpreted the information correctly.

The use of a pie graph to represent the number of each colour Smartie for the whole class provides a powerful visual image (Figure 1.12). Children can 'see' at a glance that each section of the graph is approximately equal. Such a pie graph would be very difficult to construct without the use of a computer-graphing program. The image also lends itself to further investigation of decimal fractions and percentages.

The teacher's role in understanding children's understandings

The challenge to teachers is to be able to interpret children's understandings correctly so as to inform teaching. Such skills can be learnt given time and practice. It is not enough, however, to simply collect samples of children's work. It is essential to know what to look for, what questions to ask, what tasks to formulate and how to interpret this information in the context of the child's mathematical growth over a long time. The task becomes more manageable if we break it down and consider at least four important components:

1. what we know about how children learn mathematics;
2. what we know about children's prior knowledge and understanding;
3. what we want them to come to know; and
4. how we can challenge them to move to the next level of understanding.

The first component can be gained through a knowledge of theories of learning and of research findings already documented, and from the accumulation of personal experiences gained over time. While theories of learning give us a general view of how children develop cognitively, research tells us how children's understanding about certain aspects (e.g. counting) develops over time.

The second component can be gained by continuously *paying attention* to children's mathematical thinking. This involves observing, listening, questioning, analysing worksamples, discussing with learners and the like. From such activities, teachers must then learn to interpret children's explanations so as to inform the next step.

The third component, knowledge of what we want them to come to know, can be built up over time and essentially comes from curriculum documents, such as syllabus and support materials, the national statements, profiles and numeracy benchmarks. Such documents provide specific statements regarding the outcomes expected of each child at various stages of schooling. However, they are only 'frameworks'—teachers need in-depth knowledge of mathematical concepts and processes so as to enrich them. While some classroom textbooks written for specific year levels are useful, they are not based on what the children in your care understand and, because they are written to be used in schools across various states, they may deviate from your state's syllabus content.

The final component concerns the experiences we provide our students. These must challenge children's existing conceptions and strategies and encourage them to reach for a more sophisticated level of understanding.

SUMMARY AND IMPLICATIONS FOR CLASSROOM PRACTICE

This chapter has sought to provide insights into children's understandings of mathematics by encouraging you to consider not only the well-established general learning theories of Piaget, Vygotsky, Dienes and others, but also your own experiences and personal theories of learning mathematics. It has also emphasised the importance of learning to pay attention to children's understandings that become evident as they communicate their ideas through spoken and written language. Hence, an important message conveyed by this chapter has been how the combined knowledge of theory, research and practice can lead us to a better understanding of children's mathematical understandings. Ultimately, such an understanding will benefit the children we teach because it will inform our instruction.

While research on teaching and learning can affect instructional practice through its findings or through its theoretical perspectives derived from the research (e.g. constructivism), it has never provided a 'magic cure' for the ills of education—nor is it likely to in the future (Silver, 1990). No matter how comprehensive a theory of learning might be, it cannot be 'applied unequivocally to all students' (Cobb, Wood & Yackel, 1990, p. 125). The challenge for teachers, then, is to make instructional decisions based on a merging of ideas drawn from both research and practical experience.

ACTION AND REFLECTION

Tape record interviews with two or three children of a similar age, individually, about their understanding of a particular mathematical concept. You might like to use one of the tasks suggested by the snapshots in this chapter or in another chapter in this book, or one of your own. Ask them to record their ideas on paper and then ask them to 'tell' you about their recordings. Question them to elicit as much information about their understanding as you can. Be careful not to be judgemental—you are there to learn from them.

Reflect on your interviews and worksamples. What do they tell you in terms of each child's understanding of the mathematics involved?

REFERENCES

Aldridge, S. & Bobis, J. (2003). Implementing beliefs, knowledge and practices: A beginning teacher's story. In L. Bragg, C. Campbell, G. Herbert & J. Mousley (Eds), *MERINO—Mathematics education research: Innovation, networking, opportunity* Proceedings of the 26th Annual Conference of the Mathematics Education Research Group of Australasia Inc., Vol. 1, pp. 65–71. Geelong: Deakin University.

Australian Association of Mathematics Teachers. (1997). *Numeracy = everyone's business.* Australian Association of Mathematics Teachers Inc.: Perth.

Australian Association of Mathematics Teachers. (2003). *Springboard into numeracy*, Proceedings of the National Numeracy Conference Australian Association of Mathematics Teachers Inc.: Hobart.

Australian Education Council. (1991). *A national statement on mathematics for Australian schools.* Melbourne: Curriculum Corporation.

Baroody, A. (1987). *Children's mathematical thinking.* New York: Teachers College Press.

Bauserfeld, H. (1988). Interaction, construction, and knowledge: Alternative perspectives for mathematics education. In T. Cooney & D. Grouws (Eds), *Effective mathematics teaching* (pp. 29–46). Reston, Virginia: NCTM & Lawrence Erlbaum Associates.

Board of Studies, NSW. (2002). *Mathematics K–6.* Sydney: Board of Studies.

Bobis, J. & Cusworth, R. (1995). Attitudinal shifts towards mathematics of preservice teachers. In S. Flavel,

I. Isaacs, D. Lee, R. Hurley, T. Roberts, A. Richards, R. Laird, & V. Ran (Eds), *GALTHA: Proceedings of the 18th Annual Conference of Mathematics Education Research Group of Australasia* (pp. 109–114), Darwin: Mathematics Education Research Group of Australasia Inc.

Bruner, J. (1986). *Actual minds, possible worlds*. Cambridge: Harvard University Press.

Carpenter, T. & Moser, J. (1984). The acquisition of addition and subtraction concepts in grades one through three. *Journal for Research in Mathematics Education, 15*, 179–202.

Cobb, P. (1994). Constructivism and learning. In T. Husen & T. Postlethwaite (Eds), *International encyclopedia of education* (2nd ed., pp. 1049–1051). Oxford: Pergamon Press.

Cobb, P., Wood, T. & Yackel, E. (1990). Classrooms as learning environments for teachers and researchers. In R. Davis, C. Maher & N. Noddings (Eds), *Constructivist views on the learning and teaching of mathematics* (pp. 125–146), Reston, Virginia: National Council of Teachers of Mathematics.

Cockcroft, W. (1982). *Mathematics counts: Report of the committee of inquiry into the teaching of mathematics in schools*. London: Her Majesty's Stationery Office.

Del Campo, G. & Clements, M. (1987). *A manual for the professional development of teachers of beginning mathematicians*. Melbourne: Catholic Education Office of Victoria and Association of Independent Schools of Victoria.

Department of Education, Training and Youth Affairs. (2000). *Numeracy, a priority for all: Challenges for Australian schools*, Commonwealth of Australia: Canberra.

Dienes, Z. (1960). *Building up mathematics*. London: Hutchinson Education.

Dockett, S. & Lambert, P. (1996). *The importance of play*. Sydney: Board of Studies NSW.

Ellerton, N. & Clements, M. (1991). *Mathematics in language: A review of language factors in mathematics learning*. Geelong: Deakin University Press.

Frid, S. (2000). Constructivism and reflective practice in practice: Challenges and dilemmas of a mathematics teacher educator. *Mathematics Teacher Education and Development, 2* (17–33).

Gelman, R. & Gelistel, C. (1978). *The child's understanding of number*. Cambridge: Harvard University Press.

Gray, E. & Tall, D. (1994). Duality, ambiguity, and flexibility: A 'proceptual' view of simple arithmetic. *Journal for Research in Mathematics Education, 25* (2), 116–140.

Griffiths, R. (1994). Mathematics and play. In J. Moyles (Ed), *The excellence of play* (pp. 145–157). Philadelphia: Open University Press.

Griffiths, R. & Clyne, M. (1994). *Language in the mathematics classroom: Talking, representing, recording*. Armidale: Eleanor Curtain Publishing.

Hiebert, J. (1990). The role of routine procedures in the development of mathematical competence. In T. Cooney & C. Hirsch (Eds), *Teaching and learning mathematics in the 1990s* (pp. 31–40). Reston, Virginia: National Council of Teachers of Mathematics.

Hughes, M. (1986). *Children and number: Difficulties in learning mathematics*. New York: Basil Blackwell.

Jaworski, B. (1998). The centrality of the researcher: Rigor in a constructivist inquiry into mathematics teaching. In A. Teppo (Ed), Qualitative research methods in mathematics education, *Journal for Research in Mathematics Education*, Monograph 9, (112–127).

Klein, M. (1999). The construction of agency in mathematics teacher education and development programs: A poststructuralist analysis, *Mathematics Teacher Education and Development, 1*, 84–93.

Lerman, S. (2001). A cultural/discursive psychology for mathematics teaching and learning. In B. Atweh, H. Forgasz & B. Nebres (Eds), *Sociocultural research on mathematics education: An international perspective* (pp. 3–18), Mahwah, New Jersey: Lawrence Erlbaum Associates.

Liebeck, P. (1984). *How children learn mathematics*. Harmondsworth, Middlesex: Penguin Books.

Maher, C. & Davis, R. (1990). Building representations of children's meanings. In R. Davis, C. Maher & N. Noddings (Eds), *Constructivist views on the learning and teaching of mathematics* (pp. 79–90). Reston, Virginia: National Council of Teachers of Mathematics.

Mulligan, J. & Mitchelmore, M. (1997). Young children's intuitive models of multiplication and division, *Journal for Research in Mathematics Education, 28*(3), 309–330.

Mulligan, J., Mitchelmore, M., Outhred, L. & Bobis, J. (1996). Children's representations and conceptual understanding of number. In P. Clarkson (Ed), *Technology in mathematics*. Melbourne: Mathematics Education Research Group of Australasia Inc.

National Council of Teachers of Mathematics. (2000). *Principles and standards for school mathematics.* Reston, Virginia: National Council of Teachers of Mathematics.

Pengelly, H. (1985). *Mathematics making sense.* Adelaide: South Australian Education Department.

Piaget, J. (1963). *The origins of intelligence in children.* New York: W. W. Norton & Company.

Pirie, S. & Kieren, T. (1994). Growth in mathematical understanding: How can we characterise it and how can we represent it? *Educational Studies in Mathematics, 26*, 165–190.

Putnam, R. & Borko, H. (2000). What do new views of knowledge and thinking have to say about research on teacher learning? *Educational Researcher, 29*(1) 4–15.

Renshaw, P. & Brown, R. (1997). Learning partnerships: The role of teachers in a community of learners. In L. Logan & J. Sachs (Eds*), Meeting the challenges of primary schools.* London: Routledge.

Serpinska, A. (1994). *Understanding in Mathematics.* London: The Falmer Press.

Silver, E. (1990). Contributions of research to practice: Applying, findings, methods, and perspectives. In T. Cooney & C. Hirsch (Eds), *Teaching and learning mathematics in the 1990s.* Reston, Virginia: National Council of Teachers of Mathematics.

Skemp, R. (1989). *Mathematics in the primary school.* London: Routledge.

Smith, T. (2003). Using case stories as a tool for listening more and telling less in mathematics teacher education. In L. Bragg, C. Campbell, G. Herbert & J. Mousley (Eds), *MERINO—Mathematics education research: Innovation, networking, opportunity* (Proceedings of the 26th Annual Conference of the Mathematics Education Research Group of Australasia Inc., Vol. 1, pp. 841–850). Geelong: Mathematics Education Research Group of Australasia.

Steffe, L. (1990). Mathematics curriculum design: A constructivist's perspective. In L. Steffe & T. Woods (Eds), *Transforming children's mathematics education* (pp. 389–398). Hillsdale, New Jersey: Lawrence Erlbaum Associates.

von Glaserfeld, E. (Ed) (1991). *Radical constructivism in mathematics education.* Dordrecht, Netherlands: Kluwer.

von Glaserfeld, E. (1995). A constructivist approach to teaching. In L. Steffe & J. Gale (Eds), *Constructivism in education.* Hillsdale, New Jersey: Lawrence Erlbaum Associates.

Vygotsky, L. (1978), *Mind and society.* Cambridge: Harvard University Press.

Wood, T. (2002). What does it mean to teach differently? In B. Barton, K. Irwin, M. Pfannkuch & M Thomas (Eds), *Mathematics education in the South Pacific* (Proceedings of the 25th Annual Conference of the Mathematics Education Research Group of Australasia Inc., Vol. 1, pp. 61–67), Auckland: Mathematics Education Research Group of Australasia.

Wright, B. (1991). What number knowledge is possessed by children beginning the kindergarten year of school? *Mathematics Education Research Journal, 3*(1), 2–16.

Wright, B., Stewart, R., Stafford, A. & Cain, R. (1998). Assessing and documenting student knowledge and progress in early mathematics. In S. Berenson, K. Dawkins, M. Blanton, W. Conlombe, J. Kolb, K. Norwood & L. Steffe (Eds), *Proceedings of the 20th Annual Meeting of the North American chapter of the International Group for the Psychology of Mathematics Education* (Vol. 1, pp. 211–16). Columbus, Ohio: ERIC Clearinghouse for Science, Mathematics & Environmental Education.

Young-Loveridge, J. (1991). *The development of children's number concepts from ages five to nine,* Vols. 1 & 2. Hamilton: University of Waikato.

Zevenbergen, R. (2001). Mathematics, social class, and linguistic capital: An analysis of mathematics classroom interactions. In B. Atweh, H. Forgasz & B. Nebres (Eds*), Sociocultural research on mathematics education: An international perspective* (pp. 201–216), Mahwah, New Jersey: Lawrence Erlbaum Associates.

Chapter 2

Challenging children to think mathematically: concepts and processes

CHAPTER OVERVIEW

In the past, mathematics has been thought of in terms of *content*—a body of facts and procedures that needed to be memorised. It is now more aptly described as a *way of thinking*, and the learning of it is characterised not only by its products but also by a growth in understanding of mathematical concepts and processes. The development of such concepts and processes is based on finding mathematical patterns and relationships. The effective use of these patterns and relationships provides opportunities for students to choose and apply mathematical understandings to a range of problem-solving situations. Because mathematical thinking is concerned primarily with processes, such as investigating and conjecturing, it is inherently linked to problem solving—a process in itself. The ability to solve mathematical problems is a central focus in the teaching, learning and assessing of mathematics today (National Council of Teachers of Mathematics, 2000; Australian Education Council, 1991; Board of Studies, NSW, 1998).

In Chapter 1 we found that paying attention to the details of children's intuitions and strategies allowed the teacher to gain a better understanding of what it is that they understand. In this chapter we will present a range of mathematical processes that children acquire when challenged to think and work mathematically and show how these processes are linked to problem-solving situations.

Most modern views of mathematics education acknowledge that children do not simply take in mathematical knowledge that is transmitted to them, no matter how well it is organised and structured. Children frequently construct and develop their *own* ways of doing mathematics—often in a manner quite different from the way it was introduced or intended to be processed. As a result, effective teaching cannot be entirely content-driven or teacher-centred. New concepts and understandings need to be linked to a child's existing knowledge base and personal experiences. Children need to be involved in the learning process, actively engaged in thinking, and encouraged to verbalise their thought processes and reflect upon their problem-solving endeavours.

What are some of the important mathematics processes we want children to acquire and develop? Most current syllabus documents identify a range of processes that occur when an individual is working mathematically. These processes may include:

+ investigating;

+ conjecturing;

+ problem solving;

+ applying and verifying;

+ using mathematical language;

+ reflecting; and

+ using technology.

When making sense of life experiences or seeking solutions to problems, individuals use such processes to communicate and reflect upon mathematics (Queensland Studies Authority, 2003). Students use mathematical thinking processes and skills in interpreting and dealing with mathematical and non-mathematical situations. In particular they:

+ call on a repertoire of general problem-solving techniques, appropriate technology and personal and collaborative management strategies when working mathematically;

+ chose mathematical ideas and tools to fit the constraints in a practical situation, interpret and make sense of the results within the context and evaluate the appropriateness of the methods used; and

+ investigate, generalise and reason about patterns in number, space and data, explaining and justifying conclusions reached.

(WA Department of Education and Training, 2000)

The authors of the NCTM's (1989) *Curriculum and evaluation standards for school mathematics* maintained that it is important for children to gain 'mathematical power' in order to become more effective problem solvers. This refers to an individual's ability to 'explore, conjecture, and reason logically, as well as an ability to use a variety of mathematical methods effectively to solve nonroutine problems' (NCTM, 1989, p. 5). Such approaches encourage children to engage in divergent and creative thinking and to produce multiple solution paths to problems. Moreover, such reasoning challenges children to find productive ways to adapt, modify and build on their knowledge base in situations that provide opportunities to engage in authentic practices as they discover, invent and use mathematics to understand the world (NCTM, 2000).

In this chapter, examples of how children use a range of mathematical processes to solve problems will be presented. It is important to recognise that these processes are not generally used in isolation—in fact, an individual may use a variety of processes in one open-ended problem-solving situation.

Children construct mathematical meaning in a number of ways and should be encouraged to:

+ relate mathematics to personal experiences;

+ use more than one strategy to solve a problem; and

+ apply mathematical understandings to both 'real-life' and new situations.

Mathematical understandings should not be taught in isolation. When acquiring and constructing mathematical ideas it is important to relate such ideas to real-life experiences or rich tasks. In order to fully understand a concept it should be applied to similar situations so that reasoning and problem-solving abilities may be challenged. If a child can use understandings and skills in real-life situations, they are more likely to develop those concepts and processes with meaning.

In this chapter mathematical processes and understandings will be presented under the following headings:

30

- ＋ thinking mathematically;
- ＋ what is problem solving?;
- ＋ problem solving and mathematical thinking; and
- ＋ mathematical thinking across a range of problem-solving activities.

The first section will examine the types of processes used by students when thinking mathematically, the second section will focus on essential components of the problem-solving process, the third section addresses the children's knowledge and problem-solving strategies, while the last section will provide examples of how teachers encourage children to actively engage in learning situations over extended periods of time.

Chapter focus questions

We trust that, by considering your responses to the following questions, you may further recognise that mathematical skills and problem solving are very much part of our everyday lives. To ensure that mathematics is meaningful, such notions should be reinforced in all learning situations.

1. Make a list of five instances in which you were required to think mathematically this week (e.g. reading a bus or train timetable, a TV guide, road map or recipe). What mathematical concepts were involved for each activity (e.g. time, mass, position)? What processes did you use during each activity (e.g. measuring, estimating, analysing)?

2. Reflect upon a problem that you have been trying to solve for some time (e.g. buying a computer, balancing the budget, planning a holiday). What mathematical processes have you used in order to propose a solution? You need to go beyond using addition or multiplication facts.

3. What type of problem-solving strategies have you used so far? Have they been effective?

4. Attempt to trace the thinking processes you have used to solve the problem. What information have you collected? Was it all useful? At what stage did you ask other people for advice? Have you abandoned your plan and started again? Do you have more than one solution?

THINKING MATHEMATICALLY

The processes developed when working mathematically have a direct link to the types of knowledge, skills and understandings required to complete a given task. As you will see in the following chapters, particular understandings may be directly related to the content areas of space, measurement, number or using data. In other instances, knowledge and skills could be used across a number of content areas. Table 2.1 examines the way in which mathematical processes mentioned above are likely to be used in problem-solving situations.

How do we know when children are thinking mathematically? Burrill (1998) suggested that specific situations could not be categorised as reasoning or thinking activities—mathematical thinking comes from what the students *do* during the activity. When children are making decisions about the type of procedures to use (see Table 2.1), or how to modify these procedures based on available resources, how to apply understandings previously learnt to new situations, they are thinking and reasoning mathematically.

TABLE 2.1 Mathematical thinking processes

Mathematical process	Problem-solving situation
• investigating and conjecturing	• proposing 'what-if' situations
• using problem-solving strategies	• using objects, concrete materials, pictures or diagrams • representing problems in a variety of ways, including pictorial and analytic forms • using a range of strategies
• applying and verifying	• checking answers and testing hypotheses • using alternative methods when necessary • suggesting when an approach could be used in other situations • choosing the most appropriate procedures • seeing relevance to real-life situations
• using mathematical language	• using words, pictures or symbols to describe patterns and relationships
• reflecting	• considering a given solution with respect to the other, different solutions • discussing the relative efficiency of a given solution and modifying it if necessary
• using technology	• using a calculator to check answers • selecting appropriate technology in order to represent something more efficiently

Following is a description of classroom-based activities providing a range of experiences in which children were challenged to think mathematically. A variety of processes are presented under the headings of investigating, using technology, conjecturing, reflection and application, and symbolising. The children were not just using a specific process in these problem-based situations; in fact, the students engaged in a range of processes in any given activity. In other words, one process is highlighted but several processes may be accessed in a particular situation. While these *other* processes are also important, they will not be treated explicitly in this chapter. However, many of them will be examined more closely in the content-based chapters of this book (Chapters 3–9). For example, Chapter 3 will detail the processes of collecting, representing and interpreting data.

Investigating

A class of Year 5 children was presented with the following situation: Jane and her family went to the Western Plains Zoo for one day in the holidays. On arrival they were given a map of the zoo area (see Figure 2.1).

In small groups, the children were encouraged to interpret the map and respond to a series of questions that were designed to encourage the children to work mathematically. The activities, presented in Activity 2.1, integrate understandings associated with space, measurement, number and data in an open-ended problem-solving environment.

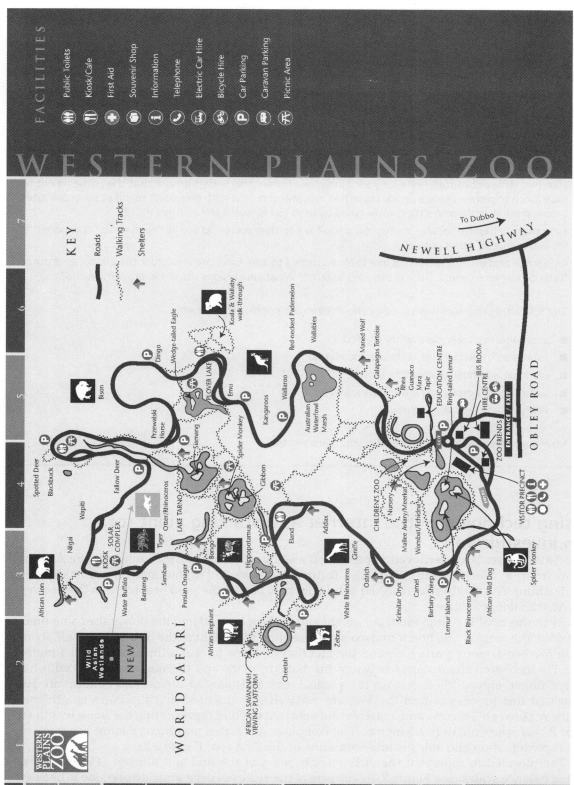

Figure 2.1 Map of Western Plains Zoo *Source:* Reprinted with permission of Western Plains Zoo.

Chapter 2 Challenging children to think mathematically

Investigating the zoo

Look at the map presented in Figure 2.1 and attempt the following questions with a small group of peers. These are the same questions that were given to the Year 5 class. As you attempt the questions, make a list of the type of mathematical processes you are required to use in order to complete the task. Remember, we are concerned not only with the type of mathematical understandings required to complete the questions but also with the actual processes used.

1. Imagine that a friend was to meet you at the zoo at 11.00 am. How could you make the map easy for someone to locate you (what about a grid, co-ordinate reference, directions involving distance)?

2. Plan two different routes—one for your family, one for another—that ensure that the parties meet to have lunch together. Draw a simple map that indicates the time each group will spend at particular sites before the lunch break. A simple table could be used to represent the planned route.

3. How many different possible routes could you take so that you could see all the animals? Compare this list with those of other groups.

4. Categorise and order the animals in a table according to size. Estimate and order the animal enclosures from largest to smallest. Do you see any patterns? What conclusions could you draw from this?

The following processes were used by the children attempting this activity:

- interpretation, representation, prediction;
- estimation, comparison, ordering, measuring;
- planning and finding alternative paths;
- justifying and explaining alternatives; and
- verifying and recording solutions.

How does this schedule compare with your personal list?

Using technology—the Internet as a starting point for an investigation

Year 3 and 4 students retrieved, represented and interpreted information about the African lion from a World Wide Web site (http://www.seaworld.org/animal-info/animal-bytes /index.htm). The children were asked to find out how much taller and heavier than themselves an African lion would be.

Ryan was unable to represent the height and mass of himself and the lion at the same time. He drew the vertical and horizontal axes representing the height of the lion and himself. Ryan then marked 1-metre parts based on the fact that he knew he was a little more than 1 metre tall. He measured the distance between his 1-metre mark and the horizontal axis with his index finger, moved his finger up the vertical axis and marked the second calibration. He repeated this process to find the 3-metre mark. He commented that the lion's length was halfway between 2 metres and 3 metres and adjusted the line representing the lion's length so that it was approximately 2.5 metres. The computer-generated graph gives more precision to his representation and aids his understanding of the data (see Figure 2.2).

Tom decided to represent the difference in mass of the lion and himself (45 kilograms) using balance scales (see Figure 2.3). The arm of the scale does not indicate one side is heavier or lighter than the other, but the bottom of the lion's tray indicates that it was much heavier.

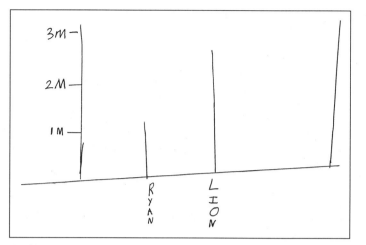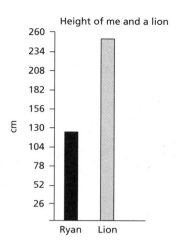

Figure 2.2 Ryan (Year 3) constructed a column graph free-hand to compare all the children's heights and then used a computer graphing package to gain a more precise representation

Figure 2.3 Tom's (Year 4) representation of the lion's mass and his own

Realising that it did not give an accurate measure, he added the electronic scales 'because they were more accurate'. He was able to make statements such as 'the lion is much heavier, 45 kilograms compared to 250 kilograms . . . this is about 50 times 4 makes 200 . . . no, 50 times 5 makes 250 kilograms. So it is more than 5 times heavier'.

From this problem-solving situation we can see that the children were using many mathematical processes. They were required to:

+ read and interpret measurement information;
+ make estimates of their own height and mass in metres and kilograms;
+ use estimation and informal units of length systematically to construct a scale on a vertical axis of a graph;

+ make comparisons and represent the relative size of themselves and the lion by constructing a column graph;

+ use technology (a computer) to gain a more precise representation of the investigation;

+ represent the relative mass of a lion and themselves; and

+ make statements about the relative mass of themselves and the lion using the language of comparison.

Conjecturing and proposing 'what-if' situations

A class of Year 4/5 children was provided with a timetable (see Figure 2.4) and the following situation.

Joel (aged 9 years) and Sara (aged 10 years) are going to the Royal Easter Show with their family on Saturday from Wollstonecraft. They intended to arrive by 9.30 am. Which train should they catch?

As a whole-class experience, the children were asked to consider what '8 26 56' meant. In addition, they were encouraged to look at a range of alternatives including 'which trains could they catch and how would they plan their return trip?' Importantly, understandings associated with the symbolism of the timetable were discussed in detail.

The children were then asked to work in small groups and were presented with the following questions to consider:

1. At what times are the most trains available to the show?
2. What if the 10.26 am is 10 minutes late? What time would they get to Olympic Park?
3. There are no trains home from the Show between 5.17 pm and 8.53 pm. Why might this be the case?
4. Which train would they catch if they wanted to be home by 5.00 pm?

The questions were specifically designed to encourage the children to propose 'what-if' situations. The following response describes the way one child in the class attempted the problem.

> We worked out that there would be less trains to the Show during the afternoon because people want to spend the whole day there. By 5.26 some people could have gone to the show in the night. In the fourth question we started with 'How would I get home if I was at the Show at 5 o'clock?' We decided to check other timetables to find alternative trains.

(Victoria, Year 4)

Encouraging children to pretend that they are 'part of' the problem or propose 'what-if' statements can help them to work through problems more easily.

Reflection and application

A Year 3/4 class was asked to investigate patterns in number sequences. The following question was proposed: 'Given the numbers 1–20, how many pairs of numbers can you find with a difference of 7?'

Initially, the children answered the question from a whole-class perspective. Then pairs and individuals set to work to find pairs of numbers with a difference of 8, 9, 10 and so on to 20. The teacher commented that patterning and number sequences motivated the students to continue the investigation. The open-ended nature of the activity (there was more than one correct

Train Timetable
Royal Easter Show

Wollstonecraft Station

Hop on a train or hop on a bus and get to the Show without any fuss.

CityRail

Further information

Train timetables available from:

- Your local station
- Phone InfoLine on 131 500 or
- visit our website at: http://www.cityrail.nsw.gov.au

Royal Agricultural Society

- For Easter Show information call (02) 9704 1000
- Visit their website at: http://www.showground.com.au

Avoid the queues and buy your ShowLink ticket in advance

How to travel with small children

- Fold prams before boarding a train
- Hold their hands when getting on & off trains
- Board the train close to the Guard's carriage which is usually in the middle of the platform. The Guard's carriage has a blue light above the door.

CityRail will make it easy for you to get to the Show

- Look out for signs at stations
- Listen for announcements at stations and on trains
- Large banners will be at stations where you have to change trains to direct you to the Olympic Park trains

---

Visit our new Internet site

http://www.cityrail.nsw.gov.au

Weekends and Public Holidays
April 4, 5, 10, 11, 12, 13, 18   1998

Train Departure Times

Wollstonecraft to Olympic Park

am 8	26	56		
9	26	45	56	
10	26	45	56	
11	26	45	56	
pm 12	26	56		
1	26	56		
2	26	56		
3	26	56		
4	26	56		
5	26			
6				
7				
8	23			

Olympic Park to Wollstonecraft

am 8	17	47
9	17	47
10	17	47
11	17	47
pm 12	17	47
1	17	47
2	17	47
3	17	47
4	17	47
5	17	
6		
7		
8	53	

Train journey time between Olympic Park and Wollstonecraft is 40 minutes.

Figure 2.4 Train timetable 1998   *Source:* Reprinted with permission of State Rail Marketing, NSW.

answer) provided opportunities for the children to engage in a range of mathematical processes.

Some of the students, for example, used calculators to generate answers. In some instances, the teacher commented that this was completed initially in an haphazard manner. Interestingly, procedures became more refined with experience.

> *Some of the children began to see patterns when they wrote solutions on paper. In the beginning they were simply punching numbers in, but soon began to estimate answers and became more refined with their trial-and-error approaches.*

(Teacher, Year 3/4)

These children were using technology to verify answers in ways that allowed them to modify their problem-solving strategies.

Other children reflected upon solutions they had generated in a quite constructive manner, and as a result were able to apply acquired knowledge to other situations. Figures 2.5 and 2.6 are samples of two children's reflective comments based on the patterns they generated to help solve the problem.

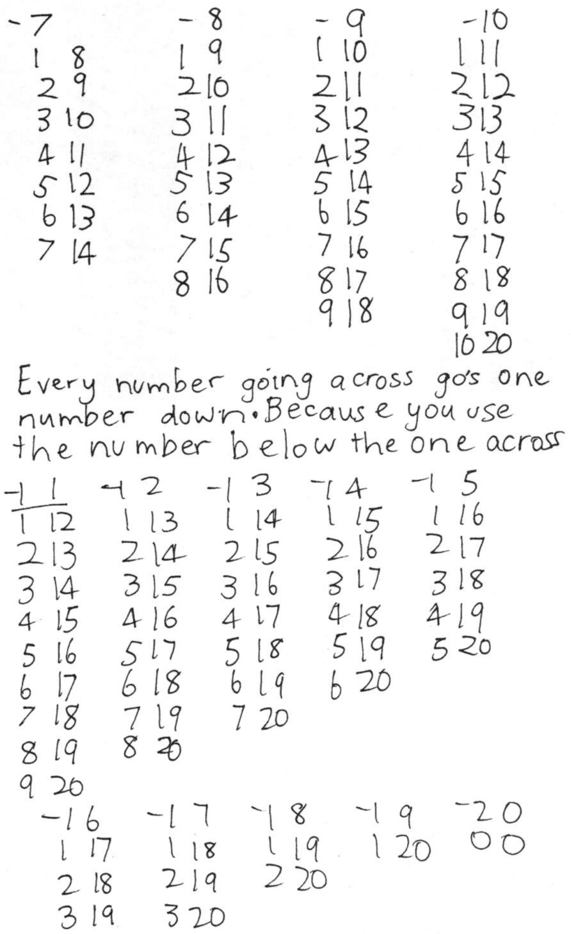

Figure 2.5 A Year 3 child's reflective comment and representation of the pattern

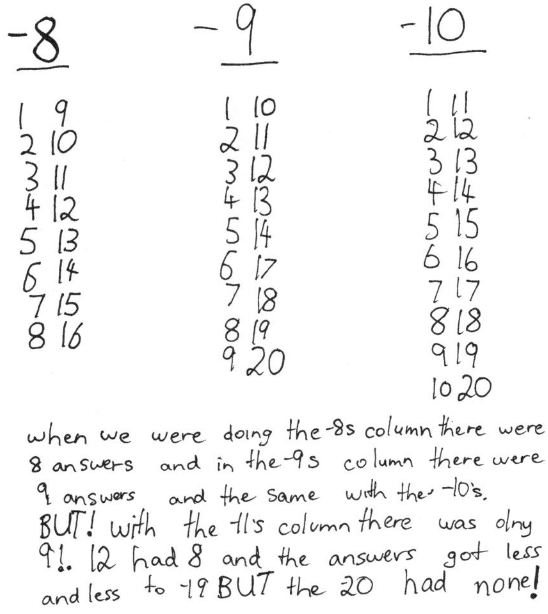

	−8			−9			−10	
1	9		1	10		1	11	
2	10		2	11		2	12	
3	11		3	12		3	13	
4	12		4	13		4	14	
5	13		5	14		5	15	
6	14		6	17		6	16	
7	15		7	18		7	17	
8	16		8	19		8	18	
			9	20		9	19	
						10	20	

when we were doing the −8s column there were 8 answers and in the −9s column there were 9 answers and the same with the −10's. BUT! with the 11's column there was olny 9!. 12 had 8 and the answers got less and less to −19 BUT the 20 had none!

Figure 2.6 A Year 4 child's working and reflective comment on the pattern generated during the investigation

One Year 4 boy looked at his 7 pattern (see Figure 2.6) and instantly recognised that for a difference of 8, as opposed to 7, he could take the first number from the first column and the second number from the second column—in other words 1 and 9, 2 and 10 and so on. He used his initial pattern, presented in a table style, to continue the investigation to numbers with a difference of 20.

Symbolising

The use of symbols provides opportunities for mathematics to be communicated in an efficient manner. Symbols allow us to represent complex relationships in concise ways. In the context of mathematical problem solving, Silver (1987, p. 40) suggests:

> *Students' problem-solving abilities might improve greatly if they could use working memory more efficiently, that is, if they learned to use automatic processing for more routine elements of an activity and thus made resources available for the controlled processing of the novel aspects of solving assigned problems.*

An average Year 2 student attempting to work out 'eight lots of four' may not automatically respond with an answer of '32'. Such a student may require concrete materials, which are grouped into eight lots of four. Children who do not count by fours may count each block individually (using one-to-one correspondence) in order to solve the problem. Most Year 6 students, on the other hand, would not consider this question to be a problem and would quickly respond with the answer '32'. These students did not need to use concrete materials because they could express the answer symbolically.

Consider the following problem:

> *74 marbles are divided so that John has 2 marbles and Mary has 5 times as many as Jim. How many marbles does each person have?*

One way to represent the problem is illustrated in Figure 2.7.

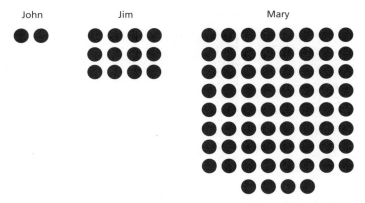

Figure 2.7 A concrete representation of the problem

One student found it useful to actually have 74 marbles (or another concrete representation of 74 objects) and a piece of paper with the names John, Jim and Mary written in a column format. The person might give John 2 marbles and then give Mary 5 marbles for every marble given to Jim. A solution is reached when there are no marbles left to distribute.

In contrast, a student who could use symbols may solve it using symbols:

$5 \times ? + \text{Jim} + 2 \, (\text{John}) = 74$
$6 \times ? = 72$
$\qquad ? = 72 \div 6$
$\qquad ? = 12$
John = 2, Jim = 12, Mary = 60.

If the previous problem stated that 182 marbles, instead of 74, were to be distributed among three people, the novice would probably find the task more difficult (needing to have 182 objects is more difficult in itself). The student who solved the problem symbolically would not have too much difficulty completing this task. The movement towards symbolic representations of mathematical ideas provides opportunities for the development of algebraic reasoning. Most syllabus documents encourage the development of such reasoning (initially through patterning activities) from the early years of school.

WHAT IS PROBLEM SOLVING?

In order to understand something we need to actively engage in it: model it with objects; have a picture or image of it; or symbolise it through language. For example, when learning to walk, a child definitely needs to go through a sequential process (doing it), which usually involves a great deal of trial and error. Similarly, using a diagram that tables streets and buildings helps us to understand how to get to a particular destination more efficiently. Third, our language provides us, or someone else (e.g. a parent or teacher), with an ability to explain situations in order to better understand how to complete tasks successfully. These three examples are actually problem-solving situations.

It will be advantageous for the teacher to provide opportunities for children to experience mathematics in real-life problem-solving situations. After all, this is how we really learn. One way of looking at a problem may involve a process where:

+ a goal is to be reached (the task solved);

+ an obstacle prevents a ready solution (the blockage to a solution);

+ the solver is motivated to reach a solution (the motivation).

Figure 2.8 gives a representation of this process.

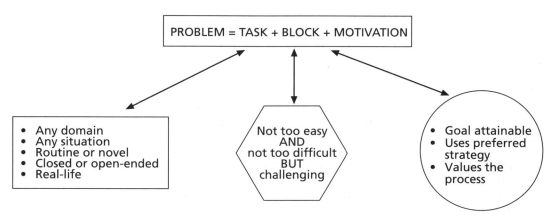

PROBLEM = TASK + BLOCK + MOTIVATION

- Any domain
- Any situation
- Routine or novel
- Closed or open-ended
- Real-life

Not too easy
AND
not too difficult
BUT
challenging

- Goal attainable
- Uses preferred strategy
- Values the process

Figure 2.8 What is a problem?

Different types of problems

Figure 2.8 indicates that problems can be presented in a variety of forms. It is important that problem-solving experiences are not restricted to one particular type of problem (e.g. word problems). Baroody (1993) identified the characteristics of 'routine word problems' and 'real problems', which may be helpful for you when you are trying to select appropriate problem-solving tasks for children (see Exhibit 2.1).

EXHIBIT 2.1 ROUTINE WORD PROBLEMS VERSUS REAL PROBLEMS

Routine word problems often found in traditional textbooks

- The unknown is specified or readily apparent.
- Only the specific information needed to calculate the answer is provided.
- One correct solution procedure is obvious.
- There is one correct answer.
- The answer is quickly computed.

Problem-solving endeavours common to everyday life and mathematics

- The unknown may not be specified or obvious.
- Too much or too little information is available.
- Many solution procedures, which may or may not be apparent, apply.
- There are a number of answers or even no answer.
- Significant problems are often time-consuming to solve.

Although routine word problems should be utilised, it is necessary to expose students to a variety of non-routine problem-solving tasks (e.g. Lovitt & Clarke, 1988; Sullivan & Lilburn, 1998). These activities allow students to work at different levels, depending on a range of factors including ability, motivation and the student's capacity to access relevant information.

The following may be considered a routine problem:

Jayne was allowed to invite eight friends to her birthday party. She decided to make a special party bag for each of her friends. Each bag contained two chocolate frogs, three snakes, two sticks of liquorice and four additional lollies. How many lollies did Jayne need for the eight bags?

There is only one answer to this problem: 88 lollies. This task could easily be modified so that it is more challenging, with children encouraged to devise a means of recording and calculating additional variables. The student could be given a relevant price list from a nearby store or supermarket that had prices of bags of lollies. An open-ended question could then be developed:

You have $15 to spend on a party. Your task is to make eight lolly bags for your friends. It is important to have the same number of lollies in each bag. What will each bag contain? If another child came, how could you arrange the lollies so that there was a fair share in each bag?

This task is more challenging and motivating, and should generate an interesting discussion. Many combinations or options could be developed. The problem solver will have to decide which option is the best value for money in order to create the best combination in each bag. A Year 3 child's response to this problem is shown in Figure 2.9.

Sullivan (2003) argued that open-ended tasks differ from closed tasks in quite significant ways. He maintained that open tasks:

+ more actively engage learners in thinking about the situation and consequently enhance the potential for construction of new knowledge;

+ are more accessible in the sense that students can use what knowledge they have in more flexible ways (children can use the knowledge they have about perimeter to explore aspects of area whereas closed questions require the recall of specific area and perimeter formulae); and

+ offer opportunities for extension of mathematical thinking because children can explore a range of options as well as consider a generalised response.

ACTIVITY 2.2

Open-ended problem solving

1. Develop two open-ended problems for someone to solve.

2. Write down the relevant knowledge and processes required to complete each problem. Consider the approach you would take to solve the problem and record your working.

3. Give the problems to the child/adult. Let that person solve the problem. You may find that he or she solved the problem in a different way from you. Encourage your subject to talk about the way he or she solved the problem. You may also like to share your method or approach. Be supportive. If the activity does not work well, do not get discouraged. Try again soon. You will be amazed at how well you can design problems in a very short time. You will also learn a great deal about the problem-solving process.

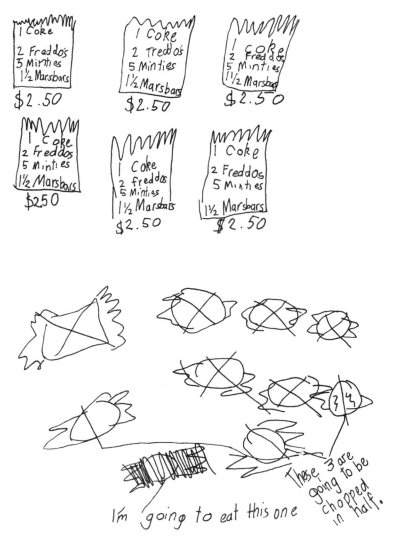

Figure 2.9 Year 3 child's solution to the 'lolly problem'

PROBLEM SOLVING AND MATHEMATICAL THINKING

Most models describe the problem-solving process in terms of:

1. the way the problem is represented;
2. relevant knowledge accessed;
3. selection of appropriate strategies;
4. affective influences; and
5. importance of reflection and metacognition. It is worthwhile looking at some of these terms in more detail.

In order to assess what children know, we need to consider a range of these elements in the process. On occasion we will be able to isolate a particular component of the process.

A student, for example, may have used an inappropriate strategy to solve a problem, or alternatively may have used an effective strategy but was not able to remember an important procedure. In contrast, a combination of factors may in fact contribute to the way in which a student solves a problem. An inefficient strategy may have been used because a student did not possess the necessary knowledge to use a more appropriate strategy. How many times have you gone the 'long way around' when solving a problem? Other factors affect the problem-solving success and also influence the way in which a person attempts to solve a problem. These elements are often termed 'affective factors' and include the participant's motivation, task persistence, beliefs and attitudes towards problem solving. These factors not only differ from individual to individual, but also differ with respect to the type of problem being solved. In the following 'examples', important elements of the problem-solving process will be investigated under the following headings:

+ representing the problem;
+ knowledge and problem-solving strategies; and
+ affective factors.

Representing the problem

A Year 6 class had volunteered to look after a vegetable garden that had not been tended for some time. The original patch was approximately 4 metres wide and 5 metres long. As part of a science unit the teacher had encouraged the children to monitor the growth rates of particular vegetables which had different natural fertilisers. Unfortunately some animals, presumably dogs, were getting into the patch and digging up the plants. The children decided that a fence needed to be erected to keep the animals out. The teacher suggested a 1-metre path around the outside of the garden so that the vegetables could be accessed easily. The following accounts show the way three children in the class represented the problem.

1. *Michelle:* The outstanding feature of Michelle's attempt to solve the 'garden problem' was the fact that she did not use any mathematical algorithms in her working. A diagram showing a garden with a surrounding pathway enabled Michelle to 'count around' the perimeter of the picture and calculate a perimeter of 26 metres. The diagram was a scaled representation of the actual problem (in this case, 1 centimetre to 1 metre). Interestingly, she made pencil marks around the outside of the picture, indicating that she used the pencil as a pointer to calculate the perimeter by going around the outside of the diagram. There were no numerals on the page to represent the length or width of the garden or paved area. All that was written was her answer: '26 m'. It was obvious that Michelle had relied almost entirely on her diagram to solve this problem (see Figure 2.10).

2. *Rebecca:* Initially, Rebecca attempted to solve this problem 'in her head'. She then used calculations to summarise the steps she took to solve the problem on paper (4 m + 2 m = 6 m; 5 m + 2 m = 7 m; 7 m × 2 = 14 m; 6 m × 2 = 12 m; 12 m + 14 m = 26 m). For some reason (possibly because of the difficulty of the problem) she used a visual method to confirm her non-visual processing (see Figure 2.11).

TR: Can you tell me why you decided to draw a diagram to solve this problem?
REB: I'm not sure really, but sometimes I mix up perimeter and area problems, perhaps that's why I checked with a picture.

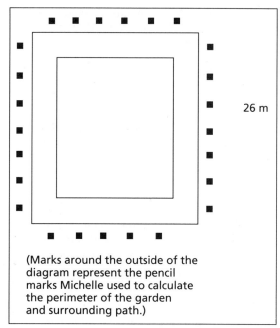

26 m

(Marks around the outside of the diagram represent the pencil marks Michelle used to calculate the perimeter of the garden and surrounding path.)

Figure 2.10 Michelle's representation of the 'garden problem'

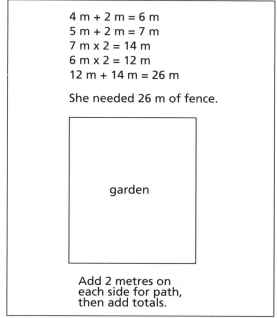

4 m + 2 m = 6 m
5 m + 2 m = 7 m
7 m x 2 = 14 m
6 m x 2 = 12 m
12 m + 14 m = 26 m

She needed 26 m of fence.

garden

Add 2 metres on each side for path, then add totals.

Figure 2.11 Rebecca's response to the 'garden problem'

TR: When you first began to work the problem out, did you have an image of a garden in your mind?

REB: No, not really.

TR: What were you thinking then?

REB: Well I realised it was a perimeter problem, so I just added one to each side and worked out the perimeter.

TR: Then you weren't sure if you were right or wrong?

REB: That's when I drew the diagram.

TR: After you drew the diagram of the garden, did you then think of any garden in particular?

REB: We have several gardens at home, and have large slabs of cement around them, so I suppose I thought about them.

3. *John:* The response from another student, John, revealed that some Year 6 children would represent the problem in a different manner. This student did not use a diagram to represent the problem.

> *If the path around the outside of the garden was 1 metre, then the perimeter of each side would be 2 metres longer than the sides of the garden. That meant that one side would be 6 metres and the other 7 metres. I added up the four sides in my head.*

(John, Year 6)

Knowledge and problem-solving strategies

The same class was given a similar problem to solve later in the week. Unlike the first problem it was open-ended in nature:

You have been asked to design a new vegetable garden for the school. You have been given 26 metres of timber that would be suitable for the outside frame of the garden. Attempt to create the largest vegetable garden possible with this much timber.

The following responses demonstrate the way in which particular individuals solved the problem.

The problem was easy; we have had one like this before. You could have two sides 7 metres long and two sides 6 metres long. I just halved 26, which is 13, and saw that you could have 7 and 6. The area would be 42 square metres.

(Peter, Year 6)

I tried working out lots of combinations by drawing diagrams of gardens with perimeters of 26 metres. I had one with sides of 8 metres and 5 metres and another 7 metres and 6 metres. This had a larger area. I then got a calculator and worked out one with sides of 7.5 metres and 5.5 metres. This area was 41.25 square metres which was not as large as the 7 × 6 = 42 square metres.

(Alice, Year 6)

I tried lots of different lengths and widths with totals of 26 metres. I drew up a table with four columns that had length, width, perimeter and total. The closer I got to a square shape, the larger the area was. I drew up a shape that was 7 metres by 6 metres. It was not a good design because you could not get into the middle of the garden without treading on all the other vegetables. I decided to make two gardens instead of one. This way you could at least get to the plants more easily. I drew lots of pictures and came up with two different gardens. One was 4 metres by 2 metres and the other was 5 metres by 2 metres. It is only 18 square metres of garden but I think it is much better.

(Bruce, Year 6)

ACTIVITY 2.3

The selection of strategies

1. Write down the names of the three children described above and list the strategies they have used to solve the problem. In two instances, a variety of strategies was used. Comment on the mathematical knowledge each child has used to solve the problem.
2. Comment on the relationship between the strategies used by the children and their mathematical thinking.
3. The three children solved the problem in different ways. Their expectations of 'what the problem was asking' were also different. How has this affected the way in which they solved the problem?

Strategies (termed 'heuristics' by Polya, 1956) do not guarantee a correct solution (English & Halford, 1995) but they may provide the problem solver with useful directions in which the solution might proceed (Silver & Marshall, 1990). Some strategies, including 'drawing a diagram' or 'using concrete materials', can be useful in a range of problem-solving contexts because they help the student to represent and link the implied relationships associated with a problem (Lowrie & Hill, 1996; Owens, 1993). Furthermore, the visual and concrete representations can overcome children's cognitive processing limitations in dealing with several aspects at once.

The teaching of specific strategies may increase the likelihood of success in problem solving (Presley & McCormick, 1995; Schoenfeld, 1987) but unfortunately teachers tend to model specific strategies in whole-class situations (Anderson, 1997). This can lead to the perception that you need to solve a problem the way the teacher has completed it. We need to be aware that students may use more than one strategy to solve a problem. Furthermore, they may begin using a particular strategy, and then modify it—or even abandon it—as relationships between attributes of a problem emerge. A student may construct a table to organise data but not complete it when a pattern or relationship between the variables is found. Nevertheless, students should be exposed to a range of problem-solving strategies that can be generalised to different situations. Importantly, children should be encouraged to monitor and reflect upon the strategies they use in particular tasks, and be challenged to consider when such approaches could be applied to different contexts.

Table 2.2 presents a range of typical problem-solving strategies and identifies where they have been used in the children's worksamples presented in this chapter. In some instances, these strategies may have been the most efficient and effective way of completing the task, whereas in other situations the strategy may have been used in conjunction with other strategies. In contrast, some of the strategies may have been weak but still provided opportunities for the student to move towards a solution.

TABLE 2.2 Strategies used by children to complete problems

Strategy	Relevant worksample
Draw a diagram	Figures 2.2, 2.10, 2.11, 2.15
Use concrete materials	Figure 2.7
Make a table	Figure 2.13
Look for a pattern	Figure 2.6
Think of a related problem	Figure 2.5
Use symbols	Figure 2.15
Act it out	Figure 2.12
Make a model	Figure 2.17

Affective factors

An individual's perception of what the problem-solving process involves may influence the way the task is represented and may even determine overall success. On occasion, these perceptions may be reinforced by events that happen in the classroom. If children, for example, are continually asked to solve problems that have one, and only one, answer it is reasonable to suggest that many of the mathematical processes highlighted in the first part of the chapter will not be developed. Furthermore, teachers may inadvertently provide children with a structured format for solving problems—limiting creativity and the desire to employ different methods or approaches. Some Year 4 children were asked how they approached a typical mathematics problem.

> *If the problem is too hard I have always been told to draw a picture because that can help you to understand the problem better.*

(John, Year 4)

> *I circle all the words that I think are important and then decide what I have to do.*

(Margaret, Year 4)

First we write down what the problem is asking, then how we are going to work it out, then we show all our working and write the answer in a word form.

(Carol, Year 4)

ACTIVITY 2.4

Children's attitudes towards problem solving

1. Comment on each individual's responses. To what extent may these opinions affect the problems that are solved?

2. To what extent were these sorts of notions expressed to you at school?

3. Can you suggest why these attitudes may limit opportunities for mathematical thinking?

ACTIVITY 2.5

Personal problem-solving approaches

1. What do you do when faced with a difficult problem? How long do you persist with the problem before giving up? Do you walk away from the situation and come back to it at a later time?

2. To what extent do you go and ask other people for advice? Do you work better in a team or by yourself?

3. How often do you attempt to find an alternative solution to a given problem? How do you determine which solution is more appropriate?

MATHEMATICAL THINKING ACROSS A RANGE OF PROBLEM-SOLVING ACTIVITIES

Research studies have indicated that involving children in problem solving promoted the development of higher order thinking skills. Schoenfeld (1987) suggested that such thinking skills are enhanced when children are encouraged to monitor or 'think about' the thinking processes they use to solve problems. These metacognitive processes (Lester, 1989) are important to successful problem solving and evolve over time (Taplin, 1994). Even young children can be encouraged to discuss and monitor their own thinking processes with instruction (English, 1991; Lowrie, 1998). One way of doing this is to present activities that encourage children to 'think aloud' when solving problems. This can be achieved in co-operative group situations (Baroody, 1993) or by encouraging children to pose their own problems.

Co-operative tasks

Well-designed co-operative learning tasks provide learners with opportunities to monitor each other's reasoning as they attempt to mutually co-ordinate ideas and processes. Even conflicts between the students' ideas and ways of approaching the problem can stimulate cognitive growth (Piaget, 1977). The need to co-ordinate sometimes conflicting ideas and approaches challenges individuals in the group situations to be more reflective about their own ideas and process. Successful problem solvers must be able to reflect on their problem-solving actions, and regulate those processes in an efficient and effective manner.

Problem posing

Problem posing (English & Halford, 1995) can enhance children's mathematical development because it actively involves children in devising their own problems, in solving open-ended problems, and in verifying and testing conjectures. Problem-posing activities also encourage children to focus on the underlying structures of problems and to use them as a source for the construction of new problems. Often, learning situations that require children to develop understandings and skills over extended periods of time provide opportunities for the integration of many of the mathematical processes described in an earlier section of this chapter.

Although reports such as those produced by the National Council of Teachers of Mathematics (NCTM, 2000) have called for an increased emphasis on problem-posing activities in the mathematics classroom, such activities are not promoted on a regular basis. As Silver (1994) argued, 'students are rarely, if ever, given the opportunity to pose in some public way their own mathematics problems' (p. 19). From a teaching perspective, problem-posing activities reveal much about the understandings, skills and attitudes the problem poser brings to a given situation and thus become a powerful assessment tool (English, 1997; Lowrie, 1999). English (1997) proposed that greater attention should be given to problem-posing processes by making greater use of problem situations set within realistic contexts. It seems to be the case that young children are more likely to be able to pose 'appropriate' problems when they have a meaningful context in which to situate the problem (Lowrie, 2002). Providing opportunities for children to scaffold their ideas and understandings is one way of ensuring that the problem-posing contexts are meaningful.

The following two classroom scenarios present long-term problem-solving activities that encourage children to utilise a diverse range of mathematical processes in stimulating learning environments. In both activities, the teacher has designed a program of activities covering a range of understandings that encourage children to consider several dynamics of the problem-solving process (representation, strategies and affective factors). Moreover, increasingly sophistical skills and understandings are required as the children move through the program.

REFLECTION ON A CLASSROOM SCENARIO A

Connections between capacity, mass and volume

A small group of Year 5 children was investigating the relationship between capacity, mass and volume. In particular, the children were looking at the relationship between litres and kilograms, and millilitres, grams and cubic centimetres. In the initial activity the children were required to construct a cubic metre using only newspaper and masking tape.

The following response, from the classroom teacher, describes how the children approached the activity.

> *The discussion went well and the students came up with the idea of a cubic metre. The estimations were way off the classroom and other large spaces. I asked them to imagine and visualise what a cubic metre would look like. The open-ended task was a fascinating thing to watch. All the students were on task and worked well in groups. In particular I observed Shaun (a less able student) taking charge of his group and saying, 'We've got to roll the newspaper out so that it's 100 centimetres long. This is only 70 centimetres long so we need another 30 centimetres to make it a metre'. All the groups were able to make a cubic metre and investigate how many students and school bags would fit inside.*

(Year 5 Teacher)

A photograph of some of the children verifying their estimations is presented in Figure 2.12.

Figure 2.12 Verifying how many students will fit inside a cubic metre

5-5-98

Volume of a Cube.

To make any cubic centimetre from Length, breath and depth you add one to the Leng breath and depth.

Great Drawing.

Length	breath	depth	=
1 cm³	1 cm³	1 cm³	1 cm³ ✓
2 cm³	2 cm³	2 cm³	8 cm³ ✓
3 cm³	3 cm³	3 cm³	27 cm³ ✓
4 cm³	4 cm³	4 cm³	64 cm³ ✓
5 cm³	5 cm³	5 cm³	125 cm³ ✓
6 cm³	6 cm³	6 cm³	116 cm³ ✓
7 cm³	7 cm³	7 cm³	343 cm³ ✓
8 cm³	8 cm³	8 cm³	512 cm³ ✓
9 cm³	9 cm³	9 cm³	729 cm³ ✓
10 cm³	10 cm³	10 cm³	1000 cm³ ✓
11 cm³	11 cm	11 cm³	1331 cm³ ✓
12 cm³	12 cm³	12 cm³	1728 cm³ ✓

Well set out Owen.

Good visual representation
Good monitoring and presentation
— found a pattern.

Figure 2.13 Owen's table format of the volume of shapes

50

In another activity, children were encouraged to explore relationships between an object's dimensions and its volume. Owen (see Figure 2.13) decided to represent his observations in a table format. Interestingly, he attempted to make a link to the previous activity by stating the number of cubic centimetres that would be in a cubic metre. Although his statement was incorrect, he was attempting to generate his own questions. Another group of children wanted to design a container that would hold 3 litres of milk and still be able to fit into a refrigerator. In that week the local Dairy Farmers had decided to release a new 3-litre container of milk and some of the children had obviously been influenced by media releases about the new shape of milk containers. The children needed to link knowledge of volume and capacity (see Chapter 7) to complete this task. One solution is presented in Figure 2.14.

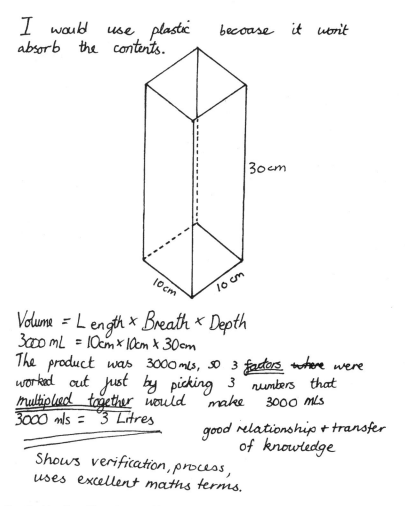

Figure 2.14 A solution for the 3L milk carton problem

An activity that required more advanced mathematical thinking saw one child attempting to calculate the volume of several rooms in her house (see Figure 2.15). One room, the bathroom, had a sloping ceiling, and she required help from her father to generate a solution. Importantly, Cailin had an excellent understanding of what the process involved, and was able to verbalise her thought processes in a sophisticated manner.

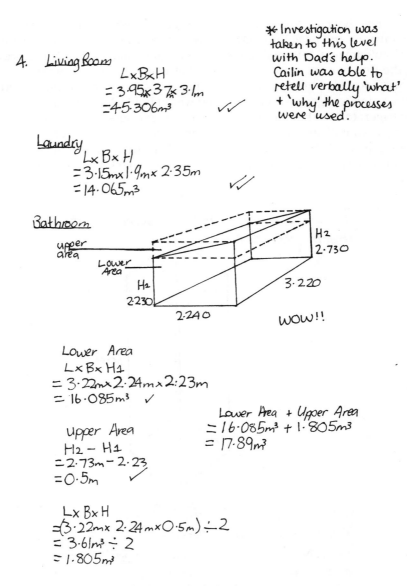

4. Living Room
    $L \times B \times H$
    $= 3.95 \times 3.7 \times 3.1m$
    $= 45.306m^3$ ✓✓

*Investigation was taken to this level with Dad's help. Cailin was able to retell verbally 'what' + 'why' the processes were used.

Laundry
    $L \times B \times H$
    $= 3.15m \times 1.9m \times 2.35m$
    $= 14.065m^3$ ✓

Bathroom

upper area

Lower Area

H_2 2.230

2.240

H_2 2.730

3.220

WOW!!

Lower Area
$L \times B \times H_1$
$= 3.22m \times 2.24m \times 2.23m$
$= 16.085m^3$ ✓

Upper Area
$H_2 - H_1$
$= 2.73m - 2.23$
$= 0.5m$ ✓

$L \times B \times H$
$= (3.22m \times 2.24m \times 0.5m) \div 2$
$= 3.61m^3 \div 2$
$= 1.805m^3$

Lower Area + Upper Area
$= 16.085m^3 + 1.805m^3$
$= 17.89m^3$

Figure 2.15 A sophisticated calculation of the volume of a bathroom

---

ACTIVITY 2.6

Children monitoring their own thinking processes

1. Examine the children's worksamples presented in Figures 2.14 and 2.15. What do you notice about the way the students have described and calculated their solutions?

2. To what extent has the use of diagrams helped them generate solutions?

3. Comment on the way each child has orchestrated a series of mathematical processes to solve the problem. Do you think a calculator was used? Why?

REFLECTION ON A CLASSROOM SCENARIO B

Links between 2D–3D representations within authentic contexts

Another group of Year 6 children was presented with a contour map and photo, and asked to identify as many features as possible. Some of the discoveries included:

+ the lines never crossed;
+ some lines have numbers on them and the numbers make up a pattern;
+ some lines make loops; and
+ the lines are unevenly spaced.

After the children had identified with some important information about key concepts associated with contour maps, small groups were required to build a model that represented a particular map (see Figures 2.16 and 2.17). Members of the group commented: 'Look how steep it is here' and 'That's right, this hill seems to be slightly higher than the other one'. In this particular activity the children were required to create a three-dimensional model of a two-dimensional diagram. They could compare these with a photo.

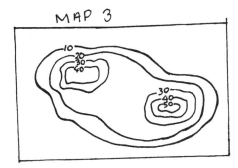

Figure 2.16 A simple contour map

Figure 2.17 A group of children creates a 3D model from the contour map

When the children had become more proficient at representing contour maps in a three-dimensional form they were challenged to interpret and analyse maps at a more sophisticated level. The children were presented with the following problem-solving situation.

The children were required to study a map of a proposed ski resort and wilderness area. In groups, they had to select appropriate sites for construction of the resort.

Some of the questions children raised were:

+ Where would be a good place for a lookout?
+ What section of the map is most suitable for skiing?
+ Where could bike and walking trails be positioned?
+ Which places should be left for wilderness areas?

Figure 2.18 shows how one student attempted the problem. Notice that co-ordinate points have been added to the map so that Liam can describe locations of sites more accurately.

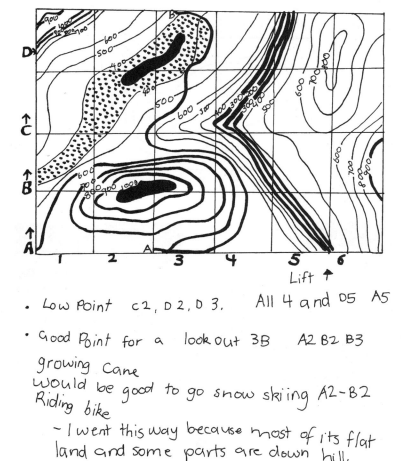

Figure 2.18 Liam's contour map of the resort

SUMMARY AND IMPLICATIONS FOR CLASSROOM PRACTICE

In this chapter we have suggested that mathematical thinking involves the selection and appropriate use of a range of processes. These processes, including investigating, representing, conjecturing, applying and verifying, reflecting and explaining, are intrinsically linked to an overarching process—the process of problem solving. Classroom teachers should provide opportunities for children to develop an extensive repertoire of mathematical processes in order to enhance their problem-solving abilities.

Classroom environments that encourage and challenge children to use a variety of processes in non-routine situations are certainly required—however, teachers need to ensure that the entire problem-solving process is addressed. Teachers need to be able to evaluate an individual's performance with respect to the understandings and processes used, and to encourage the students to apply these processes to new situations (Stacey et al., 1993). In this chapter we have suggested that mathematical concepts and processes are based on the search for patterns and relationships. The effective use of these patterns and relationships provides opportunities for students to choose and apply mathematical understandings to a range of problem-solving situations. 'Mathematical power' is achieved when individuals are able to adapt or modify these patterns and relationships to other, more novel, situations. This is more likely to take place if children are encouraged to monitor their thinking and have some control over the type of investigations presented in the classroom.

In most instances, the mathematical processes presented in this chapter should not be viewed in isolation. A range of processes may be accessed by children in any given situation. Furthermore, individual students may use varying combinations of processes to solve the same open-ended task. The selection of processes will often be influenced by the nature of the task, but could also be determined by the availability of resources, an individual's or group's understanding of the problem, problem representation, or a range of affective dimensions including attitudes or task persistence.

ACTION AND REFLECTION

1. Create a list of the processes children used when solving the activities described in the classroom scenarios above (use the processes presented in Table 2.1 as a guide).

2. In most instances, children used a range of processes to think mathematically. Create a 'web' that represents the 'chain of events' that took place in each scenario. Are there any patterns that emerge from this exercise?

3. Attempt to explain the difference between a strategy and a process in a peer-group situation. Attempt to illustrate differences with specific examples (hint: use Table 2.2).

REFERENCES

Anderson, J. (1997). Teachers' reported use of problem solving teaching strategies in primary mathematics classrooms. In F. Biddulph & K. Carr (Eds), *People in mathematics education*. Proceedings of the 20th Annual Conference of the Mathematics Education Research Group of Australasia Conference, Rotorua, New Zealand.

Australian Education Council. (1991). *A national statement on mathematics for Australian schools*. Melbourne: Curriculum Corporation.

Baroody, A. J. (1993). *Problem solving, reasoning, and communicating: Helping children think mathematically*. New York: Macmillan.

Board of Studies, NSW. (1998). *Mathematics K–6 outcomes & indicators*. Sydney: Board of Studies.

Burrill, G. (1998). Let's talk about mathematical thinking and reasoning. *NCTM News Bulletin*, January.

English, L. (1991). Young children as independent learners. In G. Evans (Ed), *Learning and teaching cognitive skills* (pp. 70–86). Melbourne: Australian Council of Educational Research.

English, L. (1997). Promoting a problem-posing classroom. *Teaching Children Mathematics, 3*, 172–179.

English, L. & Halford, G. (1995). *Mathematics education: Models and processes*. Hillsdale, New Jersey: Lawrence Erlbaum Associates.

Lester, F. (1989). Reflections on mathematical problem-solving research. In R. I. Charles & E. A. Silver (Eds), *The teaching and assessing of mathematical problem solving* (pp. 115–124). Hillsdale, New Jersey: Lawrence Erlbaum Associates.

Lovitt, C. & Clarke, D. (1988). *Mathematics curriculum and teaching program activity bank*, Vols I and II. Melbourne: Curriculum Corporation.

Lowrie, T. (1998). Developing metacognitive thinking in young children: A case study. *Gifted Education International 13*(1), 9–16.

Lowrie, T. (1999). Free problem posing: Year 3/4 students constructing problems for friends to solve. In J. Truran & K. Truran (Eds), *Making a difference* (pp. 328–335). Mathematics Education Research Group of Australasia Incorporated: Panorama, South Australia.

Lowrie, T. (2002). Young children posing problems: The influence of teacher intervention on the type of problems children pose. *Mathematics Education Research Journal, 14*(2), 87–98.

Lowrie, T. & Hill, D. (1996). The development of a dynamic problem-solving model. *Journal of Science and Mathematics Education in South-east Asia*, XIX, 1–11.

National Council of Teachers of Mathematics (1989), *Curriculum and evaluation standards for school mathematics*. Reston, Virginia: National Council of Teachers of Mathematics.

National Council of Teachers of Mathematics. (2000). *Curriculum and evaluation standards for school mathematics*. Reston, Virginia: National Council of Teachers of Mathematics.

NSW Department of Education. (1989). *Mathematics K–6*. Sydney: NSW Department of Education.

Owens, K. D. (1993). Spatial thinking processes employed by children in mathematical problem solving. Unpublished PhD dissertation. Geelong: Deakin University.

Piaget, J. (1977). *The equilibrium of cognitive science*. Chicago, Illinois: University of Chicago Press.

Polya, G. (1956). *How to solve it*. Princeton, New Jersey: Princeton University Press.

Queensland Studies Authority. (2003). Mathematics Year 1 to 10 Syllabus DRAFT. http://www.qsa.qld.edu.au/yrs1_10/kla/mathematics/syllabus.html

Presley, M. & McCormick, C. (1995). *Cognition, teaching and assessment*. New York: Harper Collins College Publishers.

Schoenfeld, A. H. (1987). *Cognitive science and mathematics education*. Hillsdale, New Jersey: Lawrence Erlbaum Associates.

Silver, E. A. (1987). Foundations of cognitive theory and research for mathematics problem-solving instruction. In A. H. Schoenfeld (Ed), *Cognitive science and mathematics education* (pp. 33–60). Hillsdale, New Jersey: Lawrence Erlbaum Associates.

Silver, E. A. (1994). On mathematical problem solving. *For the Learning of Mathematics, 14*(1), 19–28.

Silver, E. & Marshall, S. (1990). Mathematical and scientific problem solving: Findings, issues, and instructional implications. In B. Jones & L. Idol (Eds), *Dimensions of thinking and cognitive instruction* (pp. 265–290). Hillsdale, New Jersey: Lawrence Erlbaum Associates.

Stacey, K., Groves, S., Bourke, S. & Doig, B. (1993). *Profiles of problem solving*. Victoria, Australian Council for Educational Research.

Sullivan, P. J. (2003). The potential of open-ended mathematics tasks for overcoming barriers to learning. In L. Bragg, C. Campbell, G. Herbert & J. Mousley (Eds), *MERINO—Mathematics education research: innovation, networking, opportunity* (pp. 812–816). Proceedings of the 26th Annual Conference of the Mathematics Education Research Group of Australasia. Geelong: Deakin University.

Sullivan, P. J. & Lilburn, P. (1998). *Open-ended maths activities: Using 'good' questions to enhance learning.* Melbourne: Oxford University Press.

Taplin, M. (1994). Development of a model to enhance managerial strategies in problem solving. *Mathematics Education Research Journal, 6*(1), 79–93.

WA Department of Education and Training. (2000). Western Australian Curriculum Framework. [http://www.curriculum.wa.edu.au/pages/framework/framework00.htm]

57

PART

2

The Growth of Mathematical Concepts and Processes

Chapter 3
Using real data to generate mathematical thinking

CHAPTER OVERVIEW

The use of real data is an easily accessible and powerful resource for developing children's mathematical knowledge. This chapter promotes the idea that mathematics learning can be reorganised to be almost completely 'data driven'. Although the explosion of information technology has fuelled the movement towards data-driven curricula, the interpretation of real data has long been recognised as a valuable basis for developing analytical skills. The development of data-handling skills is now considered essential for survival in societies dependent on information technology.

The inclusion of data handling in mathematics curricula worldwide has become increasingly important over the past decade (Curriculum Corporation, 2000; National Council of Teachers of Mathematics [NCTM] 1996; 2000). In Australia, Numeracy Benchmarks (Curriculum Corporation, 2000) formally highlight the importance of data exploration in the Measurement and Data strand, as critical to numeracy.

> *Students collect and organise information to answer specific questions and display their findings in simple graphs. They interpret and comment on information presented in simple tables and graphs.*
>
> **(Curriculum Corporation, 2000, p. 37)**

The inclusion of a 'data' strand in current Australian mathematics curricula focuses on the processes of collecting, organising, representing and interpreting data in a variety of forms.

> *Data addresses the need for all students to understand, interpret and analyse information displayed in tabular and graphical forms. Students learn to ask questions relevant to their experiences and interests and to design ways of investigating their questions. They need to recognise when information has been displayed in a misleading manner that can result in false conclusions. By providing students with some experience in working with data they will be better able to understand statistical arguments and recognise the sound and unsound use of statistics.*
>
> **(Board of Studies, NSW, 2002)**

Furthermore, using real data helps children to see the relevance of mathematics and integrates many aspects of mathematics learning that might traditionally be taught in a disconnected way (Board of Studies, NSW, 1993; Folkson, 1996).

The inclusion of a data strand in mathematics curricula is relatively new to many teachers. In this chapter, fundamental aspects of data exploration and handling are highlighted to support teachers in developing a broader understanding of descriptive statistics and some aspects of inferential statistics. However, the integration of probability (chance) and statistics is encouraged because they are conceptually linked (Watson & Kelly, 2002). Chapter 9, 'Exploring chance and probability', is devoted to the development of probability ideas and the relationship between chance and data handling.

Chapter focus questions

The use of real data exemplifies important links within mathematical strands and integrates content and processes across other key learning areas. This chapter will address some important questions regarding data handling and its use for the teaching and learning of mathematics at the primary school level. Consider your responses to these focus questions before reading further and, if possible, share them with your peers:

1. What skills do children develop as they handle real data?
2. In what ways can we make use of real data to generate mathematical thinking?
3. Rather than teaching each part of the syllabus separately, how can we integrate aspects of number, space and measurement with explorations in data handling and interpretation?
4. do we need to look for when assessing data-handling processes?

REFLECTION ON A CLASSROOM SCENARIO

Using real data in the classroom

Students from a large metropolitan school ranging from preschool to Year 6 and a rural school participated in a project about a school census. The children were asked to collect and record data on the population of school children by grade level and gender. Figures 3.1 and 3.2 show how Years 3 and 4 children from the rural school represented the data. Notice that Figure 3.1 shows a sketch graph drawn without a vertical axis or numerical values. Figure 3.2 shows a column graph with each unit marked on the vertical axis. Figure 3.3 shows how the graphing function of a database was used to display the information in a variety of representations: a column graph showing frequency by grade, and a pie chart showing proportion of students by grade level.

After completing the activity the teachers discussed the students' work.

Well I was absolutely amazed at what my class did with the information. I got lots of different graphs, pictures, tallies and bar graphs . . . Some children didn't arrange the numbers on the axes but they had the right idea. Some even wrote a page of questions to further the investigation. Nomiki asked why there were fewer children in kindergarten compared with Grade 4. That sparked a lot of discussion in the classroom.

(Year 4 teacher, rural school)

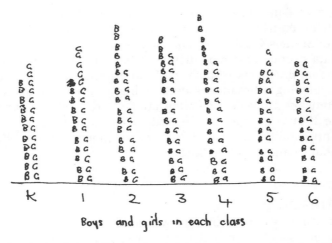

Figure 3.1 Year 3 (rural school) drew, freehand, a sketch graph using symbols B and G for boy and girl as frequencies

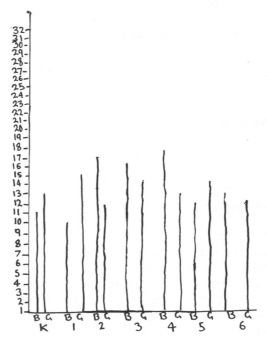

Figure 3.2 Year 4 (rural school) represent the same data as a column graph using symbols B and G as labels

I helped my children enter the information into a database, and we used the graphing function to display it in different ways. We were able to split the data by boys and girls, combine classes, and do all sorts of data exploration. The children were particularly excited because it was their own data that they had collected. The computer sorted the data and drew the graphs so quickly that we were able to spend most of our time talking about what each graph meant, deciding which was the best way to represent different information, and posing new questions to be answered from the data.

(Teacher, Year 6, metropolitan school)

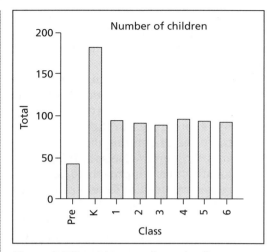
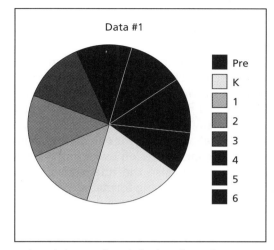

Figure 3.3 Year 6 (metropolitan school) computer-generated a column graph and pie chart from the same data

The graphs constructed by Years 3, 4 and 6 children (Figures 3.1–3.3) cannot be treated as isolated mathematical concepts. They were constructed in response to a social context—a school census—and are therefore more meaningful to the children than if they were required to graph irrelevant data generated by an adult or provided by a traditional textbook. The children were actively involved in collecting, organising and representing the data. Australian research by Watson & Moritz (1999; 2001) has emphasised the power of embedding abstract mathematical concepts in the everyday experiences of children to enhance their understanding. While all the graphs are visually different, they are representations of the same real-life data that are familiar to the children.

The Year 4 teacher encouraged her students to explore various representations without imposing restrictions. As a whole class and in small groups, they discussed and compared their graphs. As a result of this feedback, some children made several attempts to record the information in more sophisticated ways. The teacher recognised the importance of children interpreting the data, analysing and formulating predictions or questions to further the investigation. Research indicates that major obstacles to teaching children data-handling skills and concepts include the lack of essential teacher knowledge and understanding of many statistical concepts, and teachers avoiding teaching these concepts due to lack of confidence (Gal, 2000). Edwards (1996) argues that concern over teachers' lack of knowledge reflects 'transmission models of teaching which emphasise the passing on of knowledge' rather than a constructivist view, which accepts teaching and learning to be 'more a process of negotiating meaning' (p. 184). The Year 4 teacher was not concerned by the fact that children's investigations were progressing in different directions.

A prime function of graphs is to communicate information by summarising and organising collections of data. As soon as there is a need to describe a set of data in a more succinct way, the notions of range, distribution, average, mode and median arise. For example, the word 'average' usually emerges in young children's discussions about data. Often it is used informally to refer to 'usual', 'typical' or 'middle'. In upper primary, we introduce the term 'mean' to refer to average, but children often confuse mean with median and mode (Mokros & Russell, 1995). By utilising the computer to generate various graphing representations of the data collected, the Year 6 teacher was able to spend more time discussing the information represented by the graphs, thus building up children's understanding of such concepts as mean, range, median and mode. McClain, Cobb and Gravemeijer (2000) also support the use of computer tools in forming an integral aspect of statistical reasoning in developing instructional sequences.

Typically, children up to about Year 3 describe data representations in terms of the number of times an observation occurs. Therefore, they are often concerned mostly with the mode or most frequent value. By Year 4 experientially–based notions of average usually emerge. However, recent research indicates that students introduced to the 'add-em-up-and-divide' algorithm for calculating average often ignore the underlying meaning of the data and concentrate on executing the procedure (Kamii, Pritchett & Nelson, 1996). Such findings emphasise the importance of adopting a constructivist approach to teaching. Rather than imposing formal algorithms from a young age, we need to develop children's intuitive understandings of data-handling concepts and help them construct new and more sophisticated ones. This is best done by allowing children time to explore and discuss among themselves the various ways of representing and interpreting data derived from their everyday experiences (National Council of Teachers of Mathematics, 2002a).

The following section uses examples of children's explorations in data handling to articulate key mathematical concepts and processes that are based on research and practice. It not only reflects current initiatives in the mathematics curriculum, but also illustrates the growth from informal to formal mathematical ideas as a dynamic and creative process.

THE GROWTH OF MATHEMATICAL UNDERSTANDING

This section will provide an overview of key mathematical processes of classifying, collecting, representing, interpreting and reporting of data. There are examples of children's attempts to classify, collect and organise data, and how their representations emerge in increasingly sophisticated ways. The more formal processes of data analysis, representation and interpretation include aspects of real statistical processes in an attempt to encourage more able children to explore their potentials and interests.

This overview might be best interpreted as a descriptive categorisation of processes that are interrelated. It is not intended to be used as a sequential 'checklist'. Children may develop different processes simultaneously, especially when encouraged to participate in experiences integrating many data-handling, representation and interpretation skills. The mathematical focus might be initiated through questions posed by the teacher or by the students. Investigations that follow could require students to suggest possibilities, make estimates and approximations, and carry out the process of data collection and handling. Allowing children to work collaboratively provides opportunities for them to test their ideas, justify and share their thinking, and work as team members.

Encouraging young children to visualise and organise data

Teachers can encourage children to develop critical skills and strategies fundamental to statistical thinking through relevant, everyday experiences. This can be promoted from an early age where preschoolers are involved in explorations that require them to pose questions and seek answers, and to organise and communicate their thinking in increasingly structured ways. For example, children who sort and classify objects can be asked to organise and draw their groupings so that the number of things in the group can be counted (or compared) easily. Children's imagination and visualisation skills are readily developed through play situations where they actively represent others, things or events—where they experiment with situations involving growth and change (e.g. draw pictures of your baby brother growing up from a baby until now; how many changes can you think of?). Data about their play situations and experiments can be readily recorded through photographs, drawings and models. Perhaps it is the teacher's role to question children about their thinking and their organisation of the data, rather than always organising and displaying the data for the children.

Children can be encouraged to represent more than simple discrete classifications of objects and things; they can represent continuous data as growth and change (e.g. growth of a plant), order and record sequences of events, and collect and analyse data in a variety of forms (e.g. how much water do I drink each day?). Visualising aspects of their data collection and how they are going to represent data is a very important process. Later, children will need to visualise and interpret the shape of data in terms of the spread or variability.

Integrating number concepts and processes through children's representations of data

Representations can take a variety of forms; many children represent data in idiosyncratic ways. Young children's scribbles might gradually be replaced by more structured and detailed drawings of real things, and icons such as dots, lines, dashes or notations to represent groups and quantities. The emergence of formal graphical representations using gradations of scale and horizontal and vertical axes might be considered somewhat disconnected with the child's 'image' of how they first see their data.

Counting, ordering, matching, grouping and partitioning processes

These processes are critical in the formation of many early mathematical concepts; explorations with data can facilitate the development of these skills in a variety of contexts. Counting in patterns and multiples, and keeping track of the number of groups (double counting), is a difficult but important process in the development of multiplication and division concepts; using equal grouping is critical in drawing graphs and accurately drawing graphs using scale and ratio. Constructing simple grids is more difficult than one might expect, with many children focusing on drawing individual squares or units rather than seeing the patterns or intersections of rows and columns. More efficient ways of counting and partitioning collections can be facilitated with the use of a calculator, and through structures such as simple arrays, grids, pegboards and materials with rows and columns. Understanding and justifying the need for a baseline and representing items in one-to-one correspondence are also encouraged through these experiences.

Allowing children to experiment with organising and displaying data

Children need to experiment with organising and representing a set of data many times over. Through trial and error children will come to realise that data need to be organised and presented so that they can be interpreted easily by others. From such experiences as making rough recordings of categories, tables, frequencies and graphs, children will identify the need for data to be represented in more precise and uniform ways. Rather than imposing precision on children by always giving them grid paper or preorganised tables or graphs, children can be encouraged to make attempts, however crude, to show their thinking. Fundamental skills and understandings about data can grow only if children are actively involved in the processes of classifying, collecting, representing and interpreting data. Although the interpretation of data collected and presented by others is important, it does not enable the child to develop critical processes independently.

Questioning the meaning of approximations

The teacher can facilitate the development of data-handling skills by posing appropriate questions that require children to demonstrate increasingly effective ways of collecting, organising and representing data. For example, if children are already able to show units on the horizontal and vertical axes easily, they might be encouraged to use scale or intervals to present the data more effectively.

Describing and comparing the shape of data

In the middle to upper primary years children can be exposed to a wider range of statistical processes by studying data in more depth. Children can find important indicators in the data: sketch graphs can easily show the range and middle data point (median) and, where appropriate, children can calculate and interpret averages (means). Constructing more formal line and pie graphs often requires children to relate fraction knowledge of scale, ratio, percentages and decimals to their representations and interpretations.

Understanding differences between continuous and discrete data

Fundamental to children's development of statistical concepts is their ability to distinguish between discrete data (things that can be counted in units such as counting children's preferences for restaurants) and continuous data (the growth of a dog). *Things that change on a continuum include measures at particular points but also the measures of change in between the data points.* Exploring changes with line graphs requires children to identify relationships between the graph, the data set or table, and their interpretation of the changes between data points. In this chapter examples of different representations of continuous and discrete data are discussed, but further exploration of rates of change involving growth, speed and time concepts are included in Chapter 8, 'Using measurement to make links'.

The growth of data-handling skills and statistical thinking is integral to mathematical understanding generally. Processes such as classifying, estimating, counting and ordering are the bases of mathematical ideas; visualising and representing mathematical relationships as pictures, diagrams or graphs involves aspects of scale and ratio. Immersing children in problem-solving situations that allow them to experiment with data promotes a more interconnected way of learning mathematics. The following discussion is organised around four main aspects of data exploration: classifying and categorising data; collecting and handling data; representing and interpreting data; and interpreting and reporting findings.

Classifying and categorising information

Young children need to be challenged to make and describe simple comparisons about data through experiences where they:

+ pose and answer questions about why things are grouped and classified in particular ways;

- identify and name collections and groups, and list things that can and cannot be grouped;
- sort, count, describe and record (draw) collections in systematic ways individually and collaboratively;
- sequence pictures, objects or events and find missing parts in a sequence;
- organise, describe and record collections according to one or two attributes; and
- organise and display classified objects so that they can be compared easily.

ACTIVITY 3.1

Examples of children classifying and ordering data

With a small group of your peers, examine Figures 3.4 and 3.5. Discuss your responses to the questions that follow.

(Left): Figure 3.5 Taylor (4 years, 10 months) draws and explains how things are grouped in his bedroom

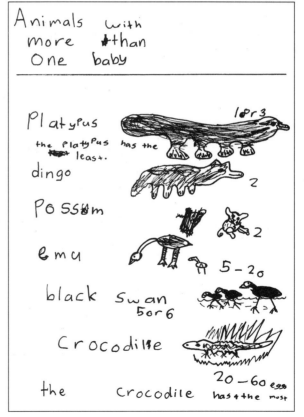

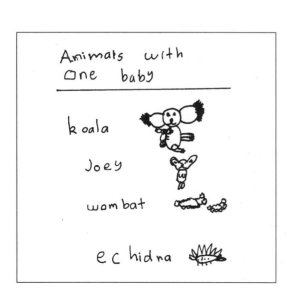

(Above and left): Figure 3.4 Classification of animals (Emma, 7 years)

- Do the worksamples show evidence that the children are describing and questioning their classifications?
- Is there evidence that they can explain and justify the purpose of their simple classifications?
- Can they describe and record similarities and differences between collections and groups?
- Is there evidence that they can talk, read and write about classifications?

Children can classify and organise information in more formal ways where they classify sequences of events, or construct a simple list, chart or table to organise data into categories. However, difficulties arise when children have to organise items using many-to-one correspondence involving simple ratio. Figure 3.4 is a good example of how Emma categorises and orders data about Australian baby animals into tables.

Further challenges are made when posing and interpreting questions of more complex comparison (e.g. 'Are there three times more dogs than cats?'). Suggesting ways to improve a classification and posing-and-answering questions arising from a new classification is even more complex. To extend children's problem-solving skills, reorganising an inadequate classification scheme into a more logical structure is quite challenging.

Collecting and handling data

ACTIVITY 3.2

Collecting and handling data

A group of Year 1 and 2 teachers listed some common aspects about data collection before assessing these aspects in their students' work (see Figure 3.6). Consider the list and determine to *what degree you think each aspect* is evident in the worksample. Teachers should number these aspects in order of importance.

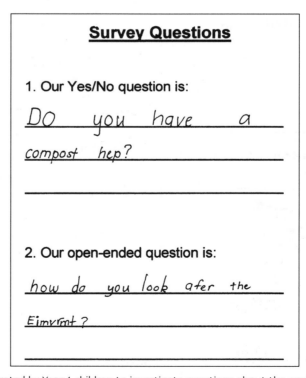

Figure 3.6 A survey generated by Year 1 children to investigate questions about the environment

- Pose simple questions about familiar things and events in order to collect and record information.
- Devise and compare informal methods for collecting and recording data at one time or over periods of time.
- Use simple grouping and counting strategies to combine and compare quantities.
- Invent methods to record data that can be interpreted by others.
- Experiment with simple diagrams and charts, tallies, and pictorial and iconic recordings of data.
- Plan, organise and conduct an investigation systematically.
- Devise and conduct a simple survey using a range of open or closed questions questions; yes or no answers, or simple multiple choice answers.
- Design data collection sheets and schedules.

Children learn to conduct an investigation and handle data in more formal ways by recording data accurately using checklists and tallies, lists, charts, one-way and two-way tables and grids, formal notations and symbols. They can investigate ways of collecting and recording data using calculators, and timing and measurement devices. Spreadsheets and the Internet can also be used as well as retrieving information from print and multimedia sources. More importantly, they need to be able to order and describe data according to highest, middle and lowest scores. They also need to be able to discuss and specify how frequencies or measurements are to be made and recorded.

Other skills include:

+ giving reasons for one collection method being better or more reliable than another;
+ showing how different information can be gained by observing events and situations involving growth and change;
+ discussing the need for consistent presentation of research questions and the possibility of the different interpretations of questions;
+ distinguishing between systematic and unsystematic collection of data, and between organised and disorganised recording of data;
+ identifying missing pieces of data and placing them in appropriate data sets;
+ comparing more than two sets of data related to the same question; and
+ discussing and evaluating data collection methods and conclusions of data collected by themselves and others.

Figures 3.7 and 3.8 on the next page show how Year 4 children categorised and represented their data about favourite restaurants as a block graph and as a bar graph.

Representing and interpreting data

Young children can be encouraged to represent and interpret data informally through pictures, icons, tallies and invented symbols by:

+ designing and constructing informal graphs with real objects, structured materials, pictures, and drawings to represent discrete and continuous data collected by themselves or others (see Figure 3.9);
+ explaining that people, things, events, movements, pictures and other iconic recordings can directly represent data; and
+ producing self-generated representations showing data that has been grouped, counted, ordered and compared.

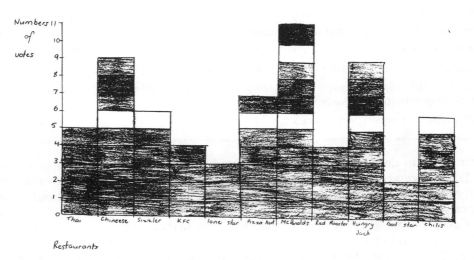

Figure 3.7 4C's favourite restaurants/bar graph, example 1

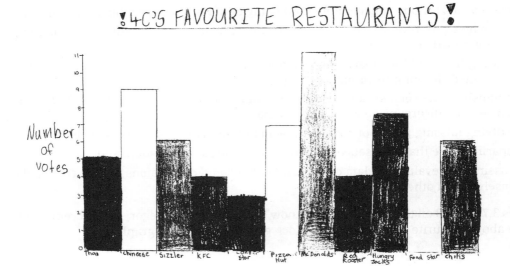

Figure 3.8 4C's favourite restaurants/bar graph, example 2

More conventional methods of representing data can emerge by structuring experiences for children where they:

+ draw and use self-constructed grids and arrays to record, organise or represent data;

+ demonstrate through trial and error a need for a baseline in drawing and making graphs;

+ show co-ordinated use of horizontal and vertical axes, columns and rows;

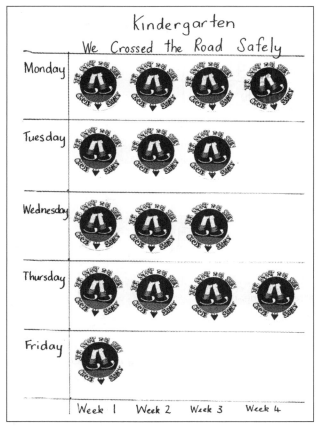

Figure 3.9 A picture graph using a grid and stickers to show the number of times Kindergarten crossed the road to play in the park over a 4-week period

+ display and summarise data initially using frequencies and measurements in whole numbers;
+ draw and construct picture graphs independently and collaboratively using one-to-one correspondence through self-generated methods of recording;
+ draw and interpret simple graphs using computer-based programs such as Kidpix; and
+ construct and interpret simple two-way tables.

Children can represent data in more formal and systematic ways through experiences where they display and interpret data in *bar and column graphs* (horizontal and vertical) where one axis shows whole numbers and the other axis shows two or more discrete categories. Similarly they may recognise the need for using a scale with multiples such as 0, 5, 10, 15. Figures 3.10 and 3.11 show Chloe's (8 years old) attempts to produce a bar graph, with and without grid paper, comparing the types of shoes worn by children in her class. She realises that her scale in Figure 3.10 is not in proportion and adjusts it in the second attempt.

More sophisticated means of summarising and displaying patterns and trends in data can be shown through:

+ constructing and interpreting lines as rating scales;
+ constructing *line graphs* to represent changes and patterns over time (continuous data);

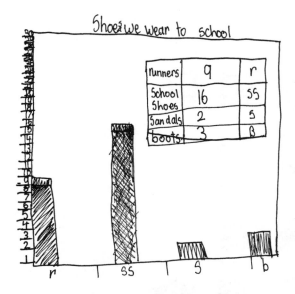

Figure 3.10 Chloe's first attempt at her graph

runners	9	r
School Shoes	16	SS
Sandals	2	S
boots	3	B

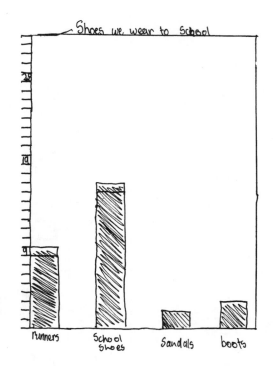

Figure 3.11 Chloe's second attempt, where she adjusts her scale

+ producing diagrams such as tree, Venn and Carroll diagrams to represent or interpret a two-way or three-way classification;
+ constructing and interpreting *pie graphs* with structured and unstructured materials showing relationships with 'fraction knowledge';
+ using visualisation skills to draw column, line and pie graphs from direct experiences and from memory; and
+ constructing and interpreting stem-and-leaf plots related to the data collected.

Figures 3.12 and 3.13 show how Tom interpreted a survey and diagram of decibel measures from print media and applied it to his own data on decibel levels. He was asked to make estimates and represent these estimates in two different graphs showing decibel levels for an ordinary day at school. Notice how he has difficulty drawing the graphs to scale with rows and columns aligned.

Interpreting and reporting findings

Young children can be encouraged to make simple interpretations and recordings about their data by:

+ discussing findings and making statements about their data collection, by counting, matching, partitioning and regrouping (see Figure 3.14);
+ reading, matching and labelling simple information from lists, charts, tallies, one-way tables, diagrams and picture graphs;

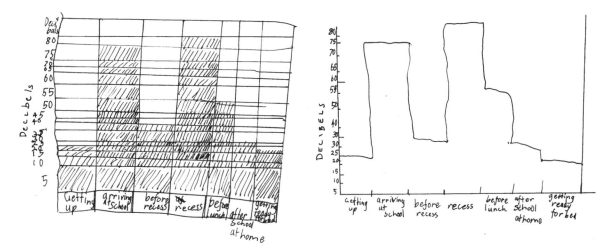

Figure 3.12 Tom's informal column graph of decibel levels during the school day

Figure 3.13 Tom's line graph of decibel levels during the school day

+ making statements and writing about information on graphs (see Figure 3.15); and
+ reclassifying pictorial information to answer questions.

Data generated by others or presented as mathematical investigations provide a range of appropriate sources for interpretation.

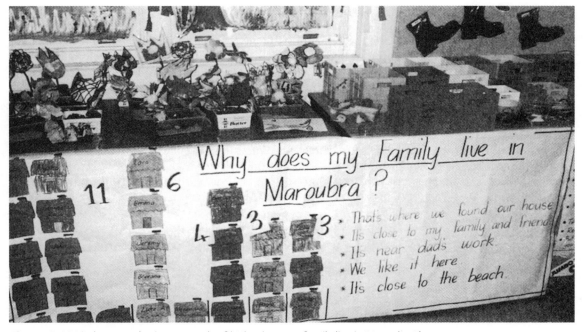

Figure 3.14 Kindergarten's picture graph of 'Why does my family live in Maroubra?'

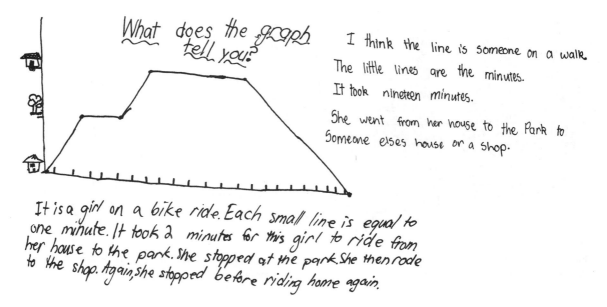

What does the graph tell you?

I think the line is someone on a walk. The little lines are the minutes. It took nineteen minutes.

She went from her house to the Park to someone elses house or a shop.

It is a girl on a bike ride. Each small line is equal to one minute. It took 2 minutes for this girl to ride from her house to the park. She stopped at the park. She then rode to the shop. Again, she stopped before riding home again.

Figure 3.15 Alex and James write stories about a line graph without direct access to the data

SNAPSHOTS OF LEARNING: LESSON PLANNING AND ASSESSMENT

The following worksamples provide 'snapshots' of how children collect, represent and interpret data from real-life investigations about themselves, their family and possessions, and their environment. They show how children can be challenged to make connections between various mathematical processes and the wider curriculum. The integrated nature of the investigations promotes a more holistic approach to developing mathematical concepts and processes, and integrates data with the use of technology. Rather than learning mathematics in compartmentalised 'bits', children develop more 'connected' understandings and processes through a range of problem situations. The investigations provide an integrated focus for many of the processes described in this chapter so far.

Many of the investigations exemplify the use of technology to assist in data exploration, for example the calculator and commercial databases such as the 'First Fleet Journal', and retrieving data from World Wide Web sites. Teachers' reflective comments about their experiences within real classroom situations are included to encourage others to question and discuss, and to experiment with new ways of facilitating mathematics learning.

1. Animals

Years 2, 3 and 4 students researched, recorded, ordered and interpreted data on baby animals in tables and bar graphs (Figures 3.16 and 3.17). The children researched and retrieved information from reference books about the number of babies mother animals gave birth to at one time (Kitchen, 1990).

Number of baby animals

Animal	Possible Number of babies	Average number of babies
Kangaroo	1 Joey	1
Black Swan	Between 2 and 9 cygnets	5
Irish Setter Dog	Between 6 and 10 puppies	10
Pig	Between 10 and 20 piglets	15
Snake	Between 10 and 80	25
Crocodile	lays 70 or more eggs	80
Frog	Thousands of tadpoles	100

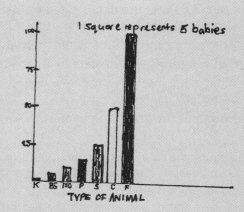

Figure 3.16 Madi orders data and presents them in a table. She records frequency in terms of range and average

Figure 3.17 Madi's bar graph showing scale of 1:5

Teachers' comments

> *They could order the number of babies from least to most but some children had difficulty explaining the range and the average. It was good to hear explanations such as 'the mother swan has about five babies each time but they could have more or less'.*

(Teacher, Year 4)

> *Some children drew the mother and babies as a picture and I had to ask them to redo it several times to get them to show it as a pictograph ... but they did it once they saw other pictographs.*

(Teacher, Year 2)

> *They still had trouble making the scale on the vertical axis to show the number of babies accurately ... grid paper helped.*

(Teacher, Year 3)

Mathematical content and processes
+ Classifies baby animals into categories.
+ Constructs and interprets ordered data in a table.
+ Expresses idea of average number (of babies) by comparing the range of possible number of births.
+ Uses counting and numeration skills: multiples of 5 and 10 to construct and interpret scale.
+ Represents tabulated information in other forms using bar or column graphs.
+ Answers and poses questions of comparison about data.

Posing key questions to assess learning
+ Which animal has the least number of babies at one time? The most babies? Why?

- List facts about the data related to 'how many times more', e.g. snakes have twice as many babies as Irish setters.
- How many more babies would an Irish setter have than a black swan?
- Can you represent the data in other ways (e.g. a picture graph or a bar graph)?
- What is meant by the 'range' (possible number of births) and the 'average' number of births?
- How does the graph show information in the table using scale?

Challenging the children's interpretations of data
- Give possible reasons for differences in the number of babies born to each mother animal at one time.
- Is the number of babies per mother related to the size of the animal?
- Devise other ways to classify and represent the data (e.g. baby animals for pets; baby animals in the wild).
- Write stories about the birth of these baby animals based on the data.

Extending children's investigations
- Conduct further research about animal statistics from books and information technology-based resources, and display information in charts and graphs.
- Use a database to create categories including animal name, location, habitat, height, mass, number of babies, type of food eaten, amount of food eaten each day, average life span and length of gestation period.
- Use the sorting and graphing functions to explore answers to questions generated by the children (e.g. is there any relationship between the type of food the animal eats and the average life span?).

2. Soft toy collection

Kindergarten, Years 1, 2 and 3 students sorted, counted, organised and represented data on soft toy collections in picture graphs using a symbol or tally to represent more than one unit. Their worksamples are presented in Figures 3.18 and 3.19.

Figure 3.18 Jan (6 years old) constructs a picture graph using computer-generated graphics

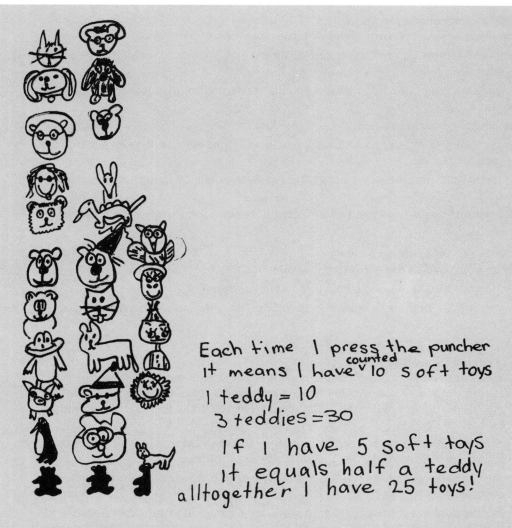

Each time I press the puncher
It means I have counted 10 soft toys
1 teddy = 10
3 teddies = 30

If I have 5 soft toys
it equals half a teddy
alltogether I have 25 toys!

Figure 3.19 Chris (8 years old) uses a teddy symbol to represent twenty-five soft toys as a picture graph. He shows direct relationships between the symbol and the toys and recognises that the symbol can be used independently

Teachers' comments

I got my students to use a calculator, and a hole puncher or (self-inking) stamp to count and record collections in one-to-one correspondence. Then they made equal groups like 2s or 5s or 10s to make it easier to count, but it was harder to co-ordinate the puncher on the count of 2, 5 or 10.

(Teacher, Year 2)

Some children didn't draw the picture graph from a baseline so counting was more difficult. They had to come up with several drafts and reasons for why it is easier to count when organised in one-to-one correspondence.

(Teacher, Year 1)

Mathematical content and processes

+ Sorts, classifies and records small or large collection of soft toys.
+ Counts collections by ones using one-to-one correspondence with a hand-held calculator as a tally.
+ Classifies toy collection by animal type and draws picture graph using computer program Kidpix.
+ Uses language of comparison to describe data.
+ Uses a symbol to represent actual objects in a picture graph where one symbol represents 10 units.
+ Calculates total number of toys represented by symbols by using simple ratios 1:5 and 1:10.
+ Makes comparisons between two different data sets (two different collections).

Posing key questions to assess learning

+ Tell me how you have organised your collections.
+ Why do you think you need a baseline in your graphs?
+ Can you represent your information in another way (e.g. in a two-way table or different graph)?

Extending children's investigations

+ Children could classify other collections and experiment with different forms of representation where one symbol or icon represents more than one unit, such as self-adhesive stickers, self-inking stamps or real objects (e.g. one drink container represents ten drinks).
+ Make a collection of graphs from the print media that use symbols representing more than one unit and discuss the suitability of their use.
+ Pose and answer questions related to the type and frequency of soft toy preferences.
+ Use a computer-graphing program to generate a range of graphs for the same data.

3. Air pollution index

Years 3 and 4 children described and interpreted a picture graph representing three levels of air pollution across three regions. The children were asked to describe and record as much information as possible about air pollution from the picture graph and to represent the information in a different way (Figures 3.20 and 3.21).

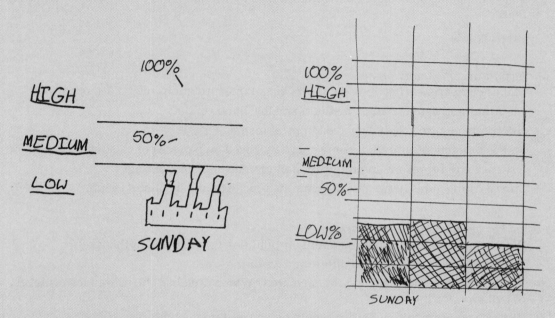

Figure 3.20 Ryan (Year 3) picture graph: pollution levels for Sunday

Figure 3.21 Ryan's column graph: pollution levels for Sunday

Ryan made two attempts to represent low pollution levels for Sunday. The second graph uses an informal scale to show level of pollution as a percentage on a column graph.

Teacher's, parent's and student's comments

> *The children hadn't looked at graphs like this from the newspaper before. Most of them could tell that the smoke stack represented the amount of pollution for the days of the week. It was more difficult to work out the meaning of the three stacks showing differences in regions. Some children made up more simple graphs with one smoke stack for each day ... then we wrote about the pollution using words like 'Tuesday had much more pollution than Saturday'.*

(Teacher, Year 3)

> *Ryan was so excited about finding picture graphs from the newspaper. He cut out about twenty examples from one paper. Some of the picture graphs were complicated but he tried to copy some and draw his own graphs. We talked about what the pictures meant in the graphs.*

(Parent, Year 3)

Sunday would be lower pollution because there's not many people at work but there's still cars on the road and some pollution . . . The lines (in the column graph) are in 10s, 5 for 50 and 5 more for 100 . . . and low means 25 for east, 30 for south-west and 20 for north-west. The 100% is when it's up to the top; and 50% would be in the middle and low would be about 20% . . . The pollution levels could be different each day because of the weather . . . wind rain, heat, dust, fire or clouds. Maybe if there's school holidays there will be too many cars going on holidays. Maybe it could go up to High if there is a bush fire polluting the air.

(Ryan, Year 3)

Mathematical content and processes
+ Makes comparisons between data from visual interpretations over a 7-day period.
+ Identifies and explains high, medium and low bands of data.
+ Interprets picture graph displayed in print media.
+ Makes predictions and represents new data based on patterns of existing data.
+ Uses scale to represent and interpret pollution levels as percentages.
+ Shows connections between self-generated pictures and a column graph.

Posing key questions to assess learning
+ What does the graph show you about air pollution for each day of the week?
+ Why is pollution different on different days of the week?
+ When was the pollution worst for each area? Which area had the overall lowest level of pollution for the week?
+ What do you think the pollution would be like on Sunday? Why?
+ Can you draw your own graph in another way to show what you think the pollution would be like on Sunday?

Extending the investigation
+ What information do you need to collect to work out whether the pollution levels would be like this every week of the year? Make a graph of this information.
+ Collect and graph information on the air pollution levels for different cities of Australia and the world (information can be obtained from newspapers and the Internet). Make comparisons about your data.
+ Do you think air pollution levels are related to the size of population, or are there other reasons for pollution levels to vary?

4. Growth of golden retriever dog

Children in Years 2, 4 and 6 examined and discussed the growth records (and photographs) of a golden retriever puppy, owned by a class member, from birth to 6 months of age. The children were asked to record and compare the growth in terms of mass at 6-week, 3-month and 6-month intervals. Figures 3.22 and 3.23 show some of their recordings.

Blaise's Growth Chart

BIRTH	430g
6 WEEKS	2.6 Kg
12 WEEKS	8.9 Kg
24 WEEKS	25.4 Kg
52 WEEKS	32 Kg

Blaise grow the most betwen 3 months and 6 months. She went from 9 kg to 25 kg. She got 16 kg hevier. When she was 6 months she wead about the same as me.

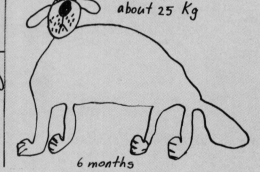

about ½ kg — birth

about 2½ kg — 6 weeks

about 9 kg — 3 months

about 25 Kg — 6 months

Figure 3.22 Picture graph (Michael, Year 2)

Teachers' comments

> *It is very difficult when you compare 430 grams to 25.4 kilograms because they cannot visualise the scale on the graph . . . but through trial and error they worked out that the best scale was 500 grams or half-kilogram parts . . . It was excellent for fractions too because they had to mark off the scale in half-kilogram lots and work out whether they had enough paper.*

(Teacher, Year 2)

> *Most of them got the idea of the dog growing a lot between 6 and 12 weeks. I'm not sure that they can calculate the proportions but the drawings were good estimates and they matched the weight correctly. Most of the predictions at 12 months were sensible. We wrote stories about it.*

(Teacher, Year 4)

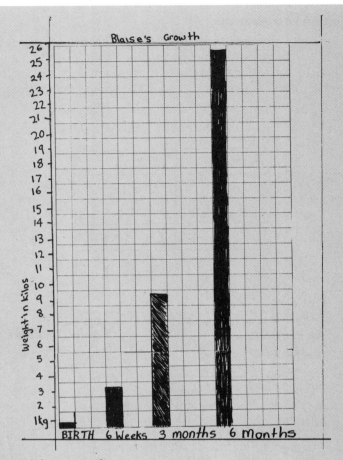

Figure 3.23 Column graph (Jane, Year 4)

Mathematical content and processes

+ Represents the relative size of the dog as picture graph, column and/or line graph using weight/time data with reasonable accuracy.

+ Describes data and poses questions about data from graphs.

+ Expresses understanding of the concept of mass in terms of weight as a measure of heaviness.

+ Explains differences between gradations of scale on column and line graphs.

+ Uses measurement units (1 kilogram = 1000 grams; 500 grams = half a kilogram; 3 months = 12 weeks; 6 months = 24 weeks; 12 months = 52 weeks) to construct scale and interpret graphs.

+ Uses and interprets language of comparison.

+ Uses multiplication expressed as 'times as many' to calculate growth factor.

Posing key questions to assess learning

Can the child justify his or her answers to the following questions?

+ Why does the column graph show growth in kilogram and half-kilogram parts while the line graph shows it in 5 kilogram parts?

- Which graph shows the information most accurately?
- Explain why the graphs look different. Give reasons for this since they show the same information.
- About how much heavier was the dog at 6 weeks old than at birth?
- About how many times heavier was the dog at 6 months old than at birth? Than at 12 weeks? You may use a calculator to show the process.
- Did the dog grow at the same rate over the first 6 months (same amount of growth each day)?

Extending the investigation
- Write a story about the growth of the dog based on the information shown in the graph.
- Collect data about the growth of different dog breeds. Extend the investigation to a comparison of weight, height and length. Record this in a table, and graph the height and weight of different breeds.
- Estimate and represent the amount and type of food eaten by the dog at the various growth points.
- Draw a timeline showing the growth of the dog every month or fortnight and describe the estimated growth spurts.

5. First Fleet convicts

Year 5 students retrieved information from a commercial database titled First Fleet Journal Ed as part of their study of early Australia. The students sorted and classified information; organised and interpreted data; and made predictions and tested hypotheses. They generated a column graph (Figure 3.24) to represent their information.

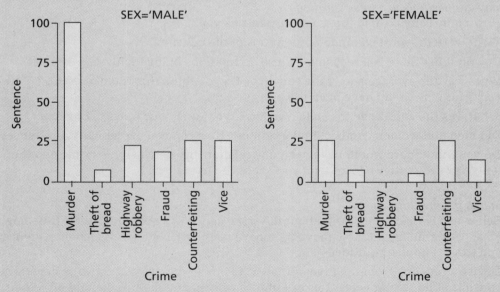

Figure 3.24 Column graph generated from database, showing convict sentences for males and females according to type of crime. *Source:* House, A. (1994) *First Fleet Journal Ed*, Know Ware

Teacher's and student's comments

The children were highly motivated to do this activity. Using the database enabled them to recognise the 'human' aspect of the convicts. It added a valuable dimension to our studies of settlement. They found it very easy to do simple sorting, like 'surname=...'. At first they had difficulty with deciding when to use 'and' and when to use 'or'. We talked about this, and once they mastered it, they were excited about the power the database gave them.

(Teacher, Year 5)

Our group investigated the hypothesis that women were given shorter sentences for the same crime than men were. To find out if this was true, we did a bar graph for the men's sentences for different crimes, and one for the women's sentences. First, we had to sort the data into men and women. We did SEX='MALE' and graphed crime and sentence. Then we did SEX='FEMALE' and did the same graph. We found that the men and women got the same sentences for the less serious crimes, like stealing bread, but that the women got lighter sentences for the serious crimes, like murder. We also found that there were no women who committed some crimes, like highway robbery.

(Student, Year 5)

Mathematical content and processes

+ Sorts and classifies data into various categories.
+ Classifies data according to two or more attributes, by using 'and/or' statements, and knowing which statement is appropriate to use for which purpose.
+ Calculates average and uses term 'age-range' with meaning.
+ Classifies information from general to more specifically defined categories (e.g. comparing crimes by gender and/or by age group).
+ Poses and investigates hypotheses.

Posing key questions to assess learning

+ How many convicts had the same surname as you?
+ What were the most common occupations of the convicts?
+ Do you think there is a reason for these occupations being highly represented?
+ What was the average age of the convicts? Do you think this is old or young? Why do you think this would have been the average age?
+ What was the age-range for male convicts? What was it for female convicts?
+ Did men and women commit similar crimes? How can you explain any differences?
+ Do you think there would have been any relationship between the crime and the length of the sentence? How can you check the hypothesis?

Extending the investigation

+ Select two convicts who were about the same age. Write about how their lives might have been similar, and how they might have been different. Use as much evidence as you can to support your ideas.
+ Devise a timeline from the time of the First Fleet to the present showing dates when convicts of particular categories or families arrived and died. Make tables or charts showing the life span of these people.

SUMMARY AND IMPLICATIONS FOR CLASSROOM PRACTICE

This chapter has emphasised the potential of using real data for developing processes fundamental to statistical thinking. Although little research has been conducted about data-handling skills of young children, constructivist-based learning principles provide a sound basis for our approach (National Council of Teachers of Mathematics, 2002b). In short, to develop children's understandings of data-handling concepts and processes, we need to capitalise on their intuitive ideas and challenge them to develop more conventional and sophisticated forms of statistical thinking. This will be accomplished more successfully if we allow children time to explore different strategies for collecting, organising and interpreting data that are derived from real-life experiences.

ACTION AND REFLECTION

Educators need to reflect on their current classroom context to recognise where opportunities for incorporating data-handling activities exist.

+ When teaching, examine your lessons and programs for the role of data exploration.
+ What data-handling skills and knowledge do the students you are teaching already possess?
+ What significant events are occurring in your educational setting that could fuel data-exploration activities? What are some of the interests your students share?
+ How can these everyday experiences be incorporated into your mathematics lessons through data-handling investigations?

Allow students the freedom to select investigations that are of interest to them. As they work, circulate among the children and question their thinking. Assess their understanding of data-handling processes and concepts by asking them to explain their reasons for each aspect of their investigation. Rather than 'showing' or 'telling' them conventional methods, have the students present their contributions and invite other students to discuss the strategies they have used. Further learning experiences can then be planned by structuring experiences that emphasise particular strategies and concepts.

Data exploration and the development of statistical thinking cannot occur in isolation or in restricted and infrequent bursts of attention. This chapter has instigated many pathways for teachers to make data exploration part of their whole curriculum.

REFERENCES

Board of Studies, NSW. (1993). *Teaching mathematics K–6: Problem solving through chance and data.* Sydney: Board of Studies.

Board of Studies, NSW. (2002). *Mathematics K–6 Syllabus 2002.* Sydney: Board of Studies.

Curriculum Corporation. (2000). *Numeracy benchmarks years 3, 5 & 7.* Melbourne: Curriculum Corporation.

Edwards, R. (1996). Teaching statistics: Teacher knowledge and confidence. In P. Clarkson (Ed), *Technology in mathematics education: Proceedings of the 19th Annual Conference of the Mathematics Education Research Group of Australasia.* (pp. 178–185). Melbourne: Mathematics Education Research Group of Australasia Inc.

Folkson, S. (1996). Meaningful communication among children: Data collection. In P. Elliot & M. Kenney (Eds), *Communication in mathematics K–12 and beyond* (pp. 29–35). Reston, Virginia: National Council of Teachers of Mathematics.

Gal, I. (2000). Adults' statistical literacy: Meanings, components, responsibilities. *International Statistical Review*, 701–751.

House, A. (1994). First Fleet Journal Ed (database). Know Ware Pty Ltd.

Kamii, C., Pritchett, M. & Nelson, K. (1996). Fourth graders invent ways of computing averages. *Teaching Children Mathematics, 3*(2), 78–82.

Kitchen, B. (1990). *Animal number*s. London: Walker Books.

McClain, K., Cobb, P. & Gravemeijer, K. (2000). Supporting students' ways of reasoning about data. In M. J. Burke & F. R. Curcio (Eds), *Learning for a new century*. Reston, Virginia: National Council of Teachers of Mathematics.

Mokros, J. & Russell, S. (1995). Children's concepts of average and representativeness. *Journal for Research in Mathematics Education, 26*, 20–39.

National Council of Teachers of Mathematics. (1996). *Teaching children mathematics—Data exploration focus issue, 2*(6). Reston, Virginia: National Council of Teachers of Mathematics.

National Council of Teachers of Mathematics. (2000). *Principles and standards for school mathematics*. Reston, Virginia: National Council of Teachers of Mathematics.

National Council of Teachers of Mathematics. (2002a*). Navigating through data analysis and probability in prekindergarten–Grade 2*. Reston, Virginia: National Council of Teachers of Mathematics.

National Council of Teachers of Mathematics. (2002b). *Navigating through data analysis and probability in Grades 3–5*. Reston, Virginia: National Council of Teachers of Mathematics.

Watson, J.M. & Kelly, J. B. (2002). Emerging concepts in chance and data. *Australian Journal of Early Childhood, 27*(4), 4–28.

Watson, J. M. & Moritz, J. B. (1999). Interpreting and predicting from bar graphs. *Australian Journal of Early Childhood, 24*(2), 22–27.

Watson, J. M. & Moritz, J. B. (2001). Development of reasoning associated with pictographs: Representing, interpreting and predicting. *Educational Studies in Mathematics, 48*, 47–81.

Chapter 4

Finding connections in space: shape, structure, location and transformations

CHAPTER OVERVIEW

Spatial abilities are employed in the performance of many tasks—from navigating an alternative route from work to home, to receiving a tennis serve, to adjusting furniture in the lounge room. Spatial abilities and perceptions are particularly important because of their relationship to most technical–scientific occupations and to the study of mathematics, science, art and engineering. Teachers should be aware that spatial settings are all around us, and not just in a geometry class (Del Grande, 1990; Owens, 1992). Children may be exposed to a range of spatial–visual experiences that draw attention to important mathematics concepts through open-ended learning situations across all key learning areas (see Lowrie, 1992; 1996). These areas could include art, drama, music, geography and physical education.

The authors of the NCTM's (1989) *Curriculum and evaluation standards for school mathematics* (National Council of Teachers of Mathematics, 1989) commented that, although mathematics is often thought to be a collection of facts and formulas, current research supports a view of mathematics as being the active construction of patterns and relationships. Many spatial relationships are commonly found in the child's day-to-day environment. It is recommended that these 'typical' experiences be linked to spatial and geometric understandings of mathematics.

> *Geometry helps us represent and describe in an orderly manner the world in which we live. Children are naturally interested in geometry and find it intriguing and motivating; their spatial abilities frequently exceed their numerical skills, and tapping these strengths fosters an interest in mathematics and improves number understandings and skills.*
>
> **(NCTM, 1989, p. 48)**

In this chapter a range of essential spatial and geometric understandings will be developed through learning activities across a number of content areas.

In Australian schools spatial and geometric understandings are often developed through the space strand of mathematics. Both *A national statement on mathematics for Australian schools* (Australian Education Council, 1991) and *Numeracy benchmarks years 3, 5 and 7*

(Curriculum Corporation, 2000) classify the space strand (or spatial sense) under headings associated with:

+ classifying shape and structure;
+ transformation and symmetry; and
+ location and arrangement.

The national statement provides the following description of each category.

Shape and structure activities assist students to develop intuition and knowledge about two- and three-dimensional shapes and their relationships to the physical world. Students should also understand shape, structure and function as basic to design through practical and challenging problems. Visualisation skills should improve as students physically manipulate objects, and represent them in two dimensions.

Situations and activities that may develop shape and structure concepts include:

+ recognising shapes close to rectangles, squares, triangles and circles in everyday things;
+ interpreting and beginning to use terms such as 'flat', 'straight', 'rolls' and 'stacks';
+ classifying shapes;
+ identifying the spatial features and things that link shape to functions such as stability, strength and storage;
+ selecting appropriate objects when given spatial features; and
+ visualising and selecting figures and objects that meet geometric criteria.

Transformation and symmetry deals with the manipulation of shapes through translation, reflection and rotation. Some transformations distort shape and size by, for example, producing 2D representations of 3D space. Students may develop and apply understandings of transformations and symmetry across curriculum areas of art, craft and technology, science and geography.

Situations and activities that may develop transformation and symmetry concepts include:

+ using a fold-line to produce symmetrical pictures by drawing freehand, folding, cutting and/or tracing;
+ using language such as turn, rotate, turn over, slide along and flip; and
+ recognising and naming rotations, reflections, translations and associated symmetries in patterns, objects and formations (e.g. fabrics, logos and dances).

Location and arrangement activities engage students in representing, locating and arranging, through sketches of their locality or through reading maps to describe position, to use bearings to define location, or to specify location with co-ordinate systems. Topological transformations, where shape, size and even straightness of lines may be distorted, are also dealt with in this strand organiser.

Situations and activities that may develop location-and-arrangement concepts include:

+ responding to and using language of position, orientation and direction (children should be encouraged to describe their movements in a particular environment);
+ placing important things in an environment on maps;

+ recognising a map as a bird's-eye view and providing this view of familiar locations such as their classroom; and

+ using location and arrangement knowledge to represent objects and images with computer software.

Visual thinking processes in space

Much of the content identified in the space strand of *A national statement on mathematics for Australian schools* (Australian Education Council, 1991) promotes visual learning. According to this document it is important that teachers provide opportunities for children to explore, actively and visually, mathematical aspects of shape and structure, transformation and symmetry, and location and arrangement. It is stated that visual approaches to mathematics are necessary to achieve a balanced curriculum, and to allow students the opportunity to develop skills which are essential not only for mathematical problem solving but also for a variety of everyday experiences.

The Curriculum Corporation (2000) describes the benchmarks that help us understand the spatial understandings that children are expected to achieve at different levels of development.

+ It is generally anticipated that *Year 3* children are able to recognise and name common 2D (squares, rectangles etc) and 3D (cubes, rectangular prisms etc) shapes and describe them in everyday language. Children are able to use grids, maps and simple plans to locate items or landmarks—particularly in authentic contexts.

+ In *Year 5* students are able to discuss 2D and 3D shapes in terms of properties and more sophisticated geometric language. Children become increasingly aware of spatial patterns and relationships and are able to more successfully interpret maps and plans outside their own environment.

+ In *Year 7* children recognise different 2D representations within 3D shapes and the characteristics of symmetry in common 2D shapes. They also recognise basic angles as corners and rotations from a point. Children can interpret simple co-ordinate systems, interpret maps to scale, and move beyond describing simple four-point compass directions.

The term 'visualising' is frequently used in curriculum statements throughout the world. Bishop (1989) suggested visualisation 'interacts in the research literature with the ideas of imagery, spatial ability, diagrams and intuition, and this literature contains a great deal of useful ideas for the potential benefit of mathematics education' (p. 7). Many of the activities and learning experiences presented in this chapter highlight the use of visual imagery in spatial and geometric reasoning.

Chapter focus questions

Before reading on, consider your responses to the following questions. They are intended to start you thinking about spatial and geometric understandings that will be addressed in the rest of this chapter.

1. Why do you think visual and spatial understandings are not given the same attention as more analytical (number) activities in many classroom situations?

2. What thinking processes are involved in solving spatial problems?

3. What are some of the similarities and differences in activities that require visual and spatial reasoning?

4. To what extent do you think technology innovations have increased the role of visual reasoning in mathematics?

5. How may spatial understandings help children solve number problems more easily?

REFLECTION ON A CLASSROOM SCENARIO

Using technology to make connections with shape

Children from a number of schools were asked to replicate a printed design using a computer paint program (represented in Figure 4.1). The program allowed the user to manipulate geometric shapes, which were located in folders on the screen, using a computer 'mouse'. The original picture of the clown had been developed from these geometric shapes, although some shapes had been enlarged, reduced, transposed, rotated or reflected. The students were expected to transform, translate or rotate the shapes in order to achieve the desired goal (which was to create an identical image of the clown originally created and printed out).

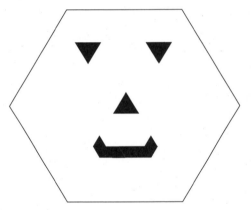

Figure 4.1 A representation of the image used for the computer-based activity

After completing the activity the children were asked to describe the approach they had used to solve the problem. Responses from children from Year 1 to Year 6 are presented below.

I used a big hexagon for the face, two triangles for the eyes, another triangle for the nose that had to be turned around. For the mouth I used a flattened hexagon for the sides and little triangles joined together.

(Matty, Year 1)

First I got a hexagon and made it a lot bigger, and then I got triangles for the eyes and another one turned the other way for the nose. Then for the mouth I made the triangles smaller, making diamond shapes with the triangles on both sides to make them even and then you get a pattern with the triangles making one up and then one down and so on.

(Rebecca, Year 3)

With this problem I firstly counted the sides of the base shape in the original picture. I found that it was a hexagon, so looked for a hexagon on the pictures at the side. I found

one and enlarged it, then put it in the middle of the page. I did similar things with the other shapes, comparing, enlarging, revolving, etc. I realised there were fourteen little triangles for the mouth. Once the size of the shape was right it was a matter of rotating some 180° in order to get the pattern right.

(Sharon, Year 6)

It was evident that the students used different approaches to solve the task in the computer-based activity. Although each of the three students started by manipulating a hexagon to represent the clown's face, the other shapes were constructed in a range of ways. Matty, the youngest child, attempted to flatten a hexagon for the sides of the mouth. Interestingly, this was achieved by rubbing out part of the hexagon. Sharon calculated the number of small triangles which were represented in the clown's mouth, fourteen in all, but Rebecca, after realising that triangles needed to be joined together to make diamond shapes, moved the triangles into position one by one.

The three students used mathematics terminology in their task evaluation. Each student used such words as 'hexagon' and 'triangle' to explain the way in which they had attempted to solve the problem. In order to describe the way the shapes were manipulated, Matty used 'turned around', Rebecca 'turned the other way' and 'one up and one down' and Sharon said 'comparing', 'enlarging', 'revolving' and 'rotating 180°'. Matty rubbed out part of a hexagon to represent the side of the clown's mouth, Rebecca realised that two triangles joined together made a diamond shape, while Sharon knew that the entire shape of the mouth was made up of fourteen triangles.

This task, then, required strategic knowledge of how to transform, rotate and manipulate shapes. The open-ended nature of the task shows children at different stages of development with respect to geometric understandings associated with analysing and representing arrangements and locations.

Examining the terminology used and the processes undertaken by the three children to complete the task reveals that they are at different developmental levels with respect to their understanding of the problem. Although each child completed the task, their knowledge of the relationship between shape, arrangement and transformation was quite different. From a theoretical perspective, the *van Hiele* model categorises student's understanding of geometry into five stages or levels. van Hiele (1986) argued that a learner moved—provided they were assisted through appropriate instructional experiences—from an initial level of visualisation to an abstract level of deduction. From a primary school perspective, children would generally be operating within one of the first three levels: visualisation, analysis and informal deductions. Importantly, it seems to be the case that exploratory and 'hands-on' activities lead to the most complete understanding of space and geometry understandings, thus enabling students to move through these three levels more easily.

At the most basic level, Level 0, understandings and concepts are viewed holistically, rather than based on components or attributes. A student would be able to recognise a square, for example, but would not be able to propose that a square had right angles, or that opposite sides were parallel.

At Level 1, an analysis of geometric concepts begins. A student would know that a square has all sides equal, and that it has 90° angles. The student would also realise that some triangles have all sides equal, whereas others have a 90° angle.

At Level 2, students understand class inclusion and are able to develop meaningful definitions about the relationships between shapes.

From a practical perspective, Pegg (1997) maintained that children do not realise that there is a relationship between squares and rectangles at Level 1, whereas at Level 2 they come to know that that every square is a rectangle and every rectangle is a parallelogram (see Figure 4.5 later in the chapter). Figure 4.6 (also later in the chapter) provides an example of how children might view elements of class inclusion with quadrilaterals. At Level 2, Pegg suggested that concepts need to have a visual basis and individual answers should have a strong real-world reference for students. With respect to Level 3, students should have an ability to develop an overview of relevant elements so that appropriate generalisations can be formed. Pegg also showed that students have an ability to work with algebraic symbols, which stand for real numbers, at this level. In summary, he suggested that the levels are:

> *Level 1: Figures are identified according to their overall appearance. Properties play no explicit role in this identification process.*

> *Level 2a: Figures are identified in terms of one single property. This property is usually some aspect associated with the length of sides but it need not be this.*

> *Level 2b: At this level several properties are known. The important feature of this list is the independent (isolated) nature of the properties to one another.*

> *Level 3: Relationships between previously identified properties of a figure are now established. There is an ordering of properties (i.e. one or more properties are seen to imply other properties). Moreover, at this level relationships between figures are established.*

> **(Pegg, 1997)**

In the 'Reflection on a classroom scenario' it was evident that the language the three students used to verbalise their ideas provided important information about the students' level of spatial or geometric understanding. We gain insight into students' mathematical development, according to the van Hiele theory, by analysing the terminology they use. For example, considering the concept of 'a square', the three levels might be expressed as follows:

> *Level 0: That window looks like a square because it has a square shape (based on a visual experience).*

> *Level 1: A square has four sides the same, two sets of parallel sides and four 90° angles (an ability to analyse components of a shape).*

> *Level 2: A square is a parallelogram with all sides equal and a 90° angle (class classification is defined).*

Critical thinking questions
Examine the mathematical language used by the three children to describe the way in which they completed the task, and reflect on the following questions:

+ Does the terminology used by each student reflect their understanding of the problem?
+ Why did Matty 'rub out' part of a shape to reproduce the desired image? Comment on this approach.
+ What type of visual processing did each child use to complete the task?
+ At what level in the van Hiele theory would you consider each of the three children to be with respect to this task?

THE GROWTH OF MATHEMATICAL UNDERSTANDING

This section provides an overview of the key mathematical understandings associated with shape and structure, transformation and symmetry, and location and arrangement. The children's worksamples provide evidence of increasingly sophisticated ways of finding connections in space. The worksamples trace the development of spatial understandings by providing insight into the way children respond to a range of problems that encourage visual and spatial reasoning.

It is important to note that the problems are open-ended in nature. As a result, the same activity, with obvious modifications, could be given to preschool children or children in the early years of high school. The activities support the needs of individuals within the usual classroom setting, and encourage more able children to apply the skills and understandings they have developed to other, more complex situations.

Curriculum documents, textbooks and multimedia resources tend to be concerned with the initial development of concepts and processes rather than the transfer to a more metacognitive and critical use of such understandings. It is important not only to have an appropriate repertoire of concepts but also to understand their representation and interrelationships. In this chapter visual and spatial concepts will be introduced using a variety of representations, with children challenged to make links between related concepts.

As a practitioner, it is important for you to have a good understanding of the main links and relationships that exist in spatial reasoning (Owens, 1995). Furthermore, it will also be necessary for you to find connections between space and other areas of mathematics. It could be argued, for example, that some teachers are uncertain about the relationship between different quadrilaterals. This is reflected in the responses of children they teach. We found, for example, that Year 6 children were certain that squares were not rectangles and were unhappy with our explanation to the contrary. Many believed it was an unnecessary complication in an area that was well understood.

If teachers are to build on what the learner already knows, they need to recognise the difficulty of reconceptualising ideas. For example, on entry to school, children are familiar with squares and this knowledge can be used as a basis for constructing an understanding of other quadrilaterals. This claim is supported by an investigation which examined the kind of knowledge that children possess on entry to school. Sixty kindergarten children were involved in the investigation, and data were obtained using the following procedure:

1. The children were shown a series of quadrilaterals and asked to colour all the shapes that were the same (see Figure 4.2).
2. The children were then asked to elaborate on why they coloured those shapes.

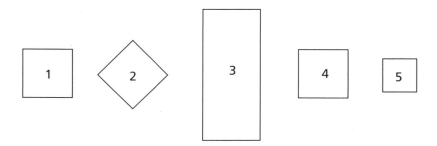

Figure 4.2 The five shapes used for discrimination

In all cases the children coloured one of the following combinations:

(a) Figures 1 and 4 (56%);
(b) Figures 1, 4 and 5 (30%);
(c) Figures 1, 2 and 4 (7%);
(d) Figures 1, 2, 4 and 5 (7%).

Respective percentages for each type of response selected by the sixty children are presented in brackets.

FOCUS QUESTIONS

1. To what extent would a kindergarten child's response to this task be influenced by typical representations of a square?

2. Some additional questions may need to be posed in order to determine the child's understanding of what a square is. What might some of these questions be?

3. It would be beneficial to present this task (Figure 4.2) to a group of young children (aged 5–8 years) and monitor their responses. Note any similarities and differences in the way children of a particular age respond to the task.

In our experience teachers adopt two main approaches when teaching children about shapes. Either they use discrete prototypes or they emphasise families of figures. The first approach focuses on typical shapes, with size and orientation excluded as critical attributes. This approach is also modelled in many elementary textbooks and is accepted wisdom in the wider population (see Figure 4.3). A teacher in this situation might set the task in Figure 4.4 with the child being asked which shape does not belong.

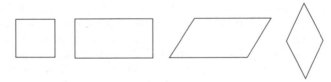

Figure 4.3 Typical textbook representations for a square, rectangle, parallelogram and rhombus

The second approach is less common and has an emphasis on defining attributes—what all members of a family have in common. This eliminates size and orientation and is probably best described as a scaffolded approach, with the membership of families being expanded to produce a hierarchy as illustrated in Figure 4.5. Children are often introduced to a family such as the one illustrated in Figure 4.6 and asked what makes them a family. In this case the answer to the question defines the attributes of rectangles and recognises that squares are a particular class of rectangles.

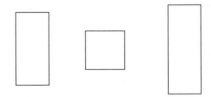

Figure 4.4 A discrimination activity with only one answer

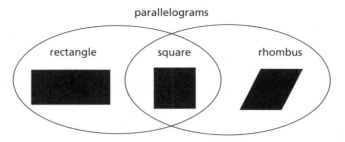

Figure 4.5 Part of the quadrilateral family

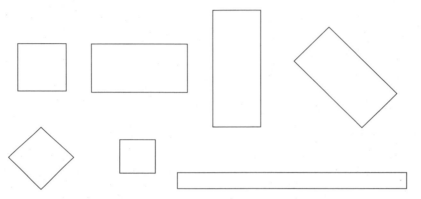

Figure 4.6 A more diverse family of quadrilaterals

Although these two approaches are different, some teachers combine them successfully. They begin with what the children already know. This is usually a restricted set of prototypes. They then set about using the second approach, eliminating size and orientation and developing an understanding of families of shapes.

Too often teachers and writers of materials have been concerned with correct naming of shapes rather than a deeper understanding of the relationships between classes of shape and the acknowledgment that single shapes may be classified at a number of levels.

FOCUS QUESTIONS

1. Why may a 'family' representation of quadrilaterals allow children to critically analyse shape and structure more easily than a more narrow 'definition' approach?

2. How may a sound knowledge of the quadrilateral family be applied to other families of shapes (e.g. the seven types of triangles)?

SNAPSHOTS OF LEARNING: LESSON PLANNING AND ASSESSMENT

There are numerous space and geometry principles that could be included in this section of the chapter. In the following snapshots of learning, we will be dealing with a number of concepts related to space in a variety of open-ended contexts that depict children at varying levels of development. Many of the reflective activities presented in this section will encourage you to describe the way in which children, at different levels of understanding, use visual and spatial reasoning to solve problems. The snapshots of learning are ordered under the following headings:

+ Shape and structure;
+ Transformation and symmetry;
+ Location and arrangement.

However, important links between the respective areas will be evident.

Shape and structure

Students should be provided with opportunities to develop practical knowledge about shapes and their relationships. Initially, this involves examining shape and structure in the children's environment. Can you name some shapes in our classroom? Why are ice-cream cones shaped the way they are? Why are most balls round? Why are some balls oval-shaped? Children should also be encouraged to describe geometric features in objects: 'This box shape has six squares in it'.

As children's geometric understandings become increasingly sophisticated, it is important to challenge them to formulate relationships between various properties of shape. Children should recognise, for example, that 3D shapes contain 2D plane figures, 1D lines and 0D points. A 2D figure contains only lines and points. A line is determined by two points and consists of a set of all points continuing in both directions. Children should recognise relationships between quadrilaterals (see Figure 4.6) and identify particular attributes of polyhedra.

ACTIVITY 4.1

As with most of the teaching–learning examples described in this book, the following snapshots provide opportunities for children to represent a problem in a number of ways. It will be beneficial to take particular notice of the different types of representations of 3D shape outlined in this snapshot. The following questions should help you to appreciate the importance of challenging children to find relationships between shapes and to construct mathematical ideas that can be applied to practical situations.

1. What is a cube?
2. Do you know of any 'families' that have a cube as one of its members?
3. Draw a diagram of a cube. Are you able to draw more than one representation of a cube?

1. Notions of 3D shapes

Children often associate 3D shapes with recognisable objects in their immediate environment. A cube, for example, is often linked to the representation of a box, whereas a cone is often compared to an ice-cream cone. In order to make these representations meaningful, children should be exposed to a range of images and characteristics. A Year 5 class was asked to investigate the properties of a cube and encouraged to represent the cube in a number of ways. The following transcript, from the classroom teacher, provides a rationale for the learning experience:

> With shapes, children have difficulty linking 'solid' and 'hollow' shapes. For example, a wooden cube and a cube they make by folding a 2D net are often seen as two representations of the same shape. I've found the following series of activities to be an effective way of building the concepts.

First, a solid cube is modelled in plasticine. Then a depression is made into one side, and the cube is developed so that, as the depression is deepened, one side is extended to form a lid. Once the lid is closed, the now hollow plasticine cube is compared to the one made from a net.

A manipulative problem with plasticine cubes is getting the faces flat, edges sharp and corners pointed. These aspects may be focused by building a 'skeleton' cube with twelve matchsticks and eight blobs of plasticine. Discussions of the solid cubes, the hollow cubes and the skeleton cubes allow effective concept development to proceed. The later consideration of 3D, 2D, 1D (lines) and 0D (points) is very much facilitated by this approach, which can be extended to other 3D shapes—with the sphere as the limiting case.

(Teacher, Year 5)

Some of these representations are presented in Figure 4.7.

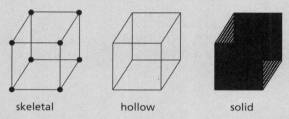

skeletal   hollow   solid

Figure 4.7 Different types of cubes

Mathematical content and processes
The children should be able to:

+ identify figures, lines and points from constructed models of cubes;
+ use appropriate mathematical language related to symmetrical aspects of a cube's properties.

Posing key questions to assess learning
Children need to be able to communicate their understandings effectively.

+ What similarities and differences between the various cubes do you notice?
+ How can you record your findings?
+ Can you design a net for the model(s) you have created?
+ Have you seen this shape (cube structures) before? (Emphasise everyday situations.)

Extending children's investigations
Children can be encouraged to:

+ construct models of other prisms and compare, discuss and name them;
+ investigate and describe nets, skeletons and cross-sections of other prisms;
+ represent other platonic solids in hollow, solid and skeletal forms. Platonic solids must have all sides identical in shape and size. There are only five platonic solids (see Figure 4.8)—including the cube, which comprises six identical square shapes.

A number of commercially developed concrete manipulatives (e.g. polydrons) can be purchased to help children construct the platonic solids, although household items including cardboard and drinking straws are worthwhile for such activities. The unique

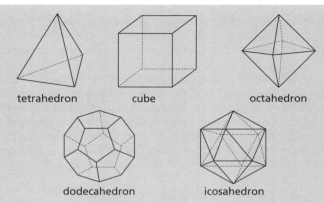

tetrahedron　　cube　　octahedron

dodecahedron　　icosahedron

Figure 4.8 The five platonic solids

properties of platonic solids—with all faces the same—ensure that these shapes can be used for dice games of chance. A dodecahedron, for example, can be used as a twelve-sided die.

2. The relationship between 2D and 3D shapes

The following problem-solving task challenged a class of Year 6 children to apply spatial concepts and processes involving shape and structure, transformation and symmetry, and location and arrangement to an architectural situation. Over a 5-week period students were required to design their 'dream home'. The following design criteria were given to the children:

1. Construct a two-dimensional house plan of your dream home. Ensure that all drawings are to scale and that relevant symbols are present.
2. Draw a three-dimensional representation of the two-dimensional plan from different perspectives (e.g. front and back views of the house). Attempt to represent these drawings in the same scale as your two-dimensional plan.
3. Design a three-dimensional model of your home.

Imagery was often evoked through these learning activities while other experiences and directed questioning techniques specifically called on students to utilise visual processing. Before some of the children's responses to this activity are presented, it will be advantageous to examine some activities used to develop the children's visual reasoning abilities.

Developing children's visual reasoning
The following activities encouraged the children to use visual imagery to represent problems in a meaningful manner. Work through these activities/questions for yourself. How do these questions help you to represent the problem and monitor your thinking? Why might it be important to do similar activities with children before allowing them to begin drawing their house plan?

+ Close your eyes and imagine walking through your own home. Which room are you in? Open the door of this room and walk through it. Which room are you in now? Walk to the kitchen—which rooms do you pass? Open the fridge and remove the milk. Which direction do you need to turn in order to get a glass from the cupboard?

+ Pretend that you are at home. Close your eyes and imagine standing outside your home. Are you at the front or back of your house? What colour is the roof of your house? Can you see it from where you are now? Walk around the outside of your house until you reach your bedroom. How many windows do you need to pass? How many windows does your bedroom have? Open your eyes and draw what your window looks like on paper.

Battista (1999) provided insights into how visual reasoning can be linked to spatial arrangements. The following activity is developed most effectively when students have the opportunity to verify solutions with pattern blocks.

How many rhombuses like this does it take to cover a hexagon? Predict, then check with blocks

Figure 4.9 Using concrete materials to verify visual reasoning

Extending children's understanding of space
Other activities related specifically to the task were also used to encourage the children to represent the problem in a meaningful manner. Attempt these questions yourself.

+ What do you think the dimensions of your bedroom are? Are there any rooms in your house which have smaller/larger areas? What are they?

+ Collect some house plans from a display home (or get a plan of your house if one exists). Look at the way windows and doors are drawn in the two-dimensional representation. Keep this in mind when drawing your own design. Does every room in your house have a window? If not, what does it have instead?

+ For homework tonight sketch the front and back of your house. Remember to draw only what you can see. What do you notice about your sketches?

At the time these activities were taking place, students were investigating perspective, the effect of shadows in pictures, and depth and dimension in drawing, during class art lessons.

Mathematical content and processes
The children were asked to complete the project in 5 weeks. Work was productive, with motivation remaining high throughout the 5-week period. Children even went to the trouble of visiting display centres on weekends in the hope of gaining additional inspiration. Class time was allocated to the project, although work at home was also encouraged.

Although the children were obviously extended by the activity, additional assessment of their work was needed to delineate the type of spatial and visual processes required to complete such a project. It is important for teachers to use a range of assessment techniques in order to monitor children's thinking (see Chapter 10). This is particularly pertinent when assessing visual and spatial thinking. As Gardiner (1983) recognised:

Children may know their way around many areas of the neighbourhood or town and, in fact, never fail to find what they are looking for. Yet they often will lack the capacity to

99

provide a map, a sketch, or an overall verbal account of the relationship among several spots. Representing their piecemeal knowledge in another format or symbol system proves an elusive part of the spatial intelligence. Or perhaps one could say: while children's spatial understanding develops apace, the expression of this understanding via another intelligence or symbolic code remains difficult.

(p. 180)

Because visual imagery is such a personal matter, children must be given time to develop their individualistic images, and be allowed to express and interpret these within a medium in which they are most comfortable. At the completion of this project some of the children were asked about strategies, approaches and techniques displayed in the development of three activities.

Students' comments
The thought and detail that went into each task could be best illustrated in a response from Chad.

I was doing rough copies of the house until they started getting better and when I got the right one I started drawing it on the board. When I did all the angles Dad took it to work and blew it up, I cut a piece of balsa wood the size of the paper, and I began to build the 2D representation. I then put support frames on my roof like the ones getting built near my house. I then imagined the lines of the house became real walls, then built the house by estimating where the windows would be.

(Chad, Year 6)

Comments from both Janelle and Justin indicated that the children used visual and spatial skills to solve problems throughout the project. Janelle tried to create a mental image of a house she had only once visited to produce 2D and 3D drafts of her plan. While Justin was somewhat more analytical, he made the walls 'stand up in (his) mind' to create a visual account of what the 3D design would look like.

My aunty has a house in Perth. I drew one side of the house and visualised that I was there. I then imagined myself in the backyard looking at the back of the house, and drew it from there.

(Janelle, Year 6)

I drew little bits of houses I liked, and then stuck them together with sticky tape. I knew where the windows were so I just made them stand up in my mind. Instead of the walls being flat you could see them standing up. I had to draw the house in perspective, like an arrow shape, making the front bigger and when it got further back I did half the scale which made it smaller.

(Justin, Year 6)

Claire created spatial images that were both large and small scale, to transform the 2D image into a 3D model. The visual imagery she used to solve problems with space indicated that such an activity required Claire to use visual and spatial processes. The authors agree with Bishop (1989) in suggesting that visual representations are essential to all aspects of the mathematics classroom. Claire is a competent designer who obviously tries to call on such visual skills when performing these tasks. Such skills need to be encouraged more fully in the classroom.

> *I thought of a plan and imagined myself walking through the house. I imagined standing in the middle, turning around and viewing each room looking at it. I then pretended to walk around the outside of the house, putting in windows and doors. I thought about how builders build a house and start from the ground up.*
>
> **(Claire, Year 6)**

Each student was required to use spatial and visual learning processes to complete the open-ended architectural project. The children were extended in a manner that allowed individuals not only to be challenged, but also to develop important mathematical concepts in a visual manner.

Extending children's investigations
Children can be encouraged to:

+ use computer-aided drawing (CAD) programs to design 2D and 3D representations of their house plan;
+ provide detailed drawings of a particular room in their house (e.g. the bathroom or the kitchen).

Transformation and symmetry

Two types of symmetry are commonly used to describe geometric shapes and figures—line symmetry and rotational symmetry. Line symmetry is associated with reflections, whereas rotational symmetry involves turns about a central point. It is important for children to be exposed to concrete manipulations of symmetry before being required to interpret other representations. For example, children should be encouraged to experiment with pattern blocks before being required to visualise or draw these figures. In a similar vein, children should be exposed to a variety of paper-folding activities before being required to draw lines of symmetry on plane shapes. Initially, young children should develop understandings of transformation and symmetry with familiar figures. A square, for example, may be translated, reflected or rotated. We may also establish that it has four lines of symmetry (see Figure 4.10).

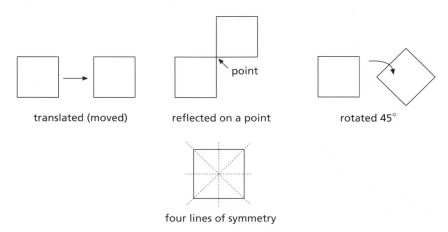

translated (moved) reflected on a point rotated 45°

four lines of symmetry

Figure 4.10 Rotations, reflections

When investigating symmetry, reflections and rotations, it is important for children to appreciate that the shape has not changed. A square may also be transformed. The shape may be changed from a square to another type of parallelogram (see Figure 4.11).

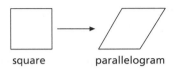

square   parallelogram

Figure 4.11 Transformations

It is important for the teacher to allow children to use a variety of different materials in order to construct relevant understandings of transformation and symmetry. Some useful materials include:

+ pattern blocks;
+ geoboards;
+ mirrors;
+ drawing and painting computer software.

The following snapshots of learning use these materials in order to promote notions of transformation and symmetry.

3. Tessellations and symmetry

A Year 2 class was creating pictures with pattern blocks. The children were required to fill an entire page with shapes and to make sure they had no spaces or overlaps on the page. The classroom teacher wanted the children to use a number of common shapes and discover relationships between the shapes.

Teacher's and student's comments

> *Before the children began putting the shapes on the paper I encouraged them to see which combination of shapes actually tessellated with each other. I felt that it was important to let them see particular relationships between the respective shapes. Because they are manipulating concrete materials they can experiment freely and make their own connections between shapes. Although they are not necessarily aware of it, they are actually doing a great deal of rotating and reflecting with the shapes.*

(Teacher, Year 2)

> *I made two patterns that I repeated all the time. In one pattern I had a hexagon in the middle, then triangles and squares, then more hexagons around the outside. In the other pattern I had diamonds and triangles. The whole thing looked like a flower.*

(Michelle, Year 2)

Mathematical content and processes
Encourage children to:

+ make patterns through flipping, sliding and turning;
+ arrange shapes in a variety of tessellating forms;
+ identify the repetitive nature of patterns;

- locate tessellations and pattern repetitions in the environment;
- find symmetrical patterns in nature;
- identify shapes and combinations of shapes that tessellate; and
- complete
patterns to gain a symmetrical result.

Posing key questions to assess learning

- What shapes tessellate with the octagonal?
- What combination of shapes do you need to tessellate with the parallelogram?
- Find patterns at home that tessellate (e.g. the tiles of the bathroom floor). What types of patterns have been used in these situations?

4. Reflections and rotations

A class of Year 3 children was given a geoboard with a rubber band that had been stretched vertically across the centre of the frame. On one side of the board, children were required to construct a four-sided figure. Typically they constructed a square although some children created other quadrilaterals (see Figure 4.12). The children were then challenged to replicate this shape in the form of a mirror image. Initially, children were encouraged to put a mirror on edge along the symmetry line and make the image while looking at the mirror.

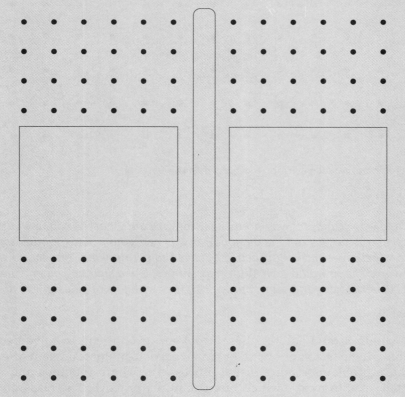

Figure 4.12 Reflection of a quadrilateral on a geoboard

With experience (and growing confidence) the children were asked to design a figure with the intention of getting a friend to replicate the mirror image. The partner was required to complete the task before using the mirror to check if the image was correct. Within a week, children were experimenting with diagonal lines of symmetry (see Figure 4.13).

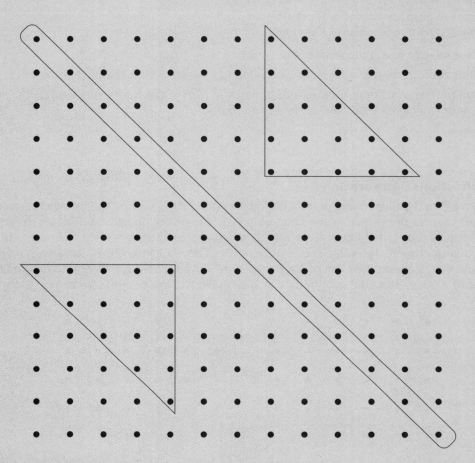

Figure 4.13 Reflection of a quadrilateral on a geoboard on the diagonal

When the line was straight it was pretty easy to work out what the shape would look like. When the line was across [on the diagonal] it was really hard. Most of the time I needed the mirror to help me, but with practice I started to get the idea. You had to really think about the way a shape would turn. With easy shapes, like a square, you only had to worry about one corner staying the same, but with shapes with lots of sides it was hard.

(Robyn, Year 3)

For many children (and adults), these problems are difficult to solve because they cannot rely on previous experiences or knowledge to help represent the problem. Essentially, these problems require visual processing—where rotations and reflections are represented 'in the mind'—which often requires practice. The classroom teacher emphasised this when reflecting on a series of these activities.

Teacher's comments

> *Initially, the children had difficulty predicting what the reflected shape would look like. It was important for the children to have a mirror to check their responses because the immediate feedback allowed them to monitor their own ideas and predictions in a supportive way. It was amazing how much most of the children had improved in such a short time. I don't think they had ever been required to visually imagine shapes before, and many of the class realised that the line of symmetry needed to be considered before anything else.*

(Teacher, Year 3)

Mathematical content and processes

The children should be able to:

+ explain why some shapes are more difficult to reflect on a particular line of symmetry than others;

+ visualise the position of reflected shapes and then test results with a mirror in order to construct a better understanding of the effect the line of symmetry has on a particular reflection; and

+ use visual imagery to describe what a reflected shape will look like if it was reflected on more than one line of symmetry.

Extending children's investigations

+ This snapshot can be replicated with the aid of the drawing and painting features on most word-processing and desktop-publishing programs. Even the cheapest programs have 'rotation', 'flip' and 'reshape' commands in the drawing tools, allowing children to make predictions about the way in which a figure will be represented once the desired command has been activated. More specialised drawing programs allow for three-dimensional representations, with a complex array of transformation and rotation features.

+ Origami (the art of paper folding) techniques and activities provide children with opportunities to develop understandings of transformation and symmetry. Children can develop techniques that encourage them to follow directions, fold along lines of symmetry, rotate figures, analyse representations and visualise transformations.

Location and arrangement

Piaget (1953) argued that when children first enter school they should be exposed to an active, exploratory period of geometric development. He suggested that children should be challenged to explore space that was concerned with their own environment. In these snapshots you will notice that specific location terminology is central to the development of mathematical understandings. Furthermore, visualisation skills and 2D drawing skills need to be fostered in children to allow them to more easily represent their 3D environment.

5. Developing 2D plans

Children were required to develop a set of instructions that could be used by another person to navigate his or her way through an obstacle course. The problem was given to Year 1 and Year 5 children.

The manner in which this activity is presented to the class depends on the age of the children. Most Year 1 children, for example, would not be expected to describe a sequence of events that would allow others to follow directions without first experimenting with, and investigating, necessary concepts and skills for themselves. Some of the important terminology and language required to create a list of navigational instructions at this level may include 'under, over, through, around, behind, below, on top of, next to, beside, sideways, right and left'.

The following transcript describes an effective way of structuring the activity in a way that provides young children with opportunities to explore and react to some of this important terminology before applying it to a problem-solving situation.

Teacher's comments

> *During the last few weeks we have been reading stories about pirates and hidden treasures and the classroom was beginning to resemble a treasure island. We had murals of palm trees, sand and the sea. With the children's help I positioned their tables and chairs in small groups around the room. I put sheets over some of the desks to represent mountains. Others held up the palm trees. Blue cellophane and coloured paper snaked around the mountains to represent the river. While it took some organising it really looked great. In a whole-class session children were asked to cross over the river, go under the tree, go through the cave, go around the mountain and so on. The children were then allowed to make up their own paths.*

(Teacher, Year 1)

The teacher then drew a simple 2D representation of the obstacle course on the chalk board (see Figure 4.14). The children were encouraged to predict what each symbol on

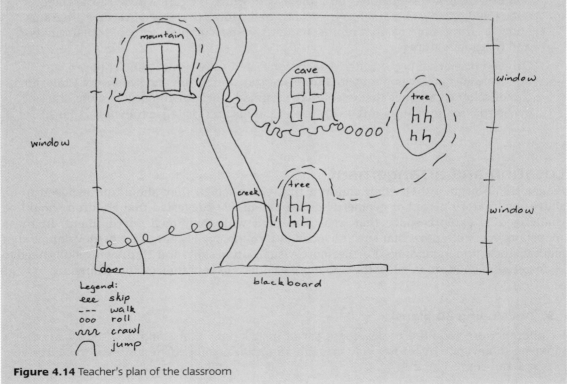

Figure 4.14 Teacher's plan of the classroom

the chalk board represented. Importantly, the children were able to point to the object on the board, and then go and find it within the classroom. The links between the symbolic 2D form and the concrete 3D form were emphasised.

The children were then provided with a sheet of A3 paper and asked to copy the diagram of the treasure map from the board. In pairs, one child navigated a path through the treasure island while his or her partner traced the path on the map. The children then changed roles. An example of one child's attempt is described below.

We walked around the big mountain, then jumped over the river, crawled under the cave and climbed over the tree. Then we walked between some trees, jumped over the river again and skipped out the door.

(Joel, Year 1)

6. 2D plans within different contexts

In a Year 2 class children were given a key or legend to follow and were asked to describe how they moved around the playground equipment in the school grounds. One child's representation is given in Figure 4.15.

A similar activity was given to a class of Year 5 children. The obstacle course was designed outside the classroom and encompassed a much larger area than that of the Year 1 group. In this activity children were able not only to use obstacles purposefully placed inside the designated area, but also to include features already present in the particular area (e.g. trees, paths, buildings). Children were asked to develop a map of the obstacle course, defining their own boundaries and creating a set of directions for a friend to follow (see Figure 4.16).

Figure 4.15 A Year 1 child's map

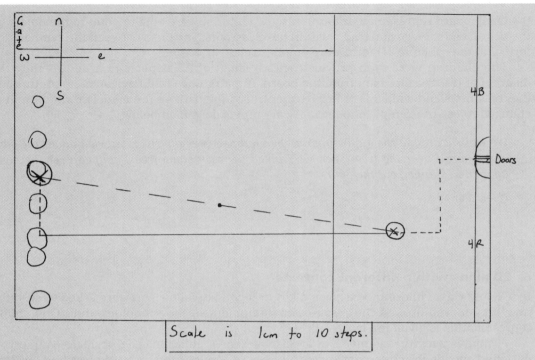

Figure 4.16 A Year 5 child's map (outside)

Student's comments

> *Start at the southern end of 4B and face west. Walk 20 steps forward and turn south. Walk 40 steps forward then turn west. Go 25 steps and stop at the tree. Put an x on the map. Continue heading west until you stop at the tree closest to the fence. Turn and face north. Go forward 30 paces and put an X on the tree closest to you. The treasure will be found in a straight line halfway between the two marks.*

(Monica, Year 5)

Mathematical content and processes

Although more conceptually challenging skills and understandings were expected from the older children, according to the Curriculum Corporation (1994) *Mathematics—A curriculum profile for Australian schools*, the following indicators trace mathematical development.

+ Responds to and uses the language of position and orientation.
+ Places important things in the environment on maps.
+ Finds paths on informal maps and mazes.
+ Recognises a map as a bird's-eye view and provides this view of familiar locations such as the classroom.
+ Uses directional language.

Extending children's investigations

As children become more confident in using location and arrangement terminology to describe position, they should be challenged to:

+ describe position in relation to directional language and co-ordinate points;
+ provide more sophisticated directions by using angle concepts (e.g. now turn 180° to the right);
+ use formal measurement units to develop more accurate maps; and
+ represent 3D space on scaled maps.

7. Exploring angles in space

Many children have great difficulty learning the angle concept (Clements & Battista, 1992). Since the concept of angle is multifaceted in nature it is important that children are able to generalise understandings and extend such understandings to further experiences. Mitchelmore and White (2000) suggested that primary-aged children:

+ first recognise superficial similarities between angles experiences and form separate angle concepts based on physical angle situations such as tiles, hills and wheels;
+ develop deeper similarities between these situations and form angle concepts related to physical angle contexts such as corner, slope and turn; and
+ establish deeper similarities between contexts and form an abstract angle concept which gradually generalises to include all angle contexts.

In the first instance they ascertain that it is important to develop an agreed language for describing various corner situations where both lines and angle are clearly visible.

A class of Year 5 children was asked to investigate different types of angles in the environment. In particular, the children were asked to identify situations where angles were fixed and instances where angles were movable. The following response from the classroom teacher presents some background activities undertaken with the children before this activity was introduced.

> I feel that it is important for children to have a range of experiences that link understandings of angle to meaningful and practical situations. There is much more to these understandings than measuring the angles of particular objects with a protractor. In fact, I do not encourage children to use a protractor until a whole series of understandings have been investigated.
>
> Initially, I ask children to find a variety of angles in both the natural and built environment. In the built environment, which would include buildings, many of the angles children explore are structured and regular. They find, for example, lots of 45°, 90° and 180° degree angles. These experiences develop understandings of solid angles. In the natural environment, there are many more variations of angle for children to explore. A great place to start is with tree branches or the veins in leaves. These experiences develop understandings associated with the relationship between two arms of an angle. Children begin to appreciate that the opening between two given lines determines the size of an angle.

The next stage is to allow children to investigate concepts of turning and slope in relation to angle. It is important for children to see that walking up a steep hill can be thought of in terms of an angle.

(Teacher, Year 5)

Students' comments
The following comments illustrate some of the processes and mathematical understandings undertaken by the children throughout this experience.

It was easy to find fixed angles. Most of them were 90° in the corners of walls, on tables and in doors. Straight lines are also angles and they are everywhere. It was much trickier to find movable angles. We thought of a compass and a circle.

(John, Year 5)

When we had to find angles that changed we decided to look for things that could move on one side and stay the same on the other. The door had an angle of 180° when closed, but we could make all kinds of angles when it was opened. We estimated 45° and 90° and when it was opened we found that it could have an angle even bigger than 90°, maybe even 150°.

(Jackie, Year 5)

The children were encouraged to draw diagrams of the objects they had classified with fixed and movable angles (see Figure 4.17). Although the children were not required to measure accurately the angle created by these objects, they were asked to predict angles (Mitchelmore & White, 1995). Importantly, these worksamples can be used as an effective assessment tool despite the fact that formal measurements were not sought.

Posing key questions to assess learning
Can the children communicate their understandings effectively by:

+ demonstrating that angles are found: (a) in corners and edges of 3D objects, (b) as 2D planes, and (c) as movements or rotations in space?
+ discussing the features of 3D shapes emphasised by and best represented in solid (with plasticine or clay), hollow (with nets) and skeleton (with plasticine and matchsticks) forms?
+ classifying angles as acute, obtuse, straight, right or reflex?
+ recognising that angle design is an important part of the construction process (e.g. building)?
+ using protractors and angle wheels to check estimates and predictions?

Extending children's investigations
Children can be encouraged to:

+ recognise and name rotations, reflections and translations in patterns and objects using angle terminology. The 'golden arches' of McDonald's might be described in terms of a shape that was reflected on an axis of symmetry or rotated 180°. Many advertising logos could be used for this purpose.

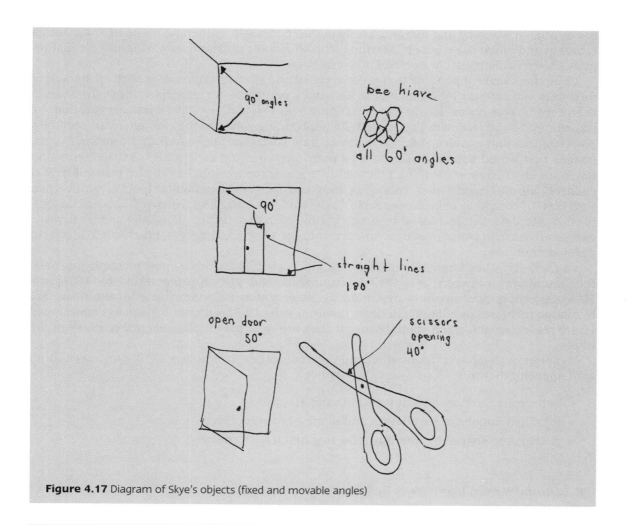

Figure 4.17 Diagram of Skye's objects (fixed and movable angles)

ACTIVITY 4.2

Symmetry in the environment

Draw an advertising logo you have seen recently. Describe, in words, relevant characteristics of the logo including details of the way lines and angles are used. Ask a colleague to describe the same logo. Compare the descriptions and note similarities and differences in the way location and arrangement terminology were used.

1. What other types of spatial language emerge from such a task? Are similar shapes rotated or reflected along common points? How many plane shapes can be found in the logo?

2. Why is this logo such an effective design?

Using computers to promote spatial awareness and geometric reasoning

One of the key statements of *Principles and standards of school mathematics* document (National Council of Teachers of Mathematics, 2000) provides insights into the way in which mathematics will be projected in the coming years. The authors acknowledge that technology is essential in teaching and learning mathematics because it influences the mathematics that is taught and enhances students' learning with such tools providing opportunities for mathematics to be investigated in rich and powerful ways.

Computers make it possible to represent visual and spatial mathematics with an amount of flexibility not offered by other media. Graphics programs, for example, allow the user to represent images accurately as either 2D or 3D representations. These images can then be transformed or rotated with precision. With appropriate software the computer can become a powerful tool that enables children to manipulate spatial arrangements and construct visual images that would usually be limited by their own drawing capabilities. As Clements and Battista (1992) commented, 'the potential of such drawing tools lies in the possibility that children will internalise such functions, thus constructing new mental tools . . . Interaction with certain computer environments may help students build less restricted concept images' (p. 452). Moreover, an increased familiarity with relevant software allows the user to investigate and construct mathematical understandings at increasingly sophisticated levels of development.

Our society is becoming increasingly reliant on visual stimulus as new technologies push the boundaries between 'real-life' environments and 2D representations of 3D space. Moreover, computers are now regarded as an essential ingredient in education and are becoming increasingly common in home environments. Children need to have well-developed visual reasoning skills and spatial sense if they are to adapt to technological changes in the future.

Experiences based on Information and Communication Technology (ICT) provide children with opportunities to:

+ appreciate relationships between 2D and 3D space;
+ establish notions of parallelism and depth perception; and
+ manipulate shapes by rotating, reflecting and transforming.

8. Computer environments in space

A Year 6 class was encouraged to use relevant computer software when investigating a range of spatial and geometric understandings.

Teacher's comments

> *Most children really enjoy using computers. Unfortunately, I feel that much of this time is devoted to playing games or using drill-and-practice software. If children are encouraged to use drawing and painting software the computer is really being used as a tool. Many measurement and space concepts can be promoted through the use of appropriate software. The computer really can become a great learning aid because children can investigate and explore in an environment that is almost limitless. Angles can be measured accurately, rotations and transformations can be undertaken with the most complex of figures and transformations can be easily reversed if needed. The flexibility allows children to develop concepts much quicker than with other approaches.*

(Teacher, Year 6)

Students' worksamples and comments
Some of the children's work is presented in Figures 4.18 and 4.19. A range of spatial understandings and skills have been employed in these activities.

Figure 4.18 Lines and patterns.

The first thing I did was make sure the grid was on my page. I decided to use 13 dots across and 13 down. I started with the second dot on the left-hand side and joined it to the top corner dot on the right. The next dot down on the left was joined to the second dot on the right. I just kept doing the pattern—4 with 3, 5 with 4 and so on. It looked like the lines were curved. I did the same on the other side, just repeating the pattern. I then did a similar pattern but this time used the top and bottom instead on the left and right. These lines looked straight but made a dark pattern in the centre where the lines crossed. It made the pattern look 3D like.

(Alicia, Year 6)

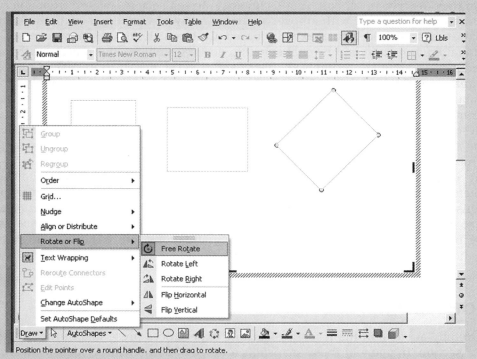

Figure 4.19 Microsoft Word file with drawing tools.

> *I drew a square and then copied it. With the copy I stretched it to make a rectangle. I then copied the square and rectangle twice so that I had six shapes. I then rotated two shapes 45° clockwise and 45° anti-clockwise. The squares really looked different than the rectangles when rotated.*
>
> **(Trevor, Year 6)**

Posing key questions to assess learning
 + Describe the position (orientation) of the shapes you have constructed with the computer.
 + How can you use the 'copy' and 'paste' functions to create symmetrical and tessellating patterns?
 + Can you 'rotate' or 'flip' your shapes using the special functions of the program?
 + What other drawing tools and commands can you use to transform your shapes?

SUMMARY AND IMPLICATIONS FOR CLASSROOM PRACTICE

This chapter has emphasised the importance of providing students with opportunities to develop spatial understandings in open-ended problem-solving situations. We have argued that spatial abilities are essential to many tasks we undertake in our daily lives, and that these skills allow children to find connections between shape, location, patterns and relationships.

Many educators would argue that geometric and spatial understandings are not given the attention they deserve in schools. In a technology-driven society—where from a very young age children are presented with an overwhelming array of visual and spatial information—spatial awareness should be contextually based. Children should be encouraged to explore their spatial environment and be challenged to observe, analyse and represent their spatial surroundings. An ability to recognise patterns and find relationships in space provides more opportunities for children to develop valuable problem-solving skills than simply recounting the number of sides or edges on a cube. Furthermore, it is more advantageous to ask children to find similarities and differences among quadrilaterals than to limit learning experiences to 'this is a square' and 'this is a rectangle'. Good teachers have the ability to reinforce important concepts and principles in ways that encourage children to apply these understandings to other problem-solving situations.

Many of the important concepts and principles discussed in this chapter should be aligned to the measurement understandings we present in Chapter 6. In fact, it will be worthwhile to revisit this chapter after studying the 'Using measurement to make links' chapter (Chapter 8) to ensure that you are able to integrate important measurement and space concepts. It will often be beneficial to formulate problem-solving situations that require children to use a combination of space and measurement understandings.

ACTION AND REFLECTION

Look carefully at some of the teaching–learning experiences presented in the 'snapshots of learning' section. In many of these snapshots a range of mathematical ideas concerned with spatial understandings are developed in problem-solving situations. In some instances, students are encouraged to construct ideas associated with shape and structure; transformation and symmetry; and location and arrangement in an integrated manner.

1. Locate the space strand in your state's mathematics syllabus and note the particular sections or strand organisers that divide the strand into content areas.

2. Write down some of the specific content areas that are associated with these sections or substrands in order to ascertain the type of mathematical understandings linked to the content areas.

3. With a small group of peers, attempt to link these content areas to the three strand organisers described in this chapter. Remember these components have been taken from *A national statement on mathematics for Australian schools* (Australian Education Council, 1991). What similarities and differences do you find with respect to the way content is described in the present chapter when compared with the way it is described in your state's syllabus?

REFERENCES

Australian Education Council. (1991). *A national statement on mathematics for Australian schools*. Melbourne: Curriculum Corporation.

Battista, M. (1999). The importance of spatial structuring in geometric reasoning. *Teaching Children Mathematics*, 5 (November), 170–177.

Bilney, B. (1997). *Plato's Jewels* [kit]: *Hands-on encounters of the 3D*. Adelaide: OZZigami Pty Ltd.

Bishop, A. J. (1989). Review of research on visualization in mathematics education. *Focus on Learning Problems in Mathematics*, 11(1), 7–16.

Burton, L. (1994). *Children learning mathematics: patterns and relationships*. Hemel Hempstead: Simon & Schuster Education.

Clements, D. H. & Battista, M. T. (1992). Geometry and spatial reasoning. In D. A. Grouws (Ed), *Handbook of research on mathematics teaching and learning* (pp. 420–465). New York: Macmillan.

Crowley, M. L. (1987). The van Hiele model of the development of geometric thought. In National Council of Teachers of Mathematics' *Learning and teaching geometry, K–12* (pp. 1–16). Reston, Virginia: National Council of Teachers of Mathematics.

Curriculum Corporation. (1994). *Mathematics—A curriculum profile for Australian schools*. Melbourne: Curriculum Corporation.

Curriculum Corporation. (1995). *Working mathematically: Space CD-ROM*. Melbourne: Curriculum Corporation.

Curriculum Corporation. (2000). *Numeracy benchmarks years 3, 5 and 7*. Melbourne: Curriculum Corporation.

Del Grande, J. (1990). Spatial sense. *Arithmetic Teacher*, 37(6), 14–20.

Del Grande, J. (1993). *Geometry and spatial sense*. Reston, Virginia: National Council of Teachers of Mathematics.

Dreyfus, T. (1991, June–July). On the status of visual reasoning in mathematics and mathematics education. Paper presented at the 15th Annual Conference of the International Group for the Psychology of Mathematics Education Conference. Assisi, Italy.

Gardiner, H. (1983). *Frames of mind*. New York: Basic Books.

Hill, J. (Ed). (1987). *Geometry for grades K–6: Readings from the arithmetic teacher*. Reston, Virginia: National Council of Teachers of Mathematics.

Hoban, T. (1998). *Shape shape shape*. New York: Greenwillow Books.

Lowrie, T. J. (1992). Developing talented children's mathematical ability through visual and spatial learning tasks. Paper presented at a joint AARE/NZARE Conference: Geelong, November.

Lowrie, T. (1996). The use of visual imagery as a problem-solving tool: Classroom implementation. *Journal of Mental Imagery*, *20*(3 & 4), 127–140.

Mitchelmore, M. C. & White, P. (1995). Abstraction in mathematics: Conflict, resolution and application. *Mathematics Education Research Journal*, *7*, 50–68.

Mitchelmore, M. C. & White, P. (2000). Development of angle concepts by progressive abstraction and generalisation. *Educational Studies in Mathematics*, *41*, 209–238.

National Council of Teachers of Mathematics. (1989). *Curriculum and evaluation standards for school mathematics*. Reston, Virginia: National Council of Teachers of Mathematics.

National Council of Teachers of Mathematics. (2000). *Principles and standards of school mathematics*. Reston, Virginia: National Council of Teachers of Mathematics.

Owens, K. D. (1992). Spatial thinking tasks place through primary-school experiences. In E. Southwell, B. Perry & K. Owens (Eds), *Space—The first and final frontier* (pp. 421–431). Proceedings of the 15th Annual Conference of the Mathematics Education Research Group of Australasia. Sydney: MERGA.

Owens, K. D. (1995). *Imagery and concepts in mathematics: Spatial activities for the primary school*. Professional development kit and video. Sydney: University of Western Sydney Macarthur, Faculty of Education.

Papert, S. (1980). *Mindstorms*. New York: Basic Books.

Pegg, J. (1997). Interpreting the extended demands of geometry questions within an extended form of the van Hiele Theory. In N. Scott & H. Hollingsworth (Eds), *Mathematics: Creating culture* (Proceedings of the 16th Conference of the Australian Association of Mathematics Teachers pp. 241-246). Adelaide: AAMT.

Phillips, E. (1991). *Patterns and functions*. Reston, Virginia: National Council of Teachers of Mathematics.

Piaget, J. (1953). How children form mathematical concepts. *Scientific American*, *189*(5), 74–78.

van Hiele, P. (1986). *Structure and insight: A theory of mathematics education*. New York: Academic Press.

116

Chapter 5
Constructing early number concepts and relationships

CHAPTER OVERVIEW

Until the 1980s number concepts and the four arithmetic operations dominated much of primary mathematics curricula. With increasing research evidence about the importance of spatial and measurement concepts, data exploration and problem solving, a more balanced curriculum has emerged. Widespread and early exposure to information technology has influenced the way children acquire mathematical concepts, highlighting the need for children to interpret such mathematical representations as models, diagrams, tables, charts and graphs (Diezmann & Yelland, 2000; Diezmann & English, 2001). Patterning and pre-algebra skills, interpretation and representation of data, and use of technology-based representations now form key components of early numeracy (Board of Studies, NSW, 2002; Groves & Stacey, 1998; National Council of Teachers of Mathematics, 2002).

Fuelled by the 'process-driven' approach to learning, the constructivist movement of the 1980s and 1990s challenged entrenched practices that focused almost exclusively on drill and practice of arithmetic. There was a shift towards understanding number concepts and processes through mental computation and number sense with an emphasis on networks and relationships between number facts and operations, such as understanding that division facts can be derived from multiplication facts. There seemed almost a movement against 'naked numbers' that was supported by the widespread use of a range of structured and unstructured concrete materials with arithmetic also embedded in situations, words, stories and pictures.

Over the past two decades there has been a large amount of research on number concepts and relationships and we now have a much clearer understanding of how children acquire these. Following the work of Piaget, the constructivists focused on the explicit assessment and development of increasingly sophisticated numerical strategies based on counting and base ten knowledge. This has been achieved through systematic and detailed investigation of children's thinking through individual interviews. Integrated with this approach has been an emphasis on developing number concepts and strategies through solving word problems that was also focused on the development of counting and arithmetical strategies. Another feature of research and practice has been on finding out how children visualise and model their notions of numerical situations rather than relying on adult-imposed representations. There has been much attention on generating and assessing pupil worksamples of mathematical ideas including drawings and diagrams of solution strategies, and explanations of how children use numerical ideas. Although the number strand of the curricula is still characterised by such aspects as numeration and place value, arithmetic number facts and operations, and fraction knowledge, these components must be seen as both interrelated and integrated across other mathematical strands. Problem-solving strands of curricula such as *Working mathematically* (Board of Studies, NSW, 2002) integrate numerical concepts and processes within broader processes such as mathematical investigating, reasoning, communicating, explaining, representing and justifying.

In Australia, *Numeracy benchmarks years 3, 5 & 7* (Curriculum Corporation, 2000) have been developed as a national priority, and these reflect three key aspects of number learning:

+ understanding number concepts so as to read and use numbers flexibly;
+ computing confidently using a variety of strategies and techniques including calculators; and
+ applying number ideas and skills in a wide variety of problem contexts involving choosing, using and justifying knowledge and strategies.

Although the *Numeracy benchmarks* describe only a limited and minimum acceptable standard of numeracy at Years 3, 5 and 7, it is intended that number learning be viewed broadly so that students are challenged no matter their age, stage or level. The development of numerical concepts and processes involves a range of complex and interrelated mathematical ideas. It is important to see these aspects developing in a connected way through using increasingly sophisticated numerical strategies.

This chapter describes the early development of key numerical concepts and processes through a constructivist-based learning framework. It is not intended to provide detailed descriptions of curriculum outcomes for the number strand. Rather, some critical aspects of number learning are exemplified through children's experiences. The following aspects will be described:

+ pre-numerical skills and intuitive notions of number;
+ key aspects of early number knowledge: counting, patterning, ordering, grouping, base ten and arithmetical strategies and procedures;
+ assessment of number knowledge and strategies through Learning Frameworks in Number; and
+ problem-based arithmetical learning.

These aspects will be exemplified through teaching/learning plans in the 'Snapshots of Learning' section: calculator patterns, base ten experiences, forming and using groups, and making links between mathematical processes.

Chapter 6 develops these aspects further by examining the role of number sense, mental computation, arithmetical operations and number relationships for whole numbers, fractions and decimals in the later primary years. Chapter 7 provides a more in-depth description of the development of fraction knowledge, ratio and proportional reasoning concepts and processes, and integrates these aspects with other strands of the curriculum.

Chapter focus questions

In this chapter several key questions are raised in order to focus our attention on critical aspects of early number learning and the way we might cater for the diverse range of abilities and interests of our students. Traditionally young children in the first year of school have engaged in a sequence of learning experiences that match curriculum expectations such as beginning with classification activities and rote counting to 10, and 'learning' numbers 1 to 10 in a lock-step fashion. We might well ask how to cater for the child who can already count, order, write and explain place value from 1 to 100 or beyond. Consider your responses to the following questions. These questions are often the subject of heated debate among educators (Bobis, 2002). The importance of contextual play and the development of numeracy skills should also be considered (Macmillan, 1999; 2002).

1. What number knowledge and skills does the child enter school with, and should we not assess this before attempting instruction?

2. How can the teacher capitalise on this knowledge in order to challenge and motivate the child?

3. What are the fundamental strategies that children need to acquire in order to develop basic arithmetical knowledge?

4. How has the early number curriculum changed in order to address a broader view of number learning?

5. Should we encourage young children to explore and develop number concepts and processes such as multiplication and division, traditionally delayed until the later years?

6. How can we use calculators to promote the development of effective number knowledge and strategies in the early years?

Throughout this chapter, and in Chapters 6 and 7, these questions will be addressed by examining examples of children's numerical thinking and reflecting upon the research that has given rise to changes in the way we approach early number learning.

REFLECTION ON A CLASSROOM SCENARIO

Visualising the hundreds chart

Year 2 students were involved in a series of regular activities to develop numeration strategies such as counting-on by tens from decades e.g. '20, 30, 40 . . .' or from various starting points (e.g. '55, 65, 75'). Some of the activities required the students to use a hundreds chart where they identified various counting patterns by covering numerals on their charts. In order to challenge the students' ability to visualise and record their patterns, the hundreds charts were removed and the students were asked to draw freehand a hundreds chart from memory. Robert, who had been covering number patterns in tens on his chart, produced the hundreds chart shown in Figure 5.1.

Robert drew a square and subdivided rows of separate squares, and then recorded numerals for 1 to 17 in the first row. He explained that he could fit 17 numbers in them. He began the second row of numbers with 18. His attempt to draw rows and columns produced single boxes, many of which had no horizontal or vertical alignment. Robert was not only unable to visualise or draw a 10-by-10 grid but also seemingly unaware that the purpose

Figure 5.1 Robert's drawing of a hundreds chart

of the hundreds chart was to represent counting numbers 1–100 in sequences of tens. Further questioning by the teacher revealed that Robert was unable to count in tens beyond 30 or from various starting points. Robert was basically a 'unitary' counter who counted everything by ones.

In comparison, Leah drew correctly a 10-by-10 grid but created an unusual arrangement of numerals. Figure 5.2 shows that she started at the bottom left-hand corner of the grid and then filled in diagonals of increasing size moving up to the top left-hand corner until reaching 62.

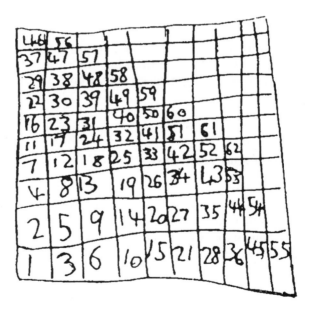

Figure 5.2 Leah's hundreds chart

Leah was later able to produce a counting pattern of tens but also seemed unaware that the purpose of the hundreds chart was to record patterns of tens. Nevertheless she made interesting patterns such as '1, 3, 6, 10, 15, 21, 28, 36, 45, 55', but was unable to identify or explain how the patterns worked.

The teacher commented on the effectiveness of this activity as an assessment strategy:

We've been using hundreds charts regularly for months and I just assumed that all the students could see and use the patterns of tens readily. I realise now that always giving the students the ready-made tens structure and the counting sequence is not getting them to think of the sequence or the patterns for themselves. I need to check whether other students like Robert are simply copying other students' patterns and whether they can draw grids because we use this skill in many other aspects of mathematics.

This activity also suggests that students would benefit from tasks that require them to explain their thinking and that expose them to a range of representations and organisational structures where they are prompted to think in different ways. A rich variety of number patterns could be constructed by the students as a basis for developing more complex numerical relationships.

Discuss this question with a peer or colleague: 'How many different ways can you show counting patterns in tens, twenties, to 100 or beyond?'

RESEARCH ON NUMBER LEARNING

Research on the development of early number knowledge in Australasia has been extensive (Diezmann & Yelland, 2000; McIntosh & Dole, 2000; Mulligan & Mitchelmore, 1996; Perry, 2000; Wright et al, 1996). A range of Australian government initiatives have supported the development of projects on number, many focused on mental computation and frameworks for developing number sense (Morony & Brinkworth, 2002). The main emphasis of research on early numeracy internationally has also been on children's developing numerical concepts and strategies, and the growth of mental computation and number sense (Anghileri, 2001; National Council of Teachers of Mathematics, 2000; Thompson, 1997; Wright, Martland & Stafford, 2000). Numerical 'strategies' refer to particular methods or skills that the child develops either intuitively or from instructional experiences. These strategies are associated with processes such as counting-on, counting-back, sharing and grouping. Number sense refers to the child's understanding and use of numerical concepts and mental computation strategies including calculator use, as well as the ability to use this in flexible ways. For young children this involves making sensible estimates and thinking about the reasonableness of an answer. This may involve applying a known strategy to a new situation such as using doubles, or combining strategies such as doubling and subtracting. Developing flexibility and number sense requires children to construct and decompose, combine and partition quantities in a variety of ways.

Some key findings from research on early number knowledge are summarised as follows:

+ Children's informal and intuitive numerical ideas, explanations and informal recordings form a very important basis for the development of numerical concepts (Hughes, 1986; Kamii, Kirkland & Lewis, 2001; Macmillan, 1999; Mulligan & Mitchelmore, 1996; Twomey-Fosnot & Dolk, 2001).

+ Children begin school with a large repertoire of counting and arithmetical strategies and can develop numeration and arithmetical concepts earlier than traditionally expected (Bobis, 2002; Wright, 1998; Young-Loveridge, 1997).

+ Children need an underlying understanding of how the number system is structured and ordered by grouping and regrouping 'tens' (Boulton-Lewis, 1998; Cobb, Yackel & McClain, 2000; Thomas, Mulligan & Goldin, 2002; Thompson, 1997).

+ Children need to develop number sense through flexibility in the way they use mental strategies (Beishuizen & Anghileri, 1998; Diezmann & English, 2001; McIntosh & Dole, 2000; Twomey-Fosnot & Dolk, 2001).

+ Children need to develop increasingly sophisticated counting and arithmetical strategies by challenging them to think abstractly rather than relying on concrete or visual models (Anghileri, 2001; Wright et al., 2002).

+ Children can develop counting and arithmetical strategies by solving and creating simple problems related to the four operations; and children can discuss, explain and record their thinking as number patterns and number sentences that approximate conventional symbolism (Carpenter et al., 1993; Carpenter et al., 1999; Mulligan & Mitchelmore 1997).

+ Children can use calculators effectively to promote their numerical concepts and skills (Groves & Stacey, 1998; Swan, 1996).

Using models and materials

A variety of concrete structured and unstructured materials and models have been used traditionally in the development of numeration and arithmetical learning: base ten blocks (Dienes' blocks), unifix cubes, bundling sticks, the abacus, ten frames, hundreds charts and place value charts. Chapter 1 referred to the process of representing mathematical ideas as the child's gradual construction from intuitive to concrete to abstract concepts. Curriculum documents and most texts about teaching mathematics to young children have extensive notes on the use of materials to teach number (see, for example, Booker et al., 2003).

Recent research shows that it is advantageous for children to use these materials only if they effectively 'map' or model their own internal mathematical ideas (Boulton-Lewis, 1998). Children need to make a connection between the representations produced externally (by the materials or textbook) and their ideas of what they represent. Therefore imposing structured materials on children might not be meaningful if the child does not make any connection between the representation or model and the mathematical idea at hand. In this chapter we have avoided the use of structured models to represent numerical ideas and relationships. Instead we have emphasised the importance of children's construction of their own models and mental strategies. However, some concrete materials can be useful for representing mathematical ideas. Some systematic methods of representing number as patterns—for example, the use of dot cards or ten frames, or hundreds charts—have been used as a catalyst for the child's interpretation and construction of numerical relationships.

Materials that provide some *structure* for children to organise their thinking are recommended, such as dot-pattern cards, simple five frames, ten frames, geoboards, grids or hundreds charts. The calculator is also a useful tool for exploration and representation of number and its use is encouraged throughout the chapter. Symbol cards using calculator digits are also important for numeral recognition. The teaching and learning of early number concepts should capitalise on the child's use of numerical representations generally, such as numerals used in real-life situations, for example compare numerals on watches, clocks, calendars or birthday cards (Clarke, 2001).

In this chapter we have taken the approach that children need to visualise and represent numerical concepts and relationships in ways that are meaningful for them. Hence the use of structured commercial material such as Dienes' blocks is not made explicit. However, interlocking structured materials such as Duplo, Lego, Unifix or Multilink cubes all provide the opportunity to model units and combine units to form other units (i.e. ten cubes makes one ten). The most powerful resource for developing early number is the child's own representation and recognition of number; in many situations this will arise through data exploration and the use of technology, such as creating graphs or pictures. It will be recalled that Chapter 3 emphasised the important role of data exploration, recording and interpretation as an effective means for representing numerical ideas and relationships.

THE GROWTH OF MATHEMATICAL UNDERSTANDING

This section describes the early growth of numerical concepts and processes by exemplifying key aspects of number: counting and notating; patterning, estimating and subitising (recognising how many items are in a small group); grouping and partitioning; mental computation; base ten and arithmetical strategies and procedures. The development of early fraction knowledge through sharing and part–whole relationships forms an integral part of these developing processes. These aspects are described in Chapter 7. No single aspect alone can determine the growth and development of number knowledge. Children's pre-calculation and mental computation strategies are based on developing these aspects with increasing levels of sophistication. Critical to this development is the growth of abstract thinking that promotes effective mental computation strategies.

It is also crucial to look at the way children establish, or fail to establish, relationships between one aspect and another. Ideally this requires that children find similarities and differences between one numerical aspect and another, such as using a counting sequence of multiples to form equal groups. Seeing these connections will enable children to develop a flexibility which enables them to develop a coherent range of arithmetical (computational) strategies and where they can move between one strategy and another. Existing strategies can be extended to solve a new, related problem or a new strategy may be constructed that builds upon prior strategies. Eventually, children can develop an *astuteness* that one strategy may be more effective, or more efficient, than another when calculating mentally or solving a simple problem. We also need to consider how individuals vary in developing their own methods for finding patterns and relationships between these key aspects and how this might influence their operating with larger numbers later.

Underpinning the effective development of key aspects of number learning and corresponding mental strategies is the child's ability to see *structure* in numerical processes and representations. Structure can be identified in a variety of ways such as by finding patterns of five on an array of 25 items rather than seeing 25 individual items. Some children impose their own structure on mathematical situations and this may enhance or impede effective solution strategies.

These aspects are fundamental to Learning Frameworks in Number, which are described later in this chapter. These frameworks form a basis for identifying and assessing features of early counting and arithmetical knowledge. The development of number sense and mental computation also involves skills in estimation, judging the reasonableness of results, and using numbers and patterns flexibly. These aspects are discussed further in this chapter and in Chapter 6, where arithmetical processes of addition, subtraction, multiplication and division are exemplified further through computational strategies and a problem-based approach.

Emergent numerical processes: classifying, matching, ordering, notating

Traditionally, pre-number learning has focused on fundamental skills of sorting and classifying, comparing and ordering, and matching and patterning before introducing children to formal number concepts and relationships. Often this occurs through informal play situations (Macmillan, 2002). While these aspects are crucial to most aspects of mathematical learning, contemporary research and practice show that a range of counting, grouping, base ten and arithmetical strategies may develop prior to formal schooling (Kamii, Kirkland & Lewis, 2001). Children's classification and notation skills shown in the next section are linked to Chapter 3 where the development of these skills was described in the context of data exploration.

FOCUS QUESTIONS

How can young children be challenged to make, order and quantify simple classifications?

In a small group of your peers examine Sam's picture graph (Figure 5.3) showing a self-generated classification and simple picture graph of the food he ate for breakfast, lunch and dinner. He draws, counts and labels items, and with assistance orders them using one-to-one correspondence. Consider the key aspects (classifying, ordering and notating) critical to the development of number concepts and relationships shown here.

Figure 5.3 Sam's (4 years, 3 months) picture graph of a number of food items

Several important aspects critical to number development were identified through the small group discussion. Sam was able to organise and explain why the items were grouped and placed in one-to-one correspondence. He could count (perceptually) by seeing the items, and record the quantities as conventional numerals; he could explain that there were more or fewer items in each group by using comparative language to describe the groupings. We agreed that Sam was already showing skills in classifying, counting, ordering and writing numerals. One teacher questioned whether Sam could recognise quantities (e.g. four items) in other contexts. Has Sam acquired an understanding of the value of numbers by recognising and comparing the quantities?

Examine the outcomes described for pre-number or early number knowledge in your relevant syllabus document. What tasks could you devise to assess early numerical processes?

Patterning, estimating and subitising

Recognising and creating patterns is also fundamental to developing number concepts and relationships. Figures 5.4 and 5.5 show estimating and subitising, where children discriminate between dot patterns to identify the quantities. Subitising is the process of immediately recognising how many items are in a small group. A series of dot pattern cards (1 to 10) were flashed and the children asked to give an estimate of the number of dots; then they were asked to match the cards that had the same number of dots and explain why one card was easier to quantify than another. Similarly other patterns of the numerals 5 to 10 were explored.

Figure 5.4 Different arrangements of dot pattern cards of 5 (Ethan, Kindergarten)

Figure 5.5 Similarities and differences between patterns of 8 (Emma, Kindergarten)

Identifying the quantities on dot cards can be extended to include many aspects of number learning by requiring children to match the patterns with objects, draw the patterns from memory, record the numerals and number names, order the cards numerically and generate new patterns such as odds and evens. Children can also be encouraged to create their own spatial arrangements. Bobis (1996) describes how a teaching program using dot patterns enabled students to successfully recognise and construct number patterns and basic combinations in the first year of school.

Other representations of number can be linked to everyday notions of number such as age or time. Figure 5.6 shows child-generated recordings of number patterns using a calendar.

Intuitive notions of number

Children's intuitive notions of number can take on many forms, such as the numbers associated with age or context; for example, 'my brother is 9 (months old), or my brother is 9 (years

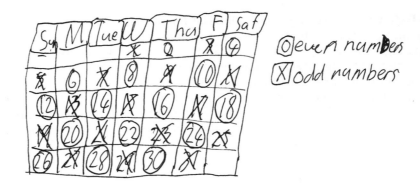

Figure 5.6 Samantha's odds and evens patterns

old)', has a very different meaning to establishing the 'nineness' of 9 counters in the classroom. Children's images of number can influence the way they count and acquire base ten strategies. The following examples show developmental points in children's pictorial and notational recordings of the number sequence 1–100.

In a study by Thomas & Mulligan (1995), children from Kindergarten to Year 4 were asked to close their eyes and to imagine the numbers from 1 to 100. Then they were asked to draw pictures that they saw in their minds. They were also asked to explain the image and their drawing.

Anthony (Figure 5.7) drew a picture of a truck and explained the image as "'cause my Dad's truck does a hundred'. This picture related his intuitive experience of the truck image to speed. Kimberley (Figure 5.8) and Mellissa (Figure 5.9) produced pictures (iconic symbols such as dots, dashes or marks used to represent the real things) of the number sequence. Kimberley's recording was of ten groups of ten circles but she could not explain her grouping, expressing it as 'just circles'. Mellissa gave a more sophisticated response related to the numeration system with her drawing of 10 rods.

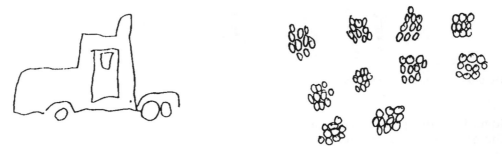

Figure 5.7 Truck image (Anthony, Year 1)   **Figure 5.8** Groups of ten (Kimberley, Year 2)

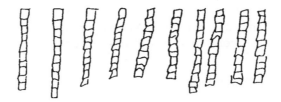

Figure 5.9 Groups of 10 (Mellissa, Year 2)

Jane (Figure 5.10) and David (Figure 5.11) both recorded the number sequence using conventional notation but in highly creative ways. Jane explained that she saw the numbers moving in a spiral formation 'going on forever'. It is important to note the structure of number segments in tens (e.g. 71–80, 81–90) that she used. David described numerals flashing one at a time, skip counting in fives up to 100.

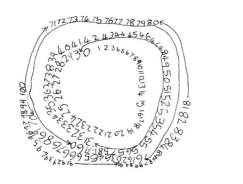

Figure 5.10 Spiral sequence (Jane, Year 1)	**Figure 5.11** Multiple sequence in fives (David, Year 4)

From further examination of children's responses it was inferred that each recording was closely linked to the child's developing structure of the number system (Thomas, Mulligan & Goldin, 2002). Anthony has not developed a base ten structure or a notion of number sequence as yet, but has a sense of the importance and size of 100. Anthony, Jane and David showed highly creative imagery that was not related to their conventional experiences in the classroom. Kimberley and Mellissa produced images that reflected aspects of classroom experiences with concrete materials.

ACTIVITY 5.1

Reflecting on children's intuitive notions of number

1. How does this visualisation of counting tasks assist the teacher in establishing the child's visualisation, counting and grouping skills, and numeration knowledge?

2. Can you trace the development in these examples from informal (or idiosyncratic) thinking to more conventional forms of counting and grouping using numerals?

3. How can this task link with other basic counting and grouping tasks?

    In a small group of your peers, try the following activity and record your responses independently: What do you visualise when you count or imagine numbers 1 to 100, 1 to 1000, 1 to 1 000 000, between 0 and 1, and before 0?

    Now try this task with some young children and try to analyse their responses in terms of the development of numeration. Why is visualisation important in establishing basic grouping strategies?

Base ten strategies and equal grouping

The numeration system is often described as a base ten number system and the structure of the system needs to be understood by children in order for them to extend the system to larger whole numbers and to include decimal numbers (Baturo, 2000; Hiebert & Wearne, 1992; Twomey-Fosnot & Dolk, 2001). Chapter 6 will extend this aspect of numeration as a system. One of the difficulties children experience is that they learn the place value of units (or ones), tens, hundreds and thousands without seeing the pattern of tens. They need to see that the system of numeration is based on the use of ten as a unit (ten ones makes one ten) and each place value position (to the left) is created by multiplying by ten. Children's flexible thinking about collections of tens and ones should precede or occur concurrently with teaching addition and subtraction of two-digit numbers. Teaching/learning experiences described in Snapshots: 'Rolls, bags and boxes' (p. 147) exemplify the process of creating the base ten numeration system.

The idea of forming equal groups, particularly groups of ten, is an advance on the early counting and mental calculation strategies. Equal grouping requires the child to form groups of equal size and use these groups as units. Children's mental computation strategies for estimating or calculating the number of items in a group can distinguish important differences between using unitary counting, additive or multiplicative ideas. Year 2 students were shown a random collection of counters with each example of increasingly difficult number size, (a) 10 items (b) 20 items or (c) 100 items. The students were asked:

> You don't need to work out how many counters there are, but can you show me an easy way of working out how many counters there are very quickly? Are there any other ways that you could group the items?

These responses to the task with 100 counters revealed a wide range of strategies with 24% of students using unitary (count by ones) strategies. For example, Amanda made several attempts to count the items by ones but lost track of her counting and the items each time. Jason used a multiple counting pattern (2, 4, 6 . . .) by placing the counters in equal groups of 2 and counting by twos to 100. Others used variations of the pattern of twos by doubling and redoubling. More than 50% of students used quinary-based strategies, showing some structural characteristics where the formation of equal-sized groups, rows or arrays of five counters allowed the students to calculate the total easily if they needed to.

One student used his hand as an informal unit of measure in such a way that he covered eight counters with one and then used the hand as a unit. He said, 'There's about 12 hands worth of counters and eight in one hand, so I would count up eight, twelve times'. Two of the most sophisticated responses showed how students used spatial patterns to form groups:

> I made an empty array by making a row of ten and a column of ten in an L shape and then you could fill it in with counters. I'd know if there were 100 because it would be ten tens.

> The counters could be placed on grid paper in rows of 10 (with squares of approximate size to the counters) and the number of rows counted using repeated addition.

The development of increasingly sophisticated grouping and calculation strategies can be enhanced when the teacher is made aware of the level of strategy use by the student. The modelling of equal groups and the associated counting patterns can assist students to move beyond unitary and simplistic counting methods to see the structure of equal groups and determine the most efficient group size, for example groups of ten are more appropriate than groups of two. This process is exemplified in a teaching/learning situation in Snapshots: 'Equal grouping' (p.145).

Critical aspects of the base ten system: curriculum frameworks

Most curricula emphasise the importance of numeration and place value as prerequisite to developing arithmetical knowledge. Refer to your mathematics syllabus section on numeration and place value. Which aspects do you consider critical to the development of basic fact knowledge and number sense?

+ Counting forwards and backwards from various starting points; unitary (by ones) or skip counting by multiples (e.g. 2, 4, 6); counting by tens.

+ Reading, writing and ordering numerals.

+ Grouping using base ten; regrouping ten ones for one ten, ten tens for one hundred.

+ Decomposing or regrouping numbers such that flexibility is assigned; for example, 23 is 2 tens and 3 ones but it is also 23 ones; 567 is 56 tens and 7 ones or 5 hundreds and 67 ones.

+ Using and interpreting place value; the value of the position of numerals increase by powers of ten from right to left for whole numbers.

+ A multiplicative idea that the value of a digit is identified by multiplying that digit by the value assigned to that position (e.g. 34 is $3 \times 10 + 4 \times 1$).

+ An additive idea that the value of the whole number is the sum of the value of the individual digits (e.g. 234 is 200 + 30 + 4).

+ Zero can be used as a place holder to identify a position between groupings.

All of these principles are commonly attributed to basic numeration knowledge. How can these principles be acquired by building on the knowledge children already have about number and place value?

Developing mental computation strategies

An increasing focus on mental computation rather than written and/or formal algorithms in the early years of schooling has been seen in many classroom studies on the early development of computation (Morony & Brinkworth, 2002). The powerful use of effective mental computation strategies and associated visual models such as the 'empty number line' are growing in regular classroom practice. Teachers are seeing the benefits of the development of efficient strong mental strategies rather than a reliance on procedural arithmetical processes. The following examples, showing a range of mental computation strategies, are drawn from classroom studies of children in the first two years of schooling.

Example 1: Counting, addition and multiplication strategies
In response to the following task, 'Start with two and the answer is ten', Kindergarten children demonstrated wide differences in the mental computation strategies they used to solve and explain relationships between the numbers 2 and 10 exemplified in the following excerpts.

Excerpt 1 (Samantha)
You start with 2 and you go 3, 4, 5, 6, 7, 8, 9, 10 (shows fingers for each count) and you have 8 more.

Excerpt 2 (Tran)
4, 6, 8, 10. Eight more makes ten (shows fingers for each count).

Excerpt 3 (Paul)
2 and 3 makes 5, and 5 more makes 10. I doubled 5 and took away the 2. 5 and 3 makes 8 altogether.

Excerpt 4 (William)
You could break the 10 into 5 bits so there's 2 in each so 5 twos make ten.

Excerpt 5 (Anna)
10 is 5 twos, so 10 is five times bigger.

These excerpts show increasingly sophisticated strategies that can be distinguished in a number of ways. Excerpt 1 shows that Samantha used a count-by-ones strategy and records the process using her fingers. This is often referred to as perceptual counting (Wright, 1998). Tran shows an advance on this strategy by using the multiple pattern of two but is still at a perceptual level. There is a marked difference in the strategies used by Paul who uses a partitioning of five and doubles to arrive at the combination of three and five. This flexibility is a basis for developing more complex mental computation strategies. Excerpts 4 and 5 are distinguished by the children's ability to use multiplicative ideas rather than counting or additive strategies where multiplication is used as an operation '10 is five times bigger'. If young children are developing these more advanced strategies in simple situations the transfer of these strategies to situations involving larger quantities can take place.

The 'empty number line' can be used as an effective tool for recording mental computation strategies. This strategy has been used widely by European educators Gravemeijer and colleagues as a semiformal routine that assists the students to move to more efficient use of mental computation. In the case of Paul (Excerpt 3) the child shows the partitioning of 10 into 5 and 5 and splits the 5 into 2 and 3. The following recording in Figure 5.12 shows Paul's use of the empty number line, the splitting of 10 and the 'jumping' of 3 and 5. The representation shows the relative size of the amounts and demonstrates how Paul arrived at '10'.

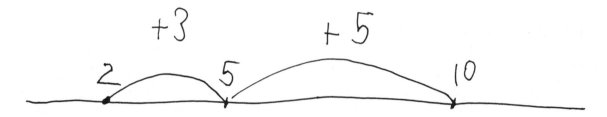

Figure 5.12 Paul's use of the empty number line

Grouping and partitioning: using interrelationships

In the following example, base ten strategies can be used to assist the child to combine and extend existing grouping and partitioning strategies. The following example shows how Timothy, aged five years, calculates 4 groups of 15 using mental strategies based on grouping, partitioning and combining tens and fives.

> *15 kids in each group and 4 groups, I can do it in tens . . . 10, 20, 30, 40 [flashes ten fingers simultaneously with count] makes 40, and the fives, 5, 10, 15, 20 [flashes five fingers simultaneously with count], 20 and 20, that's 40, 50, 60 . . . that's 60 kids all together.*

Susie, aged six years, uses an alternative but equally sophisticated strategy, based on partitioning tens and fives and doubling, which is shown in the following example:

> *15 and 15, that's 10 and 10 makes 20, and 5 and 5 makes 10 . . . 20 and 10 makes 30 . . . so for 4 groups, it would be 30 and 30 . . . 30, 40, 50, 60 [tapping ten fingers on table simultaneously with count].*

These examples show how children combine their counting and base ten strategies with the notion of equal grouping. These children can reorganise the quantities according to the structure that is most efficient for them; that is, they can work in fives and tens. Tim partitions 15 into 10 and 5; Susie collects the tens and fives separately and then combines. We would not normally expect children of this age to represent and calculate 4 × 15. The promotion of multiple counting and base ten strategies in the first year of schooling enabled these children to apply their knowledge of counting, partitioning and mental computation strategies effectively.

ACTIVITY 5.2

Arithmetical knowledge: assessment tasks

Some student teachers were comparing a range of activities they used for assessing children's mathematics in Year 1. They were required to develop some key tasks to assess children's place value and arithmetical knowledge. The following examples (Figures 5.13 and 5.14) and responses were elicited from the group.

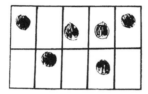

Figure 5.13 Example of ten frames to show patterns to ten

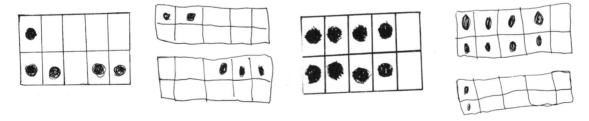

Figure 5.14 Year 1 students' combinations to 5, 10, 20

I chose the ten frame because it has so many possibilities for visualising and constructing patterns of 10 and working out addition and subtraction combinations. Also you can use the 'ten' cards to check understanding of adding on by tens (e.g. 14 plus 10 is 24), so does the child add on from the 14 by ones or add on the 10 immediately?

(Carl, student teacher)

I wanted to see whether my students were able to create and explain a variety of number combinations for 5, 10, 20. Did any of their combinations show patterns, or odds and evens?

(Felicity, student teacher)

I just used coloured plastic money boxes and 5c, 10c, 20c, 50c, $1 and $2 coins to see if they could add and subtract with money without seeing the coins. I wanted to bring in some problem solving so I asked students the following task:

Show two empty plastic money boxes, place 5 coins in one, 4 coins in the other, and the total of each money box is $2.00. What possible combinations of 5 coins and 4 coins could there be in each box?

(Deslee, student teacher)

Compare the three assessment tasks above.

■ Do these examples lend themselves to developing important principles of commutativity such as 4 + 6 = 6 + 4 or associativity such as 2 + 3 + 4 = 3 + 2 + 4?

■ How would you encourage further exploration of these principles so that children could explain these relationships?

■ How do these activities link to Learning Frameworks in Number?

The assessment tasks are linked closely with base ten strategies in the framework. It would be important for children to explore a variety of number combinations as parts of a number (e.g. 8 is formed by 2 + 2 + 4 or 3 + 3 + 2 and so on).

Young children could also be encouraged to find similarities and differences between number combinations. Gervasconi shows how ten frames and the 'Think Board' are used effectively for representing mathematical ideas through visualisation (Gervasconi, 1999). Figure 5.15 shows a Think Board to allow students to record symbols, words, pictures and materials in the four segments.

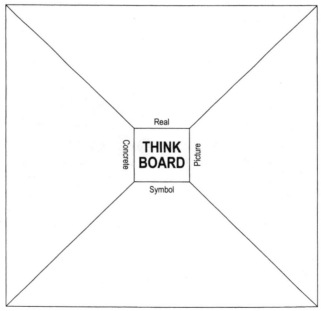

Figure 5.15 Model of a 'Think Board'

Arithmetical strategies and procedures

Students need to be challenged sufficiently in order to develop more sophisticated and efficient strategies. At the same time, base ten knowledge of place value and using ten as a unit are critical to developing addition and subtraction processes. Children's early addition, subtraction, multiplication and division knowledge is based fundamentally on the development of counting sequences and arithmetical strategies, along with skills of combining, partitioning and patterning. These processes and associated arithmetical strategies can also be elicited through word problems that distinguish between fundamental types of addition and subtraction, multiplication and division ideas.

Addition and subtraction processes

Addition and subtraction are inverse relationships where $3 + 4 = 7$ is represented as $7 - 4 = 3$ or $7 - 3 = 4$. The important notion of associativity (shown in Activity 5.3) means that children need to combine and partition numbers to construct addition and subtraction facts. Counting skills and strategies are critical to developing addition and subtraction facts.

ACTIVITY 5.3

Addition and subtraction combinations

A group of Year 2 students were asked to find as many strategies as they could to add 9 and 8. Figure 5.16 shows the wide variety of strategies exhibited by the students.

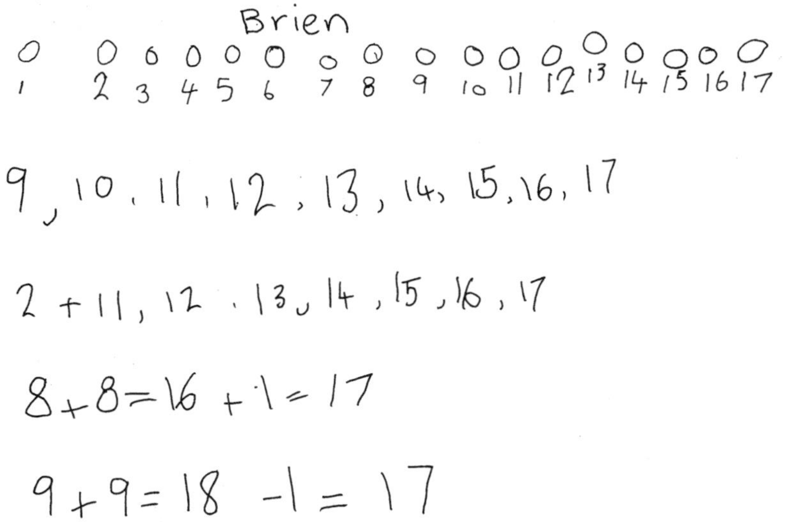

Figure 5.16 Strategies for solving 9 + 8 by Year 2 students

Can you match these strategies to the categories listed below and order them for increasing complexity?

- Counts from 1 to 17 using counters.
- Counts-on from the smaller or larger number by ones.
- Builds to ten then counts-on.
- Derives fact from knowledge of doubles.
- Derives fact by other means.
- Uses compensation.
- Partitions quantities using part-part-whole relationships.

Multiplication and division processes

The concepts of multiplication and division are not only interrelated but are closely linked to addition and subtraction strategies, and early fraction learning. However, multiplication and division concepts differ from addition and subtraction mainly because they depend on the child's ability to use equal groups as 'composite units'. A composite unit is a collection or group of individual items that must be viewed as one thing. For example, a child must view three items as 'one three' in order for the unit 'three' to be a countable unit. Multiplication is not simply a process of repeated addition; nor is division simply a process of repeated subtraction or sharing. For a true understanding of multiplication and division the child needs to eventually co-ordinate groups of equal groups and recognise the overall pattern, that is composites of composites (e.g. 'three sixes' and 'six . . . three times'). Snapshots: 'Using Arrays' (p. 146) exemplifies how to assess the use of composite units using an array pattern for multiplication.

Multiplication and division are inverse relationships where $3 \times 4 = 12$ is represented as $12 \div 4 = 3$ or $12 \div 3 = 4$ and, like addition and subtraction, these processes can be developed simultaneously. These relationships are exemplified further through the categories of equal grouping, partition and quotition in Exhibit 5.3 (p. 140). It is important to distinguish the difference between partition and quotition problems. *Partition problems* refer to a group of items to be shared into equal groups; *quotition problems* refer to a group of items shared into equal groups where the number of groups is known but not the number in each group. Multiplication and division facts can be gradually constructed and derived through increasing counting skills: skip counting and double counting where visible items are gradually replaced by counting and using composite groups (e.g. 3 groups of 4), repeated addition and subtraction, and then using multiplication and division more generally as operations.

ACTIVITY 5.4

Multiplication and division combinations

A group of Year 2 students was asked to use as many strategies as they could to find multiplication and division number combinations for 24. Figure 5.17 shows the wide variety of strategies exhibited by the students.

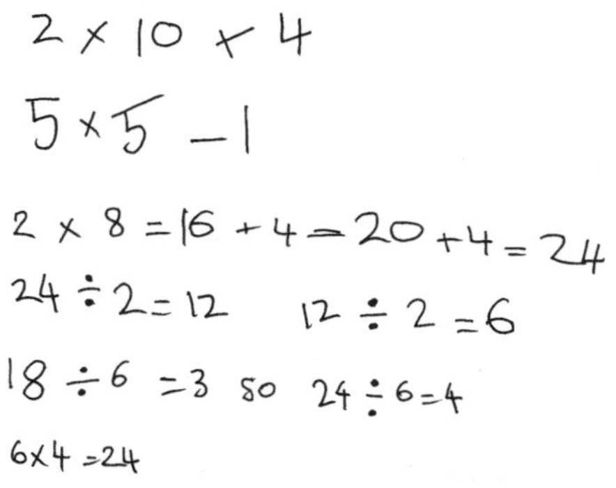

$$2 \times 10 + 4$$

$$5 \times 5 - 1$$

$$2 \times 8 = 16 + 4 = 20 + 4 = 24$$

$$24 \div 2 = 12 \qquad 12 \div 2 = 6$$

$$18 \div 6 = 3 \quad \text{so} \quad 24 \div 6 = 4$$

$$6 \times 4 = 24$$

Figure 5.17 Strategies for finding combinations for 24 by Year 2 students

Can you match these strategies to the categories listed below and order them for increasing complexity?

- Makes combinations by sharing and counting visible items in one-to-one correspondence.
- Uses trial and error to make combinations.
- Uses knowledge of addition and subtraction facts to make combinations.
- Skip counts using counters.
- Uses base ten strategies.

- Derives facts from knowledge of doubles.
- Derives division fact from multiplication fact by other means.
- Uses compensation.
- Partitions quantities using part–part–whole relationships.

How did these aspects show increasing sophistication of strategy development?

How can you ascertain whether the child has a broad understanding of multiplication and division concepts as operations rather than just repeated addition or sharing models? Turn to Snapshots: 'Equal grouping' (p. 145) and 'Using arrays' (p. 146). Notice how these examples reinforce basic strategies in developing multiplication and division such as co-ordinating equal groups in rows and columns.

The acquisition of basic number facts needs to focus on the systematic use of strategies to encourage increasingly more sophisticated number fact knowledge. It is also important for children to find similarities and differences between number facts by recording and finding patterns and relationships between facts. Making connections is critical to basic fact knowledge.

LEARNING FRAMEWORKS IN NUMBER

Australian government initiatives in early numeracy, such as the New South Wales 'Count Me In Too' project (CMIT) and the Victorian 'Early Years Numeracy Program' (ENRP), and the 'Early Numeracy' project in New Zealand have assisted teachers in developing pedagogical knowledge in order to support students' development (Clarke et al., 2000; Thomas, Tagg & Ward, 2002; Wright & Gould, 2002a). Frameworks for early number learning have been developed to provide a basis for teachers to assess and promote the advancement of numerical strategies. Similarly, other frameworks such as '"First Steps" to Numeracy' in Western Australia, the 'Diagnostic Net' in Queensland, and a mental computation framework in Tasmania focus on the assessment and development of early numeracy.

A Learning Framework in Number (LFIN), based on the work of Wright (1998) and Mulligan (Mulligan & Wright, 2000), is integral to the 'Count Me In Too' project in New South Wales (NSW Department of Education and Training, 2000). This provides a basis for teachers to promote the development of increasingly sophisticated arithmetical strategies such as counting, base ten and the four operations. Children are engaged in mathematical tasks that challenge their current level of thinking, including aspects of classifying, counting, base ten strategies, addition, subtraction, multiplication and division.

The LFIN exemplifies five key aspects of arithmetical development of young children:

1. arithmetical strategies such as counting-on,
2. number word sequences such as counting forwards and backwards,
3. base ten strategies such as using tens and units simultaneously,
4. arithmetical procedures such as combining and partitioning and patterning, and
5. early multiplication and division where equal grouping is developed.

A key feature of the LFIN is the development from a perceptual level where the child relies on counting individual items to a level where the child can use advanced counting strategies abstractly. Each successive level shows the child's cognitive advances as well as new conceptual understandings. Once basic counting processes are in place the key aspects, grouping and partitioning, base ten and equal grouping form the core of the framework. See Exhibit 5.1.

EXHIBIT 5.1 LEARNING FRAMEWORK IN NUMBER (LFIN)

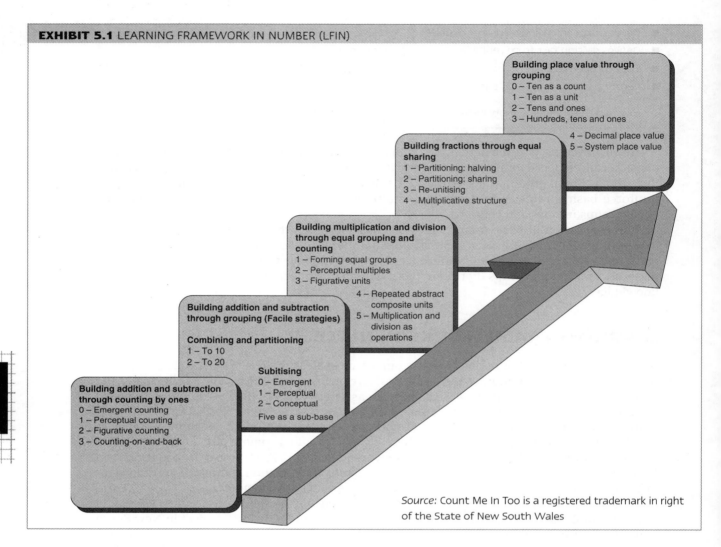

Source: Count Me In Too is a registered trademark in right of the State of New South Wales

Building addition and subtraction through counting by ones focuses on development of abstract counting (without visible items), and counting-on (e.g. adding 4 + 9 where the child counts 10, 11, 12, 13). Building addition and subtraction through grouping uses combining, partitioning and patterning, as well as other early arithmetical strategies of addition and subtraction, and can be effectively linked with the development of multiplication and division strategies. Building multiplication and division through equal grouping and counting develops concepts of multiplication and division through the idea of a 'composite' unit. Building place value through grouping is a basis for constructing and using ten as a unit, which is fundamental to numeration and place value. Children who have progressed to counting-on (arithmetical strategies) are likely to be developing the idea of equal grouping, necessary for multiplication and division. Children who are able to partition using five and ten as a base, including quinary-based strategies, make 'five', partitioning 'five', and counting in fives using equal groups, are also likely to be developing 'composite' units (equal groups).

As the focus of the project is the advancement of students' mathematical solution strategies, assessment of this growth attempts to show the most advanced strategies a student can elicit. The comparison of the rates of change of strategy between the initial and final assessments suggests that the 'Count Me In Too' project has progressed students' development of solution strategies from less efficient to more efficient, ahead of expectations (Wright & Gould, 2002b). This growth can be seen primarily in terms of the students' ability to develop more sophisticated counting and arithmetical strategies based on a teaching program incorporating efficient counting and patterning. Students making considerable progress are developing a more effective range of strategies and stronger number sense.

The Victorian 'Early Years Numeracy Program' (EYNP) (Department of Education and Training, Victoria, 2002) has also been developed for professionals to assess children's early numeracy by creating a framework of key growth points in numeracy learning. The EYNP framework encompasses growth points in number, measurement and space, organised into Number (counting, place value, strategies for addition, subtraction, multiplication and division), Measurement (time, length, mass) and Space (shape, visualisation and orientation). The growth points for counting, place value, addition and subtraction resemble those of the CMIT in New South Wales. Similarly the importance of mental computation strategies based on efficient counting is highlighted.

For example the growth points for addition and subtraction are described as follows:

1. Count-all (Counts all to find the total of two collections).
2. Count-on (Counts on from one number to find the total of two collections).
3. Count-back/count-down-to/count-up-from (Given a subtraction situation, chooses appropriately from strategies including count-back, count-down-to and count-up-from).
4. Basic strategies (doubles, commutativity, adding 10, tens facts, other known facts).
5. Derived strategies (near doubles, adding 9, build to 10, fact families, intuitive strategies).

Assessing key aspects of number

The CMIT and ENRP frameworks form a basis for assessing young students' development of arithmetical strategies and procedures. How would you assess these? Sample items from the CMIT early assessment schedule are shown in Table 5.1 on the next page. Beginning with early counting, interview a few young children to assess whether they have acquired some basic strategies and procedures identified in the frameworks. Can the children use counting-on effectively? Now attempt to match the strategies the child has used within the frameworks.

FOCUS QUESTIONS

A group of teachers and maths consultants were reviewing their implementation of the CMIT learning framework in number. Two Kindergarten teachers suggested that the framework was particularly helpful in assessing whether most of her students had acquired necessary counting and arithmetical strategies. Because the structure of the framework allowed them to ascertain at which stage the children were, they could also challenge the students with more complex tasks and extend their activities beyond the framework. How are the key aspects of number integrated in the framework: counting, grouping, partitioning, base ten and arithmetical strategies? How is counting critical to most other aspects of the framework? It is important to recognise that several aspects of the framework are developing simultaneously.

PROBLEM-BASED NUMBER LEARNING

The following discussion builds upon the ideas presented through the 'Growth of mathematical understanding' and 'Learning Frameworks in Number' sections to show how arithmetical concepts can be developed through word problems.

TABLE 5.1 Sample items from the assessment schedule for early number

Aspect of the framework	Sample item from assessment schedule
Perceptual counting	Use a pile of at least 30 counters all of one colour. Q. Get me 5 counters from the pile. Q. Get me 14 counters from the pile.
Forward number word sequence	Q. Start counting from . . . I'll tell you when to stop. (1) 1 . . . 32 (2) 62 . . . 73 (3) 86 . . . 103
Backward number word sequence	Q. Count backwards from 10 to 1. Q. Count backwards from 23. Q. What number come before: (1) 5? (2) 9? (3) 16? (4) 20? (5) 47? (6) 13?
Addition sequence	Q. I have 5 apples and I get another 3 apples. How many apples do I have altogether? Q. Here are 9 counters. (Display briefly and then screen.) Here are 4 counters. (Display briefly and then screen.) How many counters are there altogether?
Subtraction strategies	Q. I have 7 bananas. I eat 2 of the bananas. How many are left? Q. I have 12 counters. (Display briefly and then screen.) I'm taking away 3 counters. (Remove 3 without displaying any.) The counters are now arranged in two screened collections. How many are left here? (Indicate the screened collection of 9 counters.)

Addition and subtraction problems

Teachers from several Kindergarten, and Year 1 and 2 classes met at a professional development workshop to discuss the progress they had been making using a problem-centred approach to learning addition and subtraction. The transition from counting to mental strategies and automatic number facts is developed through a variety of arithmetic problem-centred situations in conjunction with open-ended problem-solving and number-sense activities. The teachers were keen to share their findings with the group. The workshop leader suggested that they focus on the strategies children used and how these matched the CMIT Learning Framework in Number (Exhibit 5.1). They examined children's worksamples and were asked to see if they could match different problem types with each example. Exhibit 5.2 (including Figures 5.18 to 5.23) compares children's worksamples from responses to a range of problem types.

EXHIBIT 5.2 ADDITION AND SUBTRACTION PROBLEMS

1. *Join (addition)*   Wendy had 6 pencils. Sue gave her 9 more pencils. How many pencils did Wendy have altogether?

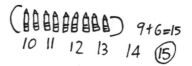

Figure 5.18 Counting-on strategy

---

2. *Separate (subtraction)* Tim had 11 lollies. He gave 7 lollies to Michael. How many lollies did Tim have left?

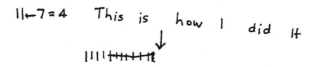

Figure 5.19 Take-away strategy

3. *Combine (subtraction)* There are 12 children in the playground—7 are boys and the rest are girls. How many girls are in the playground?

Figure 5.20 Comparison strategy

4. *Combine (addition)* Sara has 4 sugar donuts in a row. She also has 9 plain donuts. How many donuts does Sara have altogether?

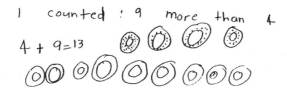

Figure 5.21 Combining groups

5. *Compare (subtraction)* Joe has 8 balloons. His sister Connie has 14 balloons. How many more balloons does Connie have than Joe?

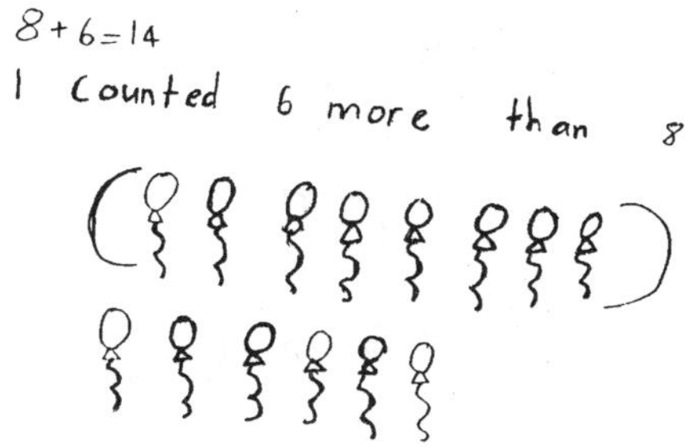

Figure 5.22 Comparing group size

6. *Join missing addend*   Kathy has 9 pencils. How many more pencils does she have to put with
   (subtraction)   them so she has 15 pencils altogether?

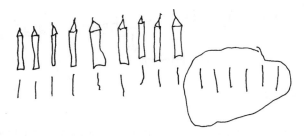

Figure 5.23 Finding the missing number

(Adapted from Carpenter & Moser, 1984)

In Figure 5.18 the child used a counting-on strategy mentally. A teacher commented on the importance of children explaining the relationship between addition and subtraction, showing how the worksample Figure 5.22 uses counting-on and the language 'more than' to solve subtraction. Research shows that this is typically more difficult to solve than other subtraction problems such as shown in Figures 5.21 to 5.23.

Multiplication and division problems

Exhibit 5.3 (including Figures 5.24 to 5.31) exemplifies multiplication and division categories with a view to using these as basic tasks for assessing and developing counting and arithmetical strategies. These examples show how relationships are embedded within problem situations. The word problems can be reorganised as assessment tasks by devising problems that are relevant to the child's language experiences and real-life contexts.

EXHIBIT 5.3 MULTIPLICATION AND DIVISION PROBLEMS

1. *Equal groups*   There are 2 tables in the classroom and 3 children are seated at each table. How
                     many children are there altogether?

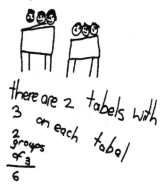

Figure 5.24 Forming equal groups

2. *Rate* If you need 7c to buy one biscuit, how much money do you need to buy 5 biscuits?

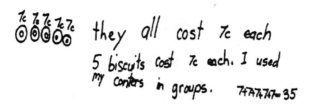

7c 7c 7c 7c 7c
they all cost 7c each
5 biscuits cost 7c each. I used
my conters in groups.
7+7+7+7+7=35

Figure 5.25 Repeated addition

3. *Comparison* Sam has 3 pencils and Rebecca has 9 times as many. How many pencils does Rebecca have?

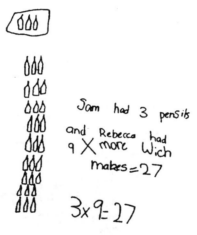

Sam had 3 pensils
and Rebecca had
9 X more Wich
makes=27
3x9=27

Figure 5.26 Multiplication as 'times'

4. *Array* There are 7 lines of children with 3 children in each line. How many children are there altogether?

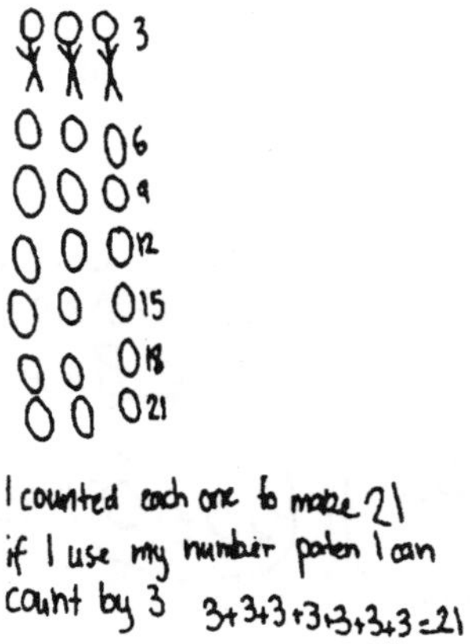

3
6
9
12
15
18
21
I counted each one to make 21
if I use my number paten I can
count by 3 3+3+3+3+3+3+3=21

Figure 5.27 Repeated addition

5. *Cartesian*   You can buy chocolate ice-cream, caramel ice-cream, banana ice-product cream or
    product   rainbow ice-cream. How many different choices can you make?

Choc

Caramel

Banana

Rambo

$4 \times 3 = 12$

Figure 5.28 Combinations of 4 × 3

6. . *Partition*   There are 12 children and 6 tables in the classroom. How many children are seated at
    each table?

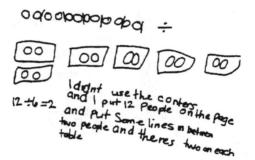

$12 \div 6 = 2$

I didnt use the conters and I put 12 People on the page and Put Some lines in between two peaple and theres two on each table

Figure 5.29 Sharing by twos

7. *Partition*   There are 24 cakes and 3 plates to put cakes on. How many cakes go on each plate
    (with the same number on each plate)?

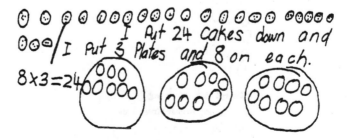

I Put 24 Cakes down and I Put 3 Plates and 8 on each.

$8 \times 3 = 24$

Figure 5.30 Sharing by eights

8. *Quotition* There are 18 children and 3 children are seated at each table. How many tables are there?

6x3 =18

I drew 18 children then I put 3 children in each table and there was 6 tables with 3 children in each table.

Figure 5.31 Dividing by threes

143

ACTIVITY 5.5

Reflecting on multiplication and division word problems

In what ways are equal grouping, partition and quotition problems linked?
Are division problems necessarily more difficult than multiplication problems?
How can we encourage children to develop the combinatorial thinking shown in the Cartesian problem? (See Chapter 9, 'Exploring chance and probability', for an explanation of combinatorial thinking.) Should we encourage children to model the situations or challenge them to think of mental strategies for solving the problems?

The group agreed that one of the main problems teachers may face when using word problems is that many children, particularly those from non-English-speaking backgrounds, will not be able to read the problem. It is important for the teacher to focus on the language of the problems. Problem contexts are often inappropriate in textbooks and tests, so the problems need to be reformulated and made relevant for the child.

SNAPSHOTS OF LEARNING: LESSON PLANNING AND ASSESSMENT

Snapshots of learning draw upon the key aspects of number learning described through examples in the chapter so far. The first snapshot focuses on the use of calculators to encourage young children to maximise their use. 'Equal grouping' and 'Using arrays' focus on core principles of determining the pertinence of groups and using the array structure to encourage multiplication. The structure of the number system is portrayed in the examples of 'Rolls, bags and boxes' while 'Making links' attempts to exemplify the importance of seeing connections between various aspects of number learning in different situations.

Groves and Stacey (1998) described an innovative approach to developing numeracy skills in young children with calculators in Victorian classrooms. The project posed challenges, namely that children can profitably begin to construct number concepts by exploring the number system well beyond the limited requirements for their age level.

Early use of the calculator does not necessarily force written symbolism. It can be matched with the children's development of concepts and problem-solving skills (Board of Studies, NSW, 1993). The snapshot, 'Calculator patterns', draws on examples of children's initial use of calculators.

1. Calculator patterns

Small groups of children from Years 1 and 2 were given calculators for the first time to explore counting and number patterns using the constant function; for example, when the child enters 3++, =, =, =, =, the calculator 'counts' by threes, giving 3, 6, 9, 12, . . .

The children recorded their patterns on coloured paper streamer rolls vertically and horizontally. Number patterns were sorted and the patterns placed into categories chosen by the children.

Teacher's and student's comments

Because we used the built-in constant function this allowed counting by any chosen number and from any starting point. This gave children the opportunity to create as many patterns as they chose to. The children should be encouraged though to predict the number pattern first before pressing away. I was impressed with the way the children could record and explain their patterns.

(Teacher, Year 1)

Our group decided to go backwards by ones from 20 and we went to minus numbers after zero. It means that the numbers start over again going the other way. Then we tried it by tens and it was quicker and we got to –150 by going back, by 10, fifteen times. It was exciting to see the numbers coming up so quickly.

(Jessica, Year 2)

Mathematical content and processes
+ Matches calculator numerals to number words.
+ Recognises and generates counting patterns, by ones or other multiples, forwards and backwards from various starting points.
+ Identifies what number comes before and after any given number.
+ Identifies place value by observing the effect of adding tens to show place value position.

Posing key questions to assess learning
+ Can you continue the pattern? Why is it a pattern?
+ If we covered up some parts of the pattern, can you work out what they were?
+ Copy and describe the pattern. Without looking at the pattern, draw it from memory.

Extending the investigation
+ Reproduce the number pattern using other methods such as a spatial arrangement of shapes.
+ Generate the pattern when it is doubled, tripled, multiplied or divided by a particular number, such as 2, 4, 6, 8 doubled is 4, 8, 12, 16.

2. Equal grouping

In this task students from Years 1 to 3 were shown a random collection of counters (or other items) with each example of increasingly difficult number size: (a) 10 items (b) 20 items (c) 100 items and so on. The students were asked to estimate how many items there were in the collection. 'Can you show me an easy way of working out how many items there are very quickly? Are there any other ways that you could group the items? How did you calculate the total number of items?'

Teacher's and students' comments

> *You just put them in twos until there are no more left and count them in twos (30 items).*

(Justine, Year 1)

> *I made them into groups of 5 and counted up in 5s.*

(Safiah, Year 2)

> *I counted them out in tens and then added up the tens to get 122.*

(Peter, Year 4)

> *You could count out one lot of 20 and then I estimated the rest would be about 5 more 20s giving a total of 120.*

(Matthew, Year 5)

> *The task was very revealing because the students had to think beyond counting by ones. I was concerned that many of my Year 2s couldn't think of groups other than 2s or 5s even when they were encouraged to think of other ways. When I compared the responses from the older students I could see that some of my Year 2s were just as able and could already group in quite complex ways. They are well and truly ready for multiplication and division tasks.*

(Teacher, Year 2)

Mathematical content and processes
+ Forms and represents groups of equal size.
+ Determines the most efficient group size (e.g. groups of 10 more appropriate than groups of 2).
+ Recognises that the total can be calculated by counting in multiples, repeated addition or derived multiplication facts.

Posing key questions to assess learning
+ Observe whether the child counts each item one by one or uses the grouping in some way to count equal groups.
+ Does the child use the group size efficiently in terms of calculating the total, for example 2 groups of 5 to make 10 rather than 5 groups of 2; 5 groups of 6 or 3 groups of 10 to make 30, rather than 15 groups of 2.
+ Ask the child to justify and explain the use of particular equal-sized groups.

Extending the investigation
Present the task as a pictorial display of random dots or as a collection of larger number size beyond 100 to ascertain whether children will form equal-sized larger groups such as 20s or 50s.

3. Using arrays

Years K, 1 and 2 students were asked to calculate the total number of blocks in an array when part of the array was screened. They were required to use the array structure to visualise another equal-sized group (e.g. one row of three blocks was visible and five rows hidden). The teacher asked, 'If you had five rows of blocks how many blocks would that be altogether?' Similarly, the task could require students to calculate the total number in the array if a row or more were added without items visible.

Teachers' and students' comments

> *If you put the counters there I can count them in rows.*

> **(Ester, Kindergarten)**

> *I just pretended that the counters were there and pointed to the spot where they would be and counted '1, 2, 3, . . . 4, 5, 6, . . . and so on 'till' I got 15.*

> **(Jason, Year 1)**

> *I counted in threes; it's 3, 6 , 9, 12, 15.*

> **(Sarah, Year 2)**

> *It's five rows of 3 . . . makes 15.*

> **(Peter, Year 2)**

> *I was surprised that there were about ten students in the class who could imagine the rows of counters and counted them by ones to 15. I suppose those students are also competent counters and they can be encouraged to learn some skip counting patterns.*

> **(Teacher, Kindergarten)**

> *I had several students who still couldn't imagine the rows and keep track of the number of items. They really need to tackle this kind of task with counters before they are 'forced' to cope without them.*

> **(Teacher, Year 2)**

Mathematical content and processes
+ Uses perceptual procedures such as pointing to imaginary items in rows, to calculate the total number of items.
+ Uses abstract thinking to visualise the structure of the array in rows and columns.
+ Uses multiple counting strategies or repeated addition to calculate number of items.
+ Recognises the multiplicative nature of the array (i.e. 3 by 5 makes 15).
+ Recognises commutativity of relationship and uses groups of 5.

Posing key questions to assess learning
+ How did you make equal groups?
+ Did you decide to count by ones? Why? Why not?
+ Do you think it is better to count in a pattern? Why? Why not?
+ Did you imagine the rows and columns of counters that you couldn't see? How did you work out how many altogether?
+ How did you use the rows and columns?

+ Did you count in the same way when the array was square, rectangular, or presented as gridlines?
+ Can you show the groups of 3 in another way?

Extending the investigation
+ Turn an array. Does the child see the array as the same formation when it is rotated at right angles? Present the child with a rectangular array (e.g. 3×4 drawn as dots). Turn the array at right angles and ask the child whether the array is the same or different.
+ Reproduce an array from memory. A simple square array made of counters or objects is revealed. The child is given five to ten seconds to examine the array. The array is then screened from the child's view. The child is asked to reproduce the array with counters and calculate the total number in the array.
+ Calculate the total number in a screened array when the number of items in each row and the number of rows is given. The child may resort to modelling or drawing a partial or full array and calculating the total using perceptual counting.

4. Rolls, bags and boxes

Years 3 and 4 were working on numeration and regrouping thousands, hundreds, tens and ones. Instead of using base ten blocks the students had made their own 'structured' materials to solve some problems. Lollies were wrapped in rolls of 10, bags of 100 (10 rolls) and boxes of 1000 (10 bags), all with transparent coverings. It is important that students first establish that there are 10 lollies in each roll. Students solve various problems requiring them to calculate whether there are enough lollies to give each student in the class or grade or school 1 lolly; for example, how many lollies are there in 3 rolls and 4 loose ones? 1 bag, 5 rolls and 17 loose ones? 1 box, 6 bags and 4 loose ones?

Teacher's and students' comments

> *We would have 166 lollies if we had 1 bag, 6 rolls and 6 loose ones and that would be enough for 6 classes cause it's $30 + 30 + 30 + 30 + 30 + 30 = 180$.*

(Emily, Year 4)

> *I could only use the rolls and singles . . . I put 10 rolls together to make a 100 'cause 10 tens make 100.*

(Steven, Year 3)

> *If you call them by their numbers like tens, hundreds, thousands it's easier to remember but it is helpful to look at the rolls, bags and boxes to remember.*

(Simon, Year 3)

> *When we had to work it out without the lollies in front of us it was hard to remember the amounts but I counted in tens and hundreds to get the answer.*

(Sarah, Year 4)

The good thing about this task is that the children made their own representations of ones, hundreds and thousands and were required to use the grouping to add and subtract amounts. My class made up a game of adding and subtracting boxes, bags and rolls and they had to use trading to work out the answers.

(Teacher, Year 3/4)

Mathematical content and processes
+ Groups and represents items in base ten structure: thousands, hundreds, tens, ones.
+ Calculates total amounts using regrouping of hundreds, tens, ones.
+ Uses notation of place value and orders and records numerals to 9999.
+ Solves problems involving regrouping and numeration to 9999.

Posing key questions to assess learning
+ Add 2 rolls to 4 single lollies. How did you count? Why is it important to count in tens?
+ How many different combinations could you make from one box of lollies? Record each combination.
+ Did you use hundreds, tens and ones at the same time?

Extending the investigation
+ Represent the value of 10 boxes as 10 000 (suggest a larger 'pack' or 'crate'). Extend to 100 000 and then 1 000 000. Can the student explain the order and structure of the groupings based on multiplying by 10?
+ Create a game where the students are required to deconstruct the box of lollies into various combinations requiring subtraction using mental computation.
+ Devise other base ten structures based on grouping common materials such as pencils or paperclips.
+ Devise a purchase 'order form' for the materials where students record quantities and calculate amounts based on groupings.

5. Making links

Year 2 children were asked to solve a range of problems that the teacher had specifically designed to assess whether the children made any mathematical connections in the way they solved the problems. The children were later asked to find similarities and differences between the problems and the strategies they used to solve them. Did they use their knowledge of one problem strategy to solve another? The following questions were asked after each problem.

+ Explain your solution strategy. Were you able to do it in your head? Why? Why not?
+ Explain or draw a picture of what you see in your mind when you solve the problem.
+ Why do you think the answer is right? Does it remind you of any other problems that you have solved? If so, how is it the same? How is it different?
+ Did you have any other ways of solving the problem?

Kim's responses are shown in Figures 5.32 to 5.36.

Problem 1: *At a local amusement park set up for the holidays, tickets for the rides were sold according to points; for example, the baby ferris wheel cost 6 points per ride. How many points were needed for three people to ride on the ferris wheel (6 points for each person)?*

Figure 5.32 Solution strategy to 'how many points altogether?'

Problem 2: *There are six different flavoured packets of chips in small, medium and large packets; how many different choices could you make? How many different packets could you buy (if you were allowed)?*

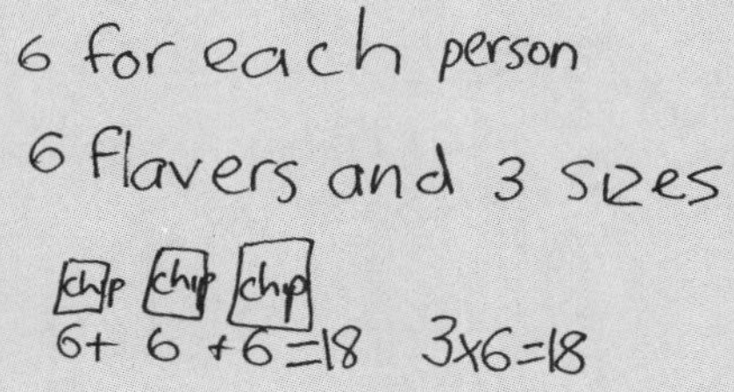

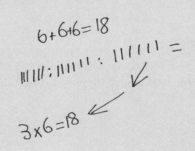

Figure 5.33 Combinations of chips

Problem 3: *How would you share equally 18 stickers between 3 children?*

Figure 5.34 Equal shares

Problem 4: *Imagine counting by threes. Now use your calculator to add 3 repeatedly. Now try it backwards. What did you notice? Can you make the pattern another way? With different numbers? With different signs? What do you see in your mind when you make a pattern of threes? Can you start at another number and then count in threes? Is it the same or different?*

149

Figure 5.35 Calculator pattern of threes

Kim visualised a spiral pattern of threes explaining that the pattern continued. She also showed how the pattern could be extended past 0 going backwards 'by the take away'.

Problem 5: *If you had to cut a 1-metre length of braiding into three equal lengths, what would the parts measure?*

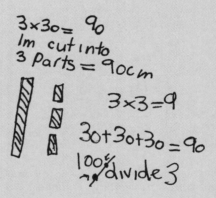

Figure 5.36 Braids in three parts

They would be littler but the same . . . about the same as my ruler, 30 centimetres long, but you wouldn't be able to use it to line up with . . . 3 and 3 and 3; 3 times 3 is 9 . . . that's like 30 and 30 and 30, with a bit left . . . and they would be called threeths I think.

(Kim, Year 4)

FOCUS QUESTIONS

Reflect on the variety of problems in 'Making links'.

1. Why did the teacher ask this combination of problems?
2. How did the responses show that the child had made some connection between the problems in terms of the numerical operations and quantities?

3. Do you think that Kim has made any connection between the problems or the way she has solved the problems?

4. Are there similarities or differences in the way the problems are solved in terms of Kim's sophistication of strategies?

5. Do you think she would have been capable of giving more sophisticated responses? Why? Why not?

Use the problems presented here or devise a series of related problems for your young students to examine how their knowledge and skills are used in a connected or disconnected way. You can assist young students to make connections between different aspects of their number knowledge by comparing their responses to similar problems. Point out, for example, how they use their counting knowledge.

SUMMARY AND IMPLICATIONS FOR CLASSROOM PRACTICE

This chapter has focused our attention on critical aspects of early number learning: counting, ordering, patterning, grouping, partitioning, base ten, and arithmetical strategies and procedures. These aspects are presented through examples of assessment tasks and children's responses, and Learning Frameworks in Number. The learning of basic number facts is presented through arithmetical strategies of addition, subtraction, multiplication and division as well as problem-based learning. One of the key points about using frameworks is to emphasise that children acquire various strategies at different rates and that they need to be challenged to use increasingly more sophisticated strategies.

The development of numerical concepts and processes involves a range of complex and interrelated mathematical ideas. This chapter has explored these aspects in terms of promoting increasingly sophisticated numerical strategies. We have also explored ways of encouraging children to build upon their intuitive notions of number to explore arithmetic through problem-based situations. Some reference to early skills such as classification and matching has been included. We have raised questions about how key aspects of number might develop in young children. The examples have provided a basis for examining how base ten and arithmetical strategies have been linked.

Children's development has been seen as promoting increasingly sophisticated strategies, beginning with an assessment of where the child is in terms of a framework. This may mean that children in their first year of school are already working with abstract counting skills, knowledge of number facts in the higher decades, base ten strategies beyond place value of tens or hundreds, and using composite groups for multiplication and division. This is not necessarily in keeping with traditional or prescriptive curricula or teaching programs. On the other hand some children may need more explicit and structured activities to promote basic counting strategies. The examples have shown that children can produce a range of solutions to arithmetical tasks and link their strategies to broader problem-solving skills. The traditional boundaries of teaching, learning and assessing have been blurred to enhance the development of meaningful number learning.

The examples shown throughout the chapter provide highlights of children's construction of mathematical ideas. Although learning frameworks give this some formal structure it does not determine a prescriptive path for the learner. Rather, it opens up more paths and possibilities. The fundamental aspects of early number learning may appear not to have changed from traditional aspects but they are portrayed in a more directed way, which encourages the growth of a rich variety of arithmetical strategies, number concepts and relationships. Mental computation and number sense has been described as integral to this growth. The mathematics curriculum has already opened up in terms of removing the boundaries of grade level restrictions on what is to be taught (Board of Studies, NSW, 2002; Curriculum Corporation, 2000). Assessing children's potential for number learning more accurately will fuel the need to remove more boundaries and create opportunities for learning number concepts and processes traditionally delayed until the later years of school.

ACTION AND REFLECTION

Refer to the LFIN and/or the EYNP and/or the 'Early Numeracy' project in New Zealand, and to the teaching–learning experiences suggested in the early number strand of your state's or region's syllabus.

With a small group of your peers, attempt to link the outcomes and/or learning experiences stated in the syllabus with the indicators appearing in the framework. What similarities and differences do you find? Does your state's syllabus emphasise the development of classification, patterning, visualising, numeral identification and counting skills? How does it focus on the development of mental computation strategies and number sense? Can you identify the key levels of the number frameworks in terms of base ten knowledge and increasingly sophisticated strategies?

REFERENCES

Anghileri, J. (2001). *Principles and practices in arithmetic teaching*. London: Open University Press.

Baturo, A. (2000). Construction of a numeration model: A theoretical analysis. In J. Bana & A. Chapman (Eds), *Mathematics education beyond 2000: Proceedings of the 23rd Annual Conference of the Mathematics Education Research Group of Australasia Inc.* (pp. 95–103). Fremantle, WA: Mathematics Education Research Group of Australasia.

Beishuizen, M. & Anghileri, J. (1998). Which mental strategies in the early number curriculum? A comparison of British ideas and Dutch views. *British Education Research Journal, 34,* 516–38.

Board of Studies, NSW. (1993). *Teaching mathematics K–6: Calculators in K–6 maths*. Sydney: Board of Studies.

Board of Studies, NSW. (2002). *Mathematics K–6 Syllabus 2002*. Sydney: Board of Studies.

http://www.bosnsw-k6.nsw.edu.au/maths/pdf_doc/maths_k6_draftsyl.pdf

Bobis, J. (1996). Visualisation and the development of number sense with Kindergarten children. In J. T. Mulligan & M. C. Mitchelmore (Eds), *Children's number learning* (pp. 17–35). Adelaide: Australian Association of Mathematics Teachers/Mathematics Education Research Group of Australasia.

Bobis, J. (2002). Is school ready for my child? *Australian Primary Mathematics Classroom, 7*(4), 4–8.

Booker, G., Bond, D., Swan, P. & Sparrow, L. (2003). *Teaching primary mathematics*. Sydney: Pearson Education.

Boulton-Lewis, G. (1998). Children's strategy use and interpretations of mathematical representations. *Journal of Mathematical Behavior, 17,* 219–239.

Carpenter, T. P., Ansell, E., Franke, K., Fennema, E. & Weisbeck, L. (1993). Models of problem solving: A study of kindergarten children's problem solving processes. *Journal for Research in Mathematics Education, 24,* 428–441.

Carpenter, T. P., Fennema, E., Franke, M., Levi, L. & Empson, S. (1999). *Children's mathematics: Cognitively guided instruction*. Portsmouth, New Hampshire: Heinemann.

Carpenter, T. P. & Moser, J. M. (1984). The acquisition of addition and subtraction concepts in grades one through three. *Journal for Research in Mathematics Education, 15*, 179–203.

Cobb, P., Yackel, E. & McClain, J. (Eds) (2000). *Symbolizing and communicating in mathematics classrooms: Perspectives on discourse, tools, and instructional design*. Mahwah, New Jersey: Lawrence Erlbaum Associates.

Clarke, D. (2001). Challenging and enjoyable mathematics for young children. *Australian Primary Mathematics Classroom, 6*(1), 20–25.

Clarke, D., Sullivan, P., Cheesman, J. & Clarke, B. (2000). The Early Numeracy Research Project: Developing a framework for describing early numeracy learning. In J. Bana & A. Chapman (Eds), *Mathematics education beyond 2000: Proceedings of the 23rd Annual Conference of the Mathematics Education Research Group of Australasia Inc.* (pp. 180–187). Fremantle, WA: Mathematics Education Research Group of Australasia Inc.

Curriculum Corporation. (2000). *Numeracy benchmarks years 3, 5 & 7*. Melbourne: Curriculum Corporation.

Department of Education and Training, Victoria. (2002). *The Early Years Numeracy Program*. Melbourne: Department of Education and Training, Victoria.

Diezmann, C. & English, L. (2001). Promoting the use of diagrams as tools for thinking. In A. A. Cuoco & F. R. Curcio (Eds), *The roles of representation in school mathematics* (pp. 77–90). Reston, Virginia: National Council of Teachers of Mathematics.

Diezmann, C. & Yelland, N. J. (2000). Developing mathematical literacy in the early childhood years. In N. J. Yelland (Ed), *Innovations in practice: Promoting meaningful learning for early childhood professionals* (pp. 47–58). Washington: National Association for the Education of Young Children.

English. L. (1999). Assessing for structural understanding in children's combinatorial problem solving. *Focus on Learning Problems in Mathematics, 21*(4) 63–82.

Gervasconi, A. (1999). Using visual images to support young children's number learning. *Australian Primary Mathematics Classroom, 4*(2), 23–27.

Groves, S. & Stacey, K. (1998). Calculators in primary mathematics: Exploring number before teaching algorithms. In L. J. Morrow & M. J. Kenney (Eds), *The teaching and learning of algorithms in school mathematics* (pp. 120–130). Reston, Virginia: National Council of Teachers of Mathematics.

Hiebert, J. & Wearne, D. (1992). Links between teaching and learning place value with understanding in first grade. *Journal for Research in Mathematics Education, 23*, 98–122.

Hughes, M. (1986). *Children and number*. Oxford: Basil Blackwell.

Kamii, C., Kirkland, L. & Lewis, B. (2001). Representation and abstraction in young children's numerical reasoning. In A. A. Cuoco & F. R. Curcio (Eds), *The roles of representation in school mathematics* (pp. 24–35). Reston, Virginia: National Council of Teachers of Mathematics.

Macmillan, A. (1999). Pre-school children as mathematical meaning makers. *Journal of Australian Research in Early Childhood Education, 6*(2), 177–192.

Macmillan, A. (2002). Numeracy play—how mathematical is it? *Australian Primary Mathematics Classroom, 7*(4), 9–15.

McIntosh, A. & Dole, S. (2000). Early arithmetical learning and teaching. In K. Owens & J. Mousley (Eds), *Research in mathematics education in Australia 1996–1999* (pp. 215–243). Sydney: Mathematics Education Research Group of Australasia Inc.

Morony, W. & Brinkworth, P. (Eds) (2002). *Springboards to numeracy: Proceedings of the National Numeracy Conference*, Hobart, 4–5 October. Australian Association of Mathematics Teachers Inc.

Mulligan, J. T. & Mitchelmore, M. C. (1996). Children's representations of multiplication and division problems. In J. T. Mulligan & M. C. Mitchelmore (Eds), *Children's number learning* (pp. 163–185). Adelaide: Australian Association of Mathematics Teachers/Mathematics Education Research Group of Australasia.

Mulligan, J. T. & Mitchelmore, M. C. (1997). Young children's intuitive models of multiplication and division. *Journal for Research in Mathematics Education, 28*, 309–331.

153

Mulligan, J. T. & Wright, R. J. (2000). Interview based assessment for early multiplication. In T. Nakahara & M. Koyama (Eds), *Proceedings of the 24th Annual Conference of the International Group for the Psychology of Mathematics Education*, (Vol. 4, pp. 17–25). University of Hiroshima, Hiroshima: Program Committee.

National Council of Teachers of Mathematics. (2000). *Principles and standards for school mathematics*. Reston, Virginia: National Council of Teachers of Mathematics.

National Council of Teachers of Mathematics. (2002). *Navigating through algebra in prekindergarten–Grade 2*. Reston, Virginia: National Council of Teachers of Mathematics.

NSW Department of Education & Training. (2000). *Count Me In Too: professional development package*. Sydney: NSW Department of Education and Training Curriculum Directorate.

Owens, K. & Mousley, J. (Eds) (2000). *Research in mathematics education in Australia 1996–1999*. Sydney: Mathematics Education Research Group of Australasia Inc.

Perry, R. (2000). *Early childhood numeracy*. Canberra: Australian Association of Mathematics Teachers Inc./Department of Education Training and Youth Affairs.

Swan, P. (1996). *Kids, calculators and classrooms*. Perth: Success Print.

Thomas, N. & Mulligan, J. T. (1995). The role of dynamic imagery in children's representations of number. *Mathematics Education Research Journal, 7,* 5–25.

Thomas, N., Mulligan, J. T. & Goldin, G. A. (2002). Children's representations and cognitive structural development of the counting sequence 1–100. *Journal of Mathematical Behavior, 2,* 117–133.

Thomas, G., Tagg, A. & Ward, J. (2002). Making a difference: The Early Numeracy Project. In B. Barton, K. Irwin , M. Pfannkuch, & M. O. J. Thomas (Eds), *Mathematics education in the South Pacific. Proceedings of the 25th Annual Conference of the Mathematics Education Research Group of Australasia Inc.* (pp. 49–57). Auckland: Mathematics Education Research Group of Australasia Inc.

Thompson, I. (1997). *Teaching and learning early number*. Philadelphia: Open University Press.

Twomey-Fosnot, C. & Dolk, C. (2001). *Young mathematicians at work: Constructing number sense, addition and subtraction*. Portsmouth, New Hampshire: Heinemann.

Wright, R. (1998). An overview of a research-based framework for assessing and teaching early number. In C. Kanes, M. Goos & E. Warren (Eds), *Proceedings of the 21st Annual Conference of the Mathematics Education Research Group of Australasia Inc.* (Vol. 2, pp. 701–709). Gold Coast, Qld: Mathematics Education Research Group of Australasia.

Wright, R. & Gould, P. (2002a). Using a learning framework to document students' progress in mathematics in a large school system. In A. D. Cockburn & E. Nardi (Eds), *Proceedings of the 26th Annual Conference of the International Group for the Psychology of Mathematics Education* (Vol. 1, pp. 197–202). Norwich, UK: Program Committee.

Wright, R. & Gould, P. (2002b). Mapping overlapping waves of strategies used with arithmetical problems. In A. D. Cockburn & E. Nardi (Eds), *Proceedings of the 26th Annual Conference of the International Group for the Psychology of Mathematics Education* (Vol. 4, pp. 418–425). Norwich, UK: Program Committee.

Wright, R. J., Martland, J. & Stafford, A. (Eds) (2000). *Early numeracy: Assessment for teaching and intervention*. London: Sage.

Wright R. J., Martland, J., Stafford, A. & Stanger, G. (Eds) (2002). *Teaching number: Advancing children's skills and strategies.* London: Sage.

Wright, R., Mulligan, J. T., Bobis, J. & Stewart, R. (1996). Research on early number learning. In B. Atweh, K. Owens & P. Sullivan (Eds), *Research in mathematics education in Australasia 1992–1995* (pp. 281–311). Sydney: Mathematics Education Research Group of Australasia Inc.

Yelland, N., Butler, D. & Diezmann, C. (1999). *Early mathematical explorations*. Needham Heights, Massachusetts: Pearson Publishing Solutions.

Young-Loveridge, J. (1997). From research tool to classroom assessment device: The development of Checkout/Rapua, a shopping game to assess numeracy at school entry. In F. Biddulph & K. Carr (Eds), *Proceedings of the 20th Annual Conference of the Mathematics Education Research Group of Australasia*, (pp. 608–615). Rotorua: Mathematics Education Research Group of Australasia.

Chapter 6

Promoting number sense: beyond computation

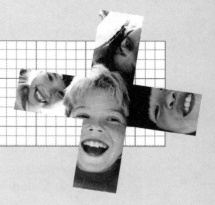

CHAPTER OVERVIEW

In an effort to create a broader view of numeracy required for effective participation in society, mathematics educators have focused on a more practical use of mathematics in curricula designed for work, life and society. The widespread use of information technologies, including calculators and computers, is changing the teaching and learning of mathematics. This is also having an impact on how children acquire number concepts and processes: students need to develop facility in choosing between mental computation, paper and pen, calculator or computer as the most appropriate method for a particular computation.

The idea of developing 'number sense' has been highlighted as a common goal of school mathematics for the 21st century (Australian Association of Mathematics Teachers, 1997; 2002; Curriculum Corporation, 2000; National Council of Teachers of Mathematics, 2000). Number sense is commonly described as the ability to understand and use numbers and operations flexibly. Number sense . . .

> *results in a view of numbers as meaningful entities and the expectation that mathematical manipulations and outcomes should make sense. Those who view mathematics in this way continually utilise a variety of internal 'checks and balances' to judge the reasonableness of numerical outcomes.*

(McIntosh et al., 1997, p. 3)

The learning of key number concepts and mental computation strategies must be seen as integral to number sense but this learning does not, in itself, ensure development of number sense. One of the widespread concerns of educators over the past decades has been that when children are faced with solving mathematical problems, they mechanically add, subtract, multiply or divide the numbers with little concern for the meaning of the problem. Furthermore, from an early age, students may develop procedures for solving algorithms with little concern for the reasonableness of an answer. The promotion of number sense is therefore critical to the basic understanding and application of mathematics.

Many researchers have focused attention on describing and assessing students' number sense (Fuson et al., 1997; Markovits & Sowder, 1994; McIntosh, De Nardi & Swan, 2002; McIntosh, Reys & Reys, 1992).

As teachers we might look for these aspects of number sense within our students' learning:

+ using numbers flexibly when mentally computing and estimating;
+ judging the magnitude of numbers and reasonableness of results;
+ moving between number representations;
+ relating numbers and symbols and operations;
+ making sense of numerical situations; and
+ looking for links between new information and previously acquired knowledge.

To develop number sense it is also important to solve mathematical problems represented through written and spoken language and to communicate mathematics with meaning. In order to promote number sense we need to provide opportunities for students to explore number concepts and operations, and patterns and relationships, and to find out whether procedures and strategies are useful and efficient. Computational skills must be based on sound number sense and conceptual understanding.

This chapter focuses on the role of number sense, mental and written computation, and number relationships, particularly in the development of more formal mathematical processes in the upper primary years. It is not intended to provide a 'list' of outcomes, but rather to explore the aspects of number sense and computational fluency. We will also focus on alternative ways of approaching number learning exemplified through research into children's experiences of number sense and a problem-centred approach. The following aspects will be described:

+ developing number sense through approximation and reasonableness of answers;
+ mental, written and calculator-based strategies for solving computations;
+ strategies for effective mental calculation and number fact knowledge: promoting addition and subtraction, multiplication and division strategies;
+ moving from non-standard to standard written algorithms: addition, subtraction, multiplication and division; and
+ developing numerical relationships through a problem-based approach.

Chapter focus questions

In this chapter several key questions are raised in order to focus our attention on critical aspects of number sense in the transition to learning more formal numerical concepts and processes. As students are required to grapple with more complex numerical situations the range of student competencies and difficulties becomes wider. One of the problems faced by teachers in the upper primary grades is catering for this diverse range of abilities of students and ensuring that students progress to secondary school with adequate basic number sense. We might also ask how to cater for the students who have acquired all of the desired curriculum outcomes for the upper years of school before entering these grades. Consider your responses to the following questions:

1. What critical number concepts and skills does the child need to have acquired so that progress in secondary school will not be hampered?
2. How can the teacher assess accurately the number knowledge acquired over six or seven years of primary schooling?

3. Should children be encouraged to use calculators as a regular means of calculating and learning number concepts?

4. What importance might be placed on the role of paper-and-pencil calculations and mental computation in the development of the number sense overall?

Throughout this chapter we will examine these questions by comparing examples of children's number sense, and mental and written computation, and reflecting upon the research that has raised serious doubts about the appropriateness of almost exclusive concentration on paper-and-pencil algorithmic techniques as critical to number learning.

THE GROWTH OF MATHEMATICAL UNDERSTANDING: NUMBER AND SENSE AND COMPUTATIONAL FLUENCY

In recent years there has been an increased emphasis on computational fluency and the importance of mental computation in mathematics curricula (Askew, 2003; Boerst & Schielack, 2003; Fuson, 2003; McIntosh, 2003; Morrow & Kenny, 1998). Mental computation can be considered to be the core of effective numeracy and should be based on number sense. Mathematics curricula across Australasia have advocated the development of mental computation through a range of strategies, and with the support of calculators.

While the emphasis in classroom practice may still be on procedures for standard written algorithms, there is now much more support for the development of non-standard written methods and the delay of formal written algorithms (Morony & Brinkworth, 2002, p. 24). McIntosh advocates a more forward-looking view expressed by many educators and curriculum developers concerning mental and written computation.

> *A reasonable goal for almost all children is to be able to deal mentally with addition and subtraction of two-digit numbers and multiplication and division by one-digit numbers. The basic addition and multiplication facts/relationships are important and children should develop near-instant recall of them—however memorisation is not enough: children need to develop strategies for efficiently reconstructing forgotten facts.*

(Morony & Brinkworth, 2002, p. 25).

However, McIntosh advises that strong and gradual development of mental computation through Years K to 4 is necessary before making wholesale changes in a school's approach to formal written algorithms.

There is growing evidence that by the time young children reach the middle primary grades they may be able to carry out mathematical procedures but do not demonstrate corresponding conceptual understanding (Boulton-Lewis, 1993; Brownell, 2003; McIntosh & Dole, 2000; Randolph & Sherman, 2001). This has become even more concerning to educators as there has been a shift towards solving mathematical problems in contexts.

A growing number of studies have indicated that specific instruction in solving computations may interfere with the development of children's natural strategies (Askew, 2003; Cooper, Heirdsfield & Irons, 1996, McIntosh, 2003). There are many who argue that written algorithms should not be taught at all, and that children should be given the opportunity to develop their own strategies and algorithms (Kamii & Dominick, 1998). Boulton-Lewis (1993), for example, argues that teachers sometimes make the task more difficult by imposing procedures that rob the problem of meaning. In contrast, when children choose their own strategies they choose strategies that are meaningful to them. Mathematics educators are now recommending that paper-and-pencil written algorithms be treated only minimally in the early years, with a much greater emphasis on mental computations, problem solving and the use of calculators (McIntosh, 2003; Morony & Brinkworth, 2002; Wright et al., 2002).

Over the past two decades, classroom-based research has shown that problem-centred number learning facilitates students' conceptual understanding and number sense and is feasible in regular classrooms (Carpenter et al., 1999; Cobb et al., 1992; Cobb, Yackel & McClain, 2000; Hiebert & Wearne, 1992; Lampert, 1990; Mulligan & Mitchelmore, 1996). Problem-centred arithmetical learning was exemplified in Chapter 5 through examples of addition, subtraction, multiplication and division problems. Problem-centred learning projects show how children who engage in meaningful arithmetic problem solving also develop autonomy and adaptability in the learning situation.

Developing number sense through approximation and reasonableness of answers

REFLECTION ON A CLASSROOM SCENARIO

Making sense of subtraction

Years 3 and 4 students were solving some word problems involving subtraction of simple combinations, where they were provided with the written problem and a space for 'working out'. Figure 6.1 shows that Jack is able to represent and solve the subtraction problem $96 - 24$ as a subtraction algorithm correctly. But in the examples shown in Figures 6.2 and 6.3, $14 - 9$ and $21 - 16$, he does not consider the reasonableness of the answer, nor does he choose an appropriate strategy. It must be questioned whether the algorithm $96 - 24$ has any meaning to Jack other than to carry out a procedure incorrectly.

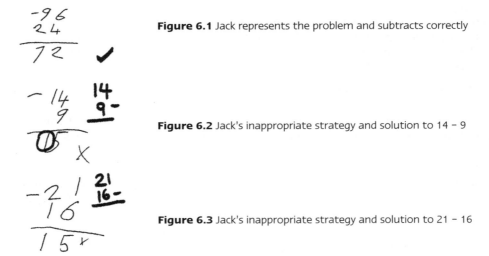

Figure 6.1 Jack represents the problem and subtracts correctly

Figure 6.2 Jack's inappropriate strategy and solution to 14 – 9

Figure 6.3 Jack's inappropriate strategy and solution to 21 – 16

Jack uses a vertical algorithm unnecessarily and he does not attempt to use mental strategies to gain a solution efficiently. In these examples the problem becomes one of meaningless calculation. He subtracts the smaller from the larger number, 4 from 9 in Figure 6.2 and, similarly, 1 from 6 in Figure 6.3. Like Jack, other children in Year 3/4 used a meaningless algorithm.

Jack's teacher commented on his responses to the subtraction tasks:

I can see that Jack has not considered the reasonableness of his answer. Rather than thinking about the easiest way to find the difference between the numbers, he has automatically attempted the algorithm. I don't think Jack's problem is simply taking the smaller number from the larger; he really needs to practise estimation and develop some number sense.

There are several fundamental problems raised by this example: is it necessary or appropriate to encourage written algorithms to solve arithmetic problems that can be computed easily by using mental strategies? Perhaps the emphasis on learning procedures inhibits the development of number sense. It might be appropriate to assist Jack in recognising and alleviating these apparent difficulties with subtraction by encouraging arithmetical strategies suggested in Chapter 5, such as 'counting on from the larger number' for basic subtraction facts to 20 (e.g. 10, 11, 12, 13, 14; $14 - 9 = 5$).

Mental, written and calculator-based strategies for solving computations

A group of Years 4, 5 and 6 teachers discussed ways of changing their mathematics program to emphasise number sense. They listed some important understandings and processes under three headings—mental computation, written computation and calculator—because they agreed that all three methods were needed.

Mental computation

+ Mentally estimates and calculates addition and subtraction to 100 using strategies based on ones and knowledge of number facts.

+ Uses alternative strategies to decompose (break up) two-digit numbers to add and subtract numbers; for example, 'to subtract 43 I took off the 40 and then 3 more', or '26 and 43 is 43, 53, 63 and 6 more is 69'.

+ Adds a list of one-digit numbers or amounts in an efficient way; for example, 76c + 49c + 14c . . . 76c + 14c makes 70, 80, 90 plus 50c is $1.40 less 1 makes $1.39.

+ Multiplies and divides by one-digit or two-digit numbers involving multiples of 10.

Written computation

+ Uses a variety of strategies to add and subtract whole numbers and money only when mental strategies are inadequate.

+ Uses regrouping in number exploration and in computations such as showing decomposition (346 is 34 tens and 6 ones or 3 hundreds and 46 ones) or when needing to subtract (46 ones becomes 3 tens and 16 ones).

+ Uses estimation and approximation to round off and justify whether sums and differences are sensible.

+ Uses multiplication and division as inverse operations and recognises the commutativity of multiplication ($36 \div 9 = 4$, $4 \times 9 = 36$).

+ Shows understanding of multiplication and division based on equal groups and uses written methods for calculating products and quotients such as expanded multiplication (e.g. 345×3 is $300 \times 3 + 40 \times 3 + 5 \times 3$) and division, such as $345 \div 3$ as $3 \times ?$ makes $300 + 3 \times ?$ makes 45.

+ Devises shorter methods for written calculation based on understanding of strategies based on groupings (as above).

Calculator

+ Uses a calculator appropriately by entering digits correctly and in the right order for all four operations.

+ Makes estimates and checks reasonableness of estimates.

+ Checks whether a prediction about numerical operations or patterns holds true when computational demands are beyond the child's levels of ability; for example, $15 + 15 = 30$, so $115 + 15 = 130$, so $115 + 115 = 230$, so $1115 + 1115 = 2230$.

+ Tests understanding of place value such as increasing digits by ten or pretending that a numerical key is inoperable.

+ Finds relationships between operations such as 45×6 is the same as $45 + 45 + 45 + 45 + 45 + 45$.

+ Finds related patterns in the number system by exploring the effect of multiplying and dividing by 10 including decimals.

+ Explores rounding-off options.

The teachers thought that the list should include traditional forms of written computation but that students should learn to automatically estimate and approximate a solution and decide which method of computation was appropriate. Learning to decide when a calculator is useful and efficient was thought to be critically important.

Strategies for effective mental computation and number fact knowledge

In Chapter 5 the development of increasingly sophisticated counting and grouping strategies were examined in terms of developing arithmetic knowledge and mental computation skills. Learning Frameworks in Number highlighted the importance of:

+ abstract counting;
+ counting-on from the larger number (rather than the first number);
+ developing number fact knowledge through base ten knowledge;
+ skip counting, equal grouping and partitioning;
+ the development of facile, fluent number fact knowledge.

The integration of mental computation skills in early number frameworks enables the development of robust number fact knowledge and informal, non-standard algorithms based on number sense. There is a well-known set of critical strategies that promote efficient number fact knowledge and good mental computation (see, for example, Booker et al., 2003; Heirdsfield, 2002; McIntosh, De Nardi & Swan, 2002). The following sections highlight these key strategies.

Promoting addition and subtraction strategies

ACTIVITY 6.1

Consider the following list of standard strategies for effective development of addition and subtraction facts. Which of these strategies do you consider to be the most intuitive? Why?

1. Count on from the larger: 12 + 39 = 39, 40, 41 . . . 51
2. Doubles: 24 + 24 = 48
3. Near doubles: 24 + 25 = 49 (25 + 25 − 1; 24 + 24 = 48 + 1)
4. Halving: 48 − 24 = 24
5. Near halving: 49 − 24 = 25 (48 − 24 = 24 + 1 = 25)
6. Commutative property: 23 + 16 = 16 + 23
7. Inverse property: changing subtraction to addition:
   52 − 38 = 14 can be thought of as 38 + 14 = 52 by adding 10 and then 4
8. Bridging to 10, 100 or nearest decade or multiple of 10:
   76 + 14 = 80 + 10 = 90
   95 + 25 = 100 + 20 = 120
9. Building up and building down from 10s, 100s (compatible pairs):
   59 + 41 =100
   200 − 46 = 154
10. Partitioning: 28 + 37 = 20 + 30 + 8 + 7 = 65
11. Compensation: 58 + 39 = 60 + 37

Critical thinking questions
+ How can these strategies assist students to develop the most efficient mental processes necessary for computational facility?
+ Which strategies do you consider to be the most critical in this development?

Adding and subtracting using semiformal routines

Common approaches used for the development of mental strategies for adding and subtracting numbers to 20 and beyond using semiformal routines can be summarised in the following ways:

1. Partitioning ('splitting') method
   For example, 38 + 46 is calculated mentally as 30 and 40 = 70; 8 + 6 = 14; 70 and 14 = 84
2. Sequencing ('jump') method
   For example, 38 + 46 is calculated mentally as 38 + 40 = 78; 78 + 6 = 84

The 'empty number line' is an effective representation for recording this process as shown in Figure 6.4 where the 'split' and 'jump' is recorded in sequence. Alternatively the process can be made more explicit as shown in Figure 6.5.

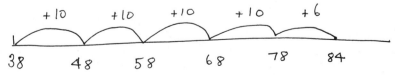

Figure 6.4 'Split and jump' shown for 38 + 46 as 38 + 10 + 10 + 10 + 10 + 6 = 84

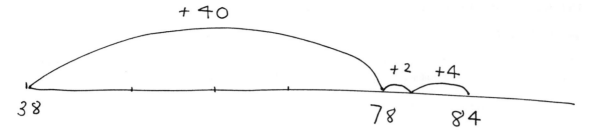

Figure 6.5 Alternative 'split and jump' shown as 38 + 40 + 2 + 4 = 84

For subtraction, the same example can be reconsidered as 84 − 38. In Figure 6.6 the student has subtracted by tens first then used their knowledge of 14 − 8 = 6 to complete the computation.

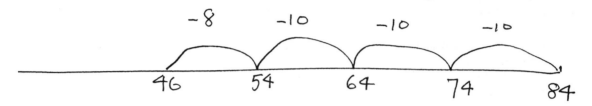

Figure 6.6 'Split and jump' shown for 84 − 38 as 84 − 10 − 10 − 10 − 8 = 46

Alternatively in Figure 6.7 the student has jumped from 84 to 54 in one go by subtracting 30 and then split 8 into 4 and 4, based on her need to jump to 50 and a doubling strategy based on 4 and 4 makes 8.

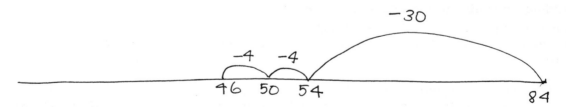

Figure 6.7 Alternative 'split and jump' for 84 − 38 shown as 84 − 30 = 54 − 4 − 4 = 46

Using the hundreds chart

The hundreds chart is a well-known representation of numbers 1–100 (or 0–99) that has a multitude of uses for developing counting, patterning, base ten, addition and subtraction, and multiplication and division fact knowledge. The use of partitioning and sequencing ('split and jump') methods can be assisted through the complementary use of the hundreds chart.

Take the examples shown in Figures 6.4 to 6.5 above. Using a hundreds chart for addition shown in Figure 6.8, students would place a marker (either transparent or opaque) on 38 and 'jump' vertically to 48, 58, 68, 78 then 6 more to 84. Alternatively they may jump 40 in one go and add on 2 and then 6.

Similarly for subtraction, any two-digit computations can be easily shown. Take the previous example of 84 − 38. To subtract 38, students may place a marker on 84 and jump vertically to 74, 64, 54, then 50 and then 46 to show − 4, − 4 to subtract 38.

1	2	3	4	5	6	7	8	9	10
11	12	13	14	15	16	17	18	19	20
21	22	23	24	25	26	27	28	29	30
31	32	33	34	35	36	37	(38)	39	40
41	42	43	44	45	46	47	48	49	50
51	52	53	54	55	56	57	58	59	60
61	62	63	64	65	66	67	68	69	70
71	72	73	74	75	76	77	(78)	79	80
81	82	83	(84)	85	86	87	88	89	90
91	92	93	94	95	96	97	98	99	100

Figure 6.8 Hundreds chart

It may be difficult for some students to find their way to 84 or to 38 because the chart 'wraps around' to the next horizontal line of numbers. This is where the empty number line or a numeral track with all numbers shown in vertical sequence may be of more complementary assistance. These methods are compared with formal algorithmic routines later in the chapter.

While the use of partitioning or 'splitting' is used in both approaches, the use of 'jumping' is proving to be a most effective model of the actual mental processes that students use (Askew, 2003; Beishuizen & Anghileri, 1998). The 'jumping' can be represented in a variety of ways to match the mental processes of the learner. Students can be encouraged to compare and contrast different methods for 'split and jump' and decide which is the most efficient method for calculating. In comparison with the traditional procedures for written algorithms the partitioning and sequencing approaches work from 'left to right' based on good partitioning strategies developed through grouping tens in early number experiences. The use of the tens frame and hundreds chart showed this in Chapter 5. When using these approaches, students should be able to mentally add or subtract any pair of two-digit whole numbers removing the need for formal written algorithms.

Promoting multiplication and division strategies

This section focuses on strategies to develop multiplication and division knowledge. Learning 'tables' has traditionally held priority in the mathematics curriculum, and a new emphasis on placing it within the context of developing effective mental computation and number sense is critical to effective numeracy. There is a wide range of teaching and learning materials available for developing number fact knowledge (e.g. see Burnett & Irons, 1998b; Booker et al., 2003; McIntosh, et al., 2002).

The following mathematical processes and relationships identify important strategies. When using these strategies students should be able to mentally multiply or divide any two-digit by one-digit whole numbers removing the need for formal written algorithms.

1. skip counting/double counting/equal grouping;
2. repeated addition (and repeated subtraction);
3. derived facts; using related facts: doubling, re-doubling, halving, re-halving;
4. commutativity;
5. inverse relationships; convert multiplication to division;
6. estimation and approximation.

FOCUS QUESTIONS

Consider this list of standard strategies for effective development of multiplication and division facts. Which of these strategies do you consider to be the most intuitive? Why? How can these strategies assist students to develop the most efficient mental processes necessary for computational facility? Consider the following game (Activity 6.2) for encouraging the strategies of skip counting/double counting/equal grouping/repeated addition.

These strategies focus on co-ordinating the use of equal groups with a skip-counting sequence. Students are encouraged to develop a 'double count' where they keep track (mentally) of the number of equal groups, and the number in each group simultaneously i.e. '3, 6, 9, 12 . . . that's four threes': for example, how many grid cards of 3 squares in length are needed to cover a numeral track stopping at (a) 21 (b) 36 (c) 42?

ACTIVITY 6.2

Prepare the following activity and trial it with a group of your peers. The following materials are needed to develop the activity: grid cards (1-cm squares joined horizontally) showing equal groups—2✕ (2 squares) to 10✕ (10 squares); 10 multiples of each required; numeral track with grid cards to fit; multiplication and division fact cards; and worksheet with small numeral tracks shown.

1. Teacher suggests beginning with 2✕, 5✕ and 10✕ and related division fact cards. Students place set of number fact cards in pile. Students sort full set of grid cards into like groups (e.g. 2 squares, 3 squares. Place numeral track (showing numerals) ready for use. Provide *blank* numeral tracks for more able students.

2. Turn over number fact card (e.g. 3 ✕ 4 = 12). Select corresponding number of grid cards to show equal grouping (i.e. 3 cards of length 4 squares).

3. Place grid cards on numeral track to show 3 groups of 4. Student verbalises skip count as cards are placed on track. Cover track. Student records skip-counting pattern and number fact on numeral track worksheet.

4. Ask students to recall the number fact, the skip-counting sequence and the number of cards taken to cover the sequence. 'I covered the pattern of threes, 3, 6, 9, 12 . . . four times, that's four cards. Teacher questions students to predict how many cards would be needed to cover 50 or 100?

Critical thinking questions

How is this strategy reinforcing the link between skip counting and equal grouping? It is important to check that students are not reverting to counting by ones to add on. Encourage the student to partition the numeral track by using the grid cards. Students who can readily recall the skip-counting sequence should be encouraged to work with more difficult counting patterns and a *blank* numeral track. Students will find skip counting by 2's 5's and 10's easier than other numbers. A number of key questions can be raised.

+ Can students explain that the grid cards partition the quantity into equal groups?
+ Can students recall the skip-counting sequence? Which sequence of multiples do they find most difficult?
+ Can students recall skip-counting sequences backwards?
+ Can students keep track of the number of groups (i.e. number of times they use an equal group while counting in sequence)?

Derived multiplication facts, using related facts, doubling and halving

Students can use known multiplication and division facts to derive unknown facts by extending arrays by one more group. If one multiple is known the next multiple can be determined by adding the multiple, for example 8×7:

$$7 \times 7 = 49$$
$$8 \times 7 = 49 + 7$$
$$8 \times 7 = 56$$

Other strategies based on knowledge of addition facts encourage the use of doubling and re-doubling such as 4×8 ($2 \times 8 = 16$; $16 + 16 = 32$) and halving and re-halving: $48 \div 4$ ($48 \div 2 = 24$; $24 \div 2 = 12$).

ACTIVITY 6.3

Play the following array card game with your peers and/or a small group of students. How effective do you think this game is in re-enforcing efficient mental computation strategies?

1. Students place the full set of array cards (array cards are square and rectangular patterns of dots in rows and columns), face up. Suggest selecting small number combinations to begin with. Student selects one card and calculates total (e.g. $3 \times 4 = 12$).
2. Ask students to think of possible ways of extending the array by one row or column and then by two rows or columns (e.g. 4×4, 5×4) by selecting the matching array card. Place smaller array card on top of larger array card to show links between small array and the extended new array.
3. Students explain and record how they extended the number fact; for example:
   '$3 \times 4 = 12$, so $4 \times 4 = 16$. I added an extra group (row) of 4'.

Critical thinking questions

This activity focuses on use of the array as a model for multiplication. The strategy is for the student to use an existing array and extend it to form new number facts. This means that the student sees equal groups (rows or columns) being added on. As well, it is important for the student to be able to partition an array is a variety of ways so that other number facts are readily 'seen' within the array. The use of screening is very important for developing mental images of the number combinations. The student should explore possible ways of covering arrays partially and recalling the number combinations that are covered. Once the student is able to visualise and recall the combinations of facts the arrays should be removed.

+ Can students extend a known multiplication fact using one or more equal groups (e.g. add on one more group 3×4, 4×4) to form a new multiplication fact?

+ Can students represent this grouping on an array?

+ Can students partition a number fact using an array into two or more smaller number facts and use a number of smaller arrays to form a larger array?

+ Can students recall from memory possible number combinations to form a larger array?

Students can select a larger array card and find all possible combinations of number facts that form the total by placing smaller cards on top of larger array cards. Students may use as many different arrays as they see possible. The activity can be extended to division by requiring students to record matching division facts.

Commutativity

Students can use commutativity as a strategy for mental calculation where $a \times b = b \times a$. Thus the number of multiplication facts (100 in total) can be reduced to 55. The emphasis is on using an array or grid as a model for multiplication and division (e.g. a gridded rectangle or an array that is 3 units by 4 units models the multiplication 3×4 or 4 times 3).

For this activity it is necessary to use two sets of array cards that consist of $\times$ pairs with products to 120 approximately and two sets of multiplication and division fact cards, with the product on one side and the matching number fact on the other. Alternatively grid paper and coloured adhesive dots can be used.

ACTIVITY 6.4

1. Place a set of array cards face up on table. Students sort cards of the same value into groups; that is, students calculate mentally the total of each array card and place with other cards of the same value (e.g. 4×5 array and 5×4 array).

2. Place a set of multiplication and division facts cards, either randomly or in order, with number fact side face down in pile (e.g. $3 \times 4 = 12$).

3. Student selects number fact card showing product (e.g. 12) and chooses matching array cards (e.g. 3 by 4 dots and 4 by 3 dots)—to show commutativity. Student turns card over to show matching number fact.

4. Student records arrays and number facts on blank grid paper.

5. Encourage students to check that they have recorded all the arrays by placing the cards (and recording them) in an organised way such as:
   2×18 18×2 3×12 12×3 4×9 9×4 6×6

Critical thinking questions

As shown in Chapter 5, arrays provide a model that helps students visualise how multiplication pairs such as 3×6 and 6×3 are related (commutativity). It is appropriate to establish a class convention for how arrays are labelled and described 3×6 (3 rows of 6) and 6×3 (6 rows of 3).

If students need to count arrays it is important to emphasise counting by groups rather than by ones; for example, 3×6 array can be counted by 6's (6, 12, 18 and so on).

+ Can students use efficient counting and calculation methods when finding the total number in an array; for example, counting in equal groups: 4, 8, 12, 16?

+ Can they explain commutativity if the array is rotated?

+ Can they recall related facts for multiplication or division with and without an array; for example, $2 \times 9 = 18$; $9 \times 2 = 18$?

+ Can students recognise that they have found all possible combinations of pairs of factors?

Students may recognise that some factors (e.g. 16, 25, 36) are squares and some factors have only two arrays (e.g. 13×1; 1×13). They can explore various patterns of factors; for example, prime numbers are those that each have only one pair of factors and only one array.

Inverse relationships: convert multiplication to division

This strategy enables the student to recognise corresponding basic division facts by using the inverse of multiplication facts. This card game can be played individually or in small groups (basic multiplication and division fact cards $2\times$ to $10\times$ are required).

ACTIVITY 6.5

Place a full set of multiplication fact cards in a pile, face down. Place full set of division cards in a pile, face down.

1. Student deals five (or more) multiplication fact cards to each player. Players conceal their hand of cards.

2. Each player turns over one multiplication fact card and one division fact card with the aim of matching these cards to any one of their hand of multiplication fact cards; that is, there are four cards that are linked (e.g. $3 \times 4 = 12$, $4 \times 3 = 12$, $12 \div 3 = 4$, $12 \div 4 = 3$. If these cards are not required by that player they return them to the bottom of the pile. Each player observes whether a card required for a match has been returned to the new pile.

3. Each player takes turns in matching a multiplication and division fact card to any one of their cards in hand. As each match of four is made the player lays the set on the table. The game continues until all multiplication fact cards in hand have a full set.

Critical thinking questions
Basic division facts rely on the inverse relationship of multiplication and division. Division by 0 is not possible. The aim of the card game is to assist students in linking the two operations of multiplication and division and recognising the four different ways that multiplication and division facts are linked.

+ Can students recognise that commutativity assists in generating and recalling multiplication facts; for example, $3 \times 4 = 12$ and $4 \times 3 = 12$ are different groupings of 12?

+ Can students relate their understanding of inverse relationships and knowledge of basic multiplication facts for division?

+ Can students explain that the groupings are the same for division but the division fact is recorded differently; for example, $3 \times 4 = 12$ means that 3 groups of 4 make 12 . . . 12 divided into 4 equal parts gives 3 in each part $12 \div 4 = 3$?

Using estimation and approximation

ACTIVITY 6.6

Some preservice teachers were comparing examples of tasks that encouraged students to round off and approximate totals rather than add a series of numbers. They discussed the two tasks with their peers and listed reasons for their preferences.

Task 1
Find the total number of children in the seven grades in our school:
(31, 29, 17, 22, 28, 26, 26)

1. Before you work it out, do you think the total will be closer to 150 or 200?
2. How do you know? Explain and record how you worked it out.
3. Do you think a calculator would be necessary to complete this task quickly?
4. If we placed all the children in teams of 10, how many teams would there be? Show how you solved the problem.
5. Are there equal numbers of boys and girls in each grade? How do you know?
6. Find out how many boys and girls there are and graph the information.

Task 2
Round off each number to the nearest 10 and approximate the total of these numbers:
(31, 29, 27, 22, 28, 26, 26)

Divide the total by 10.

They compared Tasks 1 and 2 and agreed that Task 1 was advantageous because it supported the idea that it is reasonable to approximate your answer by giving cues, for example 'before you work it out'. Task 2 also encouraged directly rounding off and approximation but there was little scope for the children to consider why they needed to do so. Task 1 also required the children to interpret a series of questions, show the solution's strategies and explain their thinking. The teachers thought that this was far more challenging than Task 2, but that Task 1 would take longer to complete than Task 2. The open-ended investigation in Task 1 also provided further opportunities for more able students. The group concluded that it was important for the children to justify the use of approximation and mental strategies when completing the task.

Multiplication and division using semiformal routines

Common approaches used for the development of mental strategies for multiplying and dividing numbers to 20 and beyond using semiformal routines can be summarised in the following ways:

+ regrouping (left-to-right aggregation);
+ partitioning.

Regrouping
Semiformal routines for multiplication of 2-digit × 1-digit numbers can be encouraged through the strategy of regrouping. This requires the 'splitting' of the number into tens and ones so that they can be multiplied separately. This strategy requires students to derive

multiplication facts (2 digit × 1 digit) by regrouping the 2-digit multiplier. This encourages use of the distributive property (i.e. 3 × 14 = (3 × 10) + (3 × 4) = 30 + 12 = 42).

This strategy encourages grouping in multiples of ten and reinforces basic number fact strategies. Calculators can be used for checking facts and addition of the total. This strategy is encouraged as an alternative to the 2-digit × 1-digit algorithm traditionally completed by right-to-left methods.

Partitioning (2-digit × 1-digit multiplication)
This strategy requires students to partition multiplication facts and their products into smaller number combinations using multiples of 10 (2 digit × 1 digit); that is, 100 can be partitioned into 20 × 2 and 15 × 4.

This strategy encourages students to develop flexible use of number fact combinations by multiplying by 10. It supports the development of 2-digit multiplication using multiples of 10 by combining known facts to form new facts. The use of addition and subtraction to 100 may also be required.

Using the empty number line
The empty number line can also assist as an aid to recording multiplication or division processes, provided that the child understands that the groups (or jumps) must be of equal size. Figures 6.9 and 6.10 show effectively multiplication of 20 × 6 and 120 ÷ 6 and 15 × 4 and 60 ÷ 4 as equal segments on the empty number line. A doubling process is used to show 2 × 15.

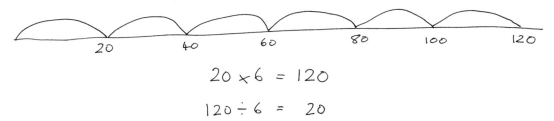

Figure 6.9 Multiplication and division 20 × 6 and 120 ÷ 6 using the empty number line

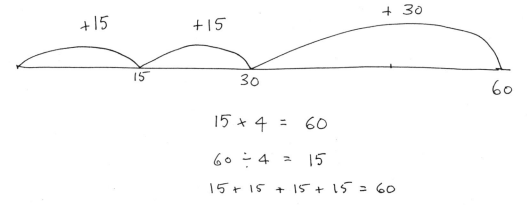

Figure 6.10 Multiplication and division 15 × 4 = 60 and 60 ÷ 4 = 15 using the empty number line

The use of the empty number line can assist students, particularly where the groups form a standard pattern of multiples such as 4 × 20.

Moving from non-standard to standard written algorithms

Common approaches used for the development of formal written algorithmic procedures for adding and subtracting numbers beyond 20 can be summarised in the following ways:

+ addition using regrouping (or renaming, trading);
+ subtraction using decomposition with regrouping (or renaming, trading);
+ subtraction using an equal addends approach.

The *addition algorithm* uses right-to-left addition of columns of digits, often called the *partial sum approach*. When students total more than ten (or hundred and so on) they need to regroup and add to the adjacent place value. For example, 15 ones becomes 1 ten and 5 ones. The *decomposition approach* is based on the idea of regrouping (or renaming, trading) the minuend using students' knowledge of base ten; that is, 53 becomes 4 tens and 13 ones. The *equal addends* approach is based on the principle of compensation where adding like amounts (i.e. tens, hundreds) to the minuend and subtrahend results in the same difference. Traditionally this can be confused with the 'borrow-and-pay-back method' which is conceptually quite different and no longer advocated in curricula because it is unreasonable. However, it appears to use similar symbolism.

Figures 6.11 and 6.12 show examples of addition using a formal vertical algorithm. Figure 6.11 shows 3-digit plus 3-digit addition without regrouping and 4-digit plus 4-digit addition without regrouping. In both cases the child adds the digits in each column from right to left. There is no need for the child to consider the whole algorithm and this may result in the child being unaware of the place value of the digits or the value of the total.

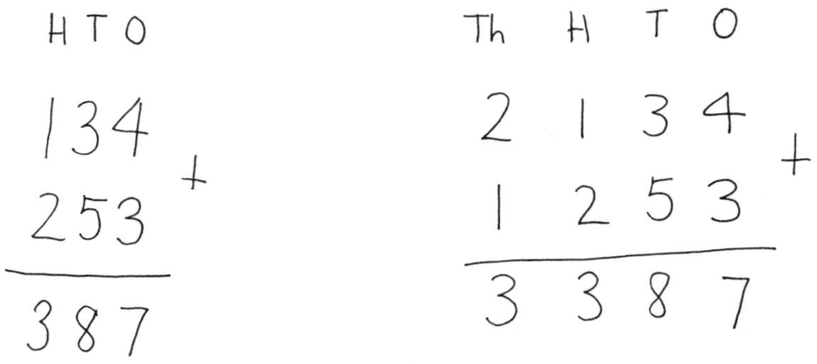

Figure 6.11 Addition of 134 + 253 and 2134 + 1253 using a formal vertical algorithm

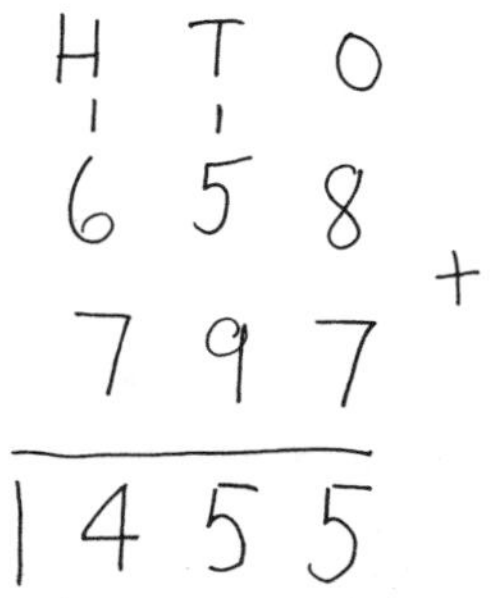

Figure 6.12 Addition of 658 + 797 using a formal vertical algorithm

Figure 6.12 shows addition of 3 digits and 3 digits with regrouping in both the tens and hundreds place. In this example the child regroups 15 ones as 1 ten and 5 ones showing the (small) one in the tens place. When adding the tens the child regroups 15 tens as 1 hundred and 5 tens showing the (small) one in the hundreds column. However, it is possible for the child to complete the algorithm without being aware of the place value of the digits or the meaning of regrouping. Semiformal algorithms may be used in the transition to this regrouping model. McClain, Cobb and Bowers (1998) exemplify 3-digit addition and subtraction using students' construction of their own personally meaningful algorithms.

Figure 6.13 compares the standard subtraction algorithm for 128 – 79 using

+ decomposition and
+ equal addends methods.

For *decomposition* the student regroups 28 as 1 ten and 18 ones; similarly 1 hundred and 1 ten is regrouped as 11 tens. The *equal addends* method shows a ten added to the minuend (the 8) and a ten added to the 7 to make 8 tens i.e. 'add ten to the top, add ten to the bottom'.

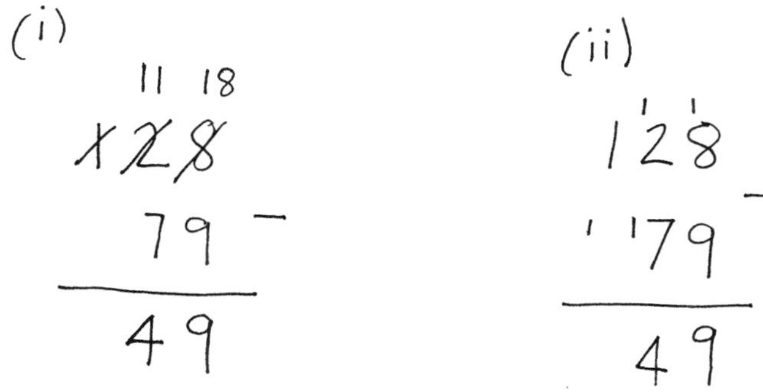

Figure 6.13 Subtraction algorithm using (i) decomposition and (ii) equal addends for 128 – 79

Figures 6.14 and 6.15 compare subtraction algorithms for *decomposition* and *equal addends* in two examples of 4-digit minus 3-digit numbers. The first example shows 1353 regrouped as 1 thousand 2 hundreds 14 tens and 13 ones or 214 tens and 13 ones. The second example shows 7001 regrouped as 6 thousands 9 hundreds 9 tens and 11 ones or 699 tens and 11 ones.

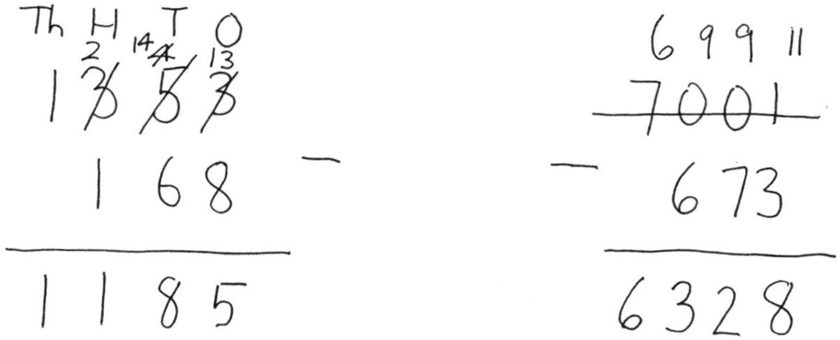

Figure 6.14 Subtraction algorithms using decomposition for 1353 – 168 and 7001 – 673

Figure 6.15 compares the *equal addends* method where, in both examples, the same amount is added to the minuend and subtrahend, that is, ten is added to 3 to make 13 and ten is added to 6 tens to make 7 tens; one hundred is added to 5 to make 15 tens and one hundred is added to 1 hundred to make 2 hundreds. The second example shows the same method; ten is added to 1 to make 11 and ten is added to 7 to make 8 tens etc.

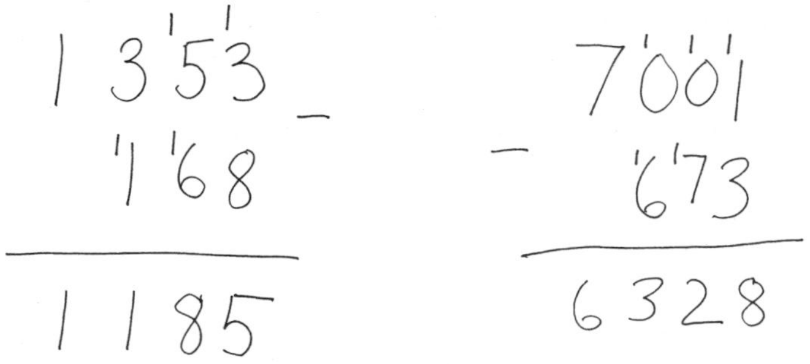

$$
\begin{array}{r}
1\ 3\ 5\ 3 \\
1\ 6\ 8 \\
\hline
1\ 1\ 8\ 5
\end{array}
\qquad
\begin{array}{r}
7\ 0\ 0\ 1 \\
-\ \ 6\ 7\ 3 \\
\hline
6\ 3\ 2\ 8
\end{array}
$$

Figure 6.15 Subtraction algorithms using equal addends for 1353 − 168 and 7001 − 673

FOCUS QUESTIONS

Educators strongly support the use of equal addends or decomposition as preferred methods in curricula. While there is strong support for mental computation strategies for all computations involving addition and subtraction of 2-digit numbers and multiplication and division by 1-digit numbers, the place of formal written algorithms is still acknowledged. The use of calculators for computations with large numbers is also considered reasonable provided that students have good computational facility and number sense.

1. What methods did you use to compute the above examples?
2. Why do you think the decomposition for subtraction is widely used?
3. What difficulties do you see with using a variety of methods?
4. At what point do you think that formal written algorithms should be introduced?
5. Should algorithms be invented by children or taught as procedures?

Common approaches used for the development of formal written algorithmic procedures for multiplying numbers beyond 20 can be summarised in the following ways:

1. standard right-to-left algorithm using regrouping;
2. expanded form;
3. partial products (from the left or the right);
4. partitioning.

The standard algorithm for multiplication uses each digit as a single multiplication fact along with regrouping. Alternative methods such as expanded form rely on good base ten strategies and the repeated addition strategy (see, for example, alternative methods advocated by Baek, 1998; Lampert, 1990; Wright et al., 2002). Such methods might include strategies such as:

+ direct modelling by ones, fives or tens in arrays, or in grids (17 rows of 4 dots; or 10 rows of 4 dots and 5 rows of 4 dots and 2 rows of 4 dots); and

+ repeated addition of the multiplicand
(13×6 as $13 + 13 = 26 + 13 = 39 + 13 = 52 + 13 = 65 + 13 = 78$). Doubling might also be used as a more efficient strategy.

Figure 6.16 shows how a 3-digit number can be expanded and aggregated from left to right so that the process of regrouping is not required.

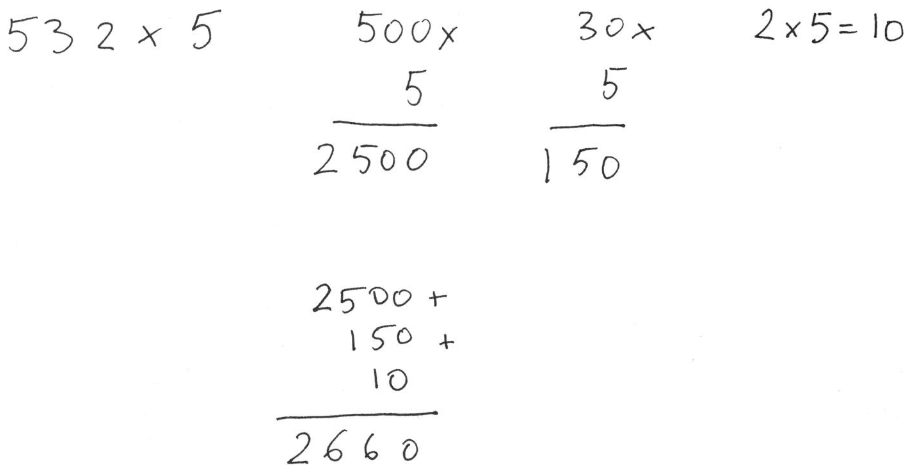

$$532 \times 5 \qquad 500 \times \atop 5 \qquad 30 \times \atop 5 \qquad 2 \times 5 = 10$$

$$\begin{array}{r} 500 \times \\ 5 \\ \hline 2500 \end{array} \qquad \begin{array}{r} 30 \times \\ 5 \\ \hline 150 \end{array}$$

$$\begin{array}{r} 2500 + \\ 150 + \\ 10 \\ \hline 2660 \end{array}$$

Figure 6.16 Multiplication algorithm using expanded form 532 × 5

Figure 6.17 shows multiplication by partial products beginning from the left (i) or the right (ii). Again, this relies on the students' ability to partition the number using base ten knowledge.

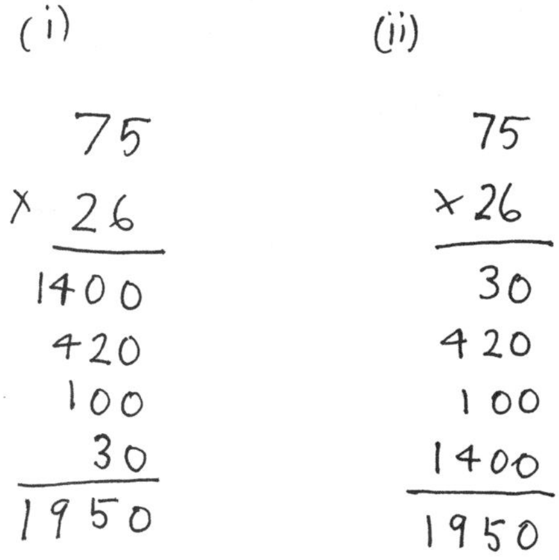

(i)	(ii)

$$\begin{array}{r} 75 \\ \times\ 26 \\ \hline 1400 \\ 420 \\ 100 \\ 30 \\ \hline 1950 \end{array} \qquad \begin{array}{r} 75 \\ \times 26 \\ \hline 30 \\ 420 \\ 100 \\ 1400 \\ \hline 1950 \end{array}$$

Figure 6.17 Multiplication algorithms by partial products beginning on the left or the right, 75 × 26

Figures 6.18 shows partitioning using expanded form for both the multiplier and the multiplicand. These methods rely on fundamental mental computation skills and number fact knowledge.

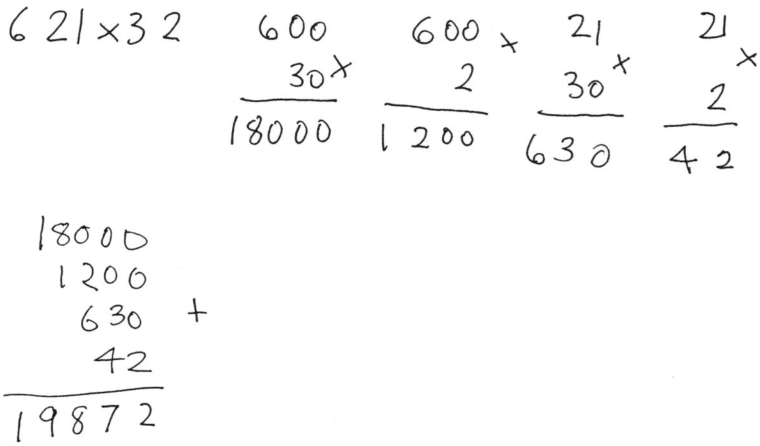

$$621 \times 32$$

$$
\begin{array}{r} 600 \\ 30 \times \\ \hline 18000 \end{array}
\quad
\begin{array}{r} 600 \times \\ 2 \\ \hline 1200 \end{array}
\quad
\begin{array}{r} 21 \\ 30 \times \\ \hline 630 \end{array}
\quad
\begin{array}{r} 21 \\ 2 \times \\ \hline 42 \end{array}
$$

$$
\begin{array}{r}
18000 \\
1200 \\
630 \\
42 \; + \\
\hline
19872
\end{array}
$$

Figure 6.18 3-digit × 2-digit multiplication algorithm 621 × 32 using partitioning and expanded form

For division the formal algorithm becomes more complex and the use of calculators is encouraged to assist in trial-and-error grouping and approximation. However strategies and recordings based on understanding that division is the inverse of multiplication can produce a variety of algorithmic methods. Some semi-alternative algorithmic methods are shown here.

1. standard division algorithm based on multiplication and repeated subtraction;
2. partitioning;
3. scaffolding with repeated subtraction;
4. 'building-up' with scaffolding.

Figure 6.19 shows traditional methods for calculating quotients based on treatment of the digits as 2-digit divided by 1-digit number facts without necessarily considering the place value of the digits. Repeated subtraction is used in the first example.

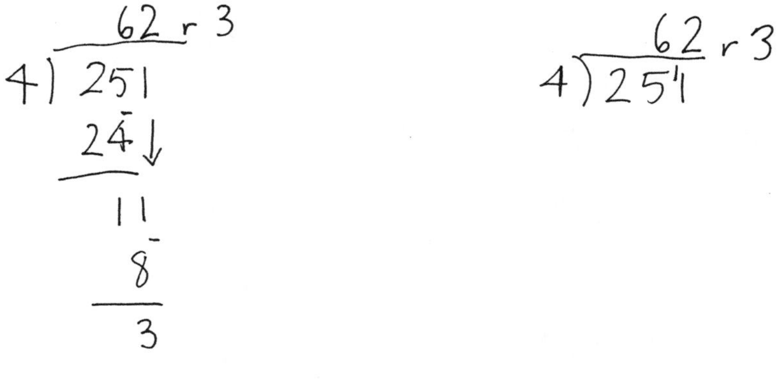

$$
\begin{array}{r}
62 \; r \; 3 \\
4\overline{)251} \\
24 \downarrow \\
\hline
11 \\
8 \\
\hline
3
\end{array}
\qquad\qquad
\begin{array}{r}
62 \; r \; 3 \\
4\overline{)25^11}
\end{array}
$$

Figure 6.19 Division algorithm using multiplication and repeated subtraction 251 ÷ 4 and traditional short division algorithm 251 ÷ 4

174

Figure 6.20 shows the same division algorithm 251 ÷ 4 using partitioning from left to right and using multiplication as the inverse.

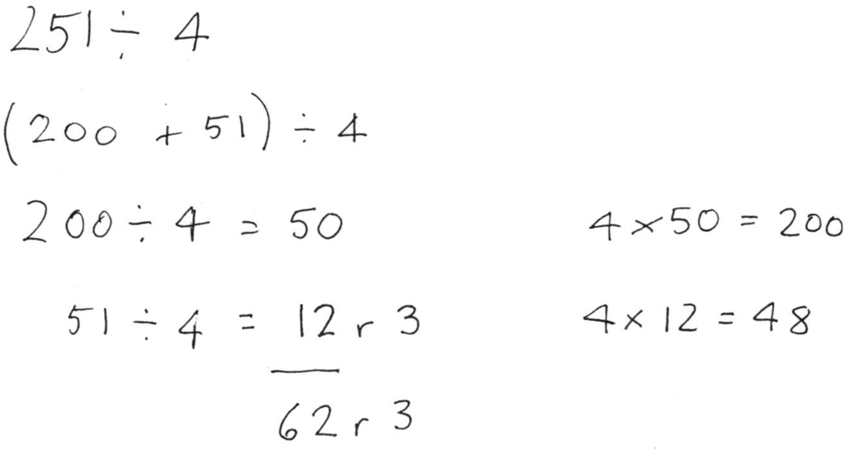

$$251 \div 4$$

$$(200 + 51) \div 4$$

$$200 \div 4 = 50 \qquad\qquad 4 \times 50 = 200$$

$$51 \div 4 = 12 \, r \, 3 \qquad\qquad 4 \times 12 = 48$$

$$62 \, r \, 3$$

Figure 6.20 Partitioning 251 ÷ 4

Figure 6.21 compares and contrasts the division algorithm 342 ÷ 26 using some scaffolding with repeated subtraction. The alternative example shows the use of 'building-up' to the dividend by a cumulative total of multiples of 26.

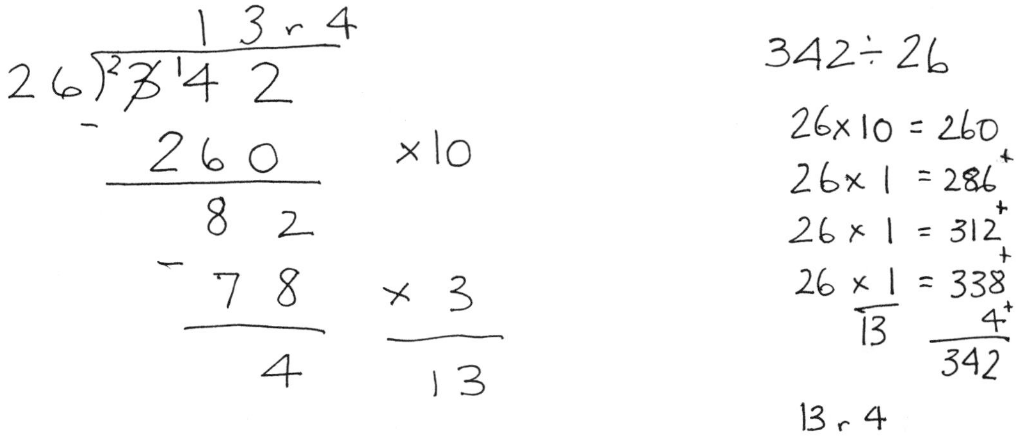

$$342 \div 26$$

$$26 \times 10 = 260$$

$$26 \times 1 = 286^{+}$$

$$26 \times 1 = 312^{+}$$

$$26 \times 1 = 338^{+}$$

$$13 \qquad 4^{+}$$

$$342$$

$$13 \, r \, 4$$

Figure 6.21 3-digit by 2-digit division using repeated subtraction and building up for 342 ÷ 26

Figure 6.22 compares scaffolding methods using repeated subtraction for 1128 ÷ 24. In these examples the multiples of 24 are subtracted gradually. A pyramid version can also be used where the multiples of 24 are recorded on top of the dividend in a vertical column rather than adjacent (to the right) of the algorithm.

It is not necessarily expected that a student will be able to approximate a solution before performing the procedures. Figure 6.23 shows a student's alternative process of approximating the answer before performing the procedure. This shows good use of mental computation and number sense.

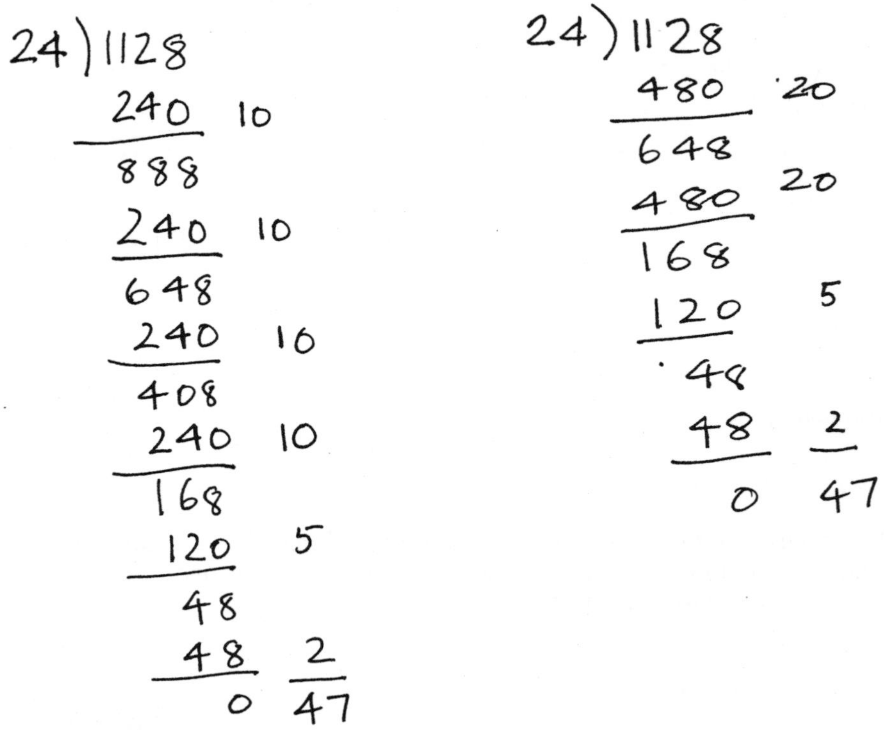

$$
\begin{array}{r}
24 \overline{)1128} \\
240 \quad 10 \\
\hline
888 \\
240 \quad 10 \\
\hline
648 \\
240 \quad 10 \\
\hline
408 \\
240 \quad 10 \\
\hline
168 \\
120 \quad 5 \\
\hline
48 \\
48 \quad 2 \\
\hline
0 \quad 47
\end{array}
\qquad
\begin{array}{r}
24 \overline{)1128} \\
480 \quad 20 \\
\hline
648 \\
480 \quad 20 \\
\hline
168 \\
120 \quad 5 \\
\hline
48 \\
48 \quad 2 \\
\hline
0 \quad 47
\end{array}
$$

Figure 6.22 4-digit by 2-digit long division algorithm 1128 ÷ 24

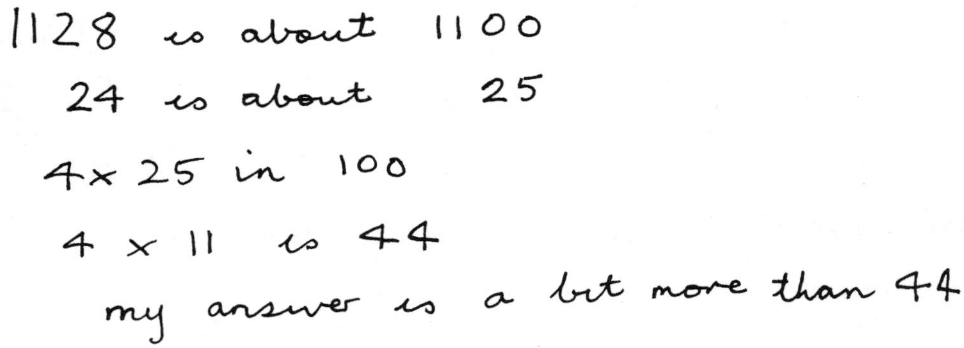

1128 is about 1100

24 is about 25

4 × 25 in 100

4 × 11 is 44

my answer is a bit more than 44

Figure 6.23 4-digit by 2-digit division 1128 ÷ 24: alternative approximation method

FOCUS QUESTIONS

1. Consider the methods for multiplication and division shown in the above examples. Discuss the similarities and differences between these approaches. Which methods do you think are most likely to be based on mental computation strategies rather than rote learnt procedures?

2. How does your state's syllabus describe the transition from mental computation to formal written algorithms?

3. How much flexibility is shown in examples of formal algorithms?

4. Reconsider the word problem examples shown in Chapter 5. How could these algorithms be matched to word problem types with meaning?

ACTIVITY 6.7

Developing numerical relationships through a problem-based approach

Children's broad conceptual basis for mathematical operations can only be fully developed by the way they represent relationships described in problem situations. It will be recalled from Chapter 5 that we discussed the importance of problem situations and questioning the child about thinking when computing. For example, Year 6 children who can recall and record standard multiplication and division tables and can order decimals to three places might be challenged to show how robust their understandings are when required to explain these relationships.

Let's take a traditional example and compare it with a problem-based approach.

Discuss the two approaches with a group of your peers and list the benefits and/or disadvantages of the two approaches.

Traditional examples
Product of 12 and 6 is _____
$12 \times 6 =$
$6 \times 12 =$
$12 \times 60 =$
$12 \times 0.6 =$
Complete the pattern: 6, ___ , 18, ___ , 30, 36
List factors of 72 _____

Problem-based and open-ended challenges
1. Make up a number story that matches $12 \times 6 =$. Explain how you got the answer. Think about how your answers would change if you changed the problem to 120×60. Would the answer be smaller or larger if it was changed to 120×0.6? Explain your thinking by recording your solutions.

2. Is 12×6 the same as 6×12? Explain your thinking by recording your solution.

3. Why is $12 + 6$ different from 12×6? Explain your thinking. Make up a problem to show how the two number facts are different.

Can the child explain that the product can be the same but the equal groupings of 12×6 and 6×12 are different?

If a number is multiplied or divided by 10, what effect does this have on the result?

The calculator can assist here in showing how the system of place value depends on multiplying or dividing by ten, such as where $120 \times 5 \div 10$ is the same as 120×0.5.

Being able to make up a word problem to match these number sentences is somewhat difficult if there is little understanding of the meaning of the symbols and operations. Figure 6.24 shows that Alex has made links between the operations but does not use division by 10 as a decimal to one place.

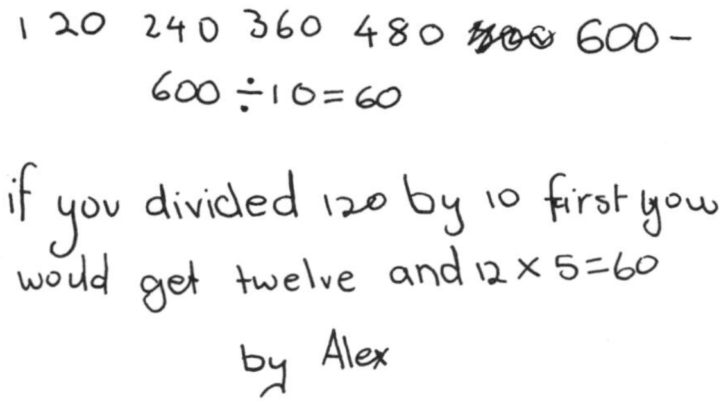

$$1 \ 20 \quad 240 \quad 360 \quad 480 \quad \cancel{500} \quad 600 -$$
$$600 \div 10 = 60$$

if you divided 120 by 10 first you would get twelve and $12 \times 5 = 60$

by Alex

Figure 6.24 Alex's representation of 120 × 5 ÷ 10

SNAPSHOTS OF LEARNING: LESSON PLANNING AND ASSESSMENT

The following section draws upon and extends key aspects of number sense discussed throughout the chapter. Examples of rich and diverse learning situations are provided as snapshots of children's developing number knowledge. Each snapshot integrates several complex number skills and processes with a view to capturing key aspects of number sense. The first example, 'Counting patterns to 1000', focuses on the use of counting patterns to develop understanding of the number system. The calculator is used to extend the investigation with decimals. Computations are presented in the snapshot 'Thinking before computing' as alternative modes of solution. An example of using real data to compare and apply large numbers is presented through the snapshot 'Air traffic investigations'. The snapshot 'Budget billions' extends the work developed in the other snapshots for more able students by using Internet sites to explore numeration and notations.

1. Counting patterns to 1000

Years 4 and 5 students investigated number patterns to 1000 and strategies for counting efficiently to 1000 (see Figure 6.25).

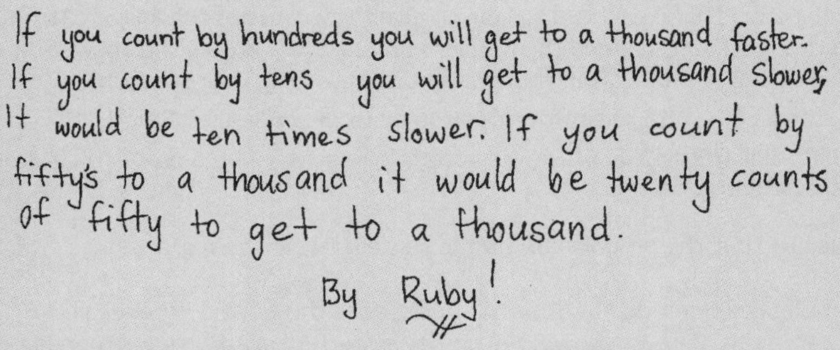

If you count by hundreds you will get to a thousand faster. If you count by tens you will get to a thousand slower. It would be ten times slower. If you count by fifty's to a thousand it would be twenty counts of fifty to get to a thousand.

By Ruby!

Figure 6.25 Ruby's comparison of counting by tens, hundreds and fifties to 1000

Teachers' comments

> *Notice how Ruby makes comparisons in terms of 'how long it takes'. I think this shows very good 'number sense' because she realises counting by tens would be ten times the number of items in the counting pattern. Also she can multiply combinations of 10, 100, 50 and 20 to show her understanding of how 1000 can be broken up into groups.*

(Teacher, Year 4)

> *I think some children need to be challenged to work out alternative number patterns by prompting, such as 'What if you counted by 5s compared with counting by 50s?' Then you would encourage children to look for combinations and to look for similarities such as the pattern of 10s and the pattern of 100s.*

(Teacher, Year 5)

Mathematical content and processes

+ Generates and compares patterns of multiples in tens, fifties and hundreds to 1000.
+ Justifies and explains counting patterns according to efficiency.
+ Shows relationship between counting in tens and hundreds as 'ten times'.
+ Uses knowledge of numeration to partition 1000 into groups.

Posing key questions to assess learning

Look at the following counting pattern:
  100, 200, 300, 400, 500, 600, 700, 800, 900, 1000

+ Write some number sentences to describe how many 100s there are in 1000?
    e.g. $100 \times 10 = 1000$
    e.g. $1000 \div 10 = 100$

+ Use the counting pattern to produce as many number combinations as possible to make 1000, e.g. $700 + 300 =$
+ If $1000 \div 100 = 10$ explain why $10\,000 \div 100 = 100$ and why $100\,000 \div 100 = 1000$.

Extending the investigation

Year 5 students made up these four pairs of examples to show some relationships:

1. $100 + 100 + 100 + 100 + 100 + 100 + 100 + 100 + 100 + 100$ $1000 \div 100$

2. 0.01×100 3. 0.01×1000 4. 1000×10
    0.001×1000 0.1×100 $1000 \div 0.1$

Use your calculator to investigate counting by 50s, 100s, 500s, 1000s and 5000s by pressing, for example, $50 + 50 = = \ldots$ and $500 + 500 = = \ldots$ What do you notice about the pattern?

+ Without using a calculator, imagine the pattern of counting in tenths (e.g. 0.1, 0.2, 0.3 . . .). What is the connection between the two patterns? Use your calculator to assist you.
+ Is it quicker to count in tenths to 10 or in hundredths to 10? Write down your reasons.

2. Air traffic investigations

Years 5 and 6 students investigated large numbers through air traffic movements at Australian airports. They researched some statistics from the airport's Airservices Australia website www.airservicesaustralia.com. Table 6.1 shows some statistics they found.

TABLE 6.1 Annual statistics: Movements at Australian Airports 2003

Location	Number of movements
Adelaide	92 104
Brisbane	127 376
Darwin	69 176
Hobart	28 014
Melbourne	144 466
Perth	85 600
Sydney	235 552

The students were asked to interpret the data, answer some key questions and pose some additional questions for their peers.

Teachers' comments

> *This was a good example of data exploration to check children's understanding of numeration to six places. Some children could see the interesting relationships in the information easily because they could compare the size of the numbers by rounding off.*

(Teacher, Year 6)

> *I got my students to approximate differences and record their own algorithms. The idea of 'times as many', as in 235 552 is about twice as much as 127 376, was a good example to start with. They used their calculators to work out the fraction of movements between cities.*

(Teacher, Year 5)

Mathematical content and processes
+ Reads, writes and compares whole numbers to six places.
+ Uses number sense to compare quantities and amounts.
+ Interprets data to find relationships between notations.

Posing key questions to assess learning
From Table 6.1 record the total number of movements and order from smallest to largest.
+ How many more movements were there in Sydney than Melbourne and Brisbane?
+ Explain why there were about one-tenth as many movements in Hobart compared with Sydney?

Extending the investigation

+ Sydney Airport handles millions of international passengers in one year. Make some estimates of the number of passengers moving through airports in capital cities of Australia (based on www.airservicesaustralia.com). Record your estimates in a table and then find some data to check your estimates. What things did you consider when you made your estimates? Did you estimate the number of passengers per flight and compare with movements?

+ Compare the data from other cities in Australia. Draw a table showing the cities in order of number of movements.

+ Examine the data for plane movements 'over 136 000 kg'. Does the order remain the same as 'total' movements for the capital cities?

+ Where would you place Canberra in this order?

3. Thinking before computing

Years 4, 5 and 6 were required to choose the most appropriate approximate form of solution and explore and record their solutions to the following algorithms. The teacher recorded their methods of solution on a chart.

Computation	Method	Students' strategy
(a) 1121 + 129	Mental	'29 + 21 makes 50, 100 + 100 makes 200, that's 1250.'
(b) 11 006 – 1102	Mental or written	'9904, you take 100 from 1006 and you get 906 but it's 2 more to take away so it's 904. Then just take another thousand so it's 9904.'
(c) 12 084 – 6796	Approximation Written Calculator	'Approximately 12 take away 7 that's 5000. Trading gives it exactly.' 'You can use your calculator to check that your answer plus 6796 gives 12 084.' 'You can do it by the "add ten" method too.'
(d) 1 368 497 + 2 679 271	Approximation Calculator Written	'That's about 1 million 400 thousand and 2 million 700 thousand but less because I rounded up each time—about 4 million dollars.'

Teacher's and student's comments

> *The students were able to judge which method was efficient and reasonable. I was impressed that they used only mental strategies in example (a) and (b). It was obviously unnecessary in example (b) but other children attempted to use an algorithm which was inefficient.*

(Teacher, Year 5)

The work we have been doing on approximating in our head is really helping us to think about the easiest way and what the answer should be like. It's great 'cause you don't need to do all the sums and the crossing out and working out.

(Student, Year 5)

Mathematical content and processes

+ Uses approximation and rounding-off to solve algorithms involving addition, subtraction, multiplication and division.

+ Chooses the most efficient mental, written or calculator strategy to solve and record solutions to computations.

+ Makes comparisons between solution strategies in order to justify advantages of one strategy over another.

+ Devises alternative strategies to solving computations involving the four operations.

Posing key questions to assess learning

+ Look at example (a) in the chart. Do you think it would be reasonable to use a calculator to solve the calculation? Why? Why not?

+ In examples (b) and (c) the student has used two different methods of calculation. Explain which method is the most appropriate.

+ Write the algorithm for example (c), and solve it using decomposition or trading. Now try it using a different method. Which method do you think is more efficient? Would you use a calculator instead? Why?

+ Try example (d) as a written vertical algorithm. Why do you think it is important to know how to add the columns correctly? Would you use another method? Why?

4. Budget billions

Year 6 students used an Internet site to discover the names of large numbers. They had been working on a thematic unit involving the Australian conventions for naming large numbers. Because the Federal Budget had just been presented with extensive reference to 'billions', the class became interested in the different naming systems and, in particular, the difference between an American billion that is commonly used in Australia, and an imperial billion, often used in the UK. Class members wondered which version of 'billion' was used in the budget deficit (or surplus). They connected to the Internet site:

http://mathforum.org/dr.math/faq/fac.largenumbers.html

From their earlier theme work and Internet research, the children constructed Table 6.2. The students' discussion of the comparisons shows how they thought about using mathematical notation to represent numbers more compactly and about how numbers might be named in each system. They still pondered about which version of 'billions' the Federal Treasurer kept referring to. What version did most Australians use when they thought of billions?

TABLE 6.2 Number systems

Number	(How many zeros)	Imperial name	American name	
1 000	(3)	Thousand	Thousand	10^3
1 000 000	(6)	Million	Million	10^6
1 000 000 000	(9)	One thousand million	Billion	10^9
1 000 000 000 000	(12)	Billion	Trillion	10^{12}

Our group wondered what the little pointy hat ^ was on the Internet site. Because the Budget was in the news, we looked at a 'billion = 10^9' on the American website and decided that it was a short way of showing how many zeros there were. Meghann thought it must be 10 multiplied 9 times and made up a name for 'pointy hat'—'times itself this many times'. Lizby said her big brother was doing stuff like that in high school but wasn't using the hat. She called 'pointy hat' 'this many zeros'.

Most of us voted the American naming system as better because there was a new number name every time you write a gap and a new bundle of three zeros. So a billion is: 'write a thousand then two bundles of zeros' and a trillion is: 'write a thousand then three bundles of zeros' and so on.

We talked about the Budget billions and thought that it couldn't be millions of millions. It was just too big! We reckoned it was just 10^9 or an American billion (like on the website) and tried to think of what it should really be called in our system. Alice thought '1 and a half-millions'. We worked it out to be 'thousands of millions' which makes sense, I think, for 1 000 000 000.

Teachers' comments

> *The children seemed to like this website because it had a nice visual appeal. The naming differences and challenges really got them in because we'd been talking about billions in the budget. The larger number names actually intrigued them and counting zeros was quite compelling but difficult for them. The children interested in number names were especially motivated by the naming differences and tried to think of other contexts for the numerical prefixes, especially from the recent space substrand we'd completed.*

(Teacher, Year 6)

> *This was very challenging for some of mine but they persisted with some help and encouragenment. It helped to go back to millions and we talked about Lotto millionaires and how some people were actually billionaires. The monetary referent really got them thinking and they laughed at the 'poverty' of an American billionaire.*

(Teacher, Year 6)

Mathematical content and processes
+ Writes numerals using SI (International System of Units) spacing conventions.
+ Appreciates that alternative naming systems exist for large numbers.

+ Devises reasons for the selection of consistent systematic number naming.
+ Uses base ten notation to compress numeral writing.
+ Has awareness of the use and appreciation of large numbers in society.

Posing key questions to assess learning
Using the data generated and extended in Table 6.2, after linking to the website:

+ What can you say about the way we write numerals?
+ What can you say about the names and nature of different systems?
+ How and where are large number names used in life?
+ How could you extend a fold-up notation strip (numeral expander) or posting cards (arrow cards) to show large numbers and assist in their reading?

Extending the investigation
The Internet site http://www.brillig.com/debt_clock/ is a running record of the US debt. See if some students can:

+ represent this figure using a form of compact notation and explain its value;
+ name the number representing the debt using both naming conventions;
+ calculate the per capita debt in the USA and compare it with Australian data.

Other Internet sites to extend thinking and investigations with larger numbers are:

+ http://mcraeclan.com/Graeme/Language/MillionsAndBillionsAndZillions.htm (phones in China);
+ http://spicerack.sr.euh.edu/~tg/numbers.html (linking large numbers to time; hyperlinks to thousands, millions, billions and very large numbers within a time context).

Filling a calculator or computer screen with digits, and then asking a partner to give it a number name, includes elements of fun, challenge and creativity. It also assesses whether students understand the system of numeration. Another creative extension might be for children to devise their own lateral thinking naming system, a little like the actual (nickname) 'googol' which is utilised for $10 \wedge 100$.

Promoting number sense in the classroom

A group of experienced teachers was asked to assess whether the snapshots of learning described above captured some key aspects of their mathematics syllabus in terms of developing numerical concepts and processes for the later primary grades. Some teachers explained that many of the processes were interrelated and it was difficult to match each particular skill and idea to a specific syllabus outcome.

It seems that number sense involves so many aspects you need to develop numeration and arithmetic operations within contexts that lend themselves to flexible thinking.

(Teacher, Year 5)

The most important aspects of number sense were exemplified through the development of strategies that challenged the child to make decisions about which methods were reasonable and efficient. Children's understanding of the number system was shown in terms of ordering, notation, place value, grouping and patterning.

SUMMARY AND IMPLICATIONS FOR CLASSROOM PRACTICE

This chapter has focused our attention on critical aspects of mental computation and number sense in the transition to more formal processes. Number sense has been exemplified through exploration of patterns and relationships within the number system and arithmetical operations. The role of calculators was highlighted as an alternative to mechanical procedures and as an instrument in developing concepts of place value of decimals. Exemplars of student work and challenges for developing number sense have been framed so that children of varying abilities can respond at their own level. Extension activities were included, particularly those utilising the Internet, to provide open-ended challenges for the students.

The main approach used in the snapshots section was to integrate many different numerical processes and understandings within contexts that encourage meaningful learning. Critical aspects of number sense were highlighted: developing number sense through approximation and reasonableness of answers; mental, written and calculator-based strategies for solving computations; strategies for effective mental calculation and number fact knowledge (promoting addition and subtraction, multiplication and division strategies); moving from non-standard to standard written algorithms (addition, subtraction, multiplication and division); developing numerical relationships through a problem-based approach; and understanding that the number system is extendable and it is based on repeated groupings of ten including decimals.

The appropriateness of almost exclusive concentration on paper-and-pencil algorithmic techniques as critical to number learning was questioned, as many exemplars in the chapter showed how mental computation strategies promoted effective number concepts and relationships.

Teaching programs could incorporate the development of informal strategies rather than focusing only on mastering number facts and computational skills that may not relate to the child's level of development. Teachers could facilitate more meaningful learning by establishing links between addition, subtraction, multiplication and division. Perhaps the teaching of these processes in an integrated fashion, based on the child's mental computation strategies and experience of a range of related problem situations, might best reflect the natural development of these processes.

Mathematics curricula have encouraged the development of number sense for many years. The importance of the problem-solving or 'working mathematically' strands of syllabuses necessitates the learning of numerical concepts and processes within contexts and not as isolated skills. Developing meaningful and efficient mental strategies, and using calculators and the Internet to enhance the learning of arithmetical strategies, have been shown in this chapter as preferable to traditional techniques.

The following chapters will develop further the key aspects of number sense presented in this chapter through other content areas of mathematics such as fractions, ratio and proportion, measurement, space, and chance and probability.

ACTION AND REFLECTION

Refer to the number strand of your state's syllabus or use numeracy benchmarks (Curriculum Corporation, 2000). Look critically at the emphasis placed on the development of paper-and-pencil computations, mental computation and estimation, arithmetic and calculator-based strategies.

1. In your view, is there a balanced emphasis placed on each of these computational strategies? If not, which one is focused on more or less than the others?
2. Do you feel that the balance depicted in your state's syllabus is also the balance occurring in most primary classrooms in your state? Why do you think this is so?
3. Does your syllabus prescribe a standard algorithm to be taught for each of the four operations? Why do you think this is the case?

REFERENCES

Askew, M. (2003). Moving from mental arithmetic to mental computation: Lessons from England. *Proceedings of the Making Sense of Computation Conference* (pp. 6–12), 2 August. Brisbane: Origo Professional Development.

Australian Association of Mathematics Teachers (1997). *Numeracy = everyone's business: The report of the numeracy education strategy development conference.* Adelaide: Australian Association of Mathematics Teachers Inc.

Australian Association of Mathematics Teachers (2002). *Standards for excellence in teaching mathematics in Australian schools.* Adelaide: Australian Association of Mathematics Teachers Inc.

Baek, J. (1998). Children's invented algorithms for multidigit multiplication problems. In L. J. Morrow & M. J. Kenney (Eds), *The teaching and learning of algorithms in school mathematics* (pp. 151–161). Reston, Virginia: National Council of Teachers of Mathematics Inc.

Beishuizen, M. & Anghileri, J. (1998). Which mental strategies in the early number curriculum? A comparison of British ideas and Dutch views. *British Education Research Journal, 34*, 516–38.

Board of Studies, NSW (2002). *Mathematics K–6 Syllabus 2002.* Sydney: Board of Studies.

Boerst, T. A. & Schielack, J. F. (2003). Toward understanding of 'computational fluency'. *Teaching Children Mathematics, 9*(6), 292–306.

Booker, G., Bond, D., Swan, P. & Sparrow, L. (2003). *Teaching primary mathematics.* Sydney: Pearson Education.

Boulton-Lewis, G. (1993). An assessment of the processing load of some strategies and representations for subtraction used by teachers and young children. *Journal of Mathematical Behavior, 12*, 387–409.

Brownell, W. (2003). From NCTM's archives: Meaning and skill—maintaining the balance. *Teaching Children Mathematics, 9*(6), 310–318.

Burnett, J. & Irons, C. (1998a). *Teaching number facts using a number sense approach: Addition and subtraction.* Narangba, Qld: Prime Education.

Burnett, J. & Irons, C. (1998b). *Teaching number facts using a number sense approach: Multiplication and division.* Narangba, Qld: Prime Education.

Carpenter, T. P., Fennema, E., Franke, M. L., Levi, L. & Empson, S. (1999). *Children's mathematics: Cognitively guided instruction*. Portsmouth, New Hampshire: Heinemann.

Cobb, P., Wood, T., Yackel, E. & Perlwitz, M. (1992). A follow-up assessment of a second-grade problem-centred mathematics project. *Educational Studies in Mathematics, 23*, 483–504.

Cobb, P., Yackel, E. & McClain, J. (Eds) (2000). *Symbolizing and communicating in mathematics classrooms: Perspectives on discourse, tools, and instructional design*. Mahwah, New Jersey: Lawrence Erlbaum Associates.

Cooper, T., Heirdsfield, A. & Irons, C. (1996). Children's mental strategies for addition and subtraction word problems. In J. T. Mulligan & M. C. Mitchelmore (Eds), *Children's number learning* (pp. 147–163). Adelaide: Australian Association of Mathematics Teachers Inc.

Curriculum Corporation. (2000). *Numeracy benchmarks years 3, 5 & 7*. Melbourne: Curriculum Corporation.

Fuson, K. (2003). Toward computational fluency in multidigit multiplication and division. *Teaching Children Mathematics, 9*(6), 300–310.

Fuson, K., Wearne, D., Hiebert, J., Human, P., Murray, H., Olivier, A., Carpenter, T. & Fennema, E. (1997). Children's conceptual structures for multidigit numbers and methods of multidigit addition and subtraction. *Journal for Research in Mathematics Education, 28*, 25–47.

Heirdsfield, A. (2002). Mental methods moving along. *Australian Primary Mathematics Classroom, 7*(1), 4–9.

Hiebert, J. & Wearne, D. (1992). Links between teaching and learning place value with understanding in first grade. *Journal for Research in Mathematics Education, 23*, 98–122.

Kamii, C. & Dominick, A. (1998). The harmful effects of algorithms in grades 1–4. In L. J. Morrow & M. J. Kenney (Eds), *The teaching and learning of algorithms in school mathematics* (pp. 130–141). Reston, Virginia: National Council of Teachers of Mathematics Inc.

Lampert, M. (1990). Connecting inventions with conventions. The teacher's role in classroom communication about mathematics. In L. Steffe (Ed), *Transforming early childhood education* (pp. 253–265). Hillsdale, New Jersey: Lawrence Erlbaum Associates.

Markovits, Z. & Sowder, J. (1994). Developing number sense: An intervention study with grade 7. *Journal for Research in Mathematics Education, 25*, 4–29.

McClain, K. Cobb, P. & Bowers, J. (1998). A contextual investigation of three-digit addition and subtraction. In L. J. Morrow & M. J. Kenney (Eds), *The teaching and learning of algorithms in school mathematics* (pp. 141–150). Reston, Virginia: National Council of Teachers of Mathematics Inc.

McIntosh, A. (2003). Moving to mental: seven steps along the computational path. *Proceedings of the Making Sense of Computation Conference* (pp. 6–12), 2 August. Brisbane: Origo Professional Development.

McIntosh, A., De Nardi, E. & Swan, P. (2002). *Think mathematically*. Melbourne: Pearson Education.

McIntosh, A. & Dole, S. (2000). Early arithmetical learning and teaching. In K. Owens & J. Mousley (Eds), *Research in mathematics education in Australia 1996–1999* (pp. 215–243) Sydney: Mathematics Education Research Group of Australasia Inc.

McIntosh, A., Reys, B. & Reys, R. (1992). A proposed framework for examining number sense. *For the Learning of Mathematics, 12*(3), 2–8.

McIntosh, A., Reys, B., Reys, R., Bana, J. & Farrell, B. (1997). *Number sense in school mathematics: MASTEC Monograph Series No. 5*. Perth: Edith Cowan University.

Morony, W. & Brinkworth, P. (Eds) (2002). *Springboards to numeracy: Proceedings of the National Numeracy Conference*, 4–5 October. Hobart: Australian Association of Mathematics Teachers Inc.

Morrow, L. J. & Kenney, M. J. (Eds)(1998). *The teaching and learning of algorithms in school mathematics*. Reston, Virginia: National Council of Teachers of Mathematics Inc.

Mulligan, J. T. & Mitchelmore, M. C. (1996). Children's representations of multiplication and division word problems. In J. T. Mulligan & M. C. Mitchelmore (Eds), *Children's number learning* (pp. 163–185). Adelaide: Australian Association of Mathematics Teachers Inc.

National Council of Teachers of Mathematics (2000). *Principles and standards for school mathematics*. Reston, Virginia: National Council of Teachers of Mathematics, Inc.

Randolph, T. & Sherman, H. (2001). Alternative algorithms: Increasing options, reducing errors. *Teaching Children Mathematics, 7*(8), 480–486.

Wright R. J., Martland, J., Stafford, A. & Stanger, G. (Eds) (2002). *Teaching number: Advancing children's skills and strategies.* London: Sage.

88

Chapter 7

Integrating fractions, ratio and proportional reasoning

CHAPTER OVERVIEW

Rational numbers, both fraction and decimal forms, have always formed an important part or strand of the primary mathematics curriculum. Student difficulties with understanding fraction concepts and performing operations with fractions and decimals have been and remain a major concern for teachers, particularly in the middle to upper primary grades and well into secondary school (Litwiller & Bright, 2002). Attempts to restrict inclusion of fractions in the primary curriculum have often resulted in either delaying or limiting fraction work. In recent years there has been a move to include more basic fractions and decimals in the primary curricula (Board of Studies, NSW, 2002; National Council of Teachers of Mathematics, 2000).

However, extensive research has now shown that children's whole number concepts often interfere with their learning of rational numbers (Behr, Wachsmuth & Post, 1985; Streefland, 1984). Many of the problems associated with fraction learning are closely linked to difficulties in the way rational number concepts are taught in school. Proficiency with symbolic representations of fractions does not mean that students are able to apply fractions in problem situations or have depth of conceptual understanding (Goldin & Passantino, 1996). Other researchers have found that young children can solve problems involving sharing and partitioning successfully (Hunting & Davis, 1991; Lamon, 1996) and that children's intuitive ideas of fractions prior to instruction form an important basis for conceptual understanding (Empson, 2003; Lamon, 1999; Saenz-Ludlow, 1994, 1995; Watanabe, 1995; Watson, Campbell & Collis, 1996). Researchers now generally support the idea that basic rational number concepts can be developed much earlier than traditionally expected and that young children are capable of using and representing fractions and decimals in a wide range of situations.

Curricula have traditionally separated out the development of common and decimal fractions as a strand or substrand; in this book we have integrated a variety of learning experiences including part–whole relationships, fractions, decimals, ratio, percentages and averages throughout the chapters. This chapter describes some critical aspects of fraction concepts and exemplifies the idea of 'ratio', 'proportion' and 'rate'.

'Ratio' usually refers to comparison between two similar quantities or amounts, such as the number of times one amount is contained in the other. For example, 1 part cordial to 4 parts water means a ratio of 1 to 4 or 1:4 but there are 5 parts altogether. Similarly we refer to things being in 'proportion' where one aspect is compared with another, such as the width and length of a house. This refers to the ratio of one to the other, and we often describe things mathematically in terms of special proportions such as a square divided into smaller squares exactly in proportion. The notion of 'rate' usually refers to comparing one amount to another of a different type such as speed and time. In Chapters 5 and 6 we also referred to the idea of 'rate' as multiplication.

This chapter does not intend to provide a detailed sequence of curriculum outcomes for teaching fractions and decimals and operations with these. An emphasis will be placed on the development of conceptual understanding of fractions and decimals and the notion of ratio and proportion. The following aspects will be addressed:

+ the concept of fair share or fairness;
+ partitioning into unequal and equal parts;
+ one-to-one, one-to-many (many-to-one), and many-to-many co-ordination of units;
+ simple ratio beyond halving and doubling;
+ constructing, representing, ordering and comparing fractions and decimals;
+ co-ordinating fractions, decimals and percentages;
+ exploring the notion of 'rate' and 'average'.

Throughout the preceding chapters we have highlighted key resources for developing mathematical concepts. In particular Chapters 5 and 6 on number concepts and Chapter 3 on data exploration refer to a rich range of resources that can be utilised for the teaching and learning of fractions, ratio and proportional reasoning. Chapter 9 on chance and probability also refers to critical aspects of fraction and ratio concepts.

In this chapter we have highlighted again the importance of using the children's own representations of fractions, ratio and proportion based on real-life experiences. Some structured materials may be useful in linking children's concepts to formal representations, but we have not encouraged the teaching of fractions solely through diagrams and models such as fraction pies, fraction bars or area models. Rather, we have encouraged children to link their intuitive notions of fractions to more formal representations. The language of fractions is critical in this process.

Continuous models, such as lengths of string, quantities of liquids, fractions of time, space, events or money, can illustrate aspects of fractions, ratio and proportional reasoning. Situations involving the use of these models or aspects of these are a most valuable resource. Devising and experimenting with recipes and cooking provide ideal integrated learning experiences. Television, newspapers, magazines, grocery packaging and clothing measurements provide a rich source of representations about fractions, decimals, ratio and proportion. Students can compare the way quantities are represented diagrammatically and symbolically.

Chapter focus questions

In this chapter several key questions are raised in order to focus our attention on critical aspects of fractions and decimals, ratio and proportional reasoning. Traditionally young children in the first years of school have engaged in a sequence of learning experiences that match curriculum expectations, such as beginning with activities that focus on part of a whole and then part of a group, usually followed by identifying common fractions such as half and quarter. We might well ask how to cater for the child who can already visualise, order and represent fractional parts in a variety of contexts. Consider your responses to the following questions:

1. How can the teacher capitalise on the child's informal knowledge of fractions in order to challenge and motivate the child?
2. What are the fundamental strategies that children need to acquire in order to develop fraction concepts, ratio and proportional reasoning?
3. Should we encourage young children to explore and develop fraction concepts and the idea of simple ratio, traditionally delayed until the later years?
4. How can we use calculators to promote the development of effective fraction and decimal knowledge, ratio and proportional reasoning?

Throughout this chapter these questions will be addressed by examining examples of children's mathematical thinking and reflecting upon the research that has given rise to changes in the way we approach fraction learning.

REFLECTION ON A CLASSROOM SCENARIO

Understanding common fractions

In order to assess students' conceptual basis for working with fractions, Year 5 students were asked to identify the fraction which represents the largest amount: 5/6, 5/7, 5/8 or 5/9. Kathryn's response, shown in Figure 7.1, shows her misconceptions about part–whole relationships.

I think that it wood be $\frac{5}{9}$ because 9 is the bigger number than 8ths.

Figure 7.1 Kathryn represents and justifies her answer

Consider the following questions:

+ Why do you think she immediately chooses 5/9?
+ Do you think she has visualised the part–whole relationship between 5 parts out of 9 compared with 5 parts out of 8?
+ What does her representation of 5/9 tell you about her conceptual difficulties?
+ What strategies would you employ to assist her in visualising, representing and ordering fractions generally?

Later, the students were engaged in a range of activities where they were required to partition lengths of paper strip, pieces of paper, three-dimensional models made of plasticine and containers of liquid into equal parts. In doing this they realised an important idea: that the more parts you have, the smaller the size of the part, so that ninths must be smaller than eighths. Very often students react immediately to the numerical values always as whole numbers, without considering their meaning in different arrangements and symbolisations.

THE GROWTH OF MATHEMATICAL UNDERSTANDING

This section describes some key aspects of fraction learning, ratio and proportional reasoning: partitioning, equal grouping, co-ordinating units and symbolising fractions. These aspects are integrated with the development of whole number knowledge fundamental to the learning framework in number, which is summarised in Chapter 5, Exhibit 5.1. The development of number sense and mental computation also involves skills in estimating, judging the reasonableness of results, and using numbers and patterns flexibly with rational numbers.

Fractional quantities and proportional relationships must be seen as interrelated with other mathematical concepts. Research on the way children develop the idea of a 'unit' or an equal group and co-ordinate units was discussed in Chapter 5, and this is critical to the development of fraction knowledge. The way that children deal with units of one and ten influences their understanding of the number system based on groupings of ten. Co-ordinating ten as one unit is critical to co-ordination of units generally; thus simple fractions can be formed and co-ordinated on this basis. For example 2/3 is two units of 1/3 of one whole unit. These parts can be grouped, counted and used as units in themselves; for example, three-thirds make a whole.

Hunting and Davis (1991) describe three levels of fraction understanding for young children:

1. Fractions are formed from idiosyncratic and intuitive experiences that are context-bound and cannot be generalised to other situations. Children may form and recognise parts of a whole or quantity but there may be little recognition of the need for equal parts.
2. Fractions become less context-bound and the child recognises the formation and need for equal parts. The numerical representation of fractions may still be emerging and inconsistent.
3. Fractions can be represented as equal parts of a whole or quantity using icons (pictures, diagrams, contexts) and numbers and symbols.

Alongside this development is the important notion of co-ordinating units, which is fundamental to understanding ratio and proportion. Watanabe (1995) describes four types of co-ordination of units: one-as-one, one-as-many, many-as-one, and many-as-many. For example one-as-many and many-as-one schemes are complementary. In this assessment task the child must co-ordinate both units:

You can trade 2 small stickers for 1 large sticker. How many small stickers would you need to trade for 4 large stickers? How many small stickers would be worth 3 large stickers and 4 small stickers?

The many-as-many scheme is more complex where the child must co-ordinate a number of units with a number of other units. For example, a paper strip divided into 2 parts is the same length as the strip divided into 3 parts. Similarly 3 small stickers are worth 2 medium-sized stickers.

The growth of fraction ideas must involve more than the traditional notion of part–whole relationships and working with common fractions in symbolic form. The idea of co-ordinating units and establishing ways of representing ratio and proportion in simple situations, such as where relationships do not always involve halving and doubling, is critical to furthering children's understanding of fraction concepts.

Developing simple ratio

In the following activity the child is encouraged to work with simple ratio. Can the child establish the relative size of the medium frame to the large frame as a many-as-many co-ordination of units?

193

ACTIVITY 7.1

Enlargement

Josh is making three photo frames (small, medium and large) to fit his photos. The small frame is only 3 centimetres wide and 4 centimetres high. The medium frame is twice as big as the small frame, and the large frame is three times bigger than the small frame. Draw each frame showing the actual measurements.

Try this activity with your students and assess whether they use the multiplicative idea of twice as long, and three times as long.

- Do students multiply (or add) the length and width of the frames?
- Do they multiply only one dimension?
- How does this aspect of simple ratio relate to measurement and proportion?
- Why do students need to develop a multiplicative notion rather than an additive one?

Developing early fraction ideas through data exploration

The early development of fraction ideas must be integrated with children's experiences of data exploration. For example, in Chapter 3 the importance of representing and interpreting data was shown as fundamental to number learning. Early fraction ideas of part–whole relationships occur when children are involved in activities where they represent discrete and continuous data using invented symbols, tallies and notations. Figure 7.2 shows how Year 1 children took a teddy symbol puncher and used a tally to represent the number of teddies at a picnic using five units in a simultaneous count of fives. In this way the children are developing skip-counting skills along with the idea that a group of things, rather than one whole thing, can be partitioned into equal groups and counted in one-to-one matching or one-to-many matching. This is fundamental to the concept of 'ratio'. Later the children may be able to articulate that they have grouped the total number of 40 teddies into 8 equal groups or 'eighths'.

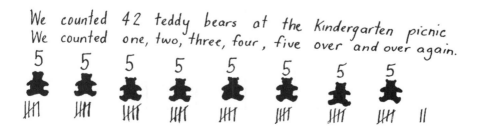

Figure 7.2 Teddy symbol used to count in fives with tally

The children have also been encouraged to produce their own representation of data where they have grouped, counted, ordered and compared.

Establishing fair shares

Several researchers have explored the concept of fair share as integral to the development of fraction ideas. Hunting and Davis (1991) and colleagues describe the preschoolers' notion of fair share and how this is a critical part of the development of fraction knowledge. Similar studies (Watson, Campbell & Collis, 1996) describe tasks where children are required to make fair shares:

+ Task 1: Cut a pancake so it can be shared fairly among three dolls.
+ Task 2: There are twelve marbles in a bag and two dolls, but there are three dolls coming to the party. Give the first doll to arrive at the party one-half of the marbles and the second doll one-third of the twelve marbles. How many marbles will the first doll get and how many will the second doll get?

The responses to these tasks show a complex development of understanding continuous (pancake) and discrete (marbles) fraction ideas. Try these tasks with your students from Kindergarten to middle primary grades and compare their types of response. Did the students show differences between the way they solved the pancake and marbles problems? Watson, Campbell and Collis (1996) found a development from simple sharing notions to the idea of fair share followed by the conservation of quantities. Later, children were able to compare equal and unequal fractional divisions of the same whole.

Partitioning

The following task, adapted from Lamon (1996), examines the child's ability to partition into halves, quarters and eighths, and assesses whether the child can co-ordinate partitioning of two whole shapes simultaneously.

There are two blocks of chocolate. Record how you would share all the chocolate fairly among 4 children so they each get the same (fair share).

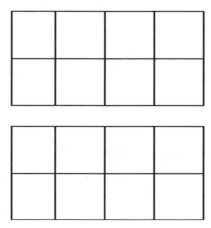

Repeat the task with a cardboard picture of two blocks of chocolate; the child shares one chocolate into four equal parts, two different ways by cutting up pieces and placing them on top.

Then repeat the process for two blocks of chocolate.

1. Does the child use halving strategies (vertical and horizontal)?
2. Does the child need to deal pieces one by one?
3. Does the child focus on sharing one chocolate at a time?
4. Can the child explain and label 1/2s, 1/4s?
5. Does the child want to fold the shape initially?

ACTIVITY 7.2

Halves and quarters

A group of Year 2 teachers discussed ways of representing simple fractions such as halves, quarters and thirds that moved away from traditional paper folding and cutting of simple objects such as fruit. A suggestion was made to expand children's notions of fractions to linear and continuous models.

The following tasks were initiated. Compare each of the teachers' suggestions.

1. (a) Use small coloured paper squares (slices of bread, circular pizza base as alternatives).
   (b) Justify that you have shown halves.
   (c) Show halves and quarters of the paper square. Is there any other way of showing halves?
2. (a) Use paper streamer/tape. Show halves and quarters of the paper streamer.
   (b) Justify the halves and quarters (fold or mark or tear).
3. (a) Use a clear container of water and four clear plastic cups.
   (b) Show a half and a quarter of the quantity of water.
   (c) Justify halves and quarters by using four cups.

■ What fundamental similarities and differences about fraction concepts are inherent in these examples?
■ How do these models influence the way children might partition or subdivide the quantities?

ACTIVITY 7.3

Finding equivalence between halves, quarters and eighths; fifths and tenths; tenths and hundredths

Students in Year 5 were asked to mark the following fractions on the strips. The idea was to enable comparison of fractions without using procedures for equivalence. Try the activity with your peers. What is the most important aspect of the activity? How could you develop this activity into problem-based situations?

Mark halves, quarters and eighths on each strip (consecutively).

Mark fifths and tenths.

Mark tenths and hundredths.

- Compare the size of the parts. Select different-sized fractional parts.
- Can the student estimate whether the parts will approximate one whole strip?
- Try an activity where the parts are added randomly by placing the segments (cut up) along one whole strip.
- Ask students to verify why a fifth is smaller than a quarter.

Developing understanding of decimals

The introduction of decimal fractions is often delayed until the middle primary grades, but moves to encourage the use of decimal notation using tenths and hundredths are supported by children's natural use of these and the demands of an increasingly technological society that relies on the use of decimal notation. Chapters 5 and 6 highlighted the importance of developing decimal number concepts through the use of calculators and open-ended investigations. In this chapter we refer to the comparison of common fractions and decimals using the notion of the bead string (see the snapshot 'Dealing with decimals' on p. 206). However, the development of decimal fractions should be integrated with the key aspects of fraction learning, ratio and proportion described here. When children are dealing with simple fractional parts they are often encouraged to use only common fraction notation. Instead, children can be encouraged to represent tenths and hundredths as one-to-many units just as tens and hundreds are described as co-ordinating units in Chapter 5. Using the calculator to reinforce place value is critical here.

ACTIVITY 7.4

Modelling, comparing and representing fractions and decimals: tenths and hundredths

A variety of materials is commonly used to show the important relationship between tenths, hundredths and thousandths. It is important that students understand that the place value system is a multiplicative system where each place shows multiplication by ten (to the left) and division by 10 (to the right). The following activity focuses on the idea of partitioning a whole into tenths and hundredths without the visual structure of rows and columns to show 100 equal parts. The students are required to construct tenths and hundredths.

■ To show hundredths, provide a paper square (or ask students to draw a square freehand). Students divide the square into 10 equal parts using rows or columns. Repeat to show 100 equal parts.

■ Do the students recognise that the process of creating much smaller parts (i.e. hundredths) is dividing each tenth into ten equal parts? Ask the students to imagine the iterative process of showing thousandths and so on.

■ To generate symbols for tenths and hundredths ask the students to divide 1 on their calculator by 10 and then by 10 again. Record the decimal notations that they have represented in their square. Use a calculator and enter $1 \div 100 = 0.01$; $1 \div 10 = 0.1$. Label parts of the square with decimal symbols.

ACTIVITY 7.5

Longer or shorter decimals: more or less?

Consider the idea that children may misconstrue the idea that decimals are 'special whole numbers' after a 'magic point' or that 'the longer the decimal the bigger it is; the shorter the decimal the smaller it is' (Stacey & Steinle, 1999).

Try to establish some connections between common fractions and decimals from an early age by using the calculator for tasks such as these:

■ Task 1: Try 2/3 as a decimal represented on the calculator. Encourage the child to round-off and explain that this fraction is about the same as 6-tenths or 66-hundredths. Can the child generate his or her own representation for this fraction in common and decimal form?

■ Task 2: Compare two different representations: 0.5111 and 0. 52. Which is larger? Why?

■ Task 3: Do you think there is anything between 0 and 1? Imagine what this might be and draw a picture of what you see between 0 and 1. Explain your picture.

Open-ended tasks such as Task 3 may provide more insight into how children form common fraction and decimal understandings and whether they relate these to a sequence of numbers. Do children establish a disconnected view of decimals and fractions as separate mathematical 'numbers' that have a 'life' of their own?

■ Task 4: This decimal challenge' introduces the difficult concept that multiplication by a fraction makes smaller, and division by a fraction makes bigger. Use calculators on a trial-and-error basis to multiply a selected number and arrive at a product in a given range. For example: What would 85 be multiplied by to get an answer between 20 and 30? What would 110 be multiplied by to get an answer around 90?

Using operations involving decimals

There has been much research interest in identifying difficulties students have with solving multiplication and division problems, especially when a decimal fraction less than one is involved. By the upper primary grades students are expected to solve problems involving decimals. Many problem situations are related also to students' knowledge of measurement concepts and an understanding of measurement facts such as 1000 metres = 1 kilometre. A sound understanding of numeration is needed to combine these aspects in problem situations. Many students find difficulty in solving the problems shown in Exhibit 7.1. The difficulties have much to do with not being able to estimate the effect of multiplying by a decimal. Figures 7.3 to 7.6 show examples of children's additive strategies for multiplication and division problem situations.

EXHIBIT 7.1 MULTIPLICATION OF DECIMAL PROBLEMS

■ Equal groups (length)

Susan used 3 pieces of ribbon each 4.6 metres long. How much ribbon did she use altogether?

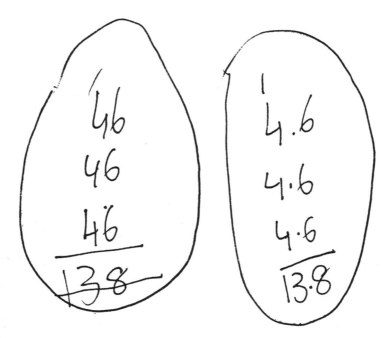

Figure 7.3 Susan's representation of 3 times 4.6 metres

■ Rate (speed)

A girl walked at an average speed of 4 kilometres per hour for 3.2 hours. How far did she walk?

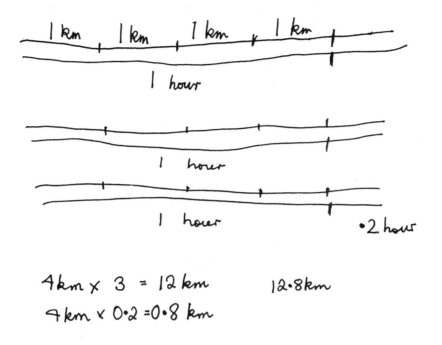

Figure 7.4 Camille's calculations and drawing of distance

• Comparison (mixture)

A painter mixes a special colour by using 3.2 times as much red as yellow paint. How much red paint should the painter use with 4 litres of yellow paint?

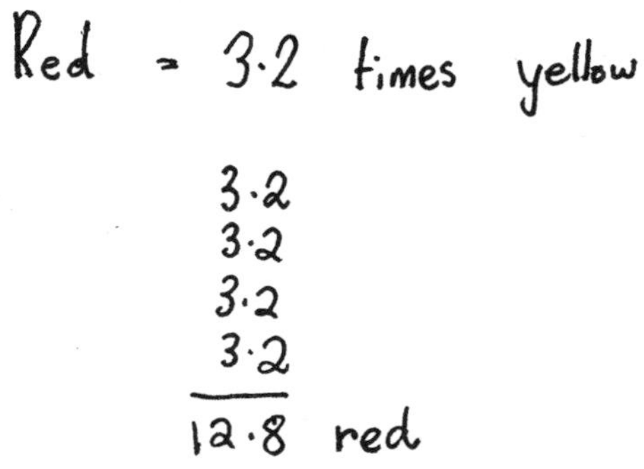

$$Red = 3.2 \text{ times yellow}$$

$$
\begin{array}{r}
3 \cdot 2 \\
3 \cdot 2 \\
3 \cdot 2 \\
3 \cdot 2 \\
\hline
12 \cdot 8 \text{ red}
\end{array}
$$

Figure 7.5 Peter's representation of 3.2 times as much paint

■ Enlargement

A photograph is made bigger (enlarged) 3 times its size. If the length of the original photograph is 5.3 centimetres, what will be the length of the big photograph?

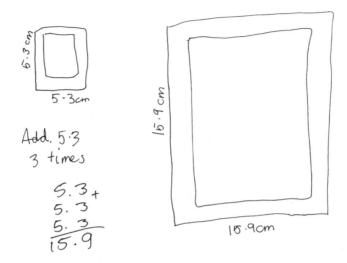

Figure 7.6 Tom's picture of the enlarged photograph and use of repeated addition

The difficulties that children experienced with operating on decimals warrant teaching emphasis on helping children to represent decimals and to solve a wide range of problem situations. Another aspect highlighted by researchers is the misconception about 'multiplication makes bigger', and 'division makes smaller'. In the Snapshots of Learning section we will examine this aspect. As well, many children experienced difficulties because of inefficient counting, or poor number fact and estimation strategies. Multiplying mixed numbers involving whole numbers and decimals also requires the children to represent the part–whole relationships shown in the quantities. This was difficult for some children who had little understanding of decimal place value. Teachers may need to identify which difficulties most influence children's responses to multiplication and division tasks.

SNAPSHOTS OF LEARNING: LESSON PLANNING AND ASSESSMENT

This section highlights some key aspects of common and decimal fractions, ratio and proportional reasoning. The first snapshot, 'Soft toy collection', focuses on representing a collection in one-to-one correspondence and as a one-to-ten ratio. The idea of one-to-many matching is extended in 'Making links with Lego® and Duplo®'. The notion of ratio as a fraction is developed in 'Food fractions'. 'Dealing with decimals' explores ways of constructing 100 equal parts and relating these to common fractions, percentages and graphs. An example of challenging students to think about the effect of multiplying or dividing involving decimals is included. A complex range of skills and understandings follows in Sandhill race, which shows a real-life problem involving number sense, ordering and interpreting data using decimal notation, applying calculation strategies and finding averages. 'Bowling strike rates' uses an Internet site to explore the concept of rate in the final snapshot.

1. Soft toy collection

Years K, 1, 2 and 3 students sorted, counted, organised and represented data on soft toy collections in picture graphs (Figure 7.7) using a symbol or tally to represent more than one unit.

Figure 7.7 Chris (8 years) uses a teddy symbol to represent twenty-five soft toys as a picture graph. He shows the direct relationships between the symbol and the toys and recognises that the symbol can be used independently

Each time I press the puncher
it means I have counted 10 soft toys
1 teddy = 10
3 teddies = 30
If I have 5 soft toys
it equals half a teddy
alltogether I have 25 toys!

Teachers' comments

> *I got my students to use a calculator, and a hole puncher or (self-inking) stamp to count and record collections in one-to-one correspondence. Then they made equal groups like 2s or 5s or 10s to make it easier to count, but it was harder to co-ordinate the puncher on the count of 2 or 5 or 10.*

(Teacher, Year 2)

> *Some children didn't draw the picture graph from a baseline so counting was more difficult. They had to come up with several drafts and reasons for why it is easier to count when organised in one-to-one correspondence.*

(Teacher, Year 1)

Mathematical content and processes
+ Sorts, classifies and records small or large collection of soft toys.
+ Counts collection by ones using one-to-one correspondence with a hand-held calculator as a tally.
+ Uses language of comparison to describe data.

+ Uses a symbol to directly represent actual objects in a picture graph where one symbol represents 10 units.
+ Calculates total number of toys represented by symbols by using simple ratio 1:5 and 1:10.
+ Makes comparisons between two different data sets (two different collections).

Posing key questions to assess learning
+ Can you count and organise collections according to one-to-many matching, such as one to five?
+ What do you notice when you draw a baseline using one-to-one correspondence to represent some data as a picture graph?
+ Can the 'toy collection' be reclassified according to two things (characteristics)?
+ Try to draw the data in a table or as a diagram. Pose some open and closed questions about the data from the graph.
+ Can you suggest ways of classifying the collections according to two or more characteristics, such as large and small toys?
+ How did you demonstrate the use of a symbol to represent more than one unit with different data?

Extending the investigation
+ Children could classify other collections and experiment with different forms of representation where one symbol or icon represents more than one unit, such as self-adhesive stickers, self-inking stamps or self-designed symbols, or real objects, for example one drink container represents ten drinks.
+ Make a collection of graphs from the print media that use symbols representing more than one unit and discuss the suitability of their use. Suggest other types of symbols that would be appropriate.
+ Design self-generated symbols or use computer-based programs that can represent information on large samples, for example one house symbol represents 1000.
+ Conduct a simple survey on the number of types of soft toys owned by children in the class, grade level or school.
+ Pose and answer questions related to the type and frequency of soft toy preferences.
+ Record the data in a number of different graphs. Suggest ideas for distributing a fraction of the soft toys, for example to more needy children at Christmas.

2. Making links with Lego® and Duplo®

Years 3 and 4 students were investigating 3D space by building models with Lego® and Duplo® blocks. They compared the number of large Duplo blocks to the number of Lego blocks to build a model of the same size and volume.

In Figure 7.8 Andrea directly compares the blocks to work out the ratio of Duplo® to Lego® blocks.

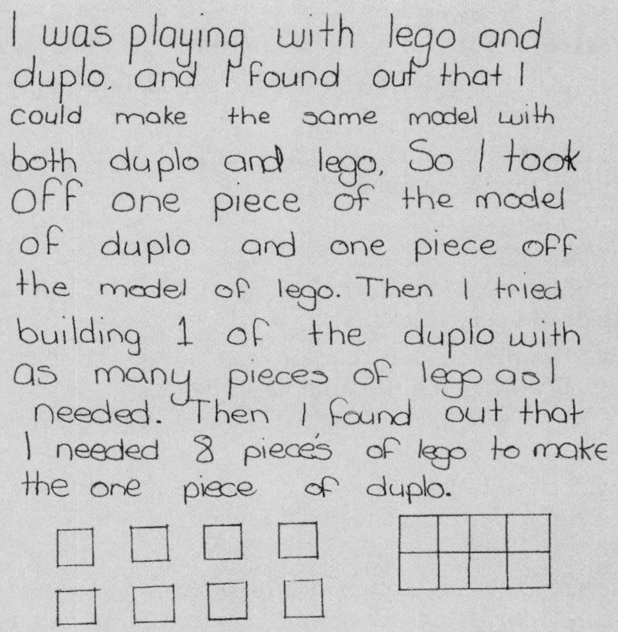

I was playing with lego and duplo, and I found out that I could make the same model with both duplo and lego, So I took off one piece of the model of duplo and one piece off the model of lego. Then I tried building 1 of the duplo with as many pieces of lego as I needed. Then I found out that I needed 8 pieces of lego to make the one piece of duplo.

Figure 7.8 Andrea's explanation of her models

Teachers' comments

This activity helped the students with understanding volume as well as comparing Duplo® to Lego®. They had to check that the Lego® model took up exactly the same amount of space as the Duplo® model. We could also use the multiplication idea that one Duplo® block is eight times bigger than one Lego® block and then I could set them to work on other tasks using this comparison.

(Teacher, Year 4)

The students could easily see the comparison because they could build it and manipulate the model to check.

(Teacher, Year 3)

Mathematical content and processes
+ Makes direct comparisons between 3D objects.
+ Uses and explains many-to-one and one-to-many co-ordination as 8 Lego® to 1 Duplo®, and 1 Duplo® to 8 Lego®.
+ Conserves volume of 3D shapes (recognises that the same amount of space is occupied when using different-sized units).
+ Visualises 3D models and calculates volume in Lego® or Duplo® units where blocks are hidden.
+ Represents models as diagrams or 3D sketches showing units.
+ Uses multiplication or division to describe the relationship between models; for example, the Lego® model uses eight times as many blocks as the Duplo® model.

+ If the model was rearranged as a different shape, how many blocks would you have?
+ If you used Lego® and Duplo® bricks to build your model, how many Lego® bricks would it equal, and how many Duplo®?
+ If you doubled or halved the number of Duplo® bricks, how would you work out the number of Lego® bricks that were needed?

Extending the investigation
+ Draw a table showing the number of Lego® bricks and Duplo® bricks needed to build models with multiples of Lego® bricks.
+ Build some Lego® and Duplo® models that are one-half or one-third the size of each other. Explain how you worked out the number of blocks.

3. Food fractions

Years 5 and 6 students were exploring a thematic unit on health and were shown a food and nutrition pyramid (Figure 7.9). Using the notion of 'serves', the children were asked to compare the layers (categories) of the pyramid in terms of ratio, which was their current topic (see Figure 7.10).

The teacher suggested that the class consider just two categories in the food pyramid—say, bread and milk—and express any comparisons using the language 'times as much' or the language of fractions.

Mathematical content and processes
+ Interprets and compares data modelled as 'serves' or units.
+ Uses common fractional notation to express simple ratio.
+ Uses understanding of multiplication as equal groups to compare number of serves.
+ Uses language and notation of ratio to make comparisons.

Posing key questions to assess learning
+ How did you use the pyramid to estimate the ratio of 'serves'?
+ Explain why the number of serves is optional and the ratio of one food type to another can be compared and changed.
+ Compare two or more categories in the food pyramid and explain the ratio of one to another.

Extending the investigation
+ Devise a food pyramid that you think is balanced and explain the way the 'unit' is used to calculate serves.
+ Use ratio notation to compare the food and nutrition plan (e.g. 1: 2: 3).
+ Use alternative notation for comparisons within the food pyramid: percentages, proportions, decimals.

204

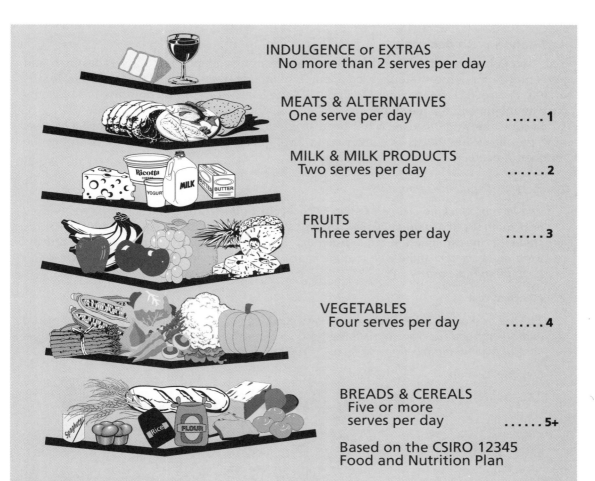

INDULGENCE or EXTRAS
No more than 2 serves per day

MEATS & ALTERNATIVES
One serve per day 1

MILK & MILK PRODUCTS
Two serves per day 2

FRUITS
Three serves per day 3

VEGETABLES
Four serves per day 4

BREADS & CEREALS
Five or more
serves per day ......5+

Based on the CSIRO 12345
Food and Nutrition Plan

Figure 7.9 Food pyramid

Source: Reproduced with the permission of CSIRO and the Cancer Council South Australia

We were learning about the food pyramid at school and it suggested 2 serves of milk and 6 serves of bread a day. So if we just bread and milk and we had to work out the fraction of the milk and bread it would be 2 milk and 6 bread, so 8 serves altogether. 3 times more bread than milk cause 2×3=6, 2 out of 8 is 2/8 or 1/4.

6 out of 8 is 6/8 or 3/4.

Milk is 1/4, bread is 3/4 of what I have.

Figure 7.10 Jessica's (Year 5) interpretation of the food pyramid

205

4. Dealing with decimals

Year 6 students were investigating ways of representing common fractions as decimals and percentages. First, the students used a length of tape marked in equal parts to show tenths of 100. Figure 7.11 shows how 1/4 and 1/3 were marked easily as portions of an arc by curving the tape into a pie shape.

Second, the students used a 100-bead string to show 100 equal parts. Figure 7.12 shows how '25 out of 100' beads is converted to 25%. The students can check by counting the number of beads.

Teachers' and students' comments

> *The idea of marking a tape or strip of cardboard into 10 equal parts can be easily used next to strips showing equivalent fractions (e.g. 1/2 = 50 or 50 parts of 100). Then the students can estimate the other fractions. Joining the strip as a circle helped students wanting to see the connection to a pie chart. I'd use the strip idea again even if we didn't turn it into a pie graph.*

(Teacher, Year 5)

> *The use of the 100-bead string was a very good way of physically comparing parts of 100 and other fractions. You can use the bead string just as a length anyway. The curving is helpful for making fractions as parts of 100 or as decimals.*

(Teacher, Year 5)

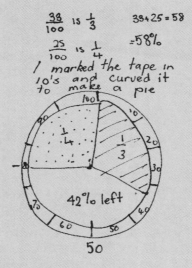

Figure 7.11 Tape marked in tenths of 100 and joined as a pie diagram

Mathematical content and processes

+ Uses linear (tape and strip) representation of tenths as segments of 100 and writes tenths as decimals.

+ Estimates and compares tenths and hundredths with simple common fractions using a 'region' model (pie chart).

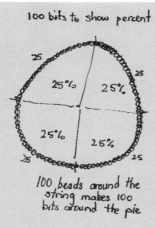

Figure 7.12 Bead diagram and graph

+ Converts common fractions to decimals and percentages by direct modelling (100-bead string).
+ Represents data in various forms on a pie chart.

Posing key questions to assess learning
+ Use a calculator to find out how to change the common fractions 1/2, 1/4, 1/3, 1/5 to decimals or parts of 100. List the ways you tried to change 1/2 into 0.5 or 50 out of 100. Explain how you got 0.5 on your calculator. Why do you think your method works?
+ What is the connection between decimal notation such as 0.5 and 50%?
+ Can you order the following fractions from smallest to largest? Use the 100-bead string and a pie chart to help you:

    2/3, 2/5, 1/2, 3/4

    Draw a pie chart to represent each fraction.

Extending the investigation
+ You have to explain to a friend how to compare a common fraction, a decimal and a percentage such as 1/2, 0.5 and 50%. Use as many different situations as you can think of to show the comparison.
+ Use a calculator to discover an efficient way of changing common fractions into decimals. Try easy examples first (e.g. 1/2 is 1 ÷ 2 = 0.5). Now try the same process with mixed numbers such as 1 1/2 and 3/2. Why are these the same amount?

5. Multiplying and dividing: bigger or smaller?

A group of very able Year 6 students were testing the misconceptions that 'multiplication makes bigger' and 'division makes smaller'. The following examples were given. Students were asked to estimate, indicate the process and say whether the answer would be bigger or smaller. After estimating they used calculators to investigate and check their solutions.

Then they generated their own examples to test.

$10 \div 2$	12×2	$12 \div 2$	16×4	$16 \div 4$	10×5	$10 \div 5$
$2 \div 10$	12×0.2	$12 \div 0.2$	$16 \div 0.4$	$16 \div 0.4$	$10 \div 0.5$	$10 \div 0.5$

Teachers' and student's comments

> *When the students compared $12 \div 2$ with $12 \div 0.2$ (a decimal less than 1) they really got stuck. It was important to let them explore it with a calculator, but they also needed to understand that the answer would be much larger than 12.*

> **(Teacher, Year 6)**

> *Some could see it was bigger because there are 5 lots of 0.2 to make 1, so it would be 5 lots of 12 to make 60.*

> **(Teacher, Year 6)**

> *I worked it out by thinking that 0.2 is 2 tenths. 12×0.2 is 12×2-tenths and then 24-tenths is 2.4.*

> **(Student, Year 6)**

Mathematical content and processes
+ Recognises that multiplication does not always mean bigger and division does not always mean smaller.
+ Recognises that multiplying a whole number by a decimal fraction less than one will always result in a number less than the whole number (dividend).
+ Recognises that dividing a whole number by a simple decimal fraction less than one will always result in a number more than the whole number (multiplier).
+ Divides a smaller number by a larger number; the answer (quotient) is a fraction of the smaller number and can be expressed as a decimal (e.g. $2 \div 4 = 0.5$).
+ Makes sensible approximations when multipying and dividing by a decimal less than 1.
+ Uses a calculator to explore and record patterns when multiplying and dividing, for example:
    $2 \div 1 = 2$
    $2 \div 2 = 1$
    $2 \div 3 = 2/3$ or 0.66

Posing key questions to assess learning
+ Explain the difference between $10 \div 2$ and $2 \div 10$. Use a diagram or picture to explain your thinking. Write a number story for each example.
+ Why is 10×0.5 one-tenth of 10×5? Make up some examples to show that this can be a pattern such as $10 \times 0.1 = 1$. What would come next in the pattern?

Mark (Year 6 student) described the way he solved $10 \div 0.5$ as 'how many halves are in 10?' and explained that you 'break up ten into halves so you would have twenty 0.5s'. Would you explain to a friend how to solve the problem this way? Can you think of another explanation? Draw a picture to show your thinking.

Extending the investigation

+ Use your calculator to continue this pattern:

$1 \div 0.1 = 10$

$2 \div 0.2 =$

What do you think the answer will be for $20 \div 0.2$? Describe your own method for working this out each time.

+ Look at the example in Figure 7.13. Do you think Holly's explanation and method is convincing? Why? Why not?

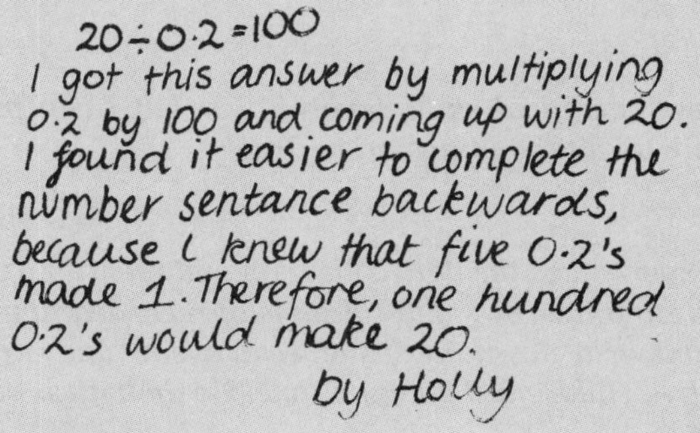

$20 \div 0.2 = 100$
I got this answer by multiplying
0.2 by 100 and coming up with 20.
I found it easier to complete the
number sentence backwards,
because I knew that five 0.2's
made 1. Therefore, one hundred
0.2's would make 20.
by Holly

Figure 7.13 Holly's method for dividing by a decimal

6. Sandhill race

Years 3, 4, 5 and 6 students in a 'family grouping' conducted an investigation and recorded, tabulated and interpreted time (in seconds to two decimal places) to find averages.

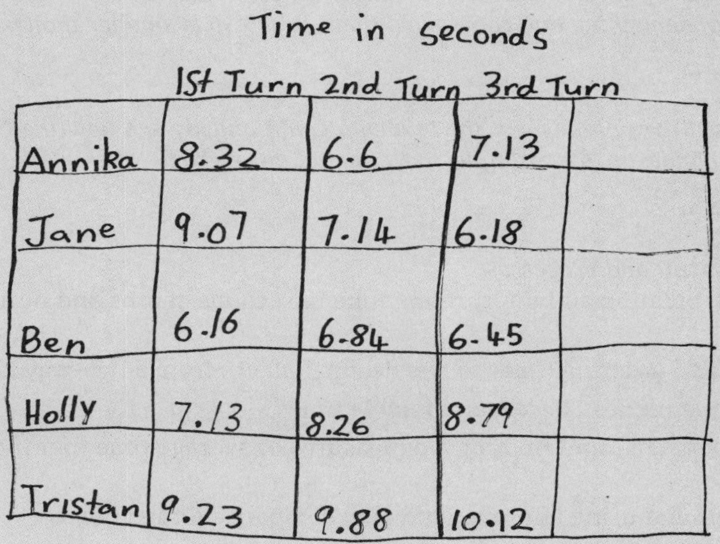

Time in Seconds

	1st Turn	2nd Turn	3rd Turn	
Annika	8.32	6.6	7.13	
Jane	9.07	7.14	6.18	
Ben	6.16	6.84	6.45	
Holly	7.13	8.26	8.79	
Tristan	9.23	9.88	10.12	

Figure 7.14 Ben's recording of the sandhill race in a table

Annika, Jane, Ben, Holly and Tristan took turns to run up the sandhill at the beach (see Figure 7.14). Annika and Jane timed each run on Jane's watch. They had three turns each. Ben recorded the times. The children compared the results and posed questions in discussion with the teacher. The following questions were devised by the children:

1. Who was the fastest runner overall?
2. Record the three best times in order.
3. Who improved their time on each turn?
4. On the third turn, by how much did Jane beat Ben?
5. About how much slower was Tristan than Ben on each turn?
6. By how much did Annika improve her time on her second turn?

Teachers' comments

> *There are so many mathematical skills involved . . . but I can pinpoint any difficulties if I ask the child to talk about the information first.*

(Teacher, Year 4)

> *If children have not experienced the data collection and recording in a table then they may have difficulty interpreting the rows and columns of recorded times . . . but you could ask children to imagine and write down the sequence of events and explain the race times, for example there were five children; their race time for their first go is in the first column downwards in seconds.*

(Teacher, Year 5)

> *Younger children could not interpret the meaning of decimal fractions but could interpret whole seconds and use a calculator to assist with calculation.*

(Teacher, Year 3)

> *What if children just show difficulty with comparing and ordering decimals and describing these in terms of faster and slower times? They need to work with data showing hundredths of something and comparing them (e.g. 6.56 is smaller than 6.59 seconds).*

(Teacher, Year 6)

> *When we used the spreadsheet the students could quickly see how the changes in data caused the changes in, for example, the sum and the average.*

(Teacher, Year 6)

Mathematical content and processes

+ Recording, tabulating and interpreting time in seconds, tenths and hundredths of a second.
+ Comparing and ordering times to two decimal places from a two-way table.
+ Identifying the highest, lowest and middle times.
+ Using number sense and finding two measures of average time (per individual, per race).
+ Rounding-off and using approximations to compare average time.
+ Using addition, subtraction, multiplication and division calculations to find exact totals, differences and averages.

- Using and interpreting the language of comparison.
- Regrouping 100 hundredths of a second as 1 second and explaining differences between 60 seconds in a minute and fractions of a second to two decimal places.
- Rounding-off fractions of a second to the whole second to find approximate times in order to make comparisons.

Posing key questions to assess learning
- Can you estimate the average by rounding-off? Can you use a calculator to calculate and check your answers?
- Can you show how you calculate average time per child and per race?
- Explain that seconds can be measured very accurately in tenths and hundredths of a second and these can be displayed as decimals on a watch.
- Why should time be measured in seconds to two decimal places?
- Can you work co-operatively in a group and participate fully in the interpretation process? Can you record your findings systematically?

Extending the investigation
- Predict and record the data for three more turns based on the outcomes of the first three turns.
- List as many facts as you can about the race, based on the data given in the table.
- Draw another table showing the information in another way, such as 'best race time for each child'.
- Draw a graph representing the data in the table and your predictions for the next three turns.
- Which type of graph would be most suitable to show this information? Why?
- Repeat the investigation. Compare the times for running uphill to running on a flat surface. What did you find? Did each person improve his or her time for each run? Why? Why not?
- Estimate the average speed for a child to run up the hill.

More challenging investigations
- Use a stopwatch, clock or wristwatch to monitor and record the time of a variety of simple events in minutes, seconds, and fractions of a second.
- Conduct some investigations by posing questions such as 'Is the tallest person the fastest runner?' Collect and represent your data to justify your answer.
- Collect data on race times from a variety of sporting events. How many different sports record time to hundredths of a second? Record your information in a table and a graph.

7. Bowling strike rates

Year 6 students are using the Internet to investigate bowling 'strike rates' and 'economy rates' of current Australian cricketers.

Year 6 is studying a thematic unit on sport. The class has already explored 'averages' and, with their teacher, the students have calculated and discussed many sporting averages. While watching a television broadcast of a test cricket match between Australia and India, the students hear reference to 'economy rate' and 'strike rate' for bowling. The teacher asks them to explore what it means in terms of other 'rates' the class has considered.

> *We thought about rates again: water rates, interest rates and land rates. Our teacher reminded us that rates compared different units of measurement, so we thought a bowling rate might be about wickets versus runs or maybe overs bowled. They were different types of things. We found a website on Australian cricket.*

> *http://www.aus.cricket.org*

> *There were lots of statistics, but you couldn't tell how they got the rates. We looked at Aussie bowlers and our teacher helped us set up a new table from the site.*

Bowler	Overs bowled	Runs	Wickets
Lee	27	103	2 (10nb)
Bracken	28	71	1
Williams	20	66	1 (1w)
MacGill	15	70	3 (1nb)
Katich	4	18	1
Waugh	9	35	1

> *Playing around dividing on the calculator you get 103 ÷ 27 = 3.81, (that's called 'eco rate'): how many runs per over are conceded. Runs and overs are different: rates again! The teacher explained that it was a rate showing how 'economical' a bowler was: again the smaller the better! 'Eco' is economy.*

Teachers' comments

> *A great motivational approach: kids love cricket. Rates are difficult for kids at this age, but the bowling rates gave them a handle. You've got to eliminate the superfluous data on the website, set up a modified table and provide calculators. It's important that the children use estimation and prediction when using calculators to divide.*

> **(Teacher, Year 6)**

> *It's good for exploring rounding decimals, and when the number of balls is not divisible by 6, it's a brilliant discussion point for decimal conventions in cricket. Just what is 6.4 overs?! Decimals are sometimes used incorrectly and this is just as important. 'Strike rate' is a more difficult concept: try more divisions later and, again, see if they can interpret the decimal quotients. They'll need help and prompts.*

> **(Central School Maths Head Teacher working with Year 6)**

Mathematical content and processes

+ Has awareness of rate as a comparison of unlike quantities.

+ Uses calculators to explore, estimate, predict and interpret rates.

212

+ Calculates and expresses rates, using correct units of measurement.
+ Selects conventional language to express comparisons in context.
+ Rounds decimals appropriately and appreciates the potential misuse of decimal values.
+ Understands the relationship between rates and averages.

Posing key questions to assess learning
What strategies do the students select in order to:

+ discover appropriate data for calculating rates, especially in sport?
+ shift data to generate calculations that expose appropriate rates?
+ calculate rates using correct language?
+ interpret rates and use them in context for decision making?

Extending the investigation
+ Children could explore data on rates for Test series matches, while enhancing their web-search skills (for example, www.cricinfo.com.au).
+ Discussion of the implications of 'economy' and 'strike' rates might enhance a simulated team selection based on bowling and batting rates, especially for limited over internationals.
+ Analysis of data in sport could enhance children's understanding of the link between rates, ratio, percentages and averages, which are used extensively, especially in cricket.

SUMMARY AND IMPLICATIONS FOR CLASSROOM PRACTICE

This chapter has focused our attention on critical aspects of fractions and decimals, ratio and proportional reasoning. The development of these concepts and processes involves a range of complex and interrelated mathematical ideas. These aspects have been explored in terms of encouraging children to build upon their intuitive notions of fractions. The examples have provided a basis for examining how base ten and arithmetical strategies have been linked to developing fraction and ratio concepts.

Assessing children's potential for learning about fractions more explicitly will fuel the need to remove more boundaries and create opportunities for earlier learning of fractions and related concepts, which are traditionally delayed until the later years of schooling. As stated earlier, it is not our intention to provide a detailed sequence of curriculum outcomes for teaching fractions, decimals and operations. Instead, an emphasis is placed on the development of conceptual understanding of fractions and decimals and how this relates to the notion of ratio and proportion. Many of the ideas fundamental to conceptual understanding of fractions have been highlighted here and in other chapters: the importance of fair share or fairness; partitioning into unequal and equal parts; one-to-one, one-to-many (many-to-one) and many-to-many co-ordination of units; representing and finding equivalent fractions and decimals; operations on decimals; and links to percentages.

The construction and representation of fractions and decimals from the child's viewpoint must be assessed so that instruction can match the child's potential for learning more complex ideas. Research is now pointing to the need for a review of the way educators perceive the relative difficulty of fractions, decimals, ratio and proportional reasoning. No longer should we be restricted by the views that these aspects are too difficult and out of bounds for most students. By focusing on integrating fraction learning within the whole number framework in the early years, new opportunities for young learners and an increased awareness of the potential of students to grasp fraction concepts will emerge.

ACTION AND REFLECTION

At the start of this chapter it was stated that 'attempts to restrict inclusion of fractions in the primary curriculum have often resulted in either delaying or limiting fraction work' in some states and territories. Refer to your state's syllabus and locate the section on decimal fractions.

1. Does it deal with operations such as multiplying and dividing with fractions or with operations involving mixed numbers?
2. Why do you think some states or territories have decided to limit this type of fraction work at the primary school level? Why do you think they have not applied the same restrictions with decimal numbers?
3. Discuss with a partner your views about whether or not it is a necessary limitation to the primary school syllabus.

REFERENCES

Behr, M. J., Wachsmuth, I. & Post, T. R. (1985). Construct a sum: A measure of children's understanding of fraction size. *Journal for Research in Mathematics Education, 16*, 120–131.

Board of Studies, NSW. (2002). *Mathematics K-6 Syllabus 2002*. Sydney: Board of Studies, NSW.

Empson, S. (2003). Low-performing students and teaching fractions for understanding: An interactional analysis. *Journal for Research in Mathematics Education, 34*, 305–343.

Goldin, G. A. & Passantino, C. B. (1996). A longitudinal study of children's fraction representations and problem-solving behaviour. In L. Puig & A. Gutierrez (Eds), *Proceedings of the 20th Annual Conference of the International Group for the Psychology of Mathematics Education*, Vol. 3 (pp. 3–10). University of Valencia: Program Committee.

Hunting, R. P. & Davis, G. (1991). *Early fraction learning*. New York: Springer-Verlag.

Lamon, S. J. (1996). The development of unitizing: Its role in children's partitioning strategies. *Journal for Research in Mathematics Education, 27*, 170–193.

Lamon, S. (1999). *Teaching fractions and ratios for understanding: Essential content knowledge and instructional strategies for teachers*. Mahwah: New Jersey: Lawrence Erlbaum Associates.

Litwiller, B. & Bright, G. (2002). *Making sense of fractions, ratio and proportions*. Reston, Virginia: National Council of Teachers of Mathematics.

National Council of Teachers of Mathematics. (2000). *Principles and standards for school mathematics*. Reston, Virginia: National Council of Teachers of Mathematics.

Saenz-Ludlow, A. (1994). Michael's fractions schemes. *Journal for Research in Mathematics Education, 25*, 50–85.

Saenz-Ludlow, A. (1995). Ann's fraction schemes. *Educational Studies in Mathematics, 28*, 101–132.

Stacey, K. & Steinle, V. (1999). A longitudinal study of children's thinking about decimals: A preliminary analysis. In O. Zaslavsky (Ed), *Proceedings of the 23rd Annual Conference of the International Group for the Psychology of Mathematics Education*, Vol. 4 (pp. 233 –240). Haifa, Israel: Psychology of Mathematics Education Program Committee.

Streefland, L. (1984). Unmasking N-distractors as a source of failures in learning fractions. In B. Southwell, R. Eyland, M. Cooper, J. Conroy & K. Collis (Eds), *Proceedings of the 8th International Conference for the Psychology of Mathematics Education* (pp. 142–154). Sydney: International Group for the Psychology of Mathematics Education.

Watanabe, T. (1995). Coordination of units and understanding of simple fractions: Case studies. *Mathematics Education Research Journal, 7*(2), 160–175.

Watson, J. M., Campbell, K. J. & Collis, K. F. (1996). Fairness and fractions in early childhood. In P. Clarkson (Ed), *Technology in mathematics education: Proceedings of the 19th Annual Conference of the Mathematics Education Research Group of Australasia*. Melbourne: Mathematics Education Research Group of Australasia.

Chapter 8
Using measurement to make links

CHAPTER OVERVIEW

Measurement concepts are frequently needed in typical day-to-day events and activities. When cooking we measure ingredients; when driving we are required to estimate distances and the relationship between distances and the speed of other cars. Generally, measurement is associated with estimates rather than with the measurement of exact quantities. We attempt to drive at about 60 kilometres per hour in many areas—if we worried about keeping the speedometer on '60' we would surely have an accident. An appreciation of the important principles associated with measurement concepts should be explored before a more formal study of those concepts. This chapter introduces a number of measurement understandings by describing:

1. general principles of measurement;
2. useful activities concerned with these principles; and
3. insights into the way children respond to these activities.

A range of measurement ideas are presented in this chapter. These complement many activities shown in other chapters where important relationships between concepts are emphasised. As this chapter title suggests, measurement experiences provide opportunities for links to other areas. The activities described in this chapter will link measurement principles to other areas of mathematics, and across other Key Learning Areas (KLA). Children's insights into these activities will be applied to everyday problem-solving situations.

Measurement is an essential component of the school mathematics curriculum. In fact, the National Council of Teachers of Mathematics (1989), *Curriculum and evaluation standards* stated that 'measurement is of central importance to the curriculum because of its power to help children see that mathematics is useful in everyday life and to help them develop many mathematical concepts and skills' (p. 51).

It is essential that measurement activities are based around everyday life experiences. Measurement concepts should begin with what children already know. When considering notions of time, for example, it may be useful to begin with cyclic descriptions of the four seasons or experiences of 'day' and 'night'. Young children come to school with intuitive notions of 'more', 'less', and 'the same'. Interestingly, it is recognised (Australian Education Council, 1991) that children have a better understanding of a 'positive' member of a pair than its 'negative' member (e.g. tall before short). This is most likely due to the language used by the child: 'I can run faster than you', 'I am getting very tall' or 'May I have some more drink please?' As a result, children should be encouraged to make comparisons from different perspectives. For example, young children should be encouraged to find objects in their natural environment that are taller, longer and heavier than themselves—but at the same time find objects that are smaller, shorter and lighter than themselves. The natural baseline is their body. A comparison is based on this natural measure.

More formal measures of quantity should not be introduced until comparison and estimation skills have been acquired. It could be argued that measurement is only ever a form of approximation. In other words, a person's ability to measure something accurately is determined by his or her capacity to use the measuring device effectively and the actual precision of the instrument itself. As a result, many measurement experiences in our day-to-day lives are based on approximation. Consider the following transcript.

Anne:	How tall are you?
Brendan:	About 180 centimetres. (to himself: Really 181 centimetres, I think)
Anne:	How much is that?
Brendan:	It's about 6 feet.
Anne:	Really, you don't look that tall.

The development of measurement understandings typically develop from the following experiences:

+ natural (body), for example 'The length of my bed is 10 hand spans';
+ informal (comparison), for example 'My big sister measured my bed and said it was 9 hand spans';
+ formal (standard units), for example 'My bed is 1.8 metres long'.

Both adults and children use natural measurements to estimate distances. The following problem was presented to a group of undergraduate students undertaking a Bachelor of Education degree. The students were asked to estimate the distances between several markers placed at varying distances in an open field. One of the activities is presented in Figure 8.1.

Figure 8.1 A representation of the distance estimation task

Marker 1 was approximately 70 metres away from Marker 2. The students were 30 metres from the first marker.

I thought the markers must have been about 65 metres apart . . . I imagined being at the start of a 100-metre race with the finish line being where the second marker was. In fact, the distance looked to be quite close to 100 metres. A distance halfway between this marker and me would not be at the first marker so I knew the distance between the markers would be greater than 50 metres; 65 seemed to be a good estimate.

(Rachael)

I imagined standing on the first marker. If I kicked a football from there I could almost get to the second marker. I can kick a ball about 60 metres so the distance between the two markers would be about 70 metres.

(Greg)

Informal measurement and comparison are used more extensively in our daily lives than more formal, standardised measures. In the early years of school most measurement experiences are associated with comparisons and informal measurement activities.

Many experiences may not require counting but rather the direct comparison of quantities. Initially children will use units of length, area, capacity, mass and time informally. They should begin to understand the idea of the repetition of a unit without overlaps and gaps and make statements about measures using language of betweenness (e.g. The room is between 6 and 7 strides wide).

(Australian Education Council, 1991, p. 139)

Measurement involves allocating numbers of units to physical quantities (length, area, volume, capacity, mass) and non-physical quantities (time, temperature). According to the authors of the Curriculum Corporation's (2000), *Numeracy benchmarks years 3, 5 & 7:*

+ Year 3 students are able to notice features of an object's length, capacity or mass, and are able to use everyday language to describe these objects. They increasingly begin to recognise the need for accuracy when measuring length (moving from informal to formal units) and have the capacity to sequence everyday events using concepts of time.
+ Year 5 students have developed skills in using metric units to estimate, measure and compare physical quantities.
+ Year 7 students are able to use a range of instruments to compare physical and non-physical quantities. They can recognise large and small standard units (litres and millilitres) and choose appropriate units for the task.

Chapter focus questions

Before reading on, consider your responses to the following questions. They are intended to challenge your thinking with respect to the relationship between formal and informal measurement.

1. Without moving from where you are, try to imagine the area a hectare would encompass. Visualise four points (include yourself as one point or marker) which would identify the perimeter of these areas.
2. Draw a picture to show where these markers would be. You may need to include recognisable landmarks such as roads, trees or buildings.
3. What is the shape of your hectare?
4. What informal procedures or techniques have you used to estimate this distance?
5. How would you go about measuring this area more formally/more accurately?
6. When would it be useful to know the area a hectare encompasses?
7. Why might this activity be more useful than getting children to actually measure the dimensions of a hectare?

REFLECTION ON A CLASSROOM SCENARIO

Linking spatial and measurement concepts

The grounds outside a Year 6 classroom were devoid of grass. Many attempts had been made to return this area to its former glory (including some quite expensive proposals), but, alas, no improvements were evident. The school's Parents and Friends committee decided that turf should be laid (for the third time) and that an underground sprinkler system should also be installed. As part of one of their mathematics projects, a teacher decided to introduce the problem to the class. It was agreed that the class should design the perfect underground watering system for the school.

An incredible amount of research was required, and the task took over four weeks to complete. In that time the students needed to consider the cost of various sprinklers, work out their respective water coverage, calculate how many fittings they would need, decide on the hose diameter and decide whether the school's water pressure could cope with the design. Additionally, the children had to consider a range of other variables including the ease with which their system could be turned on, the implications of one sprinkler head being broken, and security issues. A range of mathematical understandings was also required in order to attempt the problem, including:

+ 2D and 3D concepts;
+ measurement concepts relating to perimeter and area;
+ specific mathematical terminology.

The students were required to draw, to scale, 2D representations of the plan.

It was not possible to have a correct answer, only a solution that was practical and met reasonable budget constraints. Some of the children worked in small groups, whereas others preferred to work by themselves. Motivation remained high throughout the activity. Importantly, some children who did not tend to solve 'regular' school problems efficiently provided some of the most practical solutions. As a class, the children were then required to decide which solution would be submitted to the school principal for consideration. This metacognitive stage was the most valuable learning experience in the process. In order to solve this problem, a number of measurement concepts related to length, perimeter and area had to be considered. In addition, spatial concepts related to position and 2D–3D representations were accessed.

The children had to consider the number and type of sprinklers they would need to adequately cover the desired area. One group of students, for example, decided they would use plastic fittings and sprinkler heads that could be purchased from any department or hardware store. Generally, the water coverage area of such equipment is not as large as that of commercial systems—but they are considerably cheaper. This group found the following information vital to their overall plan:

+ full-circle sprinkler: water coverage 3-metre radius;
+ half-circle sprinkler: water coverage 3-metre radius.

Before we tried to draw our system on paper we decided to see what it looked like in real life. We got a stack of witches' hats and spread them out over the grassed area. We also asked our teacher if we could borrow all the skipping ropes from the sports room. We tied two short ropes together and put blue chalk marks on the rope at 1, 1.5 and 3 metres. We measured 3 metres in from one corner and put a witch's hat down. We then measured out

3 metres for the diameter of the full circle and put other ropes down to form a large circle. Sally then paced out how many steps it was from one end of the circle to another, making sure she went through the centre. We put another hat down in a straight line from the first one. We kept doing this, making sure we had some overlap between each circle area. We ran out of skipping ropes—but it didn't matter because we picked them up and moved them. As long as the witches' hats stayed where they were we could work out how many sprinklers we would need.

(Nathan, Year 6)

The classroom teacher commented on the way this group of children attempted to solve the problem:

This group of children used a form of trial and error to work out their pattern. They processed the relevant information on-site, actually using a true 1:1 scale; that is, doing all their measurements in the designated area. Although this approach was relatively effective for this task, it would have been quite laborious if the area had been larger. They were not able to draw a scaled diagram to complete the task without first doing it in a more informal manner. Once they had worked out the problem in a concrete way they had the confidence to then represent it in a scaled version. It is important to allow children to solve the problem this way. Making these children do scaled drawings in the first instance would not have worked—conceptually they were not ready for this.

(Teacher, Year 6)

Another group of students represented their proposal through a scaled diagram (Figure 8.2). This group actually shaded the proposed area of water each sprinkler would cover. Importantly, they also indicated the lengths of hose required between each sprinkler and calculated the total amount of piping they would need for the project.

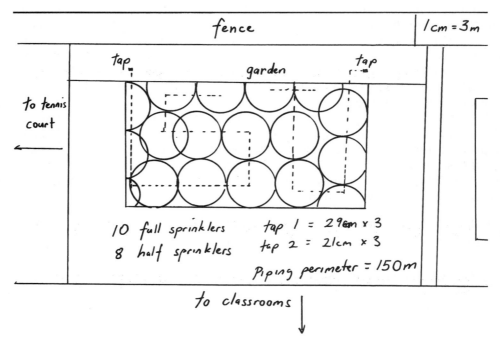

Figure 8.2 Year 6 children's scaled drawing

What could be concluded from the approaches used by the two groups of students? The first group of students:

+ developed a concrete understanding or awareness of the size of the grassed area in order to represent the problem scene;
+ used a combination of formal and informal techniques to measure distances (the rope was marked at intervals with a metre ruler while other measurements were paced out);
+ relied on approximations once a pattern for placing the markers was established;
+ did not attempt scaled drawing until a concrete one-to-one comparison was established.

ACTIVITY 8.1

Assessing children's understanding of measurement

It could be argued that the second group of students was working at a higher level of development.

■ What are some of the mathematical understandings these students have demonstrated from the worksample?

THE GROWTH OF MATHEMATICAL UNDERSTANDING

As children get older their measurement skills—in particular their ability to measure accurately—should continue to develop. In this section you will notice that many of the activities described could be applied to classroom situations across all primary grades. The main differences between the activities are (1) the students' understanding of the use of measurement units; and (2) the processes used to solve the problems.

> *Their understanding of the use of units should develop considerably during these years and they should be helped to articulate generalisations about units. For example, they may say, 'It took 19 of these squares to cover the book, but it only took 12 of the rectangles. That was because the rectangle was bigger than the square. It always works that way. The smaller the unit, the more it takes to cover the shape'.*

(Australian Education Council, 1991, p. 144)

Formal experiences follow a similar pattern. Irrespective of whether children use informal or formal units of measurement they should reflect upon and make decisions about:

+ which quantities should be measured for the task at hand;
+ which units to use (that is, how accurate you need to be); and
+ the measuring tool most appropriate.

(Australian Education Council, 1991, p. 144)

The concept of time

Conceptual understandings related to time involve much more than merely being able to tell the time. The notion of time is a very difficult concept for children to grasp because it involves ideas related to both measurement and spatial understandings. The underlying understandings of time concepts relate to duration, sequencing and cycles. Time is measured:

+ as an occurrence; and
+ by length of duration.

For small children it is important to develop meaningful understandings of time related to their everyday experiences.

One of the most beneficial ways to allow children to construct understandings of time is through children's literature. In some instances literature promotes the universal aspects of mathematics (Bishop, 1988), with activities such as counting and measuring forming the foundations of mathematics in culture. Literature-based activities can place conceptual understandings of time in realistic and imagined situations, as illustrated in the following examples.

Linking time concepts to children's literature

Important mathematical ideas related to the past, present and the future aspects of time can be challenged through literature. For small children these notions must go beyond yesterday, today and tomorrow. Aboriginal myths and legends describe beautifully such aspects of time. *The rainbow serpent* (Roughsey, 1975), for example, exposes children to ideas such as 'before', 'after', 'daytime' and 'night-time' (see Figure 8.3). The book can be used as a catalyst for children to actually paint and draw day and night scenes and to look at which animals are awake in the daytime and night-time.

Important sequential and cyclic aspects of time concepts are treated in *The very hungry caterpillar* (Carle, 1970). The book traces the movements of the caterpillar from its egg through the cycle of life.

> *One Sunday morning the warm sun came up and pop! out of the egg came a tiny and very hungry caterpillar.*
> *Then he nibbled a hole in the cocoon, pushed his way out and . . . he was a beautiful butterfly.*

Figure 8.3 Day and night drawings

In this book the children are provided with a real-life example of the cyclic nature of time. The beauty and simplicity of the book is appropriate for young children with the climax of the text encouraging discussion about the life cycle of other animals.

> *On Monday he ate through one apple. But he was still hungry.*
> *On Tuesday he ate through two pears . . .*

Importantly, the numeration concepts of one, two, three, four and five are represented visually (with apples, pears, plums, strawberries and oranges) so that children can see the relationship between the whole number and its name.

Within the literature-based activities described above the children are exposed to an extensive mathematics vocabulary for concepts associated with time. Many of these terms need to be learnt in order to discuss the way in which time is sequenced. The caterpillar eats particular varieties of fruit on a specific day. The enthusiasm generated by the book provides children with a stimulus that helps them remember the sequence for the days of the week.

Other literature-based texts can be used to promote concepts of duration and the regularity of events. More symbolic concepts associated with telling the time emerge from these activities (Figure 8.4).

Figure 8.4 Timeline

---

1. Goldilocks and the three bears

Consider the story of Goldilocks and the three bears. The following transcript demonstrates the way in which telling-the-time skills can be introduced in a meaningful manner.

Teacher's and student's comments
T: Why did the three bears go for a walk in the forest?
S: Because they wanted their porridge to cool down.
T: At what time in the day do you usually have breakfast?
S: About 7 o'clock.
T: How long would it take for porridge to cool down? (temperature concepts)
S: About half an hour.
T: Let's see what 7 o'clock looks like on our clock. Who can show me what time would be on the clock when the bears had come back from their walk?

Mathematical content and processes
Before being encouraged to tell the time, young children should be exposed to activities that require them to:

+ use and understand terms such as daytime, night-time, yesterday, today, tomorrow, all day, a long while, a little while, morning, afternoon;

+ sequence events within a day;

+ sequence events over more than a day;

Temperature

A great deal of what small children know and learn about temperature comes from real-life experiences, such as knowing what types of appropriate clothing to wear. The weather, therefore, has a significant impact on their ability to compare temperatures. When it comes to more formal measures of temperature they can readily relate to experiences of being ill. When they have a sore throat or a headache mum and dad often take their temperature. Children soon realise that mum or dad can determine how sick they are (if they are too hot) based on this measuring device: 'You have a temperature so we better take you to the doctor'. With such occurrences reinforced over time, even young children begin to appreciate that particular temperatures are normal, whereas higher temperatures indicate they have a fever. Similarly, adults will indicate the type of clothes children should wear for the day based on weather forecasts. Children begin to understand that a temperature of 30°C is hot.

The process of measuring temperature is directly related to comparison activities. The Celsius temperature scale, for example, uses the freezing temperature (0°C) and boiling temperature (100°C) of water as benchmarks. The formal scale is, therefore, associated with a common platform or baseline. These activities should challenge children not only to compare the respective temperatures of objects, but also to appreciate that these comparisons are relative. Consider the following situation.

> *A Year 1 child orders an iceblock from the school canteen one winter's day. Because the iceblock is too cold to hold she asks for some paper towelling to wrap around the plastic. The same child orders an iceblock in the summer time and does not require the paper towelling.*

Temperature ideas and understandings should be based on experiences the children can readily identify with. In the first instance, temperature comparisons should be related to a number of fundamental experiences such as iceblocks are cold—toasted sandwiches are hot; it is usually warm in summer—cool in winter.

2. Multiple comparisons with temperature

The children's body temperature can be used as a platform to compare the temperature of different containers of water. In this activity Year 1 children were asked to order three containers of water from hottest to coldest (Figure 8.5), using one of their fingers as a thermometer.

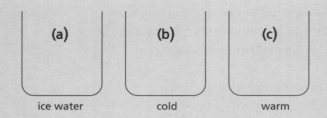

(a)   (b)   (c)

ice water   cold   warm

Figure 8.5 Containers holding water of three different temperatures

Children can then be asked to place one hand in container (a) and the other hand in container (c) and hold them there for one minute. On removing both hands from the containers, they are then required to place them immediately into container (b) and asked:

+ how the water feels to the hand that was placed in container (a)—ice water; and
+ how the water feels to the hand that was placed in container (b)—warm water.

Students' comments

> *One of my hands felt much colder than the other. It stung like when you put your feet in the bath on a cold day. My other hand felt warm.*

(Jayce, Year 1)

> *One hand was hot and the other was cold. After a while they felt the same.*

(Krista, Year 1)

Understandings of heat and temperature can be developed through such investigations.

3. Hot and cold

The following example, which is quite challenging, was given to a class of Year 1 students. In this particular activity the children are asked to draw a picture of something they considered to be 'hot' and something else they considered to be 'cold'. The children are then asked to draw another object that is hotter than their first picture and colder than their second (see Figure 8.6).

Multiple comparisons are required for this activity. Some children will not be able to propose alternative measures because the first item drawn may actually be the hottest thing they know. If Matt had drawn the sun first he may not have been able to draw something hotter than the sun. In such instances a student could be encouraged to draw an object that was colder than their hot object and warmer than their cold object.

Mathematical content and processes

+ Compares temperatures with varying 'baseline' measures.
+ Develops notions of 'heat' and 'temperature'.
+ Examines the effect of temperature on daily routines.

Figure 8.6 Year 1 child comparing temperatures

Posing key questions to assess learning
Are the children able to:

+ use terminology including 'this is hotter than that' and 'this is colder than that' to describe the temperature of two or more objects?
+ discuss and order the temperature of three objects?
+ describe that a particular object is hotter than a certain object and colder than another?
+ recognise the limitations of using their senses to measure temperature?

Linking time and temperature

A Year 1/2 class is asked to predict how long it would take for ice in a set of ice cubes to melt. The water in the container had been frozen with black, brown, green, yellow and white colouring (see Figure 8.7). In addition, the children were asked if any colours would melt more quickly or slowly than the others.

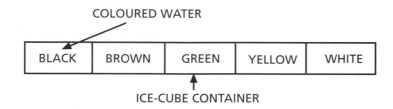

Figure 8.7 Illustration of the ice-cube example

Notions of temperature and time

■ Predict the likely responses children of this age may have for the activity above.

■ What experiences or understandings may these initial ideas be based on?

■ Conduct a similar experiment and test your own hypothesis. How are ideas associated with temperature and time linked through this activity?

Developing standard units

Before developing ideas for standard units it is necessary to choose 'the appropriate physical attribute when comparing and measuring things and units which relate to that attribute' (Australian Education Council, 1994, p. 44). Generally, the selection of a standard unit arises from the student's ability to measure more than one object with the same informal unit. Kindergarten children, for example, begin measuring and comparing things in relation to themselves. The child's own body becomes the baseline unit to compare things against. Important measurement understandings emerge from such activities. Initially these comparisons are on a one-to-one basis:

I found that the door is bigger than me and my table is smaller than me.

(Rohan, Kindergarten)

Extension activities provide children with opportunities to describe quantities associated with measurement. For example, the same child may state, 'You need two of me to be as tall as the door'. The notion that measurement describes quantities of a unit (whether it be a formal or an informal unit) emerges from such understandings.

It is important that students appreciate that they need to count the number of units that describe a given attribute. This is necessary when measuring both informally and formally.

The table is 8 hand spans wide and the table is 88 centimetres wide.

Importantly, such statements allow students to recognise inverse relationships between the number of units and the size of units.

---

4. Informally comparing length

The following activity describes the development of length concepts from the use of informal units to comparing lengths, through to the application of a standard unit for measuring.

Children are asked to make or create their own informal measuring unit. Children often select a stick, a book, their pencil case or even their school bag. It is necessary that the children use this, and only this, unit to measure various objects. This unit becomes their baseline instrument.

A Year 2 child measured the following lengths with her baseline instrument—her reading folder. Her results are displayed in Figure 8.8. Notice the first statement made by this student (Figure 8.8). A direct comparison has been made using the baseline device. She

228

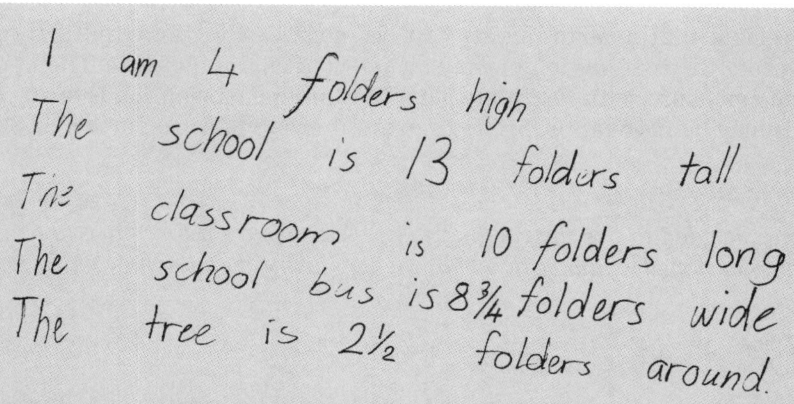

I am 4 folders high

The school is 13 folders tall

The classroom is 10 folders long

The school bus is 8¾ folders wide

The tree is 2½ folders around.

Figure 8.8 Reading folder used as a measuring device

has compared her height with the height of the folder, and worked out the difference in a similar way to the way we might with formal units (centimetres).

At this stage of development the student could be asked to estimate distances and then test them with their unit measure. Children could be asked to estimate the length they can jump. With support from the classroom teacher results could be recorded on scattergrams (see Figure 8.9). The student would draw a line that indicated her height in reading folders and the distance she could jump in reading folders. At the intersection she would put a cross or other appropriate mark. The scattergrams can be used to demonstrate the relationship or lack of relationship between the height of a person and the distance he or she could jump. In groups, children could make predictions about how far friends could jump, based on their heights.

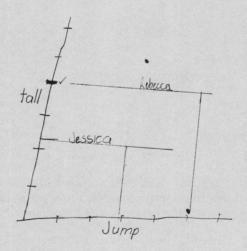

Figure 8.9 Scattergrams with height-length relationships

It is important to note that only one child's baseline instrument can be used for this activity. Previously children would have been using their individual instrument. As a group, the children would need to select a uniform measure. At this stage of development children should appreciate that measurements can be more easily compared if the same unit is used. As a result, the reading folder may be selected as the measure. The appropriateness of the baseline measure, with respect to what they are measuring, leads to an understanding that one unit may be more appropriate than another to measure particular objects.

Student's comments

> *Our group decided to use my reading folder because we didn't have to use big numbers. Jayne said her pencil would be good but we kept losing count of how many pencils we could jump.*

> **(Rebecca, Year 2)**

A similar activity to the one described above could be initiated, at a higher grade level, with the use of standard units. Again, children need to be aware of choosing the appropriate unit to measure with. Generally, children are encouraged to measure in metres, before centimetres and millimetres. Understandings that smaller units provide for greater accuracy are constructed in similar ways. In Figure 8.8 Rebecca stated that she was about 4 folders high. As an extension she was asked to write a statement about this observation (see Figure 8.10).

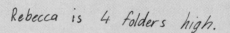

Figure 8.10 Statement from Rebecca

Several important understandings can be developed from such a representation. The statement 'Rebecca is 4 folders high' indicates that the student is aware of the repetition associated with measurement, and that measurement describes 'how many' of a particular item or unit something is.

Posing key questions to assess learning
Are the students able to:

+ make reasonable estimates of the length of objects using an informal measure?
+ develop statements that describe reciprocal accounts of length and distance (the desk is four folders high and I am 6 folders high)?

+ estimate, order and sequence a number of objects?

+ select the most appropriate informal unit to measure items?

+ associate informal measures with formal units of centimetre and metre?

Extension activities

As the children become increasingly competent in using informal measures they should be challenged to:

+ use a metre rule (or tape) to determine objects that are more than 1 metre, less than 1 metre, or about the same as 1 metre. The formal unit 'metre' should be investigated before the 'centimetre' unit because estimates can be compared to actual measurements more easily. Furthermore, difficulties associated with precision and accuracy do not occur with the larger unit.

+ estimate and then measure the number of particular objects that make up 1 metre (e.g. five of my reading folders are about 1 metre). Such activities reinforce the notion that repetition is associated with measurement units.

+ investigate instances where formal units are used in advertisements across the media. These activities should help children become familiar with the mathematical language involved in measurement.

+ recognise the need for a unit smaller than the metre. The introduction of the centimetre unit is often linked to the language children use to describe the length of objects. Such statements as 'I am in between one metre and one and a half metres' or 'This is three and a bit metres long' indicate that the children may need to be introduced to another more accurate formal unit.

ACTIVITY 8.3

Selecting units for measurement

■ What other indicators may be important in determining whether children should be introduced to another formal unit (e.g. the centimetre)?

■ What type of informal units could be used to assist the children in developing an understanding of this unit?

■ What type of objects should the children begin measuring informally/formally?

5. Balancing a see-saw

Years 3 and 4 children were asked to predict what would happen to a see-saw when particular children were positioned on either side of the beam. The activity was designed to assess the children's understanding of mass. A wooden fulcrum was placed in the centre of a ruler that had been labelled with three dots on each side of the fulcrum to model the problem (see Figure 8. 11).

A series of challenging questions was used to test the children's understanding of mass and balance.

The see-saw was held in position with three children seated as shown (see Figure 8.11). Children were asked to predict what would happen to the beam once the beam was released. In other words, the children had to decide whether the beam would remain

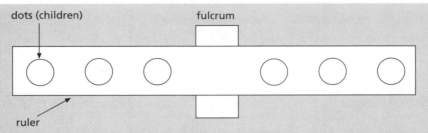

Figure 8.11 A representation of the see-saw

balanced, or fall to one side (to the left or to the right). Generally, the activities increased in complexity where different numbers of children sat on the beam.

All of the children in the class correctly answered the questions, but several children queried the position of the children in relation to balance.

Teacher's and students' comments

Kyle: It will fall this way (indicates to the left).
            (The beam is released and falls to the left.)
Teacher: How did you know that would happen?
Kyle: It is heavier on that side because it has more children.
Teacher: Good, what helped you know this?
Kyle: Well, it's like on a see-saw—the heaviest person's side goes down.

The following two examples reveal different levels of knowledge with respect to the situation.

> *It will fall this way (to the right) because it is heavier on that side. There are more children on that side.*

> **(Sharon, Year 3)**

> *I think it will drop down this way (to the left) because there are more children at the end of the beam. It will be close.*

> **(Sandra, Year 4)**

The following response, predicted before attempting a very difficult question, shows that this particular student has a sound understanding of the relationship between mass/distance/balance.

> *The beam will balance perfectly. The left side has a weight of '4' children and so has the right side. They are even so the beam shouldn't move.*

> **(Thomas, Year 4)**

This student has used the dots on the ruler to calculate a numerical value for each side of the balance. He has calculated the left side as 2 weights $\times$ position 2 = 4; and the right side as 4 weights $\times$ position 1 = 4. His conclusion, therefore, is much more advanced than responses based on the number of weights or position of the weights at the end of the ruler. Importantly, position numbers for the dots were not marked on the ruler—the student has constructed this formula with assistance from the teacher (see Figure 8.12).

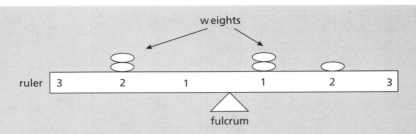

Figure 8.12 A representation of the balance problem

Mathematical content and processes
+ Places two or more objects in order according to mass.
+ Uses a balance to compare mass.
+ Compares masses using an equal arm balance.

Posing key questions to assess learning
Are the students able to:
+ interpret the action of a balance by considering the mass and distance on each arm?
+ develop understandings of the relationship between the mass of a number of objects and their distance from a fulcrum?
+ develop a rule to determine the mass on each side of the balance beam?
+ develop problems based on mass and distance for peers to solve?

Identifying relationships between measurement concepts and attributes

The development of measurement sense is ideally developed in situations where children are challenged to make connections between several measurement concepts. The following sections describe children engaging in rich activities that promote links between measurement ideas including authentic activities that examine relationships between *length–perimeter–area* and *volume–capacity*. Before moving towards these multiple frameworks, children should be provided with opportunities to consider understandings within measurement concepts prior to looking at relationships between these concepts. For example, before presenting children with activities that consider relationships between perimeter and area they should explore the notion of different shapes having the same area. Although such activities certainly lend themselves to perimeter–area relationships the central focus would be of different shapes having the same area.

The following activities illustrate *within*-concept exploration before broadening ideas to *between*-concept understandings. Figure 8.13 considers the notion of different shapes having the same area, while Figure 8.14 considers relationships between perimeter and area. Similarly, Figure 8.15 identifies different shapes having the same volume, while Figure 8.16 makes connections between volume and area. Although older children will be able to accurately draw the 2D shapes, concrete manipulatives can be used to represent the shapes. The 2D shapes can be constructed using pattern blocks while the 3D shapes can be built with Unifix cubes.

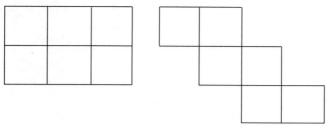

This shape has an area of 6 square units

This shape has an area of 6 square units

Draw/construct other shapes that have an area of 6 square units

Figure 8.13 Developing understandings of area

These shapes have the same area but different perimeters

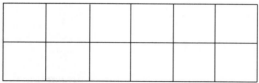

A = 12 square units
P = 16 units

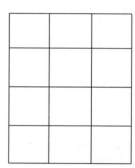

A = 12 square units
P = 14 units

Draw shapes that have the same area but different perimeters
OR
Draw shapes that have the same perimeter but different areas

Figure 8.14 Developing relationships between perimeter and area

These two shapes have a volume of 8 cubic units

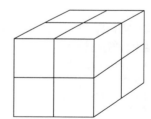

1. Build other shapes that have the same volume
2. Make a table and describe the length, width and height of each shape

Figure 8.15 Developing understandings of volume

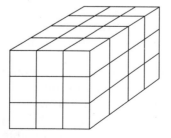

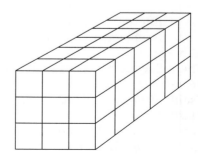

1. Which shape has the most blocks?
2. How could you check without counting all the blocks?

Figure 8.16 Developing relationships between volume and area

234

Once these measurement–sense understandings have been established children should be exposed to authentic activities that provide them with opportunities to use these ideas in both rich and lifelike contexts. The following sections present such contexts.

Using relationships—length, perimeter and area

In order for measurement concepts to be associated with practical skills and relevant problem-solving strategies, it is advantageous to develop activities that encourage children to use a number of measurement understandings to solve problems. Concepts related to length, perimeter and area are often confused by children. Similarly, concepts of area, surface area and volume are sometimes misrepresented. Activities that require the combination of two or more attributes can help children see how these attributes are related or how one attribute is not dependent on the other. When asked to describe or draw a square metre many primary-aged children will respond with the representation in Figure 8.17.

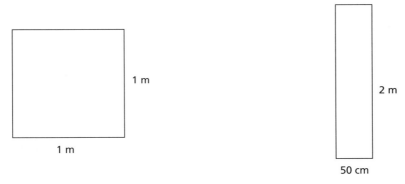

Figure 8.17 Typical representation of 1 m^2

Figure 8.18 A more uncommon representation of a square metre

When asked whether or not the diagram illustrated in Figure 8.18 is also a square metre, younger children may respond 'no' because 'it is not a square shape so it cannot be a square metre'.

The understanding that a square metre 'covers' a specific area, independent of its perimeter, should be reinforced through a variety of formal and informal comparisons. For example, investigating the number of square metres a large carpeted area covers can help children appreciate that the shape of a square metre can be different.

Students' comments

> *Our square metre was long and thin. We needed 12 of this shape to cover the whole carpeted area. The next group's square metre was shaped like a square. They also needed 12 to cover the whole area.*

(Jenna, Year 4)

> *Our square metre was shaped like an 'L'. We had to make sure that we turned it different ways so there were no gaps between or spaces on the carpet. We needed 12. Every group came up with the same answer.*

(Dion, Year 4)

Because the children are able to recognise, visualise and represent the dimensions of one square metre, the relationship between length, perimeter and area can be developed in a meaningful manner that enhances the children's understanding of not only the respective attributes but also the respective commonalities between attributes. It is much more difficult, however, for children to experience such relationships with larger areas. The following activity investigates the area of a hectare.

---

6. How big is a hectare?

How many minutes would it take you to run around the outside of a hectare paddock?

This problem was given to a group of Year 5/6 children at a rural primary school. Initially, most of the children in the class approached the problem in the same manner. The following transcript was typical of the process undertaken by children working in groups to complete the problem.

Jim: How big is a hectare anyway?

Rachael: I think it is 100×100 so it must be a thousand metres.

Sarah: Isn't it about the size of an acre?

Glen: No, it is 2.2 acres—which is pretty big. [Fact: Hectare is equal to 2.47 acres.]

Jim: But how big is it in metres?

Rachael: It is 100×100.

Jim: What do you mean 100×100?

Rachael: You know, 100 metres long and 100 metres wide.

Glen: That's it, it looks like this. (Glen draws a picture of a square and labels two sides.)

Rachael: That's what I said—one thousand metres squared.

Jim: Yes, it has to be squared metres and it is a square shape. That will be more than 1000 metres; it will be 10 000 metres squared.

Rachael: That can't be right.

Glen: Yes it can, I told you it was pretty big.

Sarah: If it is more than 2 acres that sounds about right.

Rachael: Anyway it doesn't matter how big it is as long as we agree it is 100 metres long and 100 metres wide.

Jim: OK, that means it is 400 metres around the outside. That's not very far for such a big area. It won't take long to run around that.

Rachael: And Sarah is the fastest runner in our group; it won't take her long. What do you think, Sarah?

Sarah: I do 'four hundreds' at athletics. About 65 seconds I suppose.

Several important observations emerge from this conversation:

+ Most of the children did not have an intuitive awareness of the size of a hectare.

+ Rachael recalled that the dimensions of a hectare were 100 metres by 100 metres.

+ Some of the children (Sarah and Glen) attempted to relate its size to an area they were familiar with. Interestingly, both children had spent time on farms. These two children demonstrated that they had some understanding of a hectare being an area or coverage, whereas some of the other children tended to be limited to the notion that it had certain dimensions. Some of the children may have focused on perimeter rather than area.

+ As a group, the children were looking for only one answer. Some of the children had a prototype of what a hectare looked like (a square shape with 100-metre sides). This type of image is typically represented in mathematics textbooks.

Mathematics processes

To help the children develop a greater understanding of the ideas associated with the hectare, this activity needs to be expanded so that the children:

+ develop strategies for effectively counting large numbers of metres (in this case the perimeter of the hectare) and square metres (area);

+ become more aware of the physical size of the particular area;

+ investigate the relationships between particular attributes of a hectare (perimeter and area).

Teacher's and students' comments

This group of Year 5/6 children was asked, as a whole class, to create an area of 1 hectare. The activity was undertaken in a large park opposite the school grounds. After some time, the children spaced themselves along imaginary lines that were approximately 100 metres long (see Figure 8.19). As the classroom teacher commented:

> *Although the activity took over 10 minutes for the children to co-ordinate, it was probably the first time many of the children had actually 'experienced' the dimensions of a hectare.*

(Teacher, Year 5/6)

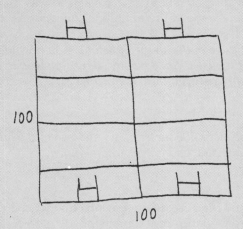

Figure 8.19 100 m × 100 m representation

The following description was typical of the children's enthusiastic response to the activity.

> *I never realised how big it actually is. It is much, much bigger than the land my house is on. It's nearly as big as all the houses in my street.*

(Joshua, Year 5)

Some of the children were then encouraged to run around the perimeter of the hectare to test their initial hypothesis. Some of the results are displayed in Figure 8.20.

Title: Running around one hectare			
Area	Perimeter	Name	Time
100m x 100m	400m	John	55 secs
100m x 100m	400m	Sally	1:05 min
100m x 100m	400m	Jane	59 secs
200m x 50m	500m	Brian	1:10 min
200m x 50m	500m	Eric	1:20 min
200m x 50m	500m	Lucy	1:18 min

Figure 8.20 Times from students running around the perimeter of the hectare

Importantly, the children were then asked to create another hectare that did not have dimensions of 100 metres. This task required some helpful input from the teacher. It was necessary for the children to understand that a hectare was 10 000 square metres. The following comments illustrate some of the initial misconceptions that had to be overcome.

I thought a hectare had to be in the shape of a square so it would be 100 metres long and 100 metres wide. I didn't realise it could be any shape that was 10 000 square metres. It will work as long as the length and width are the proper size.

(Alice, Year 5)

We could have two of the sides 200 metres long and two of the other sides 50 metres long. You just double 100 on one side and halve it on the other.

(Carmon, Year 6)

As a group the children could then create dimensions that were 200 metres by 50 metres in order to represent a hectare with different dimensions. Children ran around the perimeter of this area and recorded results. These results could then be compared with the children's times by children for the previous activity. Although no direct correlations or comparisons should be made between the two sets of results, such activities provide children with opportunities to experience differences between the particular attributes associated with area. Because understandings related to larger areas are more difficult to grasp, such explorations are most beneficial.

Posing key questions to assess learning
Are the students able to:

+ appreciate that a hectare has an area of 10 000 square metres and that the perimeter of a hectare can vary?

- estimate the size of hectares and square kilometres using a variety of problem-solving strategies?
- compare the size of particular areas to that of a hectare (a hectare is about the size of two football fields)?

Using relationships—an application of volume and capacity

At about the same time every year, public swimming pools all over the country are filled with water, in preparation for the swimming season. How much water does it take to fill an Olympic-sized swimming pool?

If asked to estimate the capacity of an object, children often attempt to compare the object with some standard measure. When estimating the capacity of a household bucket, for example, children will often say, 'How many litre containers of water would it take to fill the bucket?' A visual representation of the container may be in the form of a litre jug commonly used at school—or it may be a milk carton.

If the household bucket holds 10 litres, upper primary children will often be able to propose a relatively accurate estimation of its capacity. When asked to estimate the capacity of something as large as an Olympic swimming pool, children cannot rely on such visual representations (or comparison measures). Interestingly, children tend to make predictions by estimating the area of such a large object. A common prediction would be 20 000 litres. In order to challenge such estimations children should be encouraged to calculate the pool's dimensions more accurately. Prior knowledge of such familiar objects provides children with opportunities to make fairly accurate estimations, such as:

- the length of the pool is 50 metres; and
- the width of the pool is 20 metres.

Similarly, the children often realise that the shallow end of the pool is approximately 1 metre deep while the deep end is close to 2 metres deep. With some support from the teacher the part of the pool with depth of 1.5 metres can be estimated.

Many important measurement concepts have already been highlighted at this stage of the problem-solving process. The children can:

- use standard measures;
- consider surface area (length × width);
- estimate an average depth for a large volume; and
- relate capacity to volume.

7. Connections between volume and capacity

Children will often draw diagrams to represent initial findings. In Figure 8.21, the student has realised that the volume of the 3D object needs to be calculated. Upper primary children generally accept that an answer of 1500 square metres is not sufficient. Importantly, children will often go back to natural or informal comparisons after this formal calculation has been made, in order to complete the problem. In other words, children revert to methods described when estimating the capacity of a household bucket. Obviously some children will know the conversion and will work out the answer in litres very quickly.

Others will need to call on their previous experience of how big a cubic metre is in order to select the appropriate conversion. The following response illustrates this process.

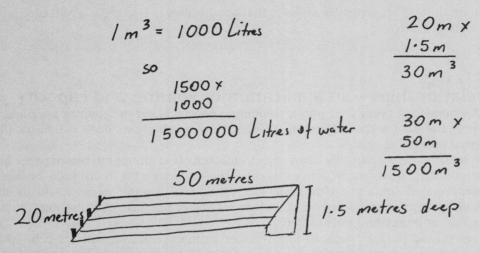

Figure 8.21 Anne's representation of a pool problem

Student's comments

> *I worked out the volume of the pool by multiplying its length by width which gave me an answer of 1000 square metres. I then multiplied it by the depth to get 1500 cubic metres. I knew the answer had to be in litres but I didn't know how many litres were in one cubic metre. I thought 1 cubic centimetre was 1 millilitre but I wasn't sure. It had to be 100 litres or 1000 litres. I tried to imagine filling it up with litres of milk. 100 were not enough. I then multiplied the 1500 by 1000 to get 1 500 000 litres. That was 1.5 million litres. It seemed to be too high. That's a lot of water.*

(Anne, Year 6)

Mathematical content and processes
This activity yielded the following observations:

+ The children were encouraged to guess first, and then check.
+ Initial estimates were based on acquired mathematical concepts (the length of the pool is 50 metres).
+ Common and standard units (metres and litres) were used.
+ Direct comparisons to known quantities were used (imagine pouring water from litre containers into the pool).
+ Area and volume calculations were utilised.
+ Conversion techniques were required (1 m³ = 1000 L).

This type of problem solving can be applied to many practical situations. The same type of processing is often used when:

+ estimating the amount of concrete you would need to order to lay a driveway or path;
+ calculating how much soil would fit into a box trailer.

Extension activities

+ Children should be encouraged to investigate situations that require them to find out the capacity or volume of large objects (water tanks, dams, ship containers). Additional measurement units can then be naturally introduced (megalitres).

+ Children can monitor their family's household water usage. How many megalitres of water are used in a year?

Additional mathematical processes

Children need to be aware that capacity is the amount of available space, while volume is the 3D space taken up by an object (e.g. a cubic metre). It is important for children to develop ideas about the relationships between volume and capacity from an early age. Literature-based texts, such as *Mr Archimedes' bath* (Allen, 1980), help children appreciate that displacement of water is directly related to volume.

In the previous activity the problem solver was required to convert volume calculated in cubic metres to litres. One of the students began with a known conversion fact, that 1 cubic metre = 1000 litres. Other children used different conversions including 1 cubic centimetre = 1 millilitre. Importantly, the children constructed their own representations to remember these conversions. Jack related 1 cubic metre to litres (it would take more than 100 litres so it must be 1000 litres). Such relationships highlight the importance of providing children with a range of informal and formal comparisons based on practical and easily identifiable experiences. It is important to establish whether the children are able to:

+ use known conversions to solve problems dealing with capacity and volume;

+ make reasonable estimates for the volume or capacity of large containers (water tanks, dams);

+ see the need for the use of a large standard unit (kilolitre).

MAKING ADDITIONAL MEASUREMENT LINKS— SCIENCE, TECHNOLOGY AND MATHEMATICS

Many mathematics concepts are directly linked to science and technology understandings. This is most evident in early concept development where conceptual understandings associated with sorting, one-to-one correspondence, comparing and classifying emerge from similar ideas and experiences. Links between subject areas should be encouraged; otherwise, students develop isolated pieces of knowledge which are not grounded in practical and real-world experiences.

Postle (1993, p. 33) indicated that:

> *Learning from experience generates knowledge. Attending to the whole experience appears to lead to the generation of realistic, useful and relevant knowledge directly supportive of human flourishings. So far as I edit, limit, deny or ignore areas of my experience, this appears to narrow what I learn from it. This restriction may aid my short-term survival, but at the cost of some detachment from reality.*

It may be argued that schooling is often devoted to short-term survival learning. Skills and understandings are fostered through a collection of specific teaching examples that require students to recall information in ways that do not relate to 'real-life' or relevant knowledge. Several weeks later students are required to reproduce attained knowledge through assessment techniques that merely reinforce and promote this narrow use of knowledge. Frequently learners are expected to apply this learnt knowledge only to artificially constructed and restricted textbook exercise 'problems'. Such problems are not usually drawn from actual examples from the 'real world', so the knowledge gained from their completion is not practical knowledge. It is worthwhile, therefore, for children to be exposed to mathematical ideas and understandings that can be readily applied to common experiences. The following activity provided children with opportunities to relate understandings of surface area and volume to ideas of mass and capacity.

8. Capacity, volume and links to science

You are to design and make a vessel constructed from a 15 centimetre × 15 centimetre square of plastic cardboard that would support the greatest load when floated in water.

A group of talented Year 4 children was given the above design brief at an enrichment weekend. Once the children had constructed the vessel, they were asked to calculate the maximum amount of sand their vessel could contain before sinking. Three main approaches, namely trial and error through concrete experiences, reasoning from everyday experiences and analytic reasoning, were observed. The following comments were typical of the approaches adopted by the children to complete the problem.

Students' comments
The concrete trial-and-error approaches included the following comments:

> *When we fold the corners we cannot waste too much paper.*

> *You need to have a large surface area so we should have sloping sides and not waste material by making corners.*

> *The higher the sides the bigger the load it will carry (the water always comes in over the sides of small boats).*

The responses that indicated children were reasoning from everyday experiences included:

> *Let's make a square barge with low sides—barges carry heavy loads.*

> *It has to look like a ship.*

> *The volume of the boat determines the load it will carry (big boats can carry more than small boats).*

More analytic processing included:

> *It won't matter what shape we make it; we've all got the same sized piece of paper.*

> *The maximum will be a cube so it must be 5 × 5 × 5.*

> *A table of values approach (14 × 14 × 1 or 13 × 13 × 2).*

The most common misconception was that volume was directly related to surface area and not related to shape. The children failed to take into account the relationship between the three dimensions (width × length × height). It seems to be important that learners have the opportunity to work through concrete materials, but more importantly that they be challenged to reason mathematically through everyday experiences. The following comment illustrates the type of reasoning evoked, and also the student's desire to relate the problem to realistic situations.

At first I thought that it wouldn't matter what shape I made the boat because we all had a piece of cardboard that was the same size. Someone else said a cube shape would hold the most sand because it had an even height, length and width. This seemed to be a good idea because high walls would mean that water could not get in to sink the boat. I was amazed at the different answers people got. Some people got over 200 millilitres worth of sand in their cup—I only got about 120 before mine sank.

(Justin, Year 4)

Such activities allow for a range of possible solutions, with children using experiences from everyday life to solve complex problems.

ACTIVITY 8.4

Volume and capacity

■ What do you think the maximum load for a 15 centimetre × 15 centimetre shape would be?

■ What mathematical knowledge would you use to solve this problem?

■ List examples of practical 'general knowledge' understandings that would influence your solution. What does this tell you about the problem-solving process?

■ How are understandings of the relationships between capacity and volume reinforced in such an activity?

SUMMARY AND IMPLICATIONS FOR CLASSROOM PRACTICE

This chapter has emphasised the importance of developing measurement concepts and processes in a problem-solving environment that encourages children to investigate and construct important mathematical understandings through everyday experiences. Measurement provides a natural link to other mathematics concepts and to other areas across the curriculum. The chapter introduced vital measurement understandings by describing the general principles of a particular concept and providing examples of useful activities concerned with the principle. These activities often began with content or resources from other learning areas including literature-based texts, children's writing, science and technology. Insights into the way children respond to these activities, through worksamples and dialogue, showed the development that is likely to occur during the primary school years.

It was argued that natural and informal comparisons should be introduced before children are required to measure with formal units. Measurement concepts are generally based on approximations so it is important for teachers to provide students with a variety of estimation and comparison skills that can be linked to everyday experiences. Formal units of measurement should be introduced only when a child sees the need for such a unit. From a teacher's perspective, the development and use of formal units should mirror that of activities associated with informal units of measurement. Measurement skills concerning accuracy and precision should also be introduced gradually, in a meaningful manner.

It is also important for children to be challenged to link measurement concepts and processes to other related understandings. For example, children should be encouraged to explore relationships between perimeter and area, surface area and volume, and volume and capacity in order to develop measurement understandings that can be applied to other curriculum areas. Measurement concepts, skills and processes should not be taught in isolation. Teachers should attempt to make strong links between measurement and other learning activities so that experiences can be applied to real-life situations.

ACTION AND REFLECTION

From the mathematics syllabus currently used in your state:

1. Select two content areas that could be integrated readily into the same unit of work (e.g. area and volume, mass and volume) and nominate a stage or grade level as a focus.

2. Look at the type of learning activities that are provided in the syllabus for these two content areas (remember to focus on a particular grade or level). Develop a series of three activities that would provide opportunities for students to develop these understandings in an open-ended problem-solving environment. It may be worthwhile examining the two examples presented near the end of Chapter 2.

3. Share your ideas with other members of your group. It would be useful to begin collecting such activity samples in a resource folder.

4. If the opportunity arises, use your unit on your next practicum or micro-teaching experience.

REFERENCES

Allen, P. (1980). *Mr Archimedes' Bath.* Sydney: HarperCollins.

Australian Education Council. (1991). *A national statement on mathematics for Australian schools.* Melbourne: Curriculum Corporation.

Australian Education Council. (1994). *Mathematics in our schools: A guide for parents and the community.* Melbourne: Curriculum Corporation.

Bishop, A. (1988). *Mathematical enculturation.* Dordrecht, The Netherlands: Kluwer Academic.

Carle, E. (1970). *The very hungry caterpillar.* Great Britain: Hamish Hamilton.

Carlson, N. (1991). *Take time to relax.* New York: Penguin Books.

Clarke, D. (1996). *The case of the mystery bone.* Sydney: Mathematical Association of NSW.

Clement, R. (1995). *Just another ordinary day*: Sydney: HarperCollins.

Curriculum Corporation. (1994). *Mathematics—A profile for Australian schools.* Melbourne: Curriculum Corporation.

Curriculum Corporation. (2000). *Numeracy benchmarks years 3, 5 & 7.* Melbourne: Curriculum Corporation.

National Council of Teachers of Mathematics. (1989). *Curriculum and evaluation standards for school mathematics.* Reston, Virginia: National Council of Teachers of Mathematics.

Postle, D. (1993). Putting the heart back into learning. In D. Boud, R. Cohen & D. Walker (Eds), *Using learning from experience.* Buckingham: The Society for Research in Higher Education and Open University.

Roughsey, D. (1975). *The rainbow serpent.* Sydney: William Collins.

Siegler, R. (1976). Three aspects of cognitive development. *Cognitive Psychology, 8,* 481–520.

Chapter 9
Exploring chance and probability

CHAPTER OVERVIEW

The notion of using real data from children's everyday experiences—experiences that require them to make decisions about chance and probability—was introduced in Chapter 3, but the links between data handling and probability were not made. Chance and data are traditionally and conceptually linked, as it is through the investigation of data gathered from real events that we can investigate chance. This chapter explores how data gathered from social and simulated or 'experimental-type' situations present opportunities for the development of children's understanding of chance and probability.

The inclusion of chance and probability in primary mathematics is relatively new to many teachers, but interest in these areas has increased markedly since the introduction of the chance and data strand of the curriculum in *A national statement on mathematics for Australian schools* (Australian Education Council, 1991). The *Statement*, like similar curriculum documents worldwide (e.g. National Council of Teachers of Mathematics, 2000), emphasises the necessity of building a strong foundation from which future understandings of probability can develop. In particular, it stresses the necessity of addressing students' misconceptions from an early age:

> *Misconceptions about chance processes are widespread. Many become established while children are still quite young and are then difficult to overcome. Therefore chance activities should be provided in schools from the earliest stages in order to help students develop more inclusive conceptions. Such activities also provide the basis for more formal study in later school years. Students should investigate chance events, estimate probabilities experimentally (that is, empirically) and determine them analytically (that is, theoretically).*

(Australian Education Council, 1991, p. 163)

Before dealing with the more formal mathematics of probability, students need to understand the concept of chance. 'Chance deals with the concepts of randomness and the use of probability as a measure of how likely it is that particular events will occur' (Australian Education Council, 1991, p. 27).

Chapter focus questions

Before reading further, consider your responses to the following questions. They are intended to start you thinking about what you already know in regard to probability and how children develop an understanding of the concept.

1. What informal conceptions do young children have about chance and probability?
2. What misconceptions do adults hold about probability?
3. What impact do these informal understandings and misconceptions of chance have on people's interpretations of situations involving probability?
4. What thinking processes are involved in solving problems of chance?
5. In what ways can we make use of real data to develop students' concepts of probability?
6. What do we need to look for when assessing children's understandings of chance and probability?

Throughout the remainder of this chapter each of the preceding questions will be addressed, either through a theoretical discussion or through an analysis of a child's work-sample, or both.

REFLECTION ON A CLASSROOM SCENARIO

It's just pot luck!

Year 4 students from a large metropolitan school enjoyed playing 'Heads or tails' whenever there were a spare few minutes before recess or lunch. The game required the whole class to stand and place their hands on either their 'head' or their 'tail'. A coin was flipped by their teacher or another student and the result was called out. If the outcome was a 'head' all the students with hands on their heads remained standing and the students with their hands on their 'tails' would sit down. If the outcome was a 'tail' all the students with their hands on their heads would sit down. The game continued in this way until there was one player, the winner, still standing. After about a week of playing this game, their teacher announced that they were now going to 'see' how clever the class was at predicting how many times a head would come up if a coin was flipped 20 times. Figure 9.1 is a copy of the class table that was generated to record students' predictions and their actual findings. Figures 9.2 and 9.3 show the records of two groups of students while conducting the investigation and their comments regarding the outcomes.

After completing their individual experiments and recordings, the students came together to discuss and reflect upon their findings as a whole class.

'Heads or tails' is a fair game because no one can tell what's going to come up next. It could be heads or it could be tails—no one knows.

(Danna, Year 4)

It's just pot luck! No one can say exactly how many heads there will be . . . but no one predicted really low numbers or numbers around 19 for heads, because it would be pretty unlikely to get that many heads or that many tails all in a row in just 20 flips.

(Karly, Year 4)

It depends on which side of the coin is facing up before you flip it. If heads is facing up to start with you nearly always get tails.

(Max, Year 10 student on work experience)

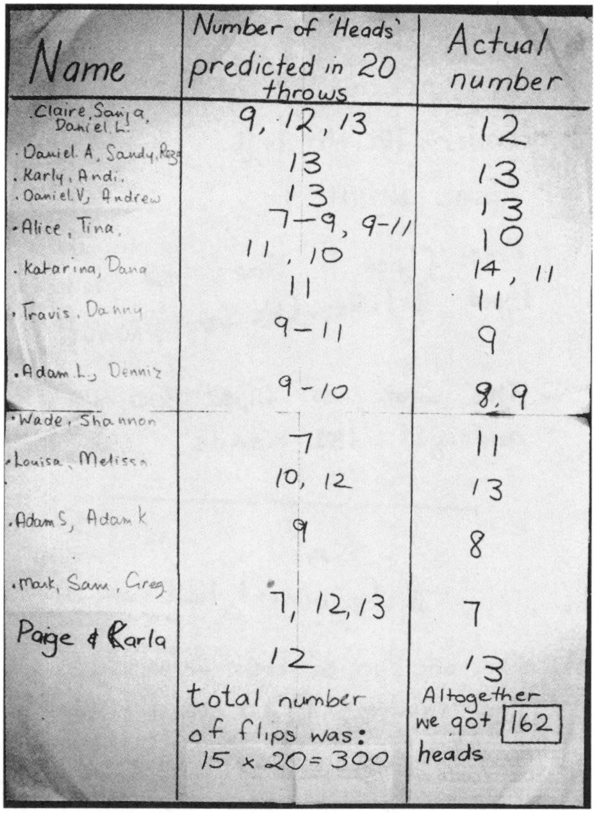

Name	Number of 'Heads' predicted in 20 throws	Actual number
Claire, Sanja, Daniel L.	9, 12, 13	12
Daniel A, Sandy, Rez	13	13
Karly, Andi.	13	13
Daniel V, Andrew	7–9, 9–11	10
Alice, Tina.	11, 10	14, 11
Katarina, Dana	11	11
Travis, Danny	9–11	9
Adam L, Denniz	9–10	8, 9
Wade, Shannon	7	11
Louisa, Melissa	10, 12	13
Adam S, Adam K	9	8
Mark, Sam, Greg	7, 12, 13	7
Paige & Karla	12	13
	total number of flips was: 15 × 20 = 300	Altogether we got 162 heads

Figure 9.1 The table constructed by the class to record students' predictions and their actual findings

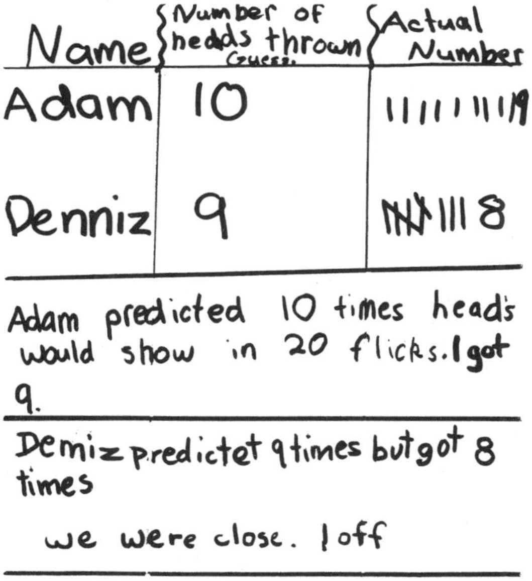

Name	Number of heads thrown (Guess)	Actual Number
Adam	10	111111119
Denniz	9	𝍸 111 8

Adam predicted 10 times heads would show in 20 flicks. I got 9.

Demiz predictet 9 times but got 8 times

we were close. 1 off

Figure 9.2 Adam and Denniz recorded their predictions and actual findings in a table similar to the class table constructed by the teacher

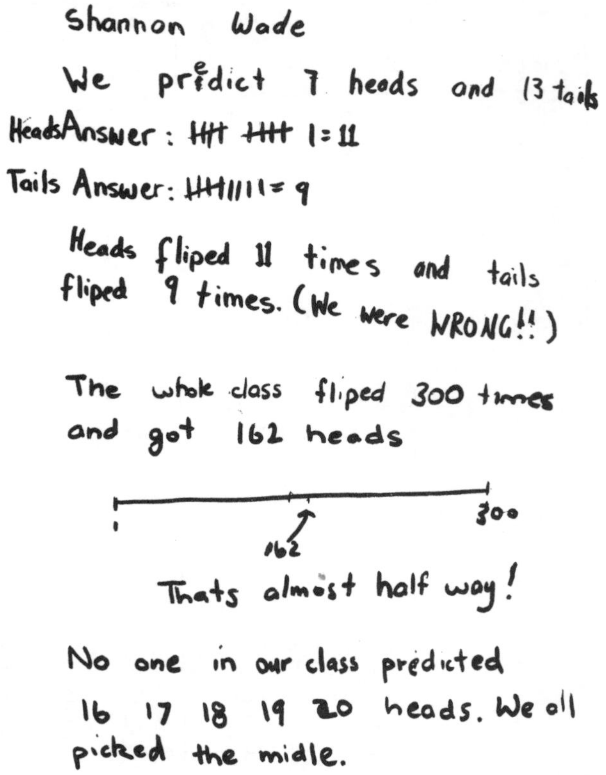

Shannon   Wade

We   prédict 7 heads and 13 tails

HeadsAnswer: ⵜⵜⵜ ⵜⵜⵜ 1 = 11

Tails Answer: ⵜⵜⵜ11111 = 9

Heads fliped 11 times and tails
fliped 9 times. (We were WRONG!!)

The whole class fliped 300 times
and got 162 heads

Thats almost half way!

No one in our class prédicted
16 17 18 19 20 heads. We all
picked the midle.

Figure 9.3 Shannon and Wade chose to record their findings in a different way from that suggested by the teacher

The class teacher later reflected upon the children's written and verbal responses.

We've been playing the 'Heads or tails' game for almost a week now and I was aware that some children were making their decisions based on some very immature thinking. Katarina consistently chose heads because she considered it to be 'lucky' and Andrew thought that it had something to do with the Earth's gravity. The coin-tossing experiment really brought a lot of their misconceptions to the surface and it challenged a few in the process. The Year 10 student on work experience seemed to have just as many misconceptions as my Year 4. I found it interesting that they all made predictions that heads would come up about half the total number of flips and that they actually recognised this fact themselves from the large class chart. Greg immediately saw how to calculate the total number of flips made by the whole class and was able to work it out mentally. He, Karly and a few others predicted that if there were 300 flips, then heads would come up about 150 times because that was half.

(Teacher, Year 4)

Understandings of probability evolve over many years as a result of exposure to countless experiences involving uncertainty. Responses of Year 4 students and the Year 10 student on work experience in the preceding scenario illustrate the range of intuitive understandings that may exist in just one classroom. Danna's response regarding the fairness of the 'Heads or tails' game is typical of children in this age range. Even children as young as 6 or 7 years relate the notion of 'fairness' to the equal likelihood of an event occurring. Karly used the everyday expression of 'pot luck' to describe her understanding of getting a 'head' every time a coin is flipped. The use of chance language among young children has been shown to range from very informal to quite sophisticated (Truran, 1995). However, this should not be taken as an indication of a child's level of understanding of chance and probability, since it is well recorded that children (and adults) are capable of providing correct responses that are actually based on quite naive or erroneous reasons (Kahneman, Slovic & Tversky, 1982).

The existence of informal understandings of probability from a young age has been documented for some time now (Fischbein, 1975; Fischbein, Nello & Marino, 1991). However, there has been some debate concerning the importance of these informal understandings on the development of children's abilities to handle more formal notions of probability. For example, Piaget and Inhelder (1975) provided a developmental perspective, claiming that children need to have reached the stage of formal operations (about the age of 12 years) before they could reason probabilistically. Fischbein, however, claimed that children could reason probabilistically *before* the stage of formal operations, but that it depended on the context in which the problems were presented and the level of verbal skills required to successfully respond.

Despite the controversy surrounding the development of children's probability concepts, researchers and educators seem to agree on at least one major point—understanding how students think about chance and probability enables the teacher to plan experiences that can facilitate the development of more formal concepts of probability (Konald, 1991; Jones et al., 1999; Watson, Collis & Moritz, 1997). With this in mind, coupled with the fact that a chance and data strand is included in *A national statement on mathematics for Australian schools* (Australian Education Council, 1991), there has been a sharp increase in research intended to inform educators and curriculum planners about young children's informal notions and the development of more formal ideas of chance and probability (e.g. Tarr & Jones, 1997; Watson, Collis & Moritz, 1997, Way, 1997, 2003). Jones et al. (1999) generated a framework that describes the typical development of students' probabilistic reasoning. The framework incorporates four levels of growth: a non-numerical or subjective level of reasoning; a transitional level, characterised by a naive quantitative reasoning ability; a third level where informal quantitative reasoning occurs; and a fourth level involving the ability to reason numerically. Jones et al. (1999) suggest that children's probabilistic reasoning will develop in accordance with the framework as 'their thinking is challenged' (p. 149). Insights into the development of children's probabilistic thinking, as provided by the framework, assist teachers to assess children's understandings and plan for effective instruction.

THE GROWTH OF MATHEMATICAL UNDERSTANDING

This section discusses important concepts and processes involved in probabilistic thinking. It illustrates the growth of mathematical thinking from informal to formal notions of probability by drawing on examples of children's explorations of this area. It will be noted that many of the investigations presented as 'snapshots' of students' developing understanding of probability will also include data-handling elements in the one activity. For example, the 'Greedy pig' snapshot (see p. 264) starts out focused on probability, but collected data lead into an analysis of a stem-and-leaf plot. Others may start with data collection, such as the 'Rolling a die' snapshot (see p. 258), to answer a question but move into a probability simulation to help explain why things happened the way they did. This emphasises the natural link between chance and data, and will help students develop an understanding of both content areas.

In the following snapshots of learning, we deal with a number of concepts related to probability and chance: likelihood, randomness, sample space, independence of events, conditional probability, theoretical probability, the law of large numbers and long-term proportion. Such 'language' of chance and probability can be conceptually difficult, especially for students from non-English-speaking backgrounds. Many terms, such as 'likely' and 'chance', are used in everyday life and usually pose little difficulty to children once they are taught explicitly within a probability context. While it is not expected that primary-aged students learn the more formal language of probability, brief definitions are provided here to enhance our understandings of the underlying concepts.

The *likelihood* of an event occurring, or its *probability*, is the number of times an event is likely to occur in relation to the total number of events that could occur. For example, the likelihood of rolling a 'six' with a fair die is one-in-six or one-sixth.

An event is said to be *random* if all possible outcomes have an equal chance of occurring. The result of flipping a coin to decide who will go first in a game is considered to be fair because either outcome (a 'head' or a 'tail') is equally likely—each person has the same chance. Hence, the outcome is determined solely by 'chance'.

When talking about *sample space*, we are referring to all the possible outcomes of a particular event. The sample space for flipping a coin consists of two outcomes—'heads' and 'tails'.

Events are said to be *independent* if the result of one event has no impact on the result of any other event, such as when a die is rolled more than once. The likelihood of getting a certain number on the second roll is independent of the outcome on the first roll as are all subsequent rolls.

Conditional probability is when the 'probability of an event has been changed by the occurrence of another event' (Jones et al., 1999, p. 149). For example, in a bag containing two blue counters and one red counter, the initial likelihood of pulling out a blue counter is 'two out of three'. However, if a blue counter is not replaced and another counter is taken from the bag, then the likelihood of it being blue is now only 'one out of two' or half.

The concepts *theoretical probability* and the *law of large numbers* are closely related. Theoretically, when tossing a coin, you would expect the likelihood of a 'head' to be a half on every toss. This is the theoretical probability. However, due to chance, it is possible to get 'heads' four times in a row. If the coin is tossed one hundred times, the number of heads is more likely to approach the expected probability of a half. The law of large numbers refers to the fact that the more trials we carry out, the closer the actual outcome will be to the theoretical probability.

ACTIVITY 9.1

Applying knowledge of concepts

With a small group of your peers, play the 'Heads or tails' game as described in the scenario at the start of this chapter. Now play the same game with two coins. If people predict 'heads' and a 'tails' to be the likely outcome they should place one hand on their head and one hand on their 'tail'. Consider the key concepts of probability described above to help you and your friends discuss responses to the following questions:

1. What strategies did you and your friends use for making decisions regarding where to place your hands in each of the games?

2. What is the sample space for the two games? How does knowledge of the sample space affect your decision making in the second game?

3. List the possible outcomes for both games. What is the theoretical probability of getting each of the possible outcomes when two coins are used? Do people express this probability in the same way? (Some may use decimal fraction notation and others may use percentages.)

4. Does knowledge of the theoretical probability help you win the game? Why? Why not?

5. If two coins were tossed two times and each time 'heads heads' occurred, what do you think the outcome would be on the third toss? Predict the reasoning behind typical 8- and 9-year-old children's decisions for this case.

SNAPSHOTS OF LEARNING: LESSON PLANNING AND ASSESSMENT

Activities depicted in the snapshots are drawn from two main contexts: *social* and *experimental*. It is important to provide students with experiences from both contexts. For many social situations, such as weather forecasts, we are not really able to quantify the likelihood of an event occurring or not, but they help to develop notions and the language of chance (see snapshots 'A chance of rain' and 'Pigs might fly' for example). On the other hand, experimental situations (see the snapshots 'Rolling a die' and 'Horse race' for example) usually lend themselves more easily to quantification and are excellent preparation for a more formal study of probability in high school. In experimental situations, data are usually generated through a modelling process or simulation, which usually requires the data-handling skills associated with collecting, organising and representing data to be utilised. In this way, activities enable children to use data as a tool for making decisions about probability. An understanding of fractions, ratio, proportion and combinatorial thinking are essential if students are to grow in their understanding of chance and probability in experimental situations.

1. Mixed-up toys

Preschoolers were exploring the computer program, *The playroom*, by Brøderbund Software (1995). One component of the program—the mixed-up toy—allows the children to design their own toy by changing its head, torso or legs. Combinations of body parts can be created randomly by clicking the mouse on the button marked with a '?' or students can make deliberate choices by clicking on selected body parts. The children liked to create their favourite mixed-up toys, print them and then make up strange names (see Figure 9.4). Their teacher asked them to make their own mixed-up toy by cutting pictures from magazines (see Figure 9.5).

Teacher's comment

> *The children cut many pictures from the magazines. Each picture was then cut into two parts and placed in the centre of the table. We thought that we'd just start with two parts rather than three, to make it simpler to talk about possible combinations. We encouraged the children to experiment with as many combinations as possible before they chose one that they wanted to glue onto their paper. When we discussed our final mixed-up toy, Matthew described how he had just placed body parts together randomly. Others, like Emily and Sarah, made deliberate choices about their combinations. They tried several possible combinations before making their final choice.*

(Preschool teacher, 3- to 5-year-old group)

Mathematical content and processes
+ Uses everyday language to describe chance.
+ Systematically collects and organises data (pictures) to create something new.

Mattnew S

Figure 9.4 Matthew's mixed-up toy 'Cloborse' created with the program, *The playroom*

M
A
A
R

B
E
A
N

Emily
Emily

Figure 9.5 Emily's mixed-up toys were created from magazine cut-outs. The names chosen for the toys are a combination of the letters from each body part

- + Uses the process of randomisation.
- + Explores different combinations.

Posing key questions to assess learning
- + Tell me about the mixed-up toys you can make on the computer.
- + How is the mixed-up toy you made from magazine cuttings different from the mixed-up toy on the computer?
- + How is your toy different from Matthew's toy (see Figure 9.4)?
- + What different combinations can you make from these two heads and this body? Can you find all the possible combinations? (Increase the difficulty of the investigation by gradually adding more toys or by cutting the toys into more pieces.)

Extending the investigation
Children can be encouraged to:
- + investigate commercially made books that utilise the mix-and-match concept, for example *Bananas in pyjamas: All mixed-up* (Australian Broadcasting Corporation, 1996).
- + investigate the existence of mythical creatures that are made from a combination of different animals (e.g. the Minotaur, Pan and the Sphinx); and
- + explore the existence of real animals that seem to be made from a combination of different animals (e.g. the platypus).

253

2. A chance of rain

Year 2 and Year 3 students recorded information about the weather for two weeks. They collected weather forecasts from newspapers each day and used a thermometer to see how accurate the reports were. The Year 3 children made a 'chance of rain' scale more complex than that used by many newspapers and used it to make their own predictions about the likelihood of rain (see Figures 9.6 and 9.7).

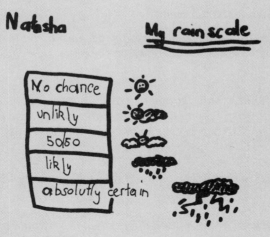

Figure 9.6 Natasha's 'chance of rain' scale

Date	Day	Temperature	Chance of Rain
3-5-97	Sat	25°C	Unlikely
4-5-97	Sun	25°C	Unlikely
5-5-97	Mon	23°C	50/50
6-5-97	Tue	23°C	likely
7-5-97	Wed	23°C	definitly
8-5-97	Thu	20°C	Likely
9-5-97	FRI	19°C	unlikely
10-5-97	Sat	17°C	definitely
11-5-97	Sun	16°C	50/50
12-5-97	MON	13-18	maybe
13-5-97	TUE	20°C	likely

Figure 9.7 Daniel recorded maximum temperatures and his personal statement regarding the chance of rain, and made drawings to indicate actual climatic conditions

Teacher's, parent's and students' comments

I think there is a fifty-fifty chance of rain today because if you look out those windows you see clouds and if you look out the windows on the other side you can't see any (clouds).

(Renai, Year 2)

On Monday the newspaper said that there was a 'chance' of rain. At first it was sunny and we all thought that it wasn't going to rain. But after lunch these black clouds were everywhere and it did rain. Nearly everyone in the class had to change their drawings.

(Daniel, Year 3)

I was absolutely certain that it was going to rain today and it did.

(Natasha, Year 3)

It's about time homework became more interesting. Gary would ask me for the newspaper the moment he got home. He was following the weather forecasts in the paper for weeks

after the project finished. He got excited when reports matched what really happened the next day.

(Parent, Year 3 child)

Studying the weather forecasts was a great way to introduce the language of chance to the children in a natural way. We brainstormed the words together and asked children with non-English-speaking backgrounds if they knew a word that meant the same thing in their own language. I felt that this helped everyone develop a better understanding for all the terms. Once everyone was familiar with the words, we used them to talk about the likelihood of other everyday events occurring, like the principal coming to visit us today, or of their parents winning Lotto.

(Teacher, Year 2/3)

Mathematical processes
+ Describes possible outcomes for familiar random events.
+ Recognises chance occurs in daily events.
+ Constructs scales to measure the likelihood of daily events.
+ Collects, records and interprets data relating to chance events.
+ Compares predictions with actual outcomes.

Posing key questions to assess learning
+ Tell me about your 'chance of rain' scale. Why have you arranged the words in that order?
+ If the weather forecast says that the chance of rain is 'likely', does that mean it will definitely happen? Why/why not?

Extending children's investigations
+ Investigate everyday sayings that involve the language of chance, for example 'Buckley's chance' and 'in a blue moon'.

255

3. The games we play

Year 3 children designed their own board games (see Figures 9.8 and 9.9 on the following pages). They made decisions regarding the use of random generators (dice, spinners or cards) and rules that would enhance the fairness of the games.

The children had been playing commercially made board games such as 'Snakes and ladders' and 'Monopoly' so that they could gain experience in using a variety of random generators. Discussions regarding *fairness* and *chance* were instigated by the class teacher before they were asked to design their own board games and random generators.

Teacher's and student's comments

Our game is 'fair' because everyone who plays has an equal chance of winning. We used two dice to make it harder.

(Melissa, Year 3)

Anna chose to use a spinner for her game. She made two—one used the numbers 1 to 6 and the other had the number 6 on it three times. She said the second spinner was to make the game go faster because a 6 would come up more often than any of the other smaller numbers. The use of spinners as well as dice turned out to be an important issue with the children that I had not thought about before. We had to discuss the whole notion of 'randomness' and 'fairness' twice—once for dice and once for spinners. They just could not make the connection between the two types of tools and would often predict different outcomes depending on the random generator used.

Both Anna's and Melissa and Kyle's games had added components of 'chance', either by writing instructions on some spaces or by requiring players to take a card with instructions for their next move written on it.

(Teacher, Year 3)

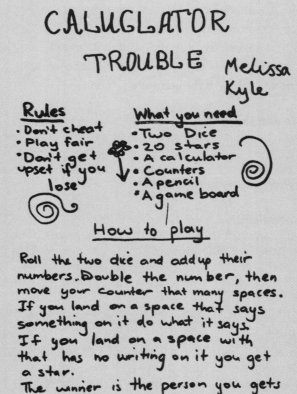

Figure 9.8 Rules and instructions for playing Melissa and Kyle's board game. There is an emphasis on 'playing fair'

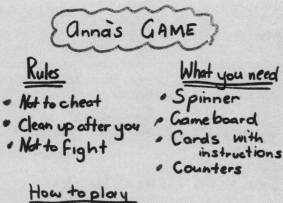

Anna's GAME

Rules
- Not to cheat
- Clean up after you
- Not to fight

What you need
- Spinner
- Gameboard
- Cards with instructions
- Counters

How to play

On the gameboard there are ? mark.

Everytime you land on a ? mark you pick a card

Spin the spinner and move your counter that number.

If you pick a card you must do what it says.

Start playing.

Figure 9.9 Anna's rules and instructions for playing her board game. The element of chance is emphasised by the use of '?' markers

Mathematical content and processes
+ Uses everyday language of chance.
+ Uses a variety of random generators.
+ Designs and makes fair and unfair games.
+ Explores elements of chance in games.

Posing key questions to assess learning
+ Why do you think your game is fair?
+ If the game is fair, will all players win an equal number of times?
+ How does 'chance' affect who wins the game?
+ Is the game still fair if one player wins three times in a row? Explain why you think this.
+ Does the use of a spinner rather than a die affect the outcome of the game? Why/why not?
+ What is the minimum number of moves needed for a 'lucky' person to win your game?

Extending children's investigations
+ Change the rules of some well-known commercial games so that they are not fair.
+ Design a game that is not fair. How do you know that it is not fair?

4. Rolling a die

Year 4 worked in pairs or small groups to conduct an experiment to see what number would come up most if they rolled a die 30 times. The teacher did not impose a special method for recording, but discussed what information they would need to keep track of before the start of the experiment. Figures 9.10, 9.11 and 9.12 show three different methods for recording the process and the final outcomes of the experiment.

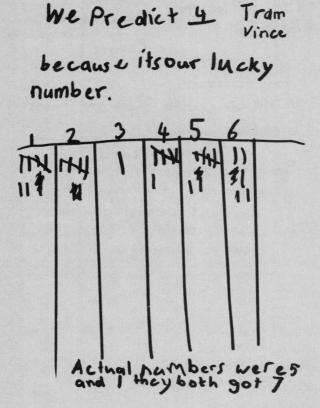

Figure 9.10 Tran and Vince used a tally system to keep a record of their outcomes

Teacher's and students' comments

> *At first we predicted that no number would come up most, but then we said that 3 would come up most. It was just a guess, because no one can really tell.*

(Karly, Year 4)

> *We predicted 4, because it's my lucky number. But 5 and 1 came up most.*

(Tran, Year 4)

> *Katarina and I predicted that 3 will come up the most because it's my lucky number. We said that it will come up 15 times because 15 is in the middle of 30. It's the logical answer. We were right—3 came up 15 times, so we were right.*

(Danna, Year 4)

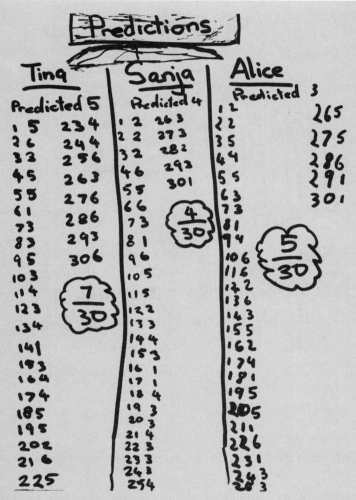

Figure 9.11 Tina, Sanja and Alice recorded the actual number rolled and then counted the frequencies at the end. The use of fractions to denote the actual frequency provided a good introduction to more formal ways of recording situations involving chance

Karla and Paige got into a big argument with Katarina and Danna over their prediction of 3 coming up 15 times. As luck would have it, it did come up 15 times and there was no way that Katarina or Danna were going to listen to Karla's view that it was 'just luck'. That's the messy bit when you deal with chance. You think you might help get rid of some fallacies associated with lucky numbers and the like when you do experiments, but because of 'chance' you can end up reinforcing them. I need to give the children more time to redo this experiment, just so we can explore their misconceptions more thoroughly.

(Teacher, Year 4)

Mathematical content processes
+ Uses everyday language of chance.
+ Predicts the likely outcomes of simple experiments.

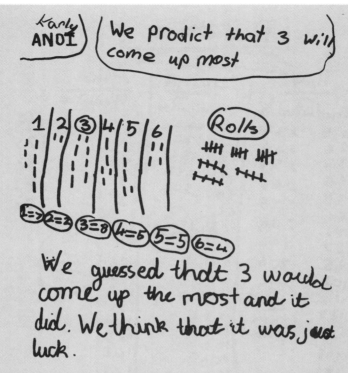

Figure 9.12 Karly and Andi used two types of tally systems to distinguish the frequency of numbers occurring from the actual number of rolls completed

+ Conducts experiments to find actual outcomes.
+ Collects, records and interprets data to inform decisions involving chance.

Posing key questions to assess learning
+ What number do you think will come up most often? Why do you think this?
+ If you rolled a '2' three times in a row, what do you think the next throw would be? Why?
+ Why do you think many commercial games require players to roll dice as part of the game?

Extending children's investigations
+ Collate data from the whole class in a table or represent them in a graph to study the impact a large number of trials has on the final outcome.
+ Repeat the experiment with a variety of other random generators such as spinners or playing cards numbered 1 to 6.
+ Investigate commercially available games that use dice as part of the game-playing procedure. Discuss the role played by the dice. What other type of random generators could be used instead of dice?

5. Pigs might fly

As part of her shared reading program, a Year 5 teacher read extracts from Emily Rodda's *Pigs might fly* (1996).

> *'Thanks, Sandy. It's really funny. I wish things like that did happen to me. Well, not pigs flying, because that's impossible, but . . .'*
>
> *'Maybe it's not impossible!' said Sandy, raising his eyebrows. 'I always say nothing you can imagine is totally impossible. It might be unlikely but that's as far as I'll go.'*
>
> *'It's all right for you to say, Sandy,' said Rachel disgustedly. 'Unlikely things happen to you all the time. But they never do to me!'*
>
> **(p. 9)**

After compiling and ordering lists of 'chance' words found in the novel, the teacher introduced the students to probability lines. The students were asked to order chance events on a scale from zero (never) to one (always)—see Figures 9.13 and 9.14. Decimal fractions and percentages were introduced when it was felt the children would make sense of them.

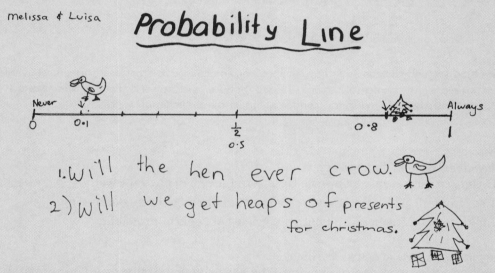

Figure 9.13 Melissa and Luisa's probability line shows an emerging understanding of how numerical notation can be used to indicate the likelihood of events

Teacher's and student's comments

> *When my mum says we are 'maybe' going to do something, it usually means we 'will'. That's about point nine on the probability line.*
>
> **(Claire, Year 5)**

> *The children were already familiar with the common fractions of one-quarter, half and three-quarters. We'd been studying decimals a lot recently too, so the probability line was a good way to link the two in a fun way. The book by Emily Rodda provided a great springboard, as I used the argument that, as in the book, we had to make up a scale to indicate to other people how likely or unlikely it was that things might happen.*
>
> **(Teacher, Year 5)**

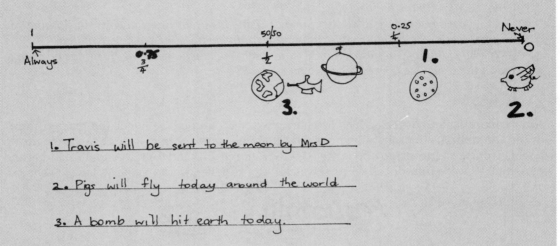

Andrew
Denniz

Probability line

1. Travis will be sent to the moon by Mrs D

2. Pigs will fly today around the world

3. A bomb will hit earth today.

Figure 9.14 Andrew and Denniz created some confusion among their classmates, as their probability line was drawn in the reverse order to everyone else's line. However, their sequencing of numbers indicate a developing understanding of numerical representations for the probability of events

Mathematical content and processes

+ Orders chance events on a scale from zero (never) to one (always).
+ Uses numerical notation to represent the likelihood of events occurring.
+ Links decimal fractions and percentages to concepts of probability.

Posing key questions to assess learning

+ Tell me about your probability line. Why have you placed that event on zero probability?
+ What is another way of writing fifty-fifty? One-quarter?
+ What things can you think of that have a probability of about 0.5 of occurring? Justify each one.

6. Horse race

Year 5/6 played the game 'Horse race' from the book *In all probability* (Great Explorations in Math and Science, 1993). Two dice are rolled and the sum of the two numbers rolled indicates what number horse gets to move forward. After playing the game a few times, the children were asked to find all the possible sums and the ways of achieving each sum (Figures 9.15 and 9.16).

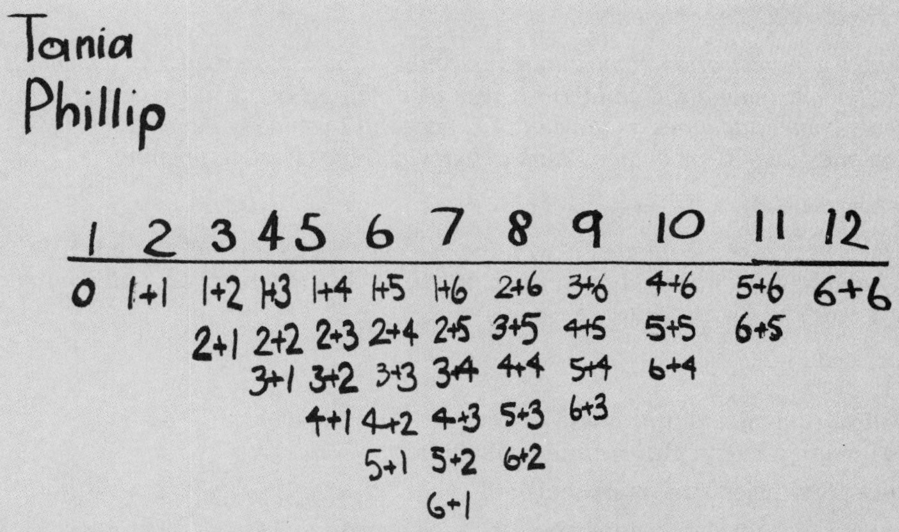

Tania
Phillip
1 2 3 4 5 6 7 8 9 10 11 12
0 1+1 1+2 1+3 1+4 1+5 1+6 2+6 3+6 4+6 5+6 6+6
2+1 2+2 2+3 2+4 2+5 3+5 4+5 5+5 6+5
3+1 3+2 3+3 3+4 4+4 5+4 6+4
4+1 4+2 4+3 5+3 6+3
5+1 5+2 6+2
6+1

Figure 9.15 Tania and Phillip systematically recorded all the possible sums

Win
Vu
2 3 4 5 6 7
3 4 5 6 7 8
4 5 6 7 8 9
5 6 7 8 9 10
6 7 8 9 10 11
7 8 9 10 11 12

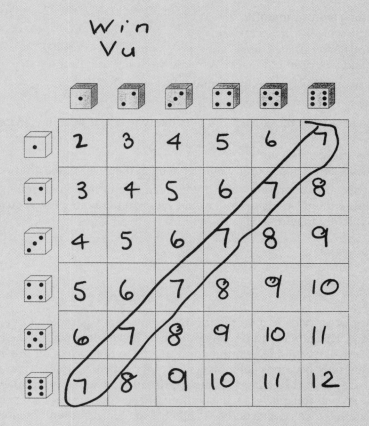

Figure 9.16 Win and Vu used a six-by-six grid provided by the teacher to help them find the possible combination and their sums

Teacher's and student's comments

> *Playing a demonstration game that involved the whole class created an enormous amount of excitement among the children. It was also helpful because I could give the weaker students some guidelines as to what to expect and I could challenge the brighter ones by asking questions to make them think about why things were happening.*

(Teacher, Year 5/6)

> *At first I bet on horse number 3 winning, because that's my lucky number. But after we found all the ways we could make each number, I decided to bet on 7 all the time. I didn't always win, but I was always close.*

(Tania, Year 6)

Mathematical content and processes
+ Uses the language of chance and probability.
+ Collects, organises and interprets data.
+ Uses data to inform decisions about chance events.
+ Lists systematically possible combinations of numbers and their sums.
+ Uses fractions to represent the expected order of likely outcomes (theoretical probability).
+ Tests predictions experimentally.

Posing key questions to assess learning
+ Which horse did you predict to win? Why did you pick that horse?
+ Which horse won? Why do you think that horse won?
+ Does each horse have an equal chance of winning?
+ How many races do you think each horse is likely to win if you play 36 games?

Extending children's investigations
+ Design your own game board that would give each horse an equal chance of winning.
+ What would the game board look like if you were to multiply the numbers on the dice instead of adding them? Which horse would be most likely to win? Which horse would be least likely to win?

7. Greedy pig

First-year primary preservice teachers had just completed a game of 'Greedy pig' (from Lovitt & Lowe, 1993). The game requires everyone to be upstanding while a die is rolled. Each time the die is rolled, players add the number on the die to the sum of all previous numbers rolled. This running total becomes each player's 'points' for that game. Players decide to sit down (and hence are out of the game) when they are satisfied with their total. If a '2' is rolled any time after the *second* roll, players still standing forfeit all their points for that game.

A stem-and-leaf plot was constructed (Table 9.1) to record students' scores for the first two games. The game and graph provided a springboard for discussions associated with randomness, fairness, independence of events and theoretical probability.

TABLE 9.1 A copy of the stem-and-leaf plot constructed by the preservice teachers to record their scores for two games of 'Greedy pig'

Game 2	Game 1	
Ones	Tens	Ones
0, 0	0	0, 0, 0, 0, 0, 0, 0, 0
6, 6, 9, 9	1	6, 6, 6
4, 4, 4, 7, 7, 7, 7	2	1, 1, 6, 6, 6, 6
1, 1, 1, 6, 6, 6	3	2, 2, 2, 2, 2
1, 1, 1	4	

The following discussion occurred between two students when the mathematics educator conducting the workshop questioned students about their strategies for winning the game.

Jan: I'll sit down after 4 or 5 throws because a 2 is bound to come up soon.

Kathy: Why?

Jan: If there's a 1 in 6 chance, we've already used some chances.

Kathy: But each throw is an independent event. Each throw has a 1 in 6 chance. You can't tell when a 2 will show—it's random.

Jan: Yeah. OK. I see . . . But the more you throw the die, the more likely you'll get a 2. I'm still going to sit down after 4 or 5 throws.

Teachers' comments

Jan's comment is fairly typical of adults who know a little about probability based on their personal experiences. Simply correcting her predictions or way of thinking will not make her understand that her reasoning is incorrect. She seems to be in a state of conflict between what she thinks should happen theoretically—because someone has told her— and what she really thinks will happen based on her informal understandings of probability. She's finding it difficult to resolve the conflict. There were probably other students in the workshop thinking the same thing, but just a little nervous about saying what they really thought. I consider it crucial to the development of their chance-and-probability concepts for me to continually challenge their understandings. At least I can get them thinking and talking about their beliefs to each other.

(Mathematics Educator)

Learning about chance and probability at uni is not like it was at high school. I hated it at school and didn't understand it. I realise that it will be my job to teach primary children about simple probability concepts so that they will understand it better than I did in high school and so that they will understand chance in their own lives better.

(Maxine, first-year preservice teacher)

I'd never seen a stem-and-leaf plot before and for a while I didn't know what was going on, but as each person entered their scores you could see how 'neat' it was. You could see exactly how many people got each score and the difference between the scores for the two games.

(Hoa, first-year preservice teacher)

Mathematical content and processes
+ Explores situations involving independent events.
+ Explores the role of chance, randomness and fairness in games.
+ Collects, records and interprets information.
+ Uses numerical notation to indicate the probability of an event.

Posing key questions to assess learning
+ Is this a fair game? Why/why not?
+ What strategies did you use to help you decide when to sit down?
+ What are the chances that a '2' will come up?
+ Is the likelihood of a '2' being rolled greater or less if the first five numbers rolled did not include a '2'? Explain your answer.
+ Why do you think this game is called 'Greedy pig'?

ACTIVITY 9.2

Assessing children's understanding

Consider the following snapshot and then respond to the questions that follow either by yourself or with a partner. Return to the definitions of chance and probability concepts presented at the start of this section to be certain that you have identified all the relevant content and processes evident in this example.

8. Pegs in a bag

During a Mathematics Fun Day, Year 1 and Year 5 were grouped together for several experiences. For the first activity, each pair of students was given a paper bag containing two pegs—a pink peg and a blue peg. The students were asked to predict the likelihood of each colour being drawn from the bag first and then asked to check their predictions. The second activity involved six pegs—three blue pegs, two pink pegs and one yellow peg. Again children were asked to predict the likelihood of each colour being drawn from the bag before trying the experiment themselves (Figures 9.17 and 9.18).

+ What chance content and processes are being developed through this experience?
+ What comments could you make about the worksamples in regard to each student's understanding of chance content and processes?
+ Predict likely responses to the second 'Peg in the bag' activity of a typical Year 5 student.
+ What questions would you ask to assess each student's understanding of the two activities?
+ How could you extend this investigation for a Year 5 student?
+ How could you change the second activity so that it would provide the students with experiences in *conditional probability*?

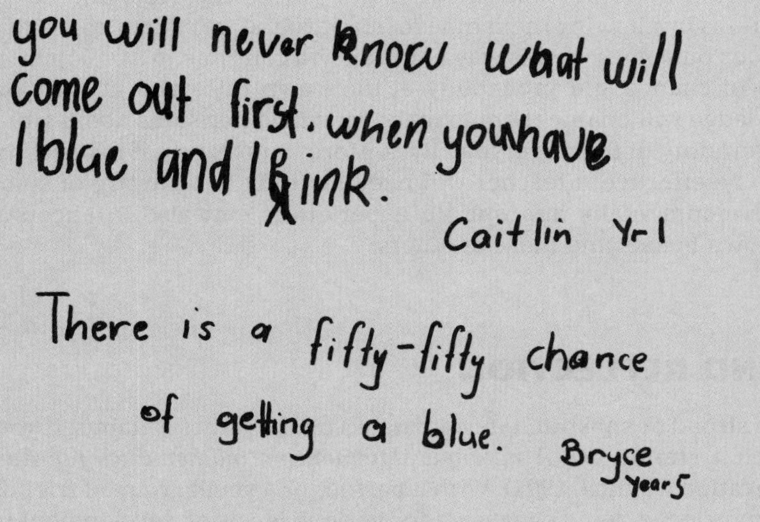

> you will never know what will
> come out first. when you have
> 1 blue and 1 pink.
>
> Caitlin Yr1

> There is a fifty-fifty chance
> of getting a blue. Bryce
> year 5

Figure 9.17 Caitlin and Bryce's responses to the first 'Peg in the bag' activity

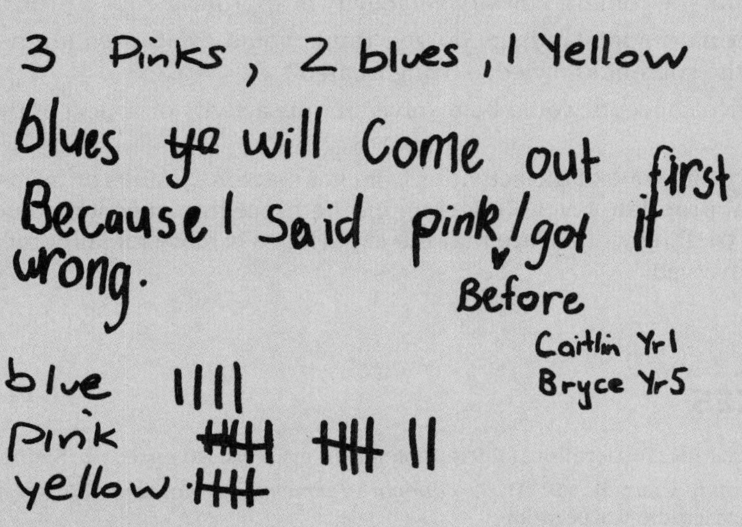

> 3 Pinks, 2 blues, 1 Yellow
> blues ye will Come out first
> Because I Said pink I got it
> wrong. Before
>
> Caitlin Yr1
> Bryce Yr5
>
> blue ||||
> pink   ‖‖‖ ‖‖‖ ||
> yellow ‖‖‖

Figure 9.18 Caitlin and Bryce's recordings of the second 'Peg in the bag' activity

SUMMARY AND IMPLICATIONS FOR CLASSROOM PRACTICE

This chapter has shown how everyday situations, such as forecasting the weather or reading children's literature, and experimental-type situations, such as rolling a die or tossing coins, present opportunities for the development of children's understandings of chance and probability. It is crucial that we challenge students' intuitive ideas, but we should not expect students to abandon their personal beliefs about probability instantly. We must allow them to experience instances when personal theories are proved incorrect and be ready to provide more formal notions by allowing them time to 'play around' with data, to make predictions and investigate various outcomes. In this way, children will continue to develop more sophisticated understandings of chance and probability at their own rates and at their own levels. Such increased knowledge will enable them to make informed decisions about situations involving chance and uncertainty in their everyday lives. More importantly, if instruction in chance and probability is to be effective, a teacher will need not only to be aware of students' intuitions and provide developmentally appropriate experiences, but also to encourage students to reflect on their own beliefs and those of others.

ACTION AND REFLECTION

Find the chance strand or substrand in your state's mathematics syllabus. If your syllabus does not contain such a strand, use *A national statement on mathematics for Australian schools* (Australian Education Council, 1991). With a partner or a small group of friends, look critically at the content knowledge being suggested for various levels of development to get an overall 'feel' for the strand. Focus on a specific activity or aspect of content and use the following questions to help guide your reflections.

1. Do you think the content knowledge/activity is appropriate for a primary-aged child?
2. What informal understandings do you think would exist in children and/or adults in regard to the content knowledge being treated?
3. What chance concepts would be involved in this activity or aspect of the content?

If possible, try out some of the activities from your state's syllabus or from this chapter with children of an appropriate level. Reflecting on the preceding questions before and immediately after your trialling will ensure that the experience is more meaningful for both you and the child(ren) involved.

REFERENCES

Australian Broadcasting Corporation. (1996). *Bananas in pyjamas: All mixed up.* Sydney: ABC Books.

Australian Education Council. (1991). *A national statement on mathematics for Australian schools.* Melbourne: Curriculum Corporation.

Board of Studies, NSW. (1993). *Teaching mathematics K–6: Problem solving through chance and data.* Sydney: Board of Studies.

Fischbein, E. (1975). *The intuitive sources of probabilistic thinking in children.* Dordrecht, The Netherlands: D. Reidel.

Fischbein, E., Nello, M. & Marino, M. (1991). Factors affecting probabilistic judgements in children and adolescents. *Educational Studies in Mathematics, 22,* 523–549.

Great Explorations in Math and Science (GEMS). (1993). *In all probability.* University of California, Berkeley: Lawrence Hall of Science.

Jones, G. & Thornton, C. (1993). *Data, chance and probability: Grades 1–3 and Grades 4–6 activity books.* Vernon Hills, Illinois: Learning Resources Inc.

Jones, G., Thornton, C., Langrall, C. & Tarr, J. (1999). Understanding students' probabilistic reasoning. In L. Stiff & F. Curcio (Eds), *Developing mathematical reasoning in Grades K–12* (pp. 146–155). Reston, Virginia: National Council of Teachers of Mathematics.

Kahneman, D., Slovic, P. & Tversky, A. (1982). *Judgment under uncertainty: Heuristics and biases.* Cambridge University Press: Cambridge.

Konald, C. (1991) Understanding students' beliefs about probability. In E. von Glasersfeld (Ed), *Radical constructivism in mathematics education* (pp. 139–156). Dordrecht, The Netherlands: Kluwer.

Lovitt, C. & Lowe, I. (1993). *Mathematics curriculum and teaching program: Chance and data investigations.* Vols I and II. Melbourne: Curriculum Corporation.

National Council of Teachers of Mathematics. (1989). *Dealing with data and chance: Addenda series Grades 5–8.* Reston, Virginia: National Council of Teachers of Mathematics.

National Council of Teachers of Mathematics (2000). *Principles and standards for school mathematics.* Reston, Virginia: National Council of Teachers of Mathematics.

Piaget, J. & Inhelder, B. (1975). *The origin of the idea of chance in children.* (L. Leake, P. Burrell & H. Fischbein, Trans.). New York: Norton. (Original work published 1951.)

Rodda, E. (1986). *Pigs might fly.* Sydney: Angus and Robertson.

Tarr, J. & Jones, G. (1997). A framework for assessing middle school students' thinking in conditional probability and independence. *Mathematics Education Research Journal, 9*(1), 39–59.

Truran, K. (1995). Animism: A view of probability behaviour. In B. Atweh & S. Flavel (Eds), *Proceedings of the 18th Annual Conference of the Mathematics Education Research Group of Australasia* (pp. 537–541). Darwin: MERGA.

Watson, J., Collis, K. & Moritz, J. (1997) The development of chance measurement. *Mathematics Education Research Journal, 9*(1), 60–82.

Way, J. (1997). Which jar gives the better chance? Children's decision making strategies. In F. Biddulph & K. Carr. (Eds), *Proceedings of the 20th Annual Conference of the Mathematics Education Research Group of Australasia* (pp. 568–575). Rotorua: Mathematics Education Research Group of Australasia.

Way, J. (2003). The development of children's reasoning strategies in probability tasks. In L. Bragg, C. Campbell, G. Herbert, & J. Mousley (Eds), *MERINO—Mathematics education research: Innovation, networking, opportunity* (Proceedings of the 26th Annual Conference of the Mathematics Education Research Group of Australasia Inc.), Vol. 1 (pp.736–745). Geelong: Mathematics Education Research Group of Australasia.

PART

3

Facilitating Mathematics Learning

Chapter 10
Linking assessment and instruction

CHAPTER OVERVIEW

The importance of linking assessment with instruction is emphasised in national and international curriculum documents (e.g. Australian Education Council [AEC], 1991; National Council of Teachers of Mathematics [NCTM], 2000). Research and the personal anecdotes of many teachers tell us that what is assessed is more highly valued by students, parents and the general community than what is not assessed (Clarke, 1988). Ideally, what and how teachers assess should be driven by *what* is taught and *how* it is taught. Traditionally, it has been the case, and often still is, that assessment 'leads' the curriculum. Increased attention to 'assessment for learning' requires teachers to deepen their understanding of assessment processes and to use more 'authentic' (Newman, 1996) and 'rich' (Clarke & Clarke, 1999) assessment tasks. Such tasks have already been provided in earlier chapters of this book through the 'Snapshots of learning' sections. However, these sections do not go into detail about strategies to collect, record and report the rich data that can be obtained through asking such questions. While these aspects will be addressed here, the main purpose of this chapter is to deepen your understanding of issues surrounding assessment and to focus on assessment practices that are designed to improve teaching and enhance children's learning.

Linking assessment and instruction is not always an easy task. In fact, research shows that beginning teachers consistently consider themselves to be less competent in both programming and assessment of students (Ewing & Smith, 2003) than in a range of other skills associated with classroom teaching. Research also tells us that teachers spend about a third of their professional time involved in assessment-related activities (Stiggins quoted by Bryant & Driscoll, 1998). Obviously, assessment and planning for learning are two key areas in teachers' work and it is critical that they develop competence in them both.

Chapter focus questions

The focus questions for this chapter provide a framework for its content. Consider the implications of each question for you as a teacher (some implications are in brackets, but you may think of more):

1. Where are the children now? (How will I know what they know? Have I selected the most appropriate task to assess this area of learning?)

2. Where do they need to go next? (Will I know in what direction instruction should take them? What is the purpose of developing this skill or knowledge?)

3. How will they get there? (Will I be able to effectively program and plan lessons that will help them achieve the intended outcomes?)

Inherent in this sequence of questions is the need to link assessment processes with planning and programming. Keeping records and reporting to parents and the children are also integral components of the process.

REFLECTION ON A CLASSROOM SCENARIO

Overcrowding the program

While on her internship during her final year of a teacher education program, Molly undertook an action research project with her Year 4 class to improve her teaching of mathematics. Figure 10.1 is a copy of the 'program' she was provided with by the classroom teacher at the start of the internship. The following entry was made in her journal in the final week of the term.

> *I believe the problem with the program the school had set was that there were too many topics to cover in too short a time. Topics were not revisited and students were introduced to many new concepts one after the other—though the students had learnt about informal aspects of length, mass and volume before being introduced to formal units. Due to whole school events, week 5 was so disrupted that there were no maths classes for the entire week! The program had to change. Revision was pushed aside since there was still new content to cover in the last week of term. This meant that I could not address the concerns I had about certain students' understandings of division before I was required to assess them. The topics will not be revisited until the next term. The students need longer periods of time to explore and understand these concepts. I wanted to address students' needs straight away, but there wasn't time in the program.*

A typical week in any primary school includes dozens of interruptions to the planned timetable. Teachers need to account for this in their program. If not, they will feel compelled to rush through the program simply to cover the content. Such an approach rarely results in effective teaching or learning. In these circumstances, it is often the case that more content results in less learning. Overcrowding of the program does not allow for meaningful development of concepts.

	Topics	Topics	Revision
Week 1	Length		Bar graphs
Week 2	Division (relate to × 4)	Division (relate × 5 & × 10)	
Week 3	Space 3D prisms		Addition facts to 20
Week 4	Multiplication (× 6)	Fractions and decimals intro 100ths	Tables × 2, × 4, × 5, × 10
Week 5	2D intro angles	Problems with money	
Week 6	Time (relate digital to analog)		
Week 7	Volume (order from largest to smallest everyday items)	Place value to 10 thousands	
Week 8	Mass—estimating 1 kilogram	Tables (intro × 9)	
Week 9	Subtraction (vertical algorithm 2 digit × 2 digit)		Subtraction algorithm 1 digit × 1 digit
Week 10	Revision		

Figure 10.1 The mathematics program Molly was required to implement on her internship

WHERE ARE THEY NOW?

Gathering the evidence

This section is about gathering the evidence a teacher needs to assess a child's knowledge and to make decisions about what instruction is required to move them to the next level of understanding. Before introducing individual strategies, we need to establish what is meant by the terms 'assessment', 'evaluation' and 'outcomes-based education'. We will also establish more clearly what the process of assessment and instruction looks like.

Assessment and evaluation

The terms 'assessment' and 'evaluation' are often used in non-educational contexts interchangeably. However, within the field of education, they are quite distinct. The easiest way to differentiate between 'assessment' and 'evaluation' in educational terms is to look at how these processes are described in your state's curriculum documents and *A national statement on mathematics for Australian schools* (AEC, 1991). These documents will no doubt iterate the focus of this chapter that 'assessment is an integral part of the learning process . . . the major purpose of assessment is the improvement of learning' (AEC, 1991, p. 21). Importantly, assessment is recognised as a 'process' whereby information is gathered to make judgements about what students can do and understand. These judgements are then used to provide feedback to parents, students and other educational stakeholders and inform teachers about what direction instruction should take. The distinction between ongoing assessment (formative), where information is gathered to provide evidence of a child's development over time, and one-off assessment tasks (summative) designed to assess learning at a particular point in the learning cycle—say at the end of a unit of work or to provide a score for a competition or entry into a selective school—is less of an issue now that the focus is on the selection of assessment strategies for specific purposes.

While assessment refers to the monitoring of student progress, evaluation relates to the teacher. Evaluation is 'the process of making judgements about the effectiveness of school/ faculty plans, teaching programs, policies and procedures' (Board of Studies, NSW, 2002, p. 138). Importantly, the distinction between assessment and evaluation processes made here are for an Australian context. The terms may have slightly different meanings in other countries.

The process of assessment and instruction

The integral nature of assessment and instruction can best be explained diagrammatically (see Figure 10.2). The process is composed of at least four phases, each of which requires important decisions to be made by the teacher so that appropriate evidence is gathered.

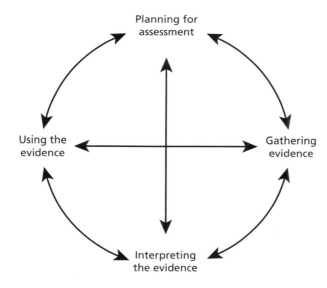

Figure 10.2. Phases of the assessment process (adapted from NCTM, 1995)

The *planning-for-assessment* phase requires teachers to consider the purposes for their assessment and to select the most appropriate strategies to suit their purpose. For example, if the purpose is to diagnose the general ability level of each child to allow ability groups to operate in the classroom, then diagnostic interviews may provide the most appropriate information (e.g. the Schedule in Early Number Assessment operating in New South Wales, the Early Numeracy Interview operating in Victoria and the School Entry Assessment in South Australia). Normally, teachers will not rely on just one type of assessment strategy to make their judgements. Whatever strategies are selected, it is essential that they provide the evidence about students' learning that is necessary to guide instruction and monitor student progress. It is also essential in this phase that teachers consider how they will record the information they gather.

The *gathering-evidence* phase involves making decisions about the nature of the tasks selected, and how and when they will be implemented. It also involves the actual implementation of the assessment tasks and the commencement of teacher recordings.

275

The *interpreting-the-evidence* phase requires teachers to examine the data they have gathered and analyse the data in terms of clearly defined criteria. Such criteria may be derived from syllabus outcomes (indicators), from established Frameworks (e.g. The Learning Framework in Number operating in New South Wales and the Early Numeracy Research Project Framework operating in Victoria) or from teacher-developed rubrics. By this phase, recordings from different data sources should be organised in a coherent manner to assist with reporting and final analysis. For example, a checklist with space for written comments may be an appropriate way to summarise data from several sources. It is also necessary at this stage for teachers to evaluate the choice of task—did it assess what was intended? Would a different strategy or task have been more appropriate or efficient?

The *using-the-evidence* phase is often the most difficult one. Teachers must now ask: Where to now? This involves decisions about planning appropriate instruction. At this phase, syllabus documents and established frameworks that detail typical learning trajectories of children provide teachers with a guide to further instruction. The decisions made in this phase will have implications for the cyclic process of assessment.

Importantly, this process is multidirectional—each phase is linked. This multidirectional process emphasises the integral nature of assessment and instruction.

Outcomes-based education

The statements describing the skills, knowledge and understandings which children typically develop in a particular area of learning (say, addition and subtraction) are referred to in most current curriculum documents as 'outcomes'. Student development on a particular strand in mathematics occurs in relation to the developmentally sequenced outcomes for that strand or substrand. Outcomes-based assessment shifts the emphasis from comparing performance of one child with that of another to an emphasis on each child's development along a continuum of described skills, knowledge and understandings (outcomes). Outcomes-based education also removes the focus on 'passing' and 'failing'. Outcomes, unlike 'benchmarks', do not provide standards of what students should be able to achieve by a particular age or grade and such statements are inappropriate where outcomes-based education is operating.

Outcomes-based assessment practices follow the principles of developmental assessment (Masters & Forster, 1996). First, progress is mapped against a sequence or continuum of outcomes that describe the typical growth trajectory of children in a particular area of learning. Second, assessment practices incorporate multiple opportunities for students to demonstrate their developing skills, knowledge and understanding of concepts and do not simply rely on one-off summative-type tasks (Spady, 1993).

While there are many ways to gather evidence of students' learning (observation, work-samples, interviews and portfolios) Callingham (2003, p. 183) makes the point that teachers can mistakenly assume from the emphasis on multiple-assessment techniques in curriculum documents that 'different assessment methods essentially provide the same information'. Her research indicates that girls usually perform better in classroom-based assessment tasks but that boys normally achieve better in examinations. She also found that students 'with high levels of mathematical skills might not apply these well in an open-ended practical situation' and that some 'students with lower levels of mathematical skills appeared to perform better' on these type of tasks (p. 189). Callingham's findings confirm previous concerns (Masters & Forster, 1996) that not all methods of assessment are fair to all students and that different methods may yield different information about a student. The implications for teachers are clear—we need to consider all tasks in relation to the purpose of the assessment (Will this task provide me with the information I need to plan further learning?) and provide a variety of assessment approaches (Are worksamples and a written test the best ways to assess this aspect of learning?).

Another factor often faced by teachers when they try to use a variety of assessment strategies is community pressure. When parents and students do not understand the purposes and usefulness of such methods they may object or request more traditional style assessment tasks and reporting mechanisms. It is important that teachers, with the support of their school administration, help parents, students and the general community to understand the significance of using a variety of methods for assessment and reporting purposes.

In the following discussion we introduce a variety of assessment strategies for gathering evidence of children's learning. While most teachers already use a variety of strategies for assessment purposes, it is often done 'on the run'. Teachers are constantly forming judgements to make choices about when and how to proceed. Such spontaneous decisions are a necessary part of every lesson. However, long-term planning should incorporate explicit strategies for generating appropriate assessment tasks, collecting relevant data and keeping systematic records. The strategies described below incorporate ideas for record keeping. This list is not exhaustive, but includes those most commonly used by primary school teachers.

Observation

While all teachers observe their students, it is usually to ensure that they are on task and are behaving appropriately. Evidence suggests that observation for the purpose of assessment, and the corresponding responses by teachers, is in fact quite a complex task (Morgan & Watson, 2002). In the past, observation has not been formally accepted (particularly by teachers) as a legitimate assessment strategy. This is partly due to teachers not structuring or systematically documenting their observations. Observational records that are not part of a systematic documentation process can be forgotten or be considered unreliable and be discarded. When done as part of a carefully planned assessment process (phase one of the assessment process described earlier), observation can be a powerful strategy.

While no one system of observational assessment will suit all teachers of all grades, it is useful to look at what other teachers do and adapt the process to suit your needs. Early childhood educators have legitimately used observational recording systems for some time. One such system focuses on a small number of children each week for observation in a range of key learning areas. Over a period of a few weeks, all children are systematically observed. Teachers often utilise small post-it notes that can easily allow records to be made 'on the run'. These notes should be transferred to an individual child's record sheet or folder and used to validate recordings on a child's checklist of outcomes (see Figure 10.3). Other systems may simply involve annotations on a class list (see Figure 10.4) or blank sheets with the 'focus' student's name at the top (see Figure 10.5).

Importantly, not all observations are worth recording. For observational notes to be useful as a basis for building individual and class profiles, it is necessary to identify significant moments that either challenge or extend the child and use these as a focus for the observation (Clarke, 1988). Clarke and Lovitt (1987) suggest that in deciding what these significant moments will be, it is helpful for the teacher to ask the question, 'Will knowing this change my subsequent teaching of that child or that lesson?' Adding a 'planning' column to observation sheets (as in the examples shown in Figures 10.4 and 10.5) will reinforce this notion of only recording those observations of significance for future instruction.

Questioning

Complementary to observation is questioning. Teachers ask many questions every day, but few could be termed 'good' questions (Sullivan & Clarke, 1990). By 'good' questions we mean those that encourage children to use higher levels of thinking and respond in ways that do not just

Indicator	Towards	Achieved	Beyond	Comments
WMS1.2 —uses a variety of strategies to solve addition and subtraction problems.			X	Used a number of complex strategies including split method, jump method, counting by 10s, 100s and multiples.
WMS1.4 —explains why an answer is correct. —changes the answer and self-corrects. —expresses a point of view about the correctness of an answer.		X X	X	Has achieved all these indicators quite well. Still lacks a little confidence with the correctness of an answer, but usually knows when to self-correct if a mistake is made.
WMS2.3 —explains the mental strategy used to solve a problem.			X	Excellent in explaining the strategies that could be used to solve a problem. Quite confident in own ability.
NS2.1 —counts backwards and forwards from any 3- or 4-digit number by 10s or 100s.		X		Highly proficient at counting by 10s and 100s from 3-digit numbers. Needs consolidation on counting from 4-digit numbers though.
NS2.2 —adds and subtracts two numbers using visual representation with and without trading. —explains and records methods for adding and subtracting. —uses split strategy for addition and subtraction. —uses an empty number line and jump strategies to represent solutions to addition and subtraction problems. —uses a jump strategy for addition and subtraction of 3-digit numbers.	X X	X X	X	Excellent in use of split strategy. Is able to explain and record methods for adding and subtracting very well, but needs consolidation on crossing the decade and century. Needs practice on adding and subtracting non-multiples of 10 as well. Is working towards utilising strategies for 3- and 4-digit numbers but a lot of work still needed. More consolidation still needed on number line work, but basic understandingg of jump method is evident. Need for introduction of more complex problems leading to work with larger numbers. Need to continue to develop confidence in using the jump method.

Figure 10.3 Individual child's checklist with annotations made from observations over a four-week period

require the recall of facts. Wood (2002, p. 64) found that 'differences in students' thinking and reasoning could be attributed to the type of questions that teachers asked'. The art of asking 'good' questions can be learnt, but it may require practice and attention to the qualities of good questions.

Questions can be described as either closed or open. Closed questions are those that usually require just one correct answer, often given from memory. According to Sullivan & Clarke (1990) and Sullivan & Lilburn (1997), 'good' questions fall into the 'open' category of questions. That is, they may have several acceptable answers and require more than remembering a fact or skill. For example, a closed question (e.g. What is the area of a rectangle 4 cm × 3 cm?) requires

Year 5 Class list Observations Term _2_ Week _3_ Topic: _Angles_

Name	Comments	Action/planning
Aldridge, Sharne	estimates accurately in ° to 360°	Protractor Work
Anderson, Judith	estimates accurately; hesitant use of protractor	consolidate protr.
Bobis, Janette	estimates well to 180°	intro >180°
Lowrie, Thomas	uses protractor correctly to measure	Construction
Mulligan, Joanne	estimates in ° to 360° well	Intro protractor

Figure 10.4 Example of an annotated class list

Observation Recording Sheet

Focus Child: _Nicholas_

Date	Notes	Planning
	Mathematics	
3/5	- trouble applying jump method to 2 digit × 2 subtraction in mental comput⁰ e.g 43-29	• Consolidate rounding to nearest ten & apply to jump method
5/5	- easily explained his strategy for estimating multiplication of 2 digits by 1 digit	• extend to 2 digits by 10
6/5	- Mastered 4× tables & knows corresponding ÷	• Introduce 4×10. ×100 ×1000 etc.
7/5	- More confident using jump method for subtract⁰. Able to jump to nearest 10 & subtract 1 or 2 to compensate	Consolidate
	English	
4/5	• completed all comprehension for Level 3 easily	Move to next level for reading group.
6/5	• Reading aloud - made errors that seemed to be due to nerves.	• Allow time to rehearse reading before reading to class /group! Check errors are only nerves!

Figure 10.5 Observational records of 'focus' student

only one correct answer, whereas the open question (e.g. How many rectangles can you draw each with an area of 12 cm²?) has multiple answers and will encourage higher order thinking.

Recently, educators have questioned the distinction between open and closed questions. Watson (2003, p. 36) found that 'what was more important was not the 'openness' of the question, but the opportunities it offered the learner to adapt, extend and refine a personal understanding of the concept', and sometimes this could be done better by a closed question. Watson recommends that teachers should also know how to 'narrow' the range of what is a possible solution to a question. By limiting the variation in answers (or narrowing the question) teachers are more likely to focus students' attention on the concepts they wish to be considered.

Rather than being concerned about a question being open or closed, it is perhaps more important that questions suit their purpose. Teachers ask questions for many reasons—to start an investigation, elicit thinking strategies, assess understanding or stimulate a discussion. For a sequence of questions to be most effective, they need to be well planned and have a clear purpose. Figure 10.6 provides a selection of questions for a range of purposes—all encourage higher level thinking. They are arranged according to the different stages of an activity and can be used as prompts for teachers to adapt in a range of contexts. For example, Figure 10.7 shows how a teacher incorporated some of these questions into a worksheet for her Year 3 class.

Starter questions

These questions are used to start an activity. They are usually open-ended, but will focus students towards investigating a particular concept or aspect of mathematics. For example:

- How many ways can you find . . .?
- The answer is . . . What might the question be?
- What patterns can you find . . .?

Questions to elicit thinking strategies

These types of questions help to focus children's thinking on the strategies they are using. They encourage children to explain their strategies, recognise patterns and build stronger relationships between concepts. For example:

- How can you group these . . .?
- Is there a pattern?
- Does that pattern help you solve the problem?
- How did you solve that?
- Have you found all the answers? How do you know?

Questions to justify their strategies and solutions

These types of questions challenge children to justify their strategies and their solutions. They help teachers to assess the level of understanding they have in regard to a particular concept, skill or strategy. For example:

- Is there another way to get that answer?
- Why do you think that?
- Which do you think is the most effective method? Why?

Questions that make the mathematics explicit ('So what?' questions)

These types of questions may be used to start a group discussion about the specific mathematics under consideration. They are used to share findings, compare strategies and make the mathematics *explicit* to the students. For example:

- Who used a different strategy to get the same answer? How can this be?
- Are everyone's answers the same? Why/why not?
- How does this activity relate to the topic . . .?
- How did this activity help you understand this topic better?
- Does it help you understand any other topic better?

Figure 10.6 Questions to encourage higher level thinking

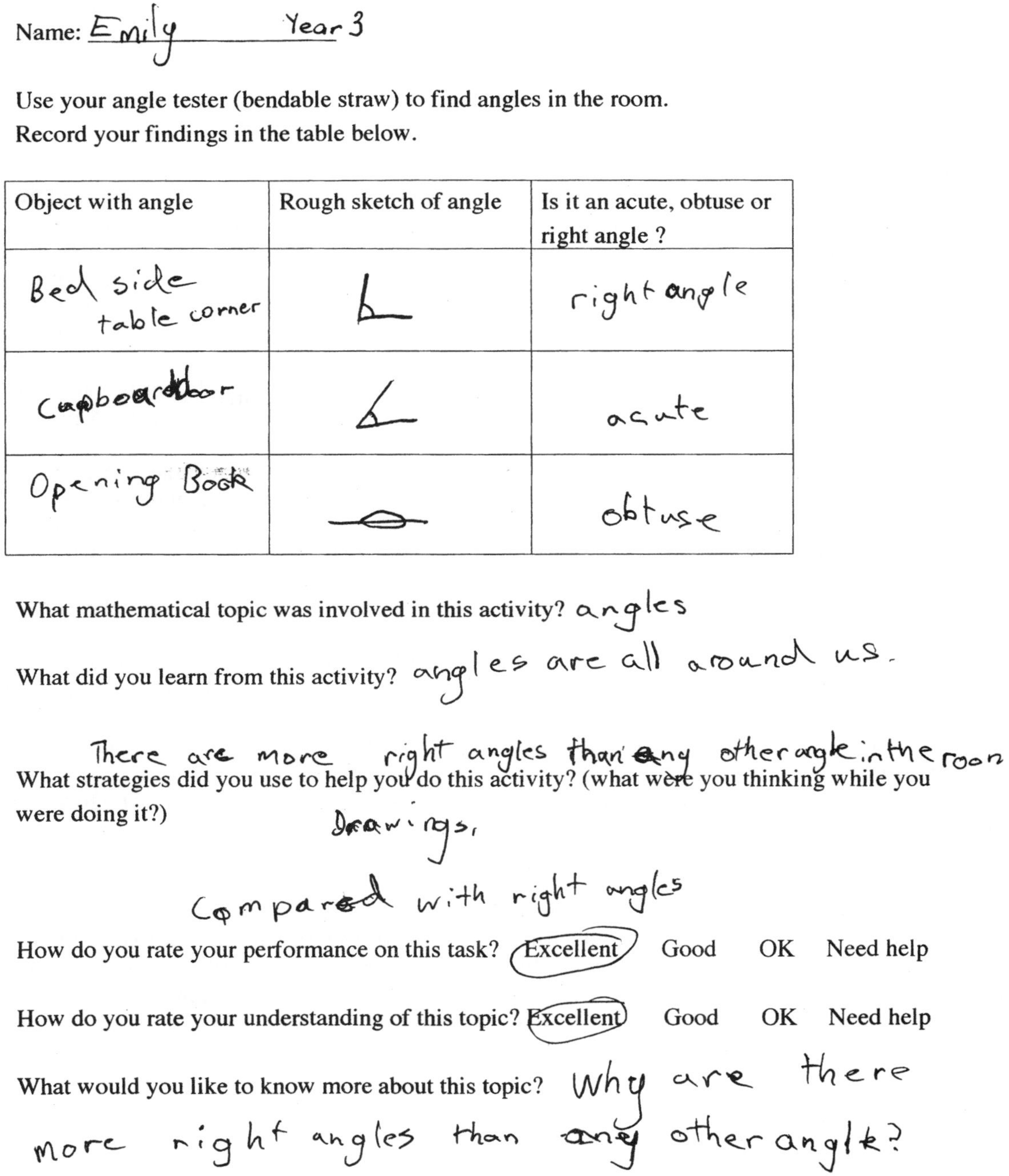

Name: _Emily_ Year 3

Use your angle tester (bendable straw) to find angles in the room.
Record your findings in the table below.

Object with angle	Rough sketch of angle	Is it an acute, obtuse or right angle ?
Bed side table corner	∟	right angle
Cupboard door	∠	acute
Opening Book	⟢	obtuse

What mathematical topic was involved in this activity? angles

What did you learn from this activity? angles are all around us.

There are more right angles than any other angle in the room

What strategies did you use to help you do this activity? (what were you thinking while you were doing it?) Drawings,

Compared with right angles

How do you rate your performance on this task? (Excellent) Good   OK   Need help

How do you rate your understanding of this topic? (Excellent) Good   OK   Need help

What would you like to know more about this topic? Why are there more right angles than any other angle?

Figure 10.7 Worksheet incorporating questions to elicit higher level thinking

An important point to remember when asking any type of question, is to give children sufficient time to think before requiring a response. Asking a series of questions quickly will only increase stress levels and encourage children to think less. One strategy to get *every* child thinking is to pose a question and ask each child to discuss his or her response with a partner. Children can then be asked to report their partner's response to the whole class. This encourages children to listen to others' answers as well as think of their own.

Worksamples

Worksamples are increasingly used in primary classrooms as a means of gathering evidence of children's learning. Much has been written to support teachers in using worksamples for the purposes of assessment and reporting (e.g. see Australian Education Council, 1994; NSW Department of Education and Training, 1998; http://www.sofweb.vic.gov.au/csf/WorkSamples). Importantly, teacher judgement of a student's achievement is not based on a single work-sample, but on their progress over time. Teachers need to consider a number of important elements when using worksamples as a strategy for assessment of progress. The *purpose* for collecting worksamples will determine the direction the other elements take. The worksamples may be required for inclusion in a portfolio to report to parents, to provide direction for instruction, or both of these. The purpose will influence the second element to be considered—*what worksamples will be collected*. Worksamples are not just 'worksheets'. They may include video and audio tapes, photographs, journal entries, teacher's anecdotal records, rough notes made by students, drawings, written tests and much more. For instance, the observation notes presented in Figure 10. 5 and the worksheet in Figure 10.7 may both be considered appropriate worksamples for collection. The worksheet in Figure 10.7 also contains elements of self-assessment. The use of student self-assessment has been described as 'one of the most constructive and empowering educational goals' (Clarke, 1988, p. 44).

Journal writing can be used as a worksample. Children can be asked to raise questions about things they do not understand or they can give a description of their thoughts and feelings about a specific learning experience or about mathematics in general. Figure 10.8 is a Year 3 child's journal entry explaining when one strategy is more appropriate to use than another.

There is a danger that the significance of worksamples collected over time may be forgotten and the sample may remain unused. Annotated worksamples help to alleviate this problem. Figure 10.9 (see p. 284) is a worksample that contains comments from a teacher (annotations) highlighting the significance of the work and providing details as to the student's developmental progress in relation to selected outcomes and indicators.

The nature of the worksamples will influence how the work samples are *collected and stored*. One system is to use some sort of folder kept in plastic tubs or a filing cabinet to store worksamples (a working portfolio). Selected worksamples can be removed according to the particular purpose of *the final product* (e.g. a portfolio for reporting to parents).

Written tests

Standardised tests

Parallel with the push for teachers to use a variety of assessment strategies has been the increased use of state-wide standardised testing in Years 3, 5, and 7 for benchmarking purposes. Unlike outcomes, which describe a child's progress along a continuum of skills, knowledge and understandings unrelated to their age or grade, benchmarks provide statements of what all students should know by the end of a particular grade. The *Numeracy*

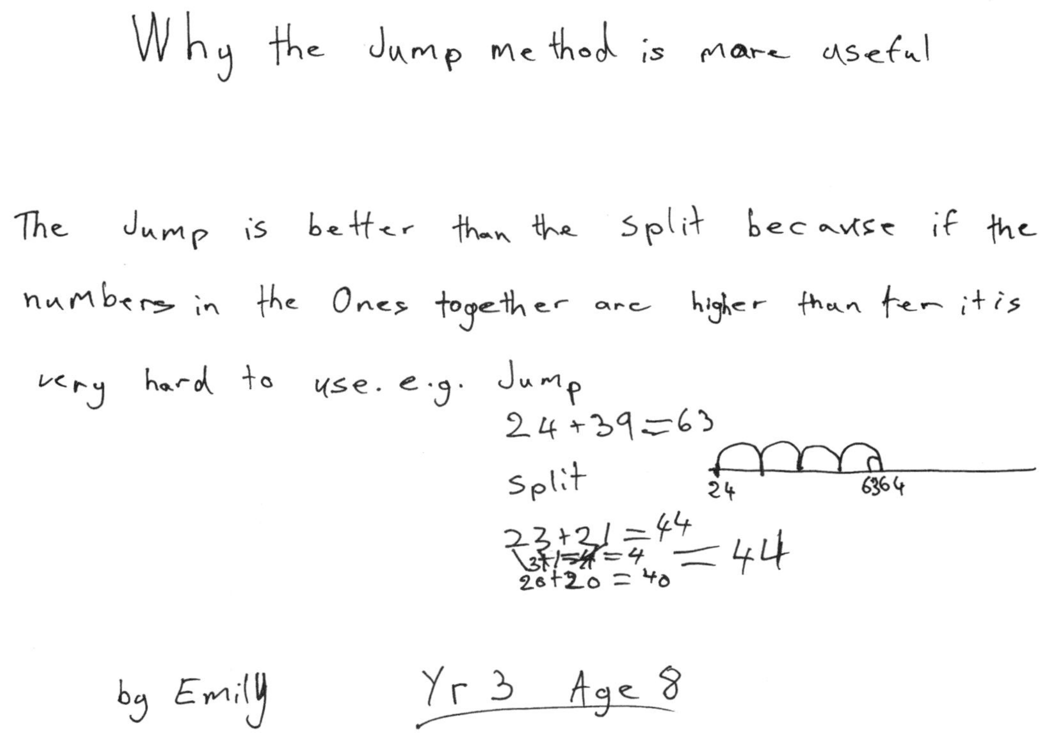

Why the Jump method is more useful

The Jump is better than the split because if the numbers in the Ones together are higher than ten it is very hard to use. e.g. Jump

$$24 + 39 = 63$$

Split

$$23 + 21 = 44$$
$$3 + 1 = 4$$
$$20 + 20 = 40$$
$$= 44$$

by Emily   Yr 3 Age 8

Figure 10.8 A Year 3 child's explanation of when one strategy is more appropriate to use than another

benchmarks years 3, 5 & 7 (Curriculum Corporation, 2000) are nationally agreed standards for these year levels. They are part of a national literacy and numeracy plan agreed to by all State, Territory and Commonwealth Ministers for Education. The benchmarks provide a basis for mathematics assessment at state level through existing testing programs such as the Basic Skills Tests for Years 3 and 5 and the Secondary Numeracy Assessment Program (SNAP) for Year 7 operating in New South Wales, and the Queensland Years 3, 5 and 7 Testing Program. It is important to realise that the *Numeracy benchmarks* only specify *minimum* levels of performance at each of these year levels and therefore may not reveal a child's true ability level. Further information about the standards-based assessment programs operating in your state can be gained from the relevant website. Figure 10.10 lists websites providing links to syllabus and assessment-related aspects for each state and territory and for New Zealand. It is advisable to become familiar with formal numeracy-assessment programs operating in your state as early as possible—they will undoubtedly impact upon your programming. When such formal tests are approaching, most teachers will modify their normal teaching strategies to prepare children for 'test-taking' processes. While we might rightly question the educational value of such learning, formal testing (for benchmarking purposes, entry into selective schools or for mathematics competitions) is still a reality and we would be disadvantaging students if we did not prepare them for aspects such as working to a time limit, answering multiple-choice questions and dealing with questions they do not know how to answer.

Teacher-constructed tests

Carefully constructed tests can be effective for collecting information about class progress and often allow students to monitor their own achievements. However, good test design must take into account many factors including suitable use of language and appropriate levels of

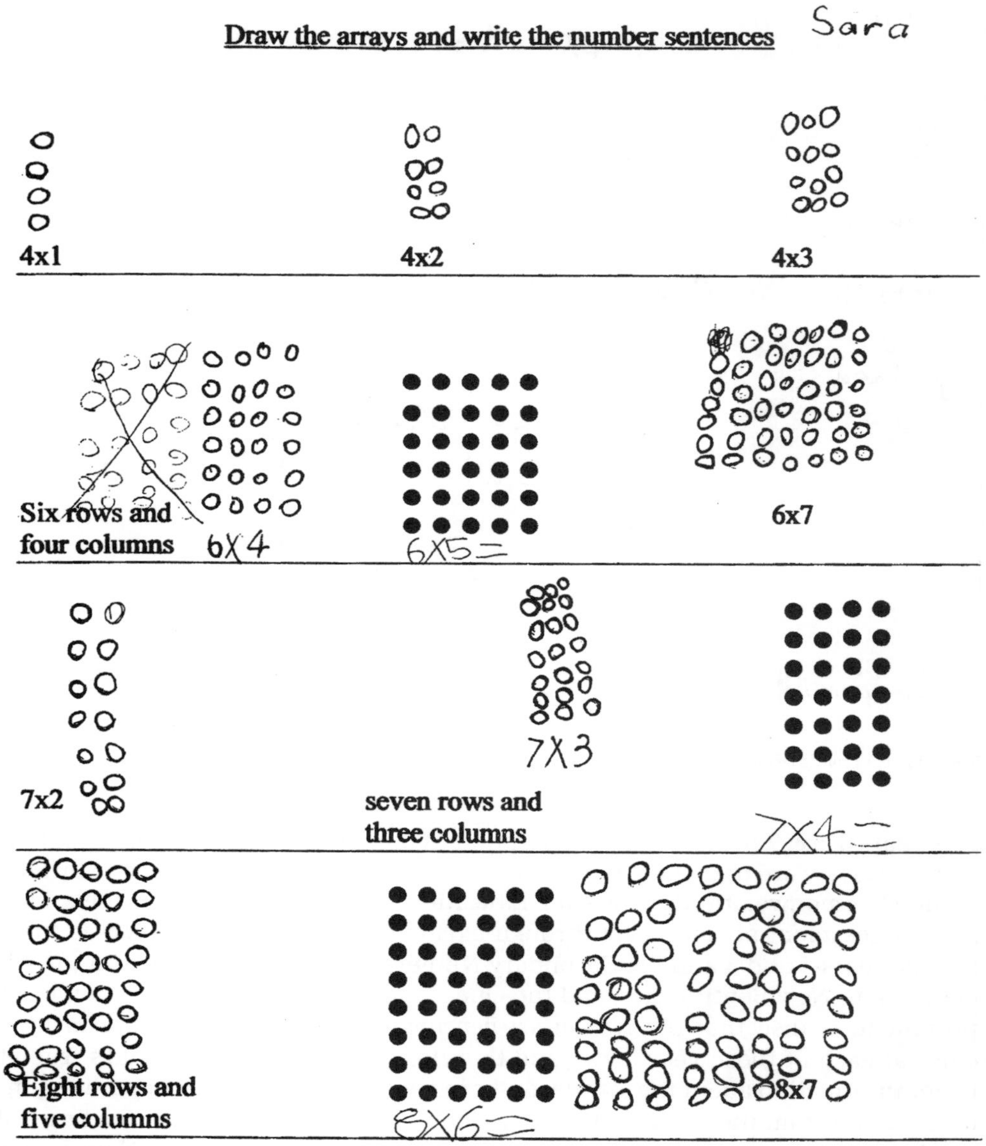

Draw the arrays and write the number sentences   Sara

4x1   4x2   4x3

Six rows and
four columns   6X4   6X5 =   6x7

7x2   7X3   7X4 =
          seven rows and
          three columns

Eight rows and
five columns   8X6 =   8x7

Outcomes and indicators	WT	A	WB
NS1.3: Uses a range of mental strategies and concrete materials for multiplication and division. • Uses columns and rows to multiply • Modelling multiplication as an array of equal rows e.g. Two rows of Three.	✓	✓	

Comments:
Initially the student encountered some difficulties doing the worksheet due to being unable to associate the relationships between number sentences and the pattern of arrays. For this reason, explicit modelling to substitute rows and columns to number sentences was required. However, once the student saw the associations and the patterns, she was able to complete the task without too much trouble. Also, this worksheet shows that the student is beginning to use columns and rows to multiply.

Figure 10.9 Annotated worksample. Provided by Gurleen Kaur and Melinda Chen

284

Queensland	http://www.qsa.qld.edu.au
New South Wales	http://www.boardofstudies.nsw.edu.au
Victoria	http://www.vcaa.vic.edu.au
Western Australia	http://www.eddept.wa.edu.au
Tasmania	http://www.tased.edu.au
Northern Territory	http://www.ntde.nt.gov.au
South Australia	http://www.sacsa.sa.edu.au
Australian Capital Territory	http://www.decs.act.gov.au
New Zealand	http://www.nzmaths.co.nz/

Figure 10.10 Websites providing links to syllabus, programming and assessment-related aspects of the curriculum

difficulty to enable all children to demonstrate their level of achievement, and care that the questions actually assess the knowledge and skills they are intended to cover. Hence, they should be constructed with specific outcomes in mind. If multiple-assessment strategies are being implemented, the need for frequent formal written tests should be reduced.

Teachers wishing to assess children's conceptual understanding, rather than just their procedural knowledge, can deviate from traditional forms of written mathematics tests. For example, a teacher wanting to assess her students' abilities to reflect on the effectiveness of different strategies to solve 2-digit by 2-digit addition gave her Year 3 class worked examples from a 'fictitious' student and asked them to comment on the strategies used (see Figure 10.11). The teacher developed a rubric for judging her students' responses (Figure 10.12).

Portfolios

I'm really proud of my students' portfolios because they were the hardest things I had to do in my first year of teaching! What made it so difficult was the fact that I had no system to manage the portfolio process.

(Beginning teacher)

A portfolio is a collection of worksamples strategically selected to provide evidence of student learning over a period of time. Different kinds of portfolios exist depending on their purpose. A *working portfolio* may contain drafts, finished products, rough notes of work in progress and the like. It is useful for a teacher and student when they want to review all the work done over a period. The work included in other types of portfolios is normally selected from a working portfolio. For instance, worksamples may be deliberately selected to exemplify a student's progress in a particular area as part of a *documentary portfolio*. The worksamples included in this type of portfolio are especially for assessment purposes and may be used as part of the reporting process to parents. Work included may not necessarily always be a student's best work, but may indicate errors and where assistance is needed.

A *show portfolio* would contain a limited amount of carefully selected work designed to reflect a student's best work. The show portfolio is often used for classroom assessment and reporting to parents. However, it is also the type of portfolio many adults, particularly teachers, compile for the purpose of employment and promotion.

In deciding what type of portfolio is necessary, Masters and Forster (1996) suggest teachers need to be familiar with four dimensions of the portfolio process. First, they need to consider the *purpose* of the portfolio (Is it mainly for formative or summative assessment?). Second,

Name: Nicky

Comment on this student's strategies for solving these problems.

1. $42 + 22 =$ **64** ✓

   correct

   42   52   62 63 64

   I would use the split or jump method. The split will work because the numbers all add up to less than 10. eg 4 2 + 2 2   good example

   4 + 2 = 6 ✓   60 + 4 = 64

   2 + 2 = 4

2. $27 + 19 =$ **46** ✓

   correct ✓

   27   37   38 39 40 41 42 43 44 45 46

   . The jump method is better because 7 + 9 is bigger than 10 and that is hard to keep in your head. It is better to jump to the next 10 and jump back 1. There are to many ones to count. good explanation

   I got the same for both questions   good explanation Nicky ✓

WM: 2.2 Selects and uses appropriate mental or written strategies, or technology, to solve problems

Indicators	Developing	Achieved	Beyond	Comment
Able to reflect on appropriateness of strategy for 2 digit addition			✓	Meaningful explanation of both strategies. Selected a more effective strategy – good reasons

Figure 10.11 Worksheet created for a Year 3 class to assess children's understanding of strategies

teachers need to consider the *content* (Should it include everything a child does or a purposeful selection of worksamples? Is the evidence relevant? Does it address the outcomes in question?). Third, a process for *selection and storage* of materials needs to be planned. Some strategies for this have already been discussed under the subheading 'Worksamples'. A number of schools are now using electronic portfolios. This enables teachers to integrate video with more traditional types of worksamples.

Finally, teachers need to have a method of succinctly recording the teacher's *judgement* of the evidence. The judgement of student achievement needs to be linked to syllabus outcomes

Working mathematically: assessment of strategies	
Outcome:	
Applying Strategies 2.2: Selects and uses appropriate mental or written strategies, or technology, to solve problems.	
Rubric	
Score	**Description of explanation**
0	Unable to provide sensible answer or no response.
1	Comments on correctness of computation only. No mention of appropriateness of strategy.
2	Meaningfully comments on appropriateness of strategy. Does not provide more effective strategy when needed.
3	Meaningfully comments on appropriateness of strategy. Provides a more effective strategy when needed.

Figure 10.12 Teacher-developed rubric for judging students' abilities to select appropriate strategies

and indicators. Indicators for assessing the contents of the portfolio may differ for separate components of the portfolio when it is composed of work from different learning areas, or a single set of indicators may apply when all the work comes from one area. Quite often, this type of judgement (summative) is communicated via a checklist (see Figure 10.3 on p. 278) or a rubric (see Figure 10.12). Care must be taken when using checklists that they are not seen simply as finite lists of skills and knowledge achieved but as a reflection of the 'whole picture' of a child's strengths and needs. The addition of comment helps to alleviate this problem and will allow for justification and elaboration that will be particularly helpful at parent–teacher interviews.

Individual interviews

The emphasis on early numeracy, combined with an interest in analysing children's strategies as well as their answers, has increased the need for students to be individually interviewed. While basically a combination of questioning and observational assessment strategies, the availability of carefully designed interviews has resulted in the development of some very powerful assessment instruments. The Early Years Numeracy Interview developed as part of the ENRP (1999–2001) in Victoria is used to assess students' numeracy for the first five years of school (Department of Education and Training, Victoria, 2002). Figure 10.13 provides examples of questions from the section on 'time'. The interview is normally conducted by the class teacher and responses can be recorded either electronically or on paper. The electronic version automatically navigates the interview for the teacher by determining pathways to be taken during the interview based on a child's responses.

Similarly, the Schedule in Early Number 1 and 2 (SENA) developed as part of the Count Me In Too program (CMIT) in New South Wales can be used to assess children's numeracy for the first five years of school (NSW Department of Education and Training, 2003). Figure 10.14 (see p. 289) provides an extract from the SENA 1 section designed to assess children's understanding of forward-and-backward counting sequences. Aspects of SENA interviews have been adapted for use in New Zealand and other states and territories in Australia.

Section E: Time

Equipment
- children's own hand-drawn clocks
- moveable yellow clock
- yellow June calendar card
- digital clock showing 12:51
- excerpt from TV guide
- blank digital and analogue clock faces

Prior to the interview, ask children to simply 'draw a clock'. If they draw a digital clock, ask them to then draw an analogue one. They bring these clocks to the interview.

38. My Clock
Depending upon the kinds of information shown in the child's drawing of a clock, ask questions like:
Tell me about your clock.
What are clocks for?
What are the numbers on your clock? (If relevant)
How do the numbers work?
What time does your clock show?
Tell me what you do at this time.

39. Telling the Time
Tell me what time these clocks show? (Use the yellow clock face.)
a) 2:00
b) 9:30
c) 2:20

40. The Days and the Months
a) Tell me the days of the week (*or* 'some days' *if the child hesitates*).
b) Tell me the months of the year (*or* 'some months' *if the child hesitates*).

41. Calendar Tasks
Show the child the yellow calendar card for June.
a) Find the 18th of June.
b) Tell me what day of the week that is.
c) Show me the last day in June.
d) Tell me what month comes after June.
e) What day of the week will the 1st of July be?

Figure 10.13 Extract from Early Years Numeracy Interview (Department of Education and Training, Victoria, 2002) designed to assess children's understanding of 'time'

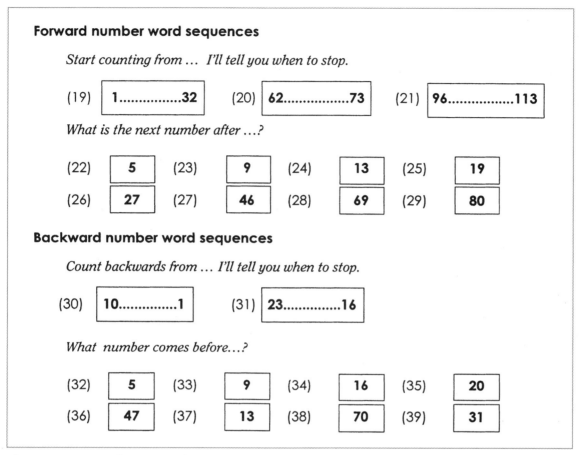

Forward number word sequences

Start counting from … I'll tell you when to stop.

(19) | 1...............32 | (20) | 62.................73 | (21) | 96.................113

What is the next number after …?

(22) **5** (23) **9** (24) **13** (25) **19**

(26) **27** (27) **46** (28) **69** (29) **80**

Backward number word sequences

Count backwards from … I'll tell you when to stop.

(30) | 10.............1 | (31) | 23.............16

What number comes before…?

(32) **5** (33) **9** (34) **16** (35) **20**

(36) **47** (37) **13** (38) **70** (39) **31**

Figure 10.14 Extract from SENA 1 (NSW Department of Education and Training, 2003) designed to assess children's understanding of forward and backward counting sequences

By themselves, interviews are simply a series of good questions. What makes them 'powerful' is the way each question or task is linked to a carefully constructed research-based framework (progress map or continuum) of mathematical development. Many of these frameworks are mentioned in the appropriate chapters earlier in this book and are briefly considered later in this chapter.

REPORTING

Reporting to parents and children

Weir (1985) describes how the principal and staff of a primary school had a 'reporting workshop' with parents. The parents were asked to tell them what information they would like to be given about their children's progress and their preferred ways of receiving this information. The parents indicated that they would like the following (Weir, 1985, p. 25):

+ the teacher's comments about how well/badly the child is progressing, areas in which the child's progress is satisfactory/needs more help, what the teacher will do about these, and what the parents could do;

+ whether there is a learning or behaviour problem, whether it is serious, what the teacher will do, and what the teacher suggests be done at home;

+ whether the child is behaving well at school, getting on with others, happy, interested in learning;

+ what is being taught/learnt and how it is taught;

+ what the child has to know;

+ what can be done at home;

+ what things the child has done well which parents can discuss with him/her after school.

The majority of the parents indicated that they would prefer to receive written reports, but that these should be two-way—a system of reply for those who wished to use it—rather than being just a one-way communication from the teacher to the parents. In order to meet the needs of parents it may be necessary to use a range of reporting strategies, such as parent–teacher interviews and sending home children's portfolios.

Giving feedback to children enables them to know where they are at in their mathematical development and how to progress further. Hence, such feedback should indicate both their strengths and weaknesses, and take account of their personal qualities and academic ability. Much of the feedback children receive is done orally and is provided every day. In addition, written comments and a teacher's actions will all communicate messages about what is valued and how the child is performing.

Reporting to others

One of the purposes of assessment is to report students' progress to others. This includes the preparation of records of development to be handed on to the next teacher as the child moves through the school. It can also include informal records and extracts from portfolios. Each school has its own requirements for keeping records of children's progress. It is advisable to find out what they are as early as possible so that you have sufficient time to plan your assessment process as you like.

As well as reporting progress to other teachers, it is often important to report to others in the educational or wider communities: principals and curriculum development officials, prospective employers and the general population are often informed about the progress of children in mathematics. The results of standardised tests, for example, are often considered as a benchmark by which to measure children's progress against a state or national norm.

WHERE TO NEXT?

Using developmental frameworks

Earlier in this chapter we reviewed the use of individual interviews as a powerful strategy for gathering evidence for the purpose of assessment. Frameworks describe the sequential development of children in a particular learning area in which growth typically occurs. Growth along a continuum is described at significant points—often referred to as 'stages', 'phases', 'growth points' or similar. Most states now provide frameworks to assist teachers in the assessment process. For example, developmental frameworks have been developed in Western Australia as part of the First Steps Numeracy Program, in Victoria as part of the Early Number Research Project (see Figure 10.15) and in New South Wales as part of the Count Me In Too program (see Figure 10.16).

1. **Not apparent**

   Not yet able to recognise and match simple shapes.

2. **Holistic recognition of shape**

   Can recognise resemblances and match some simple shapes, using standard 'prototypes'.

3. **Classification of shapes, attending to visual features**

   Can sort and compare shapes, using some geometrical language to describe features.

4. **Identification of 'classes of shapes' by some properties**

   Uses properties of shapes to classify shapes into classes, using appropriate language.

5. **Definition of shapes using properties**

   States and understands conditions for defining key shapes.

Figure 10.15 ENRP growth points for the domain of properties of shape (Department of Training, Victoria, 2002)

1. **Emergent counting stage**

   Knows some number words but is not able to count visible items. Either does not know the correct sequence of number words or cannot coordinate the words with items.

2. **Perceptual counting stage**

   Can count perceived items but not those in concealed collections. Perceptual counting includes seeing, hearing or feeling items.

3. **Figurative counting stage**

   Can count concealed items but counts from one.

4. **Counting-on stage**

   Can use advanced count-by-one strategies. Counts on rather than counting from one.

5. **Facile stage**

   Can solve simple addition and subtraction tasks using a range of non-count-by-one strategies.

Figure 10.16 Learning Framework in Number for the aspect of Early Arithmetical Strategies (NSW Department of Education and Training, 2003)

Frameworks provide teachers with a progress map or guide as to where children are at and where they should go to next. For example, Figure 10.17 is an extract of a teacher's individual analysis for a child in her class. The teacher conducted an individual interview (SENA 2), analysed the results in terms of the Learning Framework in Number (New South Wales Department of Education and Training, 2003) and then used the same framework to map some guidelines for instruction. Similarly, the Year 2 Diagnostic Net in Queensland requires teachers to validate observational assessment data with specifically designed assessment tasks. Teachers are required to use evidence from the observations and assessment tasks to monitor and report children's progress using developmental continua. The continua provide teachers with the basis for developing Individual Student Profiles. These profiles allow teachers to make decisions about the direction instruction should take for each child.

Once sufficient data have been gathered and analysed, teachers need to start thinking about how to help each child progress. The use of frameworks with carefully described indicators of progress helps teachers to make these judgements. However, even experienced teachers find the next phase in the assessment process the most difficult one of all—how will they get there? Figure 10.17 emphasises the importance of linking these two phases.

Student: Murray
Sena 2 Assessment: 11/3
Year: 3

Aspect to be developed	Where are they now?	Where to next?	Outcomes and Indicators	How?	Why?
Early Arithmetic Strategies	*Stage 3: Counting on.* Uses larger number and counts on to find the answer. Also displaying some strategies from Stage 4 e.g. partitioning.	*Stage 4: Facile.* Strengthening the known strategies and developing strategies that apply when working with 2- and 3-digit numbers in addition and subtraction.	NS2.2 Using mental and written strategies for addition and subtraction involving 2-, 3- and 4-digit numbers. • Uses patterns to extend number facts. • Explains and records methods for adding and subtracting	Using activities that will focus on developing these strategies while eliciting the most efficient strategy for the particular task. Teaching Point: Encourage the use of known strategies and encourage the exploration of more efficient strategies for completing the task. Consolidation: Explore the use of addition and subtraction strategies, such as jump and split method, through working with 2-digit numbers on the number line and through trading and non-trading using concrete materials, such as base ten blocks.	It is important that the student learns and explores more efficient counting strategies and that they have opportunities to practise these strategies, otherwise they would continually revert to using inefficient strategies and they would have difficulty solving large number problems.
Numeral Identification	*Level 5: 1–1000.* Recognises numbers up to 1000. Student was unable to confidently identify numbers after 10000.	*Level 6: to 100000.* Ability to recognise numbers up to 100000. (I think going further than this at this stage would not allow for the student to confidently understand these numbers)	NS3.1 Orders, reads and writes numbers of any size. • Reads, writes and says large numbers • Writes numbers presented orally	These activities will focus on exploring, naming and identifying numbers up to 100000. Teaching Point: Encouraging the exploration of numbers up to 100000, through reading, writing and saying them, while questioning the student. Consolidation: Through using place value charts, numeral expanders and base ten materials.	The extent of the number system is not fully understood unless students encounter large numbers, which are necessary, for example, in population figures and counting crowds. Through working with larger numbers, the student would be able to manipulate large numbers and gain a better understanding of place value.
Counting by 10s and 100s	*Level 2: Off decade by 10s* Counts forwards by 10s on the decade, but struggles with counting by 10s when off the decade.	*Level 2: Off decade by 10s* The student needs to have a few consolidating activities so that they are confident and able to count by tens off the decade.	NS2.1 Counts, orders, reads and records numbers up to four digits. • Counting forwards and backwards by tens or hundreds, on and off the decade.	Through providing consolidating activities for counting by tens and hundreds, the student will become more confident with it. Teaching Point: Exploring the hundreds chart and looking for number patterns when counting forwards and backwards. Consolidation: Using activities that explore the hundreds chart, such as putting strips of the hundreds chart back together, eg the strip 7, 17, 27, 37 etc.	It is important that the student learns the patterns of the number system when counting by tens and hundreds. This will provide the student with more efficient and flexible strategies for counting and solving problems mentally. It will also help the student to learn the place value of numbers and the structure of the number system.

Figure 10.17 Extract from a teacher's analysis of a student's results on the SENA 2. The links made to the Learning Framework in Number and the syllabus outcomes provide the teacher with a guide as to where the child needs to go next. Extract provided by Elizabeth Kerr.

HOW WILL THEY GET THERE? PROGRAMMING FOR LEARNING

Planning at different levels

Planning for mathematics occurs at various levels. These might include:

+ programming for a year (e.g. scope and sequence chart);
+ programming for a term;
+ programming a unit of work;
+ planning a day or week (perhaps using a daybook); and
+ planning a lesson.

It has already been noted that programming is an area in which teachers, particularly beginning teachers, consider themselves to be less competent than in a range of other skills associated with classroom teaching (Ewing & Smith, 2003). Planning, documenting and implementing a mathematics program is a challenging and time-consuming experience for most teachers. You will find that requirements for programming may differ from school to school. Hence it is difficult and undesirable to provide models that will suit all teachers in all contexts. However, we can provide some generic guidelines that will assist the process. Before presenting such models, it is important to consider exactly what a mathematics program is and why teachers need one.

A program is a *working document* that reflects as much about a teacher's beliefs about mathematics as it does about his or her knowledge of mathematical content (or syllabus content). Remembering that programming is part of the assessment-for-learning process, a good program should have as its starting point the needs of the children. Other factors that need to be considered include mandatory state or national curriculum documents, the school context and the teacher's own expertise. Among the many benefits, programs assist with the day-to-day running of the classroom. For this reason, they should be flexible and practical. In addition, programs help to keep teachers accountable to parents, principals and other stakeholders in the educational community. Programs are professional documents that explicitly record the knowledge and learning experiences provided to all students. They also provide the basis from which further learning will be monitored, assessed and reported.

Programming for a year

Most schools devise their own *scope-and-sequence* charts. These charts provide a guide for teachers of different year levels and are based on syllabus outcomes for each stage. They are particularly helpful in large schools, where there are multiple classes for each grade. However, a problem with scope-and-sequence charts is that teachers may equate 'topics covered' with actual learning. Figure 10.18 is an example of how teachers of Years 1 and 2 at one school used syllabus outcomes to plan a scope-and-sequence chart for the measurement strand.

Programming for a term

Most teachers program on a term-by-term basis. Many teachers find this period to be too long to be trying to 'guess' what level of mathematics children will be achieving ten weeks in advance, so they plan for shorter periods of time. This may involve devising a number of smaller units of work.

Outcome / Week	Term 1										Term 2										Term 3										Term 4									
	1	2	3	4	5	6	7	8	9	10	1	2	3	4	5	6	7	8	9	10	1	2	3	4	5	6	7	8	9	10	1	2	3	4	5	6	7	8	9	10
Length **MS1.1** Estimates, measures, compares and records lengths and distances using informal units, metres and centimetres.		✓	✓																																✓	✓				
Area **MS1.2** Estimates, measures, compares and records areas using informal units.						✓	✓																													✓	✓			
Volume and Capacity **MS1.3** Estimates, measures, compares and records volumes and capacities using informal units.													✓	✓																										
Mass **MS1.4** Estimates, measures, compares and records the masses of two or more objects using informal units.									✓												✓	✓									✓	✓								
Time **MS1.5** Compares the duration of events using informal methods and reads clocks on the half-hour.													✓										✓																	

Figure 10.18 An example of a scope-and-sequence chart for the measurement strand (printed with permission from Julie Horngold, Brighton-Le-Sands Public School).

Programming a unit of work

A unit of work normally consists of a series of developmentally linked lessons designed around a central topic, theme or concept. Figure 10.19 is an excerpt from a literature-based unit on Mass for a Year 1 class. Numerous prepared units of work can be located on the web. For example, the New Zealand website, http://www.nzmaths.co.nz/, provides links to units of work for each strand. Besides providing a suggested teaching sequence of about a week's duration, each unit is structured to include details about resources and outcomes, and specific questions designed to elicit mathematical thinking and encourage the development of understanding. In addition, some units provide homework activities. Similarly, the Victorian website, http://www.vcaa.vic.edu.au/csfcd/smp/sp.htm, provides sample units designed to act as a framework for teachers to create their own program according to individual needs and teaching approaches.

Formats for programming units of work vary enormously. Figures 10. 19 and 10.20 are two examples using different formats. There is no *one* way to program; however, school administrators may sometimes prescribe a format or require a particular pro forma to be used.

Planning a week or day

Experienced teachers often plan on a daily basis using a combination of their program and a daybook (see Figure 10.21 for an example of a teacher's daybook). Teachers with experience may not need to record the structure of every lesson in as much detail as a beginning teacher. This is because they will have established routine teaching strategies applicable for most classroom situations (e.g. settling students and assigning tasks). However, even experienced teachers may need to document their lesson plans more extensively when required to teach a topic for the first time or when implementing a lesson requiring high levels of organisation.

ACTIVITY 10.1

Planning effective lessons

One way we can improve our teaching of mathematics is to critically reflect on our own teaching and the teaching of others. Have you ever considered what an effective mathematics lesson looks like? Think back to a lesson you remember as being 'good'. You could have been either the teacher or a student in the class at school or at university. Describe the scenario to a friend if it helps you remember the important elements of the lesson. List why you consider it to have been such a memorable lesson. Share this list with your peers and develop a list of elements for 'good lessons'. Could you incorporate similar elements in your next lesson plan?

Planning a lesson

While you will no doubt be able to develop quite a long list of elements for 'good lessons', this section will focus on identifying a smaller number of general components. When combined, these individual components form a useful pro forma or template for effective mathematics lessons. While we do not support the notion of providing a 'recipe' for all occasions, we agree with Sullivan (2002) that such templates have the potential to simplify tasks considered quite complex, particularly by beginning teachers. Lesson templates assist teachers by providing an overall structure, while still allowing them the freedom to adapt to different contexts.

Essentially, lesson plans need to convey information about the topic, intended outcomes and indicators, major phases of the lesson and resources, and provide prompts for evaluation and future planning. Consideration of lesson phases is most crucial to effective teaching. An effective lesson sequence consists of at least three phases:

Mathematics and Literature Unit: Who Sank the Boat? (Mass)

Weeks: 1–3   **Year:** 1

Theme: What is Mass?

Outcomes: MS1.4: estimates, measures, compares and records the masses of two or more objects using informal units.
Working mathematically integrated throughout unit.

Indicators	Learning Experiences	Resources	Assessment Strategy
Children able to:	Introduce text and unit via: • Discuss cover and pictures (text masked) • Add own text to pictures • Read text together and compare children's words with text	Who Sank the Boat? Masks on text Pen	Observe terminology and understanding children have of mass
	Present pictures of text out of sequence. Students order them and explain their order. Make books from pictures.	Pictures from text Scissors, glue	Worksample
• Use everyday language to describe and explain mass (communicating)	Introduce word MASS (e.g. "*Who Sank the Boat* is a book which helps us understand a special maths word . . .") • Present two items of obviously different masses. Question children to elicit meanings of mass. Relate to everyday term: weight • Find words in text describing the animals' masses. Start word bank.	Text Word Bank	
• Compare mass of two or more objects by estimating and hefting			
• Order mass of two or more objects using equal-arm balance (applying strategies) • Recording findings using pictures and words (communicating)	Apply knowledge of mass to classroom objects. • Children collect three objects and supply words to describe/compare mass. Add words to word bank. • Select one item. Stand next to someone you think has an object of similar mass. Check by hefting & then equal arm balance. • Order all three items according to mass using hefting. Check with equal-arm balance. Record using pictures & words.	Collection of suitable items	Observation notes & recordings

Figure 10.19 Example of a unit format

296

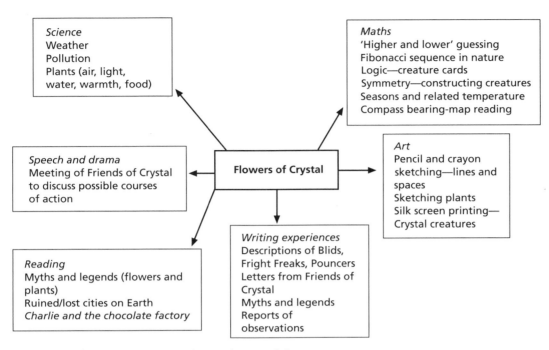

Science
Weather
Pollution
Plants (air, light,
water, warmth, food)

Maths
'Higher and lower' guessing
Fibonacci sequence in nature
Logic—creature cards
Symmetry—constructing creatures
Seasons and related temperature
Compass bearing-map reading

Speech and drama
Meeting of Friends of Crystal
to discuss possible courses
of action

Flowers of Crystal

Art
Pencil and crayon
sketching—lines and
spaces
Sketching plants
Silk screen printing—
Crystal creatures

Reading
Myths and legends (flowers and
plants)
Ruined/lost cities on Earth
Charlie and the chocolate factory

Writing experiences
Descriptions of Blids,
Fright Freaks, Pouncers
Letters from Friends of
Crystal
Myths and legends
Reports of
observations

Figure 10.20 Example of a unit planned around a central theme

Term 2 Week 3   Monday   Date   3/6

Morning Session:
9–10 : Math Intro of MASS unit. (Equal-arm-balance)
10–10.20: Spelling List & Homework
10.20–11 : Reading Groups.
        (4 parents helping)

Midday Session:
11.30 – 12.15 :   Library   (RFF)

12.15– 1pm : HSIE – part 2 Environment of Coastal Region
                Brainstorm Session

Afternoon Session:
  DEAR (15 mins)
  2.15 : Music : Recorder practice for assembly
  2.30 : Fitness & skills (Ropes, balls, witches' hats)

Figure 10.21 Example of a teacher's daybook

1. An introductory phase involving the whole class. This phase may consist of revision via a game, discussion or a series of carefully selected questions (ones that do not just require recall of facts). It may also develop a context for the introduction of new content.

2. A phase involving focused teaching of a particular concept, skill or knowledge. This can be done most effectively if children are arranged in small groups with similar needs. Alternatively, if individual work is assigned, the teacher is free to move around the classroom and engage in discussions as required.

3. A final phase involving the whole class in sharing and reflection on the learning is desirable. This phase will assist making the mathematics more explicit to the children. Prepared questions will help this process. For instance: What did you learn in this lesson that you did not know before? What would you like to know more about?

The lesson plans shown in Figures 10.22 and 10.23 utilise the components outlined by this structure, but in two different formats.

SUMMARY AND IMPLICATIONS FOR CLASSROOM PRACTICE

The main purpose of this chapter has been to deepen your understanding of issues surrounding assessment and to emphasise the importance of linking assessment and instruction. A framework for the chapter was provided by the three questions:

1. Where are the children now?
2. Where do they need to go next?
3. How will they get there?

Consideration of this sequence of questions will assist teachers to understand how assessment practices can inform teaching and enhance children's learning. Planning and assessment lie at the centre of good teaching. This chapter has provided an overview of commonly used assessment strategies and has given guidelines as to the essential elements for effective planning. However, all this information should be considered in the light of school context and the needs of children.

ACTION AND REFLECTION

1. What would you do if your principal or a parent asked you to describe your mathematics program and justifications for your program? Prepare a brief hypothetical presentation for the principal or parent/s to outline what you have been doing, why, and where this will lead in the children's future learning.

2. Describe your own philosophy for teaching mathematics. In particular, describe the aspects of mathematics teaching that you believe to be important, and give reasons for your beliefs.

Class: 2F   **Topic: Number/Place Value**   **Week: 2**   **Date: 3/5**

Anticipated outcomes:
NS1.1: Counts, orders, reads and represents 2- & 3-digit numbers
Working Mathematically

Activity/purpose/Class structure	Indicators	Resources	Assessment
1. *Introduction: Consolidation/revision of counting by 10s off decade.* **Whole Class** (a) Select number on 100s chart and count forwards & backwards by 10s on & off decade. Significant questions • What patterns do you recognise? Explain. • How many times do you need to add 10 to 33 to get to 73?	Able to: • Count forwards by 10s off the decade for 2-digit numbers. • Explain/describe patterns (communicating, reasoning)	100s chart Worksheet	Worksample
2. *Exploration of patterns to introduce counting by 10s off decade using 3-digit numbers.* **Ability Groups** *Triangles:* (with parent) • Roll die and start counting from 10 (orally). • 100 chart. Colour patterns of 10s off decade to 100. • Take turns describing patterns. *Squares:* (with parent) • Number chart 101–200. Colour pattern of 10s off decade. Chn select 3 different starting numbers • Dot-to-dot by 10s off the decade for 3-digit numbers. *Circles:* (with teacher) • Use calculator – enter start number (e.g. 135) & count by 10s. Record on long strips of paper. Include forwards & backwards counting.	• Explore & record patterns when counting by 10s off decade for 2- & 3-digit numbers. • Using calculators to generate patterns (applying strategies)	Calculators Number Charts 101 to 200 & 100s chart Strips of paper Textas Dot-to-dot sheet	
3. *Closure: Consolidation & reflection on learning.* **Whole class** • Think of how you would explain your activity to a child in Year 1. What would you say? Tell partner. • Think of something new you learnt today or an interesting pattern you or someone else discovered. Write about it in your journal. Specific questions for different groups: • How did you know that you correctly counted by 10s off the decade? (picture is formed) (Squares) • What would be the next 3 numbers in your pattern? (Circles & triangles) How do you know?	• Explain patterns & new knowledge (communicating, reasoning)	Journals	Journal entries
4. *Evaluation of lesson* Were tasks appropriate for different abilities in class? Where to now for each group?			

Figure 10.22 An example of a lesson plan using a horizontal format

Topic: Multiplication & Division   **Class:** 3/4 M   **Date:** 7 August

Outcomes:
NS2.3: Uses mental and informal written strategies for multiplication and division.
Patterns & Algebra 2.1: Generates, describes and records number patterns using a variety of strategies and completes simple number sentences by calculating missing values.

Indicators:
- Linking multiplication facts to find total in arrays (reflecting)
- Justifies the method used to obtain an answer (reasoning)
- Describes and records methods used to solve multiplication and division problems (communicating, reasoning)
- Uses multiplication facts to work out division facts (reflecting, applying strategies)

Resources:
Array cards, multiplication and division cards, bingo boards and worksheet

Activity 1: *Introduction (Whole class)*
Aim: To consolidate students' knowledge of arrays from previous lesson and revise commutative property of multiplication using arrays.
Significant Questions: How can I find out how many dots are in an array without counting them all? Which method is the quickest? What do you notice about the array when we look at it from the other direction?
Steps
- Show a partial array on card (only contains one horizontal row of dots and one vertical row of dots e.g. 4×6). Students find total number of dots using multiplication as a strategy.
- Student writes the multiplication fact on board and records partial array.
- Turn array to demonstrate commutative property of multiplication. Ask student to record new fact and partial array on board.
- Ask children to suggest other examples and to explain relationships.

Activity 2: *Introduction of new content (Whole Class)*
Aim: To explore the inverse relationship of multiplication and division using arrays. Children are already familiar with some division facts.
- Select child to demonstrate the construction of an array for 3 × 4 with counters on magnetic board.
- Record multiplication fact including answer.
- Discuss its (inverse) relationship with 12 ÷ 3 = 4 & 12 ÷ 4 = 3. Use array to model relationship.
- Repeat with 3 × 6.
- Children explain relationship for class recording on board.
- Use pre-made array cards as flash cards.
Significant Questions/tasks: Tell me all the division and multiplication facts for this array. How do you know you have listed all the facts?

Activity 3: *(Small Groups)*
Aim: Consolidation of commutative property and understanding of relationship between multiplication & division.
Group 1 & 2: Match Array cards to multiplication and division fact cards. Memory & snap.
Group 3: Multiplication & Division Bingo.
Group 4: Worksheet revision of commutative property.
Group 5: With teacher for extension.

Activity 4: *Sharing and reflection*
How can knowledge of the relationships between multiplication and division facts help us in mathematics?

Evaluation:
Did the tasks cater for the different abilities within each group?
Were indicators achieved?

Figure 10.23 An example of a lesson plan using a vertical format

REFERENCES

Australian Education Council. (1991). *A national statement on mathematics for Australian schools.* Melbourne: Curriculum Corporation.

Australian Education Council. (1994). *Mathematics—Work samples.* Melbourne: Curriculum Corporation.

Board of Studies. NSW. (2002). *Mathematics K-6.* Sydney: Board of Studies.

Bryant, D. & Driscoll, M. (1998). *Exploring classroom assessment in mathematics: A guide for professional development.* Reston, Virginia: National Council of Teachers of Mathematics.

Callingham, R. (2003). A comparison among three different approaches to mathematics assessment. In L. Bragg, C. Campbell, G. Herbert & J. Mousley (Eds), *MERINO—Mathematics education research: Innovation, networking, opportunity* (Proceedings of the 26th Annual Conference of the Mathematics Education Research Group of Australasia Inc., Vol. 1, pp. 183–190). Geelong: Mathematics Education Research Group of Australasia.

Clarke, D. (1988). *The Mathematics curriculum and teaching program: Assessment alternatives in mathematics.* Canberra: Curriculum Development Centre.

Clarke, D. & Clarke, B. (1999). Developing and using rich assessment tasks: Some models, some lessons. In K. Baldwin & J. Roberts (Eds), *Mathematics, the next millennium* (Proceedings of the 17th Biennial Conference of the Australian Association of Mathematics Teachers, pp. 266–273). Adelaide: Australian Association of Mathematics Teachers.

Clarke, D. & Lovitt, C. (1987). MCTP assessment alternative in mathematics. *The Australian Mathematics Teacher, 43*(3), 11–12.

Curriculum Corporation. (2000). *Numeracy benchmarks years 3, 5 & 7 with professional elaboration.* Melbourne: Curriculum Corporation.

Department of Education, Training and Employment, South Australia (1998). *Quality assessment tasks.* Adelaide: Department of Education, Training and Employment.

Department of Education and Training, Victoria (2002). *The early years numeracy program.* Melbourne: Department of Ed & Training.

Ewing, R. & Smith, D. (2003). Beginning teacher survey—2002 cohort analysis of questionnaire data. Unpublished report to the Faculty of Education and Social Work, University of Sydney.

Masters, G. & Forster, M. (1996). *Assessment resource kit (ARK).* Melbourne: Australian Council of Educational Research.

Morgan, C. & Watson, A. (2002). The interpretative nature of teachers' assessment of students' mathematics: Issues for equity. *Journal for Research in Mathematics Education, 33*(2), 78–110.

National Council of Teachers of Mathematics. (1995). *Assessment standards for school mathematics.* Reston, Virginia: National Council of Teachers of Mathematics.

National Council of Teachers of Mathematics. (2000). *Principles and standards for school mathematics.* Reston, Virginia: National Council of Teachers of Mathematics.

Newman, F. (1996). *Authentic achievement: Restructuring schools for intellectual quality.* San Francisco: Jossey-Bass.

NSW Department of Education and Training (1998). *Using work samples in mathematics K-6,* Sydney: NSW Department of Education and Training.

NSW Department of Education and Training (2003). *Count me in too: Professional development package,* Sydney: NSW Department of Education and Training.

Spady, W. (1993). *Outcomes-based education.* Canberra: Australian Curriculum Studies Association.

Sullivan, P. (2002). Teaching mathematics: Describing effective approaches. *Reflections, 27*(1), 34–39.

Sullivan, P. & Clarke, D. (1990). *Communication in the classroom.* Geelong: Deakin University Press.

Sullivan, P. & Lilburn, P. (1997). *Open-ended maths activities: Using good questions to enhance learning.* Melbourne: Oxford University Press.

Watson, A. (2003). Opportunities to learn mathematics. In L. Bragg, C. Campbell, G. Herbert & J. Mousley (Eds), *MERINO—Mathematics education research: Innovation, networking, opportunity* (Proceedings of the 26th Annual Conference of the Mathematics Education Research Group of Australasia Inc., Vol. 1, pp. 29–38). Geelong: Mathematics Education Research Group of Australasia.

Weir, M. (1985). 'To whom it may concern'. *Primary Education*, July/August, 25–26.

Wood, T. (2002). What does it mean to teach differently? In B. Barton, K. Irwin, M. Pfannkuch & M Thomas (Eds), *Mathematics education in the South Pacific* (Proceedings of the 25th Annual Conference of the Mathematics Education Research Group of Australasia Inc., Vol. 1, pp. 61–67), Auckland: Mathematics Education Research Group of Australasia.

Chapter 11
Managing the learning environment

CHAPTER OVERVIEW

The mathematics that children learn is essentially linked to *how* they learn it. The environment in which children learn affects their conception of what mathematics is, how it is learnt and, ultimately, their view of themselves as learners and users of mathematics. Historically, instruction in mathematics has required students to be passive receivers of knowledge, working silently and individually to copy and solve numerous computations from a text or blackboard. This chapter advocates the now generally accepted view that learning is best achieved when students are actively involved in the teaching and learning process.

The Mathematical Sciences Education Board (in Lappan, 1993, p. 525) refers to learning environments conducive to the development of 'mathematical power for all students' as those that:

+ encourage students to explore;
+ help students to verbalise their mathematical ideas;
+ show students that many mathematical questions have more than one right answer;
+ teach students through experience the importance of careful reasoning and disciplined understanding; and
+ build confidence in all students that they can learn mathematics.

> *In reality, no one can teach mathematics. Effective teachers are those who can stimulate students to learn mathematics.*
>
> **(National Research Council, 1989, p. 58)**

This chapter is about stimulating children to learn mathematics by providing them with an environment that will maximise their potential for learning. A range of aspects concerning learning environments will be described to support the establishment and maintenance of conditions most conducive to learning mathematics in a variety of contexts. Research and practical issues related to the use of collaborative group work, games, resources and technology will be discussed.

Chapter focus questions

Before proceeding, consider the following questions and, if possible, discuss your ideas with others.

1. What is a learning environment?
2. How do we establish one that is conducive to the development of 'mathematical power' in students?
3. How do we encourage our students to be autonomous learners within this environment?
4. What is the teacher's role in this environment?

While there is obviously no definitive approach to teaching mathematics successfully, we can be informed by research findings and the 'wisdom of practice' regarding how children learn mathematics and about the conditions which are most beneficial for learning to occur.

THE LEARNING ENVIRONMENT

In this chapter, we take the view that the learning environment is more than the designated room or physical space in which instruction occurs. The learning environment is also created by the hidden messages conveyed about what is important in learning and doing mathematics—Silence or discussion? Speed or accuracy? Procedures or understanding? Hidden messages about mathematics are also sent to students via assessment. What and how we assess tells our students what is most valued in mathematics. This means that the mathematics learning environment is not only physically but also socially and emotionally constructed. To describe such an environment, we must broaden our view of the educational setting to include aspects of social, emotional and cultural development.

The vision of mathematics depicted in current syllabus documents from around the world requires students to view mathematics differently from what is conveyed to them by current classroom practices—as a static body of knowledge governed by rules and procedures that, when executed correctly, yield one right answer. There is international agreement that, for meaningful mathematics to occur, students should be actively involved in solving problems, explaining their reasoning, justifying their assertions, hypothesising, discussing, questioning and reflecting on their own thinking and the thinking of others (Australian Education Council, 1991; National Council of Teachers of Mathematics, 2000). Research suggests that within classrooms where instruction reflects such ideals, and where teachers are familiar with children's mathematical thinking, the students' views of mathematics 'coincided with the goals of the current reform documents', and their 'ability to explain and justify their answers' was particularly impressive (Franke & Carey, 1997, p. 23). Perhaps the overarching factor in an environment conducive to learning mathematics in this way is a focus on *making sense* of the mathematics.

Factors that determine the nature of the learning environment

Consider your response to the following episode.

Two Year 5 pupils were having a heated argument. They had been asked to devise their own strategies for multiplying decimals, and had found that their methods had given two different answers. Frustrated, they asked their teacher, 'Who is right?'

If you were the teacher in question, how would you respond to this question? What would you suggest they do next? The answer to each of these questions depends on the type of learning environment that has been established in the classroom.

In this particular instance, the teacher suggested that they use a calculator to determine whose answer was right. Having established this, the children were able to check back and find out where one had gone wrong. When they finally agreed that they thought they had a 'foolproof' method, the teacher asked them to use the calculator to see whether this method would always work.

Ultimately, the learning environment is influenced by a number of interrelated factors, including teachers' beliefs about mathematics, their knowledge of content, their knowledge of pedagogy, and their understanding of how children learn mathematics. In the episode just presented, the manner in which the teacher handled the situation is indicative of a problem-solving environment. She encouraged the children to find their own mistakes, thus empowering them to make their own decisions rather than always relying on her. The manner in which the children were encouraged to use a calculator to check what they had already done and then to extend their work by extending its applicability to other numbers was also indicative of an environment in which technology was integral to instruction.

However, the nature of the learning environment is not always controlled solely by the person facilitating the learning. It can also be influenced by a number of external constraints, such as the prior experiences of the children, parent expectations and school policy. A major obstacle to beginning teachers or educators wishing to instigate changes in classroom practice can be the culture that already exists—such cultures are usually determined by tradition at schools and nurtured by staff or groups of parents who are determined to maintain familiar practices. In such circumstances, it may take a great deal more effort and time to 'construct' a learning environment that is aligned to one's beliefs and expectations.

Determining the existing environment

Before we can establish an environment approximating that advocated in current syllabus documents and more conducive to learning mathematics, we need to examine more closely some factors that are likely to determine the nature of the learning environment. Figure 11.1 summarises the many factors that may have an impact on the nature of the learning environment.

Teachers' beliefs and their knowledge of content, methods and materials influence the decisions they make concerning instruction—decisions which determine the type of learning environment created (Fennema & Franke, 1992; Thompson, 1992). In turn, the learning

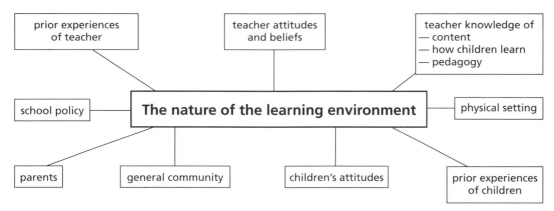

Figure 11.1 Factors that may have an impact on the nature of the learning environment

environment or 'ethos' established in a classroom has been shown to have an impact on the attitudes of students and ultimately on their achievement levels in mathematics (Bishop & Nickson, 1983; Ernest, 1988).

Obviously, a teacher cannot teach what she or he does not know. It is therefore imperative that a teacher has in-depth knowledge of mathematical content at a level beyond that at which they need to teach their students. The knowledge of what mathematical content to follow is crucial if a teacher wishes to lay the foundations for knowledge expected in the future. A teacher's understanding of mathematics needs to be strong enough to enable him or her to recognise and capitalise on opportunities that provide potentially rich mathematical experiences.

ACTIVITY 11.1

What makes an effective teacher of mathematics?

While important, a positive attitude and extensive content knowledge of mathematics do not necessarily guarantee that a teacher will be a 'good' teacher of the subject. They must also have knowledge about *how children learn* and *think* when solving mathematical problems (Fennema & Franke, 1992). Consider the following episode from a Year 2 classroom. How does the teacher's knowledge of how children learn help her assist the boy to use a more sophisticated counting strategy?

A young child attempting to find the total shown on two dice was heard by his teacher counting all the dots starting from '1'. The teacher was aware that the child was capable of counting-on from numbers other than one and sought to encourage the child to utilise this strategy in the current activity. When it was the child's turn again, he rolled a '5' and a '3'. Before he had time to start counting each dot, the teacher placed her hand over the die showing '5'. 'How many dots did you see on the die under my hand?' The boy responded immediately, '5'. The teacher then asked the boy if he could think of a quick way to find out how many dots there were altogether now that he knew that there were five on one die. 'Yes,' he replied after a short pause. 'I can go 5 . . . 6, 7, 8.'

The teacher was aware of the boy's level of strategy development and by hiding the number on one die forced the child to utilise the more sophisticated strategy of counting-on. Knowing something about the strategies children use to solve simple arithmetical problems such as this allows teachers to structure experiences that will encourage children to reach a more sophisticated level of understanding and strategy use.

Another essential component of teacher knowledge represented in Figure 11.1 is *pedagogical knowledge*. This type of knowledge refers to the general teaching and learning strategies teachers decide to utilise before, during and after instruction. Such decisions influence the physical arrangement of the learning space, the organisation of children, the selection of activities, the assessment procedures to be implemented and the like. This type of knowledge is built up through a variety of experiences over time.

ACTIVITY 11.2

Reflecting on the impact of teacher knowledge and beliefs on the learning environment

During a mathematics activity in a Year 4 classroom, a student approached his teacher and asked, 'What's 7 times 6? I used to know but I just can't remember'.

How would you answer this child's question? What is more important in answering this child's question—knowledge of content, pedagogy or of how children learn mathematics?

When a group of preservice teachers was asked this question they listed the alternatives available to them and then decided on which strategy they were likely to adopt. In so doing, they communicated their understanding and beliefs of how children learn mathematics and their knowledge of both content and pedagogy. Responses included:

+ Tell the child the answer immediately.
+ Tell the child directly or get the child to use a calculator or to look up a times table chart.
+ Ask the child to think of a strategy to help him or her find out. If the child knows what 6×6 equals, ask the child to use that information to work out 7×6.
+ Get another child in the class to tell the child.

Generally, preservice teachers rationalised their final strategy for adoption by commenting on the context. For example, if the aim was to enable the child to solve a more complex problem, most agreed that the immediate response should be to help the child derive a correct answer quickly, so that the child could direct more attention to the task requiring higher order thinking. However, most agreed that the question might be indicative of a general lack of understanding or poor learning strategies and should therefore be addressed in another context. Hence, student teachers agreed that knowledge of pedagogy and of how children learn mathematics were more important than content knowledge in this instance.

With the increasing emphasis on allowing students to be more actively involved in the teaching and learning process, their potential for influencing the instructional decisions of teachers will probably grow in significance in the future. However, a common problem facing many teachers wishing to establish a learning environment based on constructivist principles is the typical traditionally modelled environment students have experienced in their past. Before a different view of mathematics can be constructed for these students it is helpful if teachers take time to explore the existing perceptions of their students. By recognising the diversity of views in the classroom, the teacher will be better informed to create an environment which is conducive to the development of mathematically 'powerful' children.

ACTIVITY 11.3

Determining students' perspectives of mathematics

Try the following activity with your peers, and then with some children of various ages.

Close your eyes and try to picture a mathematics classroom. Where is the teacher? What is the teacher doing? Where are the children? What are they doing? What objects or instruments are the teacher and children using? Open your eyes and draw a picture of what you imagined. Compare your drawing with a friend's drawing. What things do your drawings have in common? What things are different?

Compare your drawings to the one prepared by a Year 5 child (see Figure 11.2).

This activity is used to help students overcome stereotypes about mathematics classrooms. Students generally picture a conservative looking teacher, wearing glasses and sitting at a desk or standing at a chalk board filled with written computations. He or she is usually using pencil and paper, books, a calculator or computer, and sometimes a ruler. The classroom is often a rather spartan-looking room, with students seated at desks in rows. The children are usually working individually from textbooks with a pencil and ruler nearby. These observations suggest that students view mathematics as a solitary endeavour that is carried out in a place very different from their everyday surroundings.

Figure 11.2 A Year 5 child's drawing in response to the question: 'What does a mathematics classroom look like?'

PHYSICALLY CONSTRUCTED LEARNING ENVIRONMENTS

The learning environment is influenced by many physical characteristics of the space available, such as the shape and size of the room. However, it is the ways in which these physical elements are utilised which reveal a teacher's educational philosophy, knowledge, beliefs and attitudes towards mathematics and how children learn mathematics. This section will discuss how the physical elements of a variety of settings may be utilised in an attempt to construct an environment conducive to learning mathematics and to the development of autonomy in children.

Setting up the learning environment—in the classroom

To encourage children to take responsibility for their own learning, we need to establish an environment that is inviting and supportive. Children need to be immersed in a setting that is both mathematically rich and well managed.

Furniture and space

The overall physical layout of the setting will reflect the philosophical base of the adult managing the environment. Large floor spaces for all age groups are extremely versatile. Early childhood settings catering for children up to 6 years of age utilise more open floor space and often incorporate the immediate outside spaces to help achieve this. Floor space is often more conducive to co-operative work and provides variation to seat work. While such expanses of free floor space may be considered a luxury to teachers trying to accommodate large classes of growing primary-aged children, a little creative thinking in regard to the configuration of furniture can often work wonders. For example, an upper primary teacher placed the two computers allocated to her room on tables with wheels. Each day the computers were wheeled outside the classroom to the enclosed veranda, where individuals or small groups of students could work independently yet still be supervised via open windows and doors. Grouping desks also makes more floor space available. Figure 11.3 illustrates how open floor space can facilitate the completion of experiments in probability requiring co-operative work in a Year 4 classroom. If school-aged children are not restricted to their 'own' seat they will make better choices when selecting the best working space for their tasks and will feel more comfortable working co-operatively with a variety of partners rather than the individual they have been 'selected' to sit beside for a period of time.

Figure 11.3 Year 4 children select to work on the floor to conduct their experiments in probability

Resources and the use of concrete materials

Issues surrounding the availability of resources—time to make and organise them, funds to purchase them and the like—repeatedly emerge as major constraints on teachers' preferred classroom practices (Bobis, 1996, 2000). However, the real power of physical resources lies in the manner in which they are utilised, rather than in the number or quality of presentation. This refers to how they are incorporated into learning experiences as well as how and where they are stored. Before responding to such organisational concerns, it is important to establish some reasons for using concrete materials to help children learn mathematics.

It has been shown that students who use concrete materials in their mathematics classes usually outperform those who do not. It has also been established that students' attitudes towards mathematics are improved when concrete materials are used (Sowell, 1989). These benefits are applicable to children from all grade levels, ability levels and topics with the proviso that the manipulative makes sense of the topic. However, the use of concrete materials is not sufficient to guarantee understanding. Like pencil-and-paper routines, students can learn to manipulate objects without understanding what they are doing.

While concrete materials such as pattern blocks, counters and base ten materials are important to learning, they actually have little intrinsic educational value 'in themselves' or on their own'. Children must be encouraged to reflect on their actions with the materials so as to construct meaningful relationships. It is important to ensure that students make connections between the conceptual work done with the materials and the procedural knowledge. It must be remembered that the use of concrete materials is a means to an end, not an end in itself. Ultimately, students should be able to solve most problems independently of concrete materials. However, the process of removing concrete supports should be a gradual one. Experienced teachers have noticed that even after content has been mastered symbolically, students often revert to using manipulatives to solve computations simply because they are available. Similarly, adults often find themselves resorting to using their fingers to add a small number to another, simply through habit. When teachers perceive the time is right, they must encourage individual children to function with symbols alone. Unfortunately, in the attempt to get students working with symbols as quickly as possible, many teachers often ignore important bridging stages between working purely with concrete materials and working solely with symbols.

When children have easy access to the resources they need and are expected to care for them, independence and responsibility are fostered. Therefore, it is essential that materials are accessible to the children at all times. Counters, calculators, measuring instruments and the like should be stored in clearly labelled tubs or on shelves that children can reach. Equipment not being used can be stored on higher shelves until it is required. The practicalities of storing resources in this manner mean that distribution and packing-away times are much shorter, and develop autonomy in the children. Many resources, such as large magnet boards, Lego boards, dart boards (where a ball is thrown instead of darts) or a hundreds chart can be fixed semipermanently to walls, and gameboards such as 'Snakes and ladders', 'Chess' or 'Hopscotch' can be painted on outdoor surfaces. In this way, resources are actually *built into* the physical environment. It frees up much-needed floor space, cuts down setting-up and packing-away time, and encourages children to utilise the resources more frequently.

Displays

Displaying children's work, as well as making the environment colourful and a cheerful place to be, can enhance self-esteem as it is often seen as a reward for work well done. If children are encouraged to take an active role in setting up, caring for and dismantling the displays they learn to take responsibility for creating and changing the physical environment. It also fosters the idea of valuing their work and the work of other children.

Displays that are regularly changed to reflect current topics being treated in the classroom can help children become more autonomous in their learning. For instance, children having difficulties could be encouraged to refer to displays before asking another child or the teacher for assistance. This behaviour will become more regular if the teacher models the practice and draws children's attention to where particular bits of information are located. Children should be encouraged to add newly acquired information to existing displays so as to reinforce the dynamic nature of their growing knowledge base.

Learning environments—outside the classroom

The home environment is an important component of almost every child's learning experiences. It is where they encounter their first and most influential teachers—their parents. While some children, for various reasons, are educated at home, this discussion is concerned more with how the home environment can be constructed to prepare young children for school mathematics and support the mathematical experiences of school-aged children that occur within the classroom.

Many daily routines involve basic mathematical concepts and skills that can help prepare young children for the more formal mathematics they will encounter at school. For example, setting the table involves counting and one-to-one recognition to ensure that the correct number of knives and forks has been arranged. Classification of items into groups occurs when cutlery is sorted into various compartments of the cutlery drawer, when socks are sorted into matching pairs and when toys or books are grouped on shelves according to a particular characteristic. Cooking, building with blocks and playing with various containers at bath time provide young children with important physical knowledge that is needed to grasp more sophisticated knowledge about space, volume, capacity and mass later in their school life. Most homes display calendars and various types of clocks (both digital and analogue). Recording special events on the calendar or setting the timer to indicate when the cake in the oven should be cooked are mathematical activities that young children can be involved in. Even at home, before starting school, parents can immerse their children in an environment filled with meaningful and purposeful mathematics.

It is important that schools support parents in trying to understand their aims and the methods of mathematics education, because the home environment remains an influential factor in children's mathematical development and success throughout their formal school life. Home mathematics kits, such as *Helping your child learn math* (www.ed.gov/pubs/parents/math/), and government-initiated websites are intended to increase the involvement and understanding of parents in their children's maths programs. Numeracy websites (e.g. www.nlnw.nsw.edu.au) provide advice to parents and teachers about how they can take a more active role in their children's education, such as engaging in family games that use a variety of mathematics skills and talking to their children about the occurrence of mathematics in everyday life.

Another learning environment outside the classroom that is underutilised by mathematics educators is simply the world around us. Showing the relevance of real-life objects or events to mathematics studied at school can make a topic more meaningful to children and can provide motivation for further study. Mathematics trails or maths walks around the local community are an effective way of increasing students' awareness of the mathematics in their immediate natural and artificial environment, and provide an ideal opportunity for the integration of mathematics into other subject areas. For example, a trail that focuses on the natural environment could integrate mathematics with science and technology.

It is important when constructing maths trails that questions have some mathematical purpose: that they do not just require students to 'count the number of petals on a flower' or 'the number of bricks in a wall', but rather challenge students to reflect on the purpose for the size and shape of petals on particular flowers or the need to arrange bricks in a certain pattern. The aim of maths trails or excursions should be to find maths in the real world and to help develop mathematical concepts.

311

SOCIALLY AND EMOTIONALLY CONSTRUCTED LEARNING ENVIRONMENTS

This section will examine socially and emotionally constructed learning environments, namely an inquiry-based environment and a technologically rich environment. Such environments are established not only by the arrangement of the physical setting, but also by the teaching, learning and assessment strategies adopted by the teacher. Instructional decisions can determine the nature of all classroom interactions and determine exactly how mathematically empowered students become. While a large part of this section describes an inquiry-based and technology-rich environment and how it might function, the rest of the section looks at the use of collaborative group work and games as instructional strategies that, when employed by teachers appropriately, can lead children to autonomous learning in mathematics.

Inquiry-based environments

Problem solving and the notion of it being the focus of school mathematics was introduced in Chapter 2. Involving students in problem-solving situations on an occasional basis is really a token gesture to the underlying principles of problem solving and can only result in a superficial treatment of the benefits such an approach can have on children's abilities to learn mathematics. The terms 'inquiry' and 'investigations' are used here rather than the term 'problem solving' as the latter often conjures up notions of textbook-type word problems, and has been used in the literature on problem solving in a generic sense to refer to any situation where a solution is not obvious. Inquiry-based learning, however, is much more than just problem solving; it is a framework, a philosophy or an approach to working with children that requires educators to pay attention to at least four important pieces of information: what we know about how children learn mathematics; what we know about the prior knowledge of children; what we would like children to come to know and understand in mathematics; and how we can challenge children to move to the next level of understanding. These four elements were discussed in Chapter 1 in relation to understanding children's mathematics.

Inquiry-based learning environments usually employ open-ended investigations where children are encouraged to find multiple solutions and to generate new lines of inquiry as they delve deeper into an investigation. In this way, children are encouraged to become autonomous learners, and teachers take on the role of facilitators and co-ordinators rather than just providers of knowledge. Franke and Carey (1997) define such an environment as one in which students have 'opportunities to consistently engage in problem solving, discuss their solution strategies and build on their own informal strategies for solving problems' (p. 10). Their research suggests that even Year 1 children can view 'mathematics as a problem-solving endeavour in which many different strategies are considered viable and communicating mathematical thinking is an integral part of the task' (p. 23). They found that children exposed to a learning environment of this nature 'assumed a shared responsibility with the teacher for their mathematics learning' and that 'success was not determined by speed and accuracy' (p. 23).

A common misconception about learning environments founded on the desire to encourage the development of autonomous learners who share in the decision making is that learning is haphazard and that teachers do not teach. Some ill-informed opponents of an inquiry approach equate it with noisy and chaotic classrooms. While this might be true of at least some classrooms where an inquiry-based focus is claimed, this situation is not conducive to efficient learning. In fact, environments where children are encouraged to be autonomous learners must in reality be highly organised to ensure that learning occurs with relatively minor obstructions. The difference between an inquiry-based approach and the traditional teacher-dominated environment is that children are actively involved and assume some responsibility for their own learning. They are encouraged to form their own hypotheses and to explore them through mental and physical activities—experimenting, observing, comparing findings, asking questions, discovering answers and posing more questions. The teacher's role is to provide experiences that will allow children to explore and develop increasingly more sophisticated ideas within a structured framework.

Any teaching approach, including inquiry-based learning, that is applied to all children without regard for individual differences and prior experiences will fail for at least some children. It is not possible to prescribe a set of steps that when followed would produce an inquiry-based environment because various contexts would require different 'ingredients' and often rely on existing conditions. However, it is possible to illustrate what an inquiry-based environment might look like in a variety of instances. What are the starting points of mathematical investigations which build upon children's natural curiosity and upon their existing mathematical understandings? What is the role of the teacher in an inquiry-based learning environment? One important starting point is to ask 'good' questions.

REFLECTION ON A CLASSROOM SCENARIO A

The answer is 20. What's the question?—A student teacher's dilemma

As part of an inquiry-based mathematics subject for their teacher education program, a group of final-year preservice teachers conducted four 1-hour sessions with a Year 4 class from an inner city state school. On their first visit they provided calculators, counters and a variety of other concrete materials to help the children investigate the problem: The answer is 20. What's the question?

The children were encouraged to work in small groups and to be as creative as they possibly could. At first the investigation did not seem to spark much enthusiasm in the class, and the student teachers starting wondering why a task that had appealed to them did not seem very motivating to Year 4 children. While moving around the room to help motivate groups of students, one preservice teacher noticed the recordings of two boys (Figure 11.4). After making a number of fairly typical responses, the boys had recorded '$d + p = 20$' and '$y - e = 20$'. At first the student teacher panicked as she thought, 'Algebra! I don't understand algebra. What do I do now?' Her first reaction was to ignore the boys and to continue encouraging the other children. But she became intrigued as to how the boys started on the 'different' line of thought. After sharing her dilemma with her peers, the group of preservice teachers decided to allow the boys to share their discoveries with the rest of the class and see where that would lead them.

The boys explained, 'We got the idea from television and a song we heard—'it's as simple as 1, 2, 3, . . . a, b, c'. So we gave every letter in the alphabet a number and then tried to add or take away letters that would equal 20'. The other children were so intrigued by this discovery that they started similar investigations themselves (Figure 11.5). The class was no longer interested in the initial investigation; the children were now all following different lines of inquiry. Some children decided to find out the total value of all the letters in their name and others made up short sentences so as to investigate the value as indicated by the letters. The children became so intrigued with their investigations that no one wanted to leave for morning tea when the bell rang.

On returning to university to report on their experiences, the preservice teachers were anxious to tell their peers 'This inquiry-based teaching really works!' They were pleased with their decision to follow the children's line of inquiry. Despite having to deviate from the security of their prepared lesson plan, they felt that the learning that had occurred was more worthwhile than they had conceived possible.

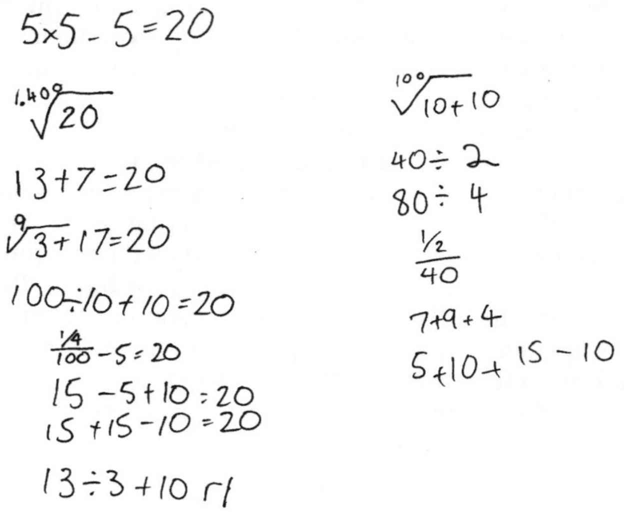

$$5 \times 5 - 5 = 20$$

$$\sqrt[1.409]{20} \qquad \sqrt[100]{10 + 10}$$

$$13 + 7 = 20 \qquad 40 \div 2$$

$$\sqrt[9]{3} + 17 = 20 \qquad 80 \div 4$$

$$100 \div 10 + 10 = 20 \qquad \frac{1/2}{40}$$

$$\frac{1/4}{100} - 5 = 20$$

$$7 + 9 + 4$$

$$15 - 5 + 10 = 20$$

$$5 + 10 + 15 - 10$$

$$15 + 15 - 10 = 20$$

$$13 \div 3 + 10 \ rl$$

Figure 11.4 Two Year 4 boys' responses to 'The answer is 20. What's the question?'

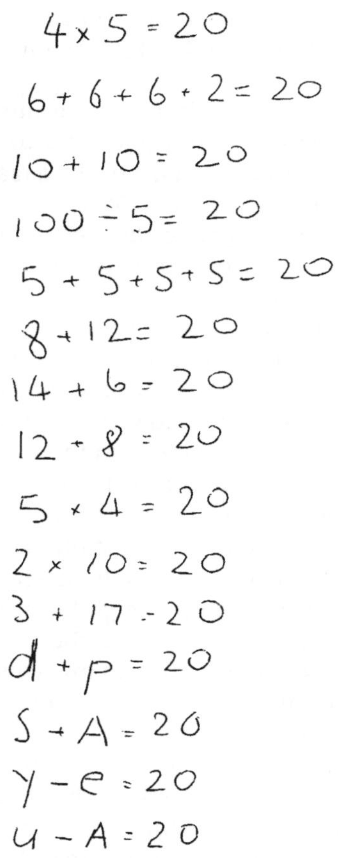

$$4 \times 5 = 20$$

$$6 + 6 + 6 + 2 = 20$$

$$10 + 10 = 20$$

$$100 \div 5 = 20$$

$$5 + 5 + 5 + 5 = 20$$

$$8 + 12 = 20$$

$$14 + 6 = 20$$

$$12 + 8 = 20$$

$$5 \times 4 = 20$$

$$2 \times 10 = 20$$

$$3 + 17 = 20$$

$$d + p = 20$$

$$S + A = 20$$

$$y - e = 20$$

$$u - A = 20$$

Figure 11.5 Year 4 investigations changed direction after learning about other children's discoveries

Part 3 Facilitating mathematics learning

In the scenario just presented, the investigation was initiated with an open-ended question. Such questions have many benefits compared with closed-type questions. Sullivan and Clarke (1991) suggested that open-ended questions are usually 'good' questions because they:

+ often involve higher level thinking, as they do not involve just the recall of facts;
+ can stimulate further investigation because they often require more than one response;
+ are suitable for a wide range of abilities, as all students can usually answer to some degree;
+ provide opportunities for further learning to occur as students go about answering the question;
+ provide opportunities for assessment as students demonstrate what they know about a topic rather than what they do not know;
+ promote discussion and collaboration as students investigate the likelihood of additional answers; and
+ challenge students' beliefs about mathematics problems only requiring one right answer.

Questions of this nature encourage children to explore mathematical situations because they are not limited by the boundaries created when questions requiring one correct answer are the focus. However, such questions require that time be provided to enable worthwhile investigations to be conducted.

While asking 'good' starter questions is important, it is also essential that teachers continue the momentum and at times focus children's attentions so that they do not bypass discoveries. Careful questioning must be used to stimulate critical reflective thinking of the mathematical properties, relationships and patterns emerging from mathematical investigations.

The role of the teacher

Teachers make hundreds of decisions regarding appropriate instructional strategies each day. The complexity of the options teachers face has been presented visually by Bredekamp and Rosegrant (1993, p. 39) as a continuum ranging from non-directive to directive behaviours (see Figure 11.6). According to the Bredekamp and Rosegrant continuum, the least directive behaviour is to withhold all interaction with a student. To stand back and observe can be a frustrating experience for many teachers as the temptation to assist is a strong urge in most adults. To give positive affirmation of a job well done is at times unnecessary and can be damaging if it is false or overused. The act of succeeding often provides enough intrinsic reward for the learner. On the other hand, acknowledging students' achievements from time to time can keep a child involved in a particular activity for a longer period.

At the other extreme, *direct instruction* may be required when it is essential that children complete a process in one particular way. For most students, few such instances would be warranted. However, it is common practice in many classrooms for teachers to prescribe specific methods for solving pen-and-paper computations, while in reality a number of written methods can derive correct solutions to such computations. Often an over-reliance on textbooks and methods learnt by rote during their own time at school directs teachers to instruct students in 'one' method.

The degree to which a particular range of behaviours is utilised more often than another is indicative of the type of learning environment operating. While an inquiry-based learning environment might herald greater use of the non-directive and mediating teacher

Non-directive	Mediating	Directive
Acknowledge / Model / Facilitate / Support / Scaffold / Co-construct / Demonstrate / Direct		

Figure 11.6 Bredekamp and Rosegrant's teaching continuum

behaviours, it is important to realise that all types of behaviours are essential components of an efficient learning environment. The difficulty arises as to which one best suits a particular child in a particular context to achieve the desired outcomes.

Given the pivotal role that instructional decisions play in determining the type of learning environment established by a classroom teacher, Bredekamp and Rosegrant (1993) suggest the term 'orchestrate' to refer to the teacher's role:

> *The teacher orchestrates the learning environment by coordinating and facilitating numerous activities, moving around, monitoring children's social and cognitive needs, assisting when needed, encouraging and acknowledging children's efforts, and challenging them to new levels of learning.*

(p. 41)

REFLECTION ON A CLASSROOM SCENARIO B
Introducing decimal fractions

Consider the way the teacher orchestrates the learning in the following scenario.

While introducing decimal fractions to Year 3, Janice demonstrated the use of skip counting by hundredths and tenths using the overhead projector calculator. One little boy became particularly intrigued by the idea of having so many numbers between whole numbers. Almost a week after the class had been introduced to skip counting by hundredths, he approached Janice with an interesting question: 'How many numbers are there between zero and one?' At this point, Janice was faced with a number of alternative strategies for satisfying this boy's curiosity. She could have embarked on an explanation of number theory and the notion that there are an infinite number of numbers between any two numbers, but the likelihood that such an explanation would induce a leap of understanding of how our number system is structured was unlikely. Instead, she decided to find out more about the boy's understanding of number and asked, 'What makes you think that there are lots of numbers between zero and one?' The boy explained his thinking: 'Well, if I draw a number line from zero to one and count by hundredths, there are still gaps between each of the hundredths'. Obviously, his understanding of there being a hundred hundredths between the two numbers had caused him to extrapolate the existence of other numbers between the hundredths. Janice asked, 'Do you think if you draw another number line from zero to one hundredth it would help you find out?' The boy returned to his desk and immediately set to work. He returned a few minutes later with a workbook illustrating a carefully drawn line that extended from one side of the page to the other. At one end of the line was the symbol for zero and at the other end was 0.01. Between the two numerals he had placed numerous pencil marks at evenly spaced intervals along the line. In attempting to explain his number line, the boy revealed his thinking process and came to new insights. 'The numbers would have to be smaller than hundredths, maybe thousandths.' Janice decided to see how far the boy's insight could go with some more prompting. 'Would there be more numbers between your thousandths then?' Almost immediately, the boy's eyes enlarged and his mouth opened slightly. He looked straight into Janice's eyes and exclaimed, 'There could be billions and billions! Wow!'

This child's thinking was challenged, his original problem was investigated, his hypothesis was tested, his interest was heightened through further investigations, and his ownership of the problem was encouraged, with the result that he was able to advance to a more sophisticated level of understanding.

Technology-rich learning environments

There is no doubt that computers and calculators are already a major part of the learning environment, and the role of technology will increase in the future. National curriculum documents are recommending that students have easy access to calculators and computers, and that they are able to make informed decisions about when it is appropriate to use these tools and how to use them efficiently (Australian Education Council, 1991). This section will examine some of the reasons for technology being so important. It will also explore some of the ways in which teachers can manage technology in the learning environment in order to make optimum use of it.

There are three ways in which the computer can affect the mathematics classroom. The first of these is to expand the program, by using the computer to introduce additional activities. The second is to replace some of the existing topics. The third is as a tool to enhance the program. The first of these is not always desirable, as the extra activity can detract from the already full program. The third, however, is the way in which the computer should be used. The power of the computer in the mathematics classroom is its function as a tool for processing information and doing calculations, thus reducing time devoted to routine tasks, and freeing teacher and pupils to engage in higher level thinking activities.

The main types of computer applications which can be used as tools to enhance the curriculum are spreadsheets, databases, programming languages such as Logo, commercial adventure games, simulations, tutorials, and drill and practice. Particular examples of how these can be used to support various topics have been described in other chapters of this book. For example, in Chapter 9 we saw how preschool children explored the concept of randomness while creating mixed-up toys using the software package *The playroom*.

To make effective use of computers, it is important that the hardware and software are managed effectively. It is not always easy to manage resources, particularly if there is only one computer in the classroom. The following scenario provides an example of one teacher who coped effectively with such a situation.

REFLECTION ON A CLASSROOM SCENARIO

Managing limited resources

The Year 4 classroom had one stand-alone computer. The children had been working on a project in which they were using the programming language Logo to draw a picture of a face, for which each part (e.g. ear, mouth) had a predetermined perimeter (see Clements et al., 1997). The teacher decided to allocate the computer exclusively to this project for the whole day. One group of children was working at the computer, entering a program which they had written, while another group was at their desks. The previous group had discovered a 'bug' in their program, and was trying to locate it, with one child playing 'turtle' and stepping out the procedures. Other children were developing or refining their programs. Others had done as much as they could until their next turn at the computer, and were doing their language contract work. The teacher was keeping an eye on the group working at the computer and, at appropriate times, would ask such questions as 'What do you think we ought to try first? Why did you choose that? What else could we do? Do you agree or disagree with that?'

The teacher had posted a roster on the whiteboard. Each group was given a maximum of 1 hour per session, and then the group saved their work on their own floppy disk. The group using the computer currently was out of turn but needed access urgently, so had negotiated some extra time with a group that was not quite ready.

In this scenario we can see that the teacher has maximised the use of the computer by having the children work in groups of three or four. Apart from increasing the access time to the computer, another reason for the children working in groups was because of the potential of Logo activities to promote interactions between children (Williams, 1994). It is important that, within the groups, each student has his or her own responsibility. For example, a child can be responsible for one of the following: keyboard operating, record keeping or monitoring consensus decision making (Stokes, 1994). In the situation described above, they were each responsible for writing the program for one part of the face, and then worked out, together, how to arrange the pieces. The children can be responsible for the changeover between groups and, if necessary, for negotiating to trade timeslots with another group.

A way of supplementing the single stand-alone computer is for the school to have a set of laptop computers that can be brought into the classroom at times when the demand is high. For example, the laptops can be used if the pupils are all needing to use databases to enter and analyse data from their own group surveys on different topics, and if necessary they can be plugged into the network for printing. If the pupils are all working at the same activity, even if they are at different stages of their projects, the interaction between groups can be very constructive. This arrangement also enables children to access the computer as soon as the need arises, rather than having to wait for somebody else to finish.

An alternative to having a computer in the classroom is to take the class to a computer laboratory. This, of course, has the advantage that all the pupils can have access to the same piece of software at the one time, and that there are enough terminals for individual or small-group use. The disadvantage is that the class has to wait until their scheduled time in the lab, and cannot have the same spontaneous access or flexibility of access as in the classroom.

The Internet

One of the most exciting recent developments is the easy accessibility of the Internet. This enables pupils to access, compare and contrast information from a variety of sources. Pupils can have direct access to first-hand, up-to-date sources of data, or they can share information with other students doing the same task across the world. Lovitt and Clarke (1992) describe an activity in which a group of pupils use the Internet to replicate Eratosthenes' famous experiment, in which he used the distances and the angles of the sun's rays to estimate the Earth's circumference (see Lovitt & Clarke, 1992, Vol. 2, pp. 371–378).

Choosing and managing software

Another important issue is choosing and managing software. Often, the first reaction of those responsible for selecting software is to choose software which is being given good reviews, and which they expect to be popular with the children. While this motivational effect is certainly important, it is even more important that the software that is selected will not be an 'extra', but will have a significant impact on the effectiveness of their teaching. It is still the teachers who are doing the teaching, not the software, and so it is important that the software will fit in with their curricula and needs. Those responsible should choose software that would enable them to use the computer in the most effective way, as a classroom resource to support the curriculum.

It is important to manage the use of the software so that it is evenly spread across grade levels. Some good drill and practice software can be used for individual or small-group remediation right across the school. Other software, such as adventure games, would be better allocated to the grade level where it is the most likely to tie in with the maths being done in the existing program for that class. This will overcome the problem that children become so familiar with some software by the time they reach upper primary school that the teacher is unable to use it effectively. Other software can be reused, but in different ways. For example, in one school, the children had used and enjoyed the adventure game *L-A mathemagical adventure* (Association of Teachers of Mathematics, 1984) in Year 5, and with the teacher's guidance had solved the mathematical problems presented in it. The Year 6 teacher realised that they could benefit from revisiting the same problems, but exploring and investigating them in much greater depth. One problem, for example, asked them to enter a password number on a calculator which had only a few buttons functioning (4, 7, $\times$, – and =). In Year 5 they just used a 'guess and check' approach for finding the correct number, because they did not have the experience and knowledge to use more sophisticated strategies. However, in Year 6 it was possible for them to revisit the problem, and compare the effectiveness of various strategies such as working back from the answer and reaching generalisations to help them to solve the problem (Dyson & McShane, 1990).

The role of the teacher

In most situations, the computer does not, and should not, replace the teacher. The role of the teacher is still an active one, in the same way as for other independent activities: as facilitator, questioner and encourager. In asking questions, it is necessary for the teacher to appear to be working with the children, rather than leading them, asking such questions as 'What could we do next?' We saw one example of this earlier, in the description of the activity in which the children were using Logo to draw a face.

There are, however, times when it is appropriate to use the computer as a replacement for the teacher, to facilitate independent learning. For example, the teacher could prepare a hypercard tutorial stack for individuals or groups to access independently. Another example can be the use of drill and practice or tutorial software for remediation. An advantage of computer-assisted learning is its potential to provide individual programs to suit the different needs and learning styles of students, in a way which would not be practical in a group lecture or tutorial. Other advantages are the availability of immediate feedback and individualised programs, and student control of pace, sequencing and content. Furthermore, regardless of the length of time or number of attempts the student needs to complete the program, all students will end up having achieved consistent outcomes, an end point which is not as easily achievable with a one-off lecture or tutorial. There are numerous examples of appropriate software programs described in Chapters 3–9 that can facilitate independent learning.

Calculators

Many critics of the use of calculators in the classroom are concerned that their use will prevent the children from using their brains. However, there are many ways in which the calculator can be used as a carefully managed resource to promote mathematical thinking and understanding. For example, it can be useful as a tool to check what the children have already done by another method. It can empower them to make their own decisions, and find their own mistakes, rather than relying on the teacher, and thus can create a problem-solving environment. It can also be used to make classroom mathematics more relevant to real-life situations, enabling children to work with the numbers that occur in real-world contexts such as shopping. Another way in which a calculator can be utilised is to investigate whether the rules or patterns children have found will always work, even with big numbers which they might not yet know how to multiply in their heads or with pencil and paper (Sullivan & Clarke, 1990). If they have the calculator to do the routine computations for them, they are able to keep their minds focused on the investigation itself. The use of the calculator does not mean that children no longer need to learn algorithms, but it does mean that there needs to be an increase in attention to developing estimation skills and strategies for mental calculation. In particular, they need to be able to recognise the 'sensibleness' of their answers (Bobis, 1991).

Often, a teacher will deliberately give only one calculator to a group, to encourage co-operation. If they have a calculator each, they are more likely to ignore each other and work independently, even though they are sitting in a group. With one child operating the calculator, it becomes necessary for the others to interact, and contribute their ideas to the group outcome.

INSTRUCTIONAL STRATEGIES FOR ENHANCING THE LEARNING ENVIRONMENT

Grouping for instruction

Basically there are three ways of grouping students for instruction: whole-class instruction, individual instruction and small-group instruction. Whole-class instruction is perhaps the most familiar instructional mode for mathematics and, while individualised instruction is rarely practical when large groups of students are concerned, it is often used when children are noted to have specific learning needs. Small-group work is also used, often when teachers wish to focus on four to six children with similar needs. While all three modes of instruction have their place in an environment emphasising rich and meaningful mathematics, it is through the use of small groups of children working collaboratively that desirable outcomes that are in accord with the views expressed in current curriculum documents may be achieved both academically and attitudinally.

The following discussion focuses on the use of collaborative group work in a variety of settings. It presents the merits of collaborative group work, strategies for grouping, guidelines for developing co-operative skills, and activities that can be used to get started.

Collaborative group work

Not all group work is collaborative. Many educators arrange their children into groups and then set tasks that are completed individually or by children working in pairs. This is often the result of a number of factors—the children may not have been taught co-operative skills, the task may not warrant or encourage children to work co-operatively, and/or a classroom code of conduct may exist that reinforces silent work. By collaborative group work, it is intended that the entire group work together towards the same goal.

A great deal of research evidence revealing the benefits of collaborative group work has accumulated in the past few decades (e.g. Dalton, 1985; Johnson & Johnson, 1990). Collectively, the findings demonstrate that when the environment is structured to allow for co-operative learning it can promote:

+ higher academic achievement;
+ divergent thinking in problem-solving situations;
+ intrinsic motivation to learn;
+ autonomous learning behaviour;
+ positive self-esteem;
+ positive attitudes towards the subject area in which it is being used and to school in general;
+ mutual respect and concern for others;
+ acceptance and understanding of individual differences.

Each of these points reflects characteristics inherent in learning environments advocated in modern mathematics syllabus documents. Additionally, the last two points have implications particularly important for teachers wanting to sensitise students to issues of gender equity, ethnicity, aboriginality, and students with special needs.

Strategies for grouping

Groups can be formed according to ability, friendships, interests, needs or simply by random assignment. Those formed in line with friendship and interests are more successful at working collaboratively, particularly when children are being introduced to the skills of co-operative learning. Coercing students to work with children of the opposite sex or of different ethnic backgrounds when they have little experience of collaborative work skills may only aggravate existing tensions.

The construction of a sociogram is one strategy that is helpful in determining which children would like to work together. This may be done simply by asking the children to list the names of children they would select to play a popular mathematics game or help solve a challenging problem. From the lists, a sociogram could be constructed similar to that presented in Figure 11.7.

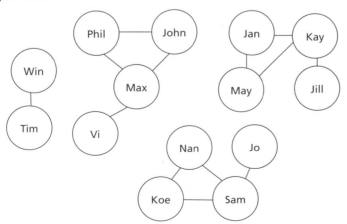

Figure 11.7 A sociogram highlighting the friendship groupings in a classroom

Once routines for working in collaborative groups are established, the learning environment can be structured so children slowly take responsibility for decision making—including decisions regarding the structure of groups. It must be noted, however, that it may take a year to teach all the skills necessary for collaborative learning to work effectively and even longer before co-operative skills are utilised by students automatically (Johnson & Johnson, 1990).

Guidelines for developing co-operative skills

Co-operative learning skills are social skills that are learnt through a process of explicit teaching, practice, feedback and reflection. Skills required to form and work in groups, to solve problems and to manage differences can be taught through a variety of strategies including role-play, games and brainstorming sessions. Whatever strategy is adopted, it needs to be accompanied by discussion to ensure that the co-operative skills witnessed have been made explicit. For instance, after playing the game 'Silence' (described on the following page) a group of Year 5 children brainstormed the following list of behaviours they believed helped their group complete the task successfully:

+ waiting for others to have their turn;
+ watching to see what pieces other people needed;
+ placing unwanted pieces in the centre for others to use;
+ helping someone else when I finished;
+ sitting in a circle so we could see everyone's pieces.

After making such behaviours explicit, it is necessary to repeat the activities to practise their application. Feedback can be provided by the teacher, but it can also be encouraged to come from other group members when they witness co-operative behaviour in practice. Of course, different situations will necessitate different co-operative skills, so the learning process will need to be repeated for a variety of contexts.

Activities that build co-operative group skills

The process of learning co-operative skills is aided if appropriate activities are provided along with guidelines on how to proceed. Hill and Hill (1990, p. 7) suggested that the 'two essential elements in any co-operative activity are goal similarity and positive interdependence'. Positive interdependence occurs when individuals believe that they can succeed only if they work together. This can be achieved by giving students specific roles to play, such as 'reporter', or by assigning group members subtasks that, when the results of each are combined, complete the group's work (see the game 'Silence' described below).

If the aim is to develop cohesiveness and co-operation in the learning environment, the activities we choose must be scrutinised carefully. The following activities were selected for their non-competitive nature and the fact that they do not rely on weaker players being eliminated for the game to proceed. While the co-operative nature of each activity engenders fun and interest, the underlying mathematical skill or concepts being practised will need to be made more explicit through discussion and other examples.

'Set and match'
Year level: Various
Maths skill: Classification of shapes

Children are given pictures of various objects such as illustrations of 2D shapes or 3D objects, or pictures of fruit or animals. Alternatively, if everyday items are chosen such as pegs and straws, the children could be given the actual object. The children move around to find other children with pictures or objects that match theirs in some way. Introducing the rule that there is to be no talking during this part of the activity encourages interesting use of non-verbal communication skills. The number of matching cards required to make a group or set can be determined by the age and ability of the children undertaking the activity. When they have found the required number of group members, they must discuss the reasons for selecting each member for entry into the set and decide on a name that best describes their set. More capable children might like to discuss the notion of each person belonging to another group at the same time. To extend the activity, ask children to find another group of people in which they feel they may also belong. In this way, the activity could continue for some time. Groups are formed randomly, regardless of the gender balance or ability levels of the children involved.

'Silence'

Year level: Various
Maths skill: Visual imagery, visual memory, flipping, sliding, turning of 2D shapes
Materials: Six cardboard shapes (circles are used here), each cut into three pieces, for example:

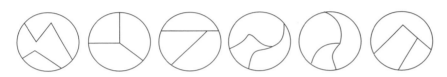

Children work in groups of six (though this can vary, depending on the number of shapes used). The cardboard pieces are shuffled and each player is dealt three pieces. There are three rules for players to follow:

1. Silence—no verbal communication is permitted.
2. Each player can have only three pieces at any one time.
3. Players cannot take a piece from another person. Pieces not wanted are placed in the centre of the table for other players to take. Players can take pieces only from this pile.

As the activity proceeds, students try to fit their pieces together to make their shape whole again, following the rules. The activity is complete once each member has successfully completed his or her shape. Co-operation is encouraged by students surrendering pieces to the centre of the table that other students need to complete their shape. Collaboration can be encouraged if groups of students pit themselves against the clock, rather than against each other.

After completing the activity a number of times, encourage the students to discuss the strategies they use to complete their shapes. Emphasise the skills of visualisation and the mathematics of flipping, sliding and turning. The activity can be made simpler by placing a thick outline around the perimeter of the shapes before cutting them into pieces or by using card that is coloured differently on the two sides.

Making group work work

While even preschool children can be taught co-operative learning skills, factors such as the appropriateness of the task, the number and composition of the group, the resources available, prior experiences with collaborative learning environments and the expectations of the educational facilitator will determine the degree of success for each activity. A number of organisational factors will also contribute to the successful implementation of group work, whether the focus is on collaboration or not. The following list provides some guidelines for organising small group work and is applicable to a variety of settings:

+ Ensure that children understand what group they are in and where they are to work.
+ Give clear instructions and ensure children understand their task and the required outcomes.
+ Keep group sizes small (about 4–6) if collaboration is required.
+ Assign roles to students (e.g. observer, recorder) to encourage participation by all.
+ Have resources ready and easily accessible to students.
+ Ensure that some groups will be able to work independently.
+ Provide adequate space to allow all members of each group to work together.
+ Establish time limits for group work at the outset.
+ Provide time for sharing group achievements with the rest of the class.
+ Establish routines for packing away materials.
+ Ensure that students know what to do if they finish before other groups.
+ Provide immediate feedback regarding co-operative skills during the group work time.
+ Provide students time to reflect on the benefits of working collaboratively and to assess their own contribution/performance.

The use of games in the mathematics classroom

Games usually have elements of play in them but proceed according to a set of rules and often rely on some degree of chance, skill, strategy or endurance, with the major goal being that of winning over an opponent. If the rules become too rigid or complex, the element of fun is lost and it may no longer be considered a game but 'hard work', particularly for young children.

From about the age of 2 years, children begin to engage in games that involve simple rules ('Ring around the roses' instructs all children to 'fall down' at the end of the game), but it is usually not until the age of 7 years that most children are able to devise strategies, and become concerned about winning and following the same rules as everyone else playing the game. This has important implications for the 'games' we provide children in the first few years of school. Mannigel (1992, p. 65) suggested that children in the 4–6-year age range be restricted to very 'simple board games and card games, where the game has a meaning for the child, and when the group is very small: only two or three play'.

Many educators have advocated the use of games for teaching mathematics (Hughes, 1986; Kamii, 1985; Skemp, 1989), but an important question must be asked: Can mathematics be taught effectively through games?

It is advocated generally that well-designed games provide students with opportunities for practice, revision, concept-and-skill development, social interaction, co-operative learning and discussion, and for having fun with mathematics in a non-threatening environment. It is also claimed that games have the potential to enhance student autonomy in learning and develop positive attitudes towards mathematics (Mannigel, 1992). While a well-designed game may help create a good environment for learning mathematics, it will not necessarily ensure that the mathematics is learnt. Research by Higgins (1992) indicates that children in the 5–6-year age range often focus on other aspects of games, such as turn-taking, rather than the mathematical experiences intended by the teacher. Experienced teachers will no doubt recall similar experiences even in upper primary classrooms. Such distractions, however, may be avoided if a few guiding principles are followed such as those outlined by Aldridge and Badham (1993). For example:

+ Use games that address specific objectives rather than as time-fillers for fast workers or rainy sport days.

+ Introduce one or two new games at a time and use only five or six games in a classroom at a time.

+ Choose games that have only a few simple rules. Too much time spent learning the rules detracts from time playing the game and experiencing the mathematics.

+ Choose games where the rules remain the same but the mathematics can be varied.

+ When new games are introduced, remove (temporarily) those that may have become tiresome. Changing the games too often may cause confusion and arguments about the rules.

+ Have an adult play with the children occasionally to model and reinforce good game-playing behaviour (see the 'well-focused attention' strategy described below).

+ Provide immediate positive feedback to children when you witness good strategy-use and game-playing behaviour.

+ Use games that involve two to four players, as this decreases the waiting time between turns.

+ Keep completion times short so that a variety of children can be 'winners'.

+ Choose games that have an element of chance. This allows weaker children to feel they have a chance of winning.

+ Choose games with goals that are challenging and intrinsically interesting.

+ Include games that require genuine mathematical thinking, rather than just computations.

+ Allow the children to make their own games.

Developing autonomy in learners through games

The instructional process in all learning settings can be facilitated when students are autonomous learners. Most children, however, remain 'dependent' learners for much of their formal school life and even into adulthood. These children are not aware of strategies that assist learning or even of how they can get help to learn. Learning environments that focus on teacher-directed and whole-class instruction reinforce behaviour that is teacher-dependent. For these children, the use of group works, games and other settings lacking in direct teacher instruction can be problematic. 'Well-focused attention' is a teaching strategy for promoting autonomy in learning (Mannigel, 1992). It is based on the idea that short periods of deliberate and focused attention from an adult can establish strategies that continue independently. The following excerpt illustrates the strategy used by a preschool teacher as two children play a card game. While both children have played the game before, the educator has deliberately placed Fran, who is in need of help, with a child considered to be an 'independent' learner.

Julie: My turn. (She turns two cards over and gets a matching pair.) Yeah! I got two fish. I remembered there was a fish there from my last turn.

Fran: Is it my go now?

T: What do you think? Has Julie finished her turn?

Fran: OK, my turn. (She turns one card over.)

T: Stop, Fran. Think. Can you remember if you've seen a cow before?

Fran: I think I can. (She slowly scans the upside-down cards in front of her.) I think it's this one. (She turns a card to reveal a second picture of a cow.) I did it! Two cows.

T: Good thinking. I liked the way you took your time to remember where the other card was.

Julie: My turn again.

Fran: Julie's turn.

The teacher in this excerpt focuses her attention on Fran and makes comments about appropriate learning strategies needed to succeed in the game. Rather than answering her question regarding whose turn it was, the teacher asked a question that required Fran to think for herself about the logical sequence occurring in the game. She also reminds her of the strategy to think about previous turns to help find a matching pair of cards. Immediate feedback is provided to promote the child's self-awareness of the learning strategy. Feedback is specific to the strategy practised rather than in the form of global statements acknowledging 'good work'. By developing children's self-awareness of effective learning strategies over extended time, teachers can encourage the development of autonomous learners.

SUMMARY AND IMPLICATIONS FOR CLASSROOM PRACTICE

This chapter has emphasised the importance of the learning environment in stimulating children to learn mathematics. A range of aspects concerning learning environments was dealt with in the attempt to support educators in establishing and maintaining conditions most conducive to learning mathematics in their particular contexts.

While physical aspects of the learning environment are influential in determining the quality of learning, they are really only reflections of the philosophical approaches adopted by educators and their associated institutions. We must increase our sensitivity to the importance of the socially and emotionally constructed environment.

As issues about what it means to be mathematically prepared for an increasingly technological society have become a more prominent concern of educational authorities and the broader community, certain expectations for curricula content and instructional style have gained in significance of late. Current curriculum documents from around the world advocate changes in teaching practices that focus on students seeking solutions, exploring patterns and formulating conjectures (National Research Council, 1989). From such a perspective, learning mathematics is seen to be 'empowering' for students. If teaching is to emphasise these processes students will need to study mathematics in an exploratory and dynamic way, not as a static, absolute body of procedures to be memorised. This perspective of teaching and learning is in accordance with a learning environment which focuses on inquiry and investigation, and utilises available resources including appropriate technology.

Within environments that focus on autonomous learning and inquiry, the teacher's role is different from what has been traditionally considered appropriate. The ideal environment in which mathematics might be learnt best means the teacher must adopt a variety of roles, such as observer, facilitator, model, director and organiser. It was suggested in this chapter that perhaps the best description for the teacher's role is that of 'orchestrator'. Creating and maintaining mathematics learning environments as advocated in this chapter is a challenge to all teachers, whether they be beginning teachers or teachers with many years of experience.

ACTION AND REFLECTION

To conclude this chapter, we would like to invite you to reflect upon your present context for learning mathematics by working through the following points. Children are learning all the time, even during transitions from one activity to another, so when we are evaluating environments we need to consider whether:

1. the physical environment has:
   + a wide range of concrete materials, both commercially and non-commercially available;
   + all materials clearly labelled and easily accessible to students;
   + posters, literature books with mathematical content, TV guides, timetables, newspapers and the like for children to access easily;
   + children's work displayed around the room;
   + spaces for children to work in groups;
   + spaces that are conducive to discussion between students and between adults and students;
   + spaces where children can work with concrete materials;
   + spaces where children can work quietly and reflect on their experiences.

2. the social environment:
   + encourages students to consistently explain and justify their ideas and thinking strategies, whether they be right or wrong;
   + provides sufficient time to allow exploration of new materials or concepts;
   + encourages adults to talk to children about the processes they use to solve problems;
   + encourages adults and children to discuss mathematics from everyday experiences, such as those occurring on food packaging and in newspapers;
   + encourages students to make sense of the mathematics they do;
   + encourages students to work independently or collaboratively to solve mathematical problems before going to the teacher;
   + fosters questions that will encourage higher order thinking rather than just recall;
   + explicitly encourages the development of skills necessary for collaborative group work;
   + encourages students to take risks by asking questions and formulating conjectures;
   + conveys open respect for student's mathematical ideas and creations;
   + accepts tasks that are open-ended with a wide variety of solutions;
   + encourages students to take time to think about problems, questions and ideas;
   + encourages students to show respect for, and listen to, other students;
   + is a friendly atmosphere that makes it an enjoyable place to be for adults and children.

327

REFERENCES

Aldridge, S. & Badham, V. (1993). Beyond just a game. *Pamphlet number 21*. Primary Association for Mathematics.

Association of Teachers of Mathematics. (1984). *L-A mathemagical adventure* at http://acorn.educ. nottingham.ac.uk//SchEd/pages/atm/software.html

Australian Education Council. (1991). *A national statement on mathematics for Australian schools*. Melbourne: Curriculum Corporation.

Bishop, A. & Nickson, M. (1983). *Research on the social context of mathematics education*. London: Nelson.

Bobis, J. (1991). Using a calculator to develop number sense. *Arithmetic Teacher, 38*(5), 42–45.

Bobis, J. (1996). *Report of the evaluation of the Count Me In Project*. Sydney: NSW Department of Education and Training. http//www.currriculumsupport.nsw.edu.au/maths

Bobis, J. (2000). *Count Me In Too Report: A Case study of implementation*. Sydney: NSW Department of Education and Training. http//www.currriculumsupport.nsw.edu.au/maths

Bredekamp, S. & Rosegrant, T. (1993). *Reaching potentials: Appropriate curriculum and assessment for young children*. Vol. 1. Washington, DC: National Association for the Education of Young Children.

Clements, D. H., Battista, M. T., Sarama, J., Swaminathan, S. & McMillen, S. (1997). Students' development of length concepts in a Logo-based unit on geometric paths. *Journal for Research in Mathematics Education, 28*(1), 70–95.

Dalton, J. (1985). *Adventures in thinking*. Melbourne: Thomas Nelson.

Dyson, S. & McShane, R. (1990). *Computers in secondary mathematics*. Melbourne: Barson Computers.

Ernest, P. (1988). The attitudes and practices of student teachers of primary school mathematics. In A. Borbas (Ed), *Proceedings of the 12th International Conference on the International Group for the Psychology of Mathematics Education*. Veszprem, Hungary: International Group for the Psychology of Mathematics Education.

Fennema, E. & Franke, M. (1992). Teacher's knowledge and its impact. In D. Grouws (Ed), *Handbook of research on mathematics teaching and learning* (pp. 147–164). New York: Macmillan.

Franke, M. & Carey, D. (1997). Young children's perceptions of mathematics in problem-solving environments. *Journal for Research in Mathematics Education, 28*(1), 8–25.

Higgins, J. (1992). Let's just get on with the game. The use of games to form mathematical knowledge and reasoning within the cultural context of the peer group. Paper presented at International Council of Mathematics Education 7, Quebec.

Hill, S. & Hill, T. (1990). *The collaborative classroom: A guide to co-operative learning*. Melbourne: Eleanor Curtain Publishing.

Hughes, M. (1986). *Children and number*. Oxford: Basil Blackwell.

Johnson D. W. & Johnson R. T. (1990) Using cooperative learning in math. In N. Davidson (Ed), *Co-operative learning in mathematics: A handbook for teachers* (pp. 103–125). Menlo Park, California: Addison-Wesley.

Kamii, C. (1985). *Young children reinvent arithmetic*. New York: Teachers College Press.

Lappan, G. (1993). What do we have and where do we go from here? *Arithmetic Teacher, 40*(9), 524–526.

Lovitt, C. & Clarke, D. (1992) *The mathematics curriculum and teaching program*. Vol. 2 (pp. 371–378). Melbourne: Curriculum Corporation.

Mannigel, D. (1992). *Young children as mathematicians: Theory and practice for teaching mathematics*. Wentworth Falls: Social Science Press.

National Council of Teachers of Mathematics. (2000). *Principles and standards for school mathematics*. Reston, Virginia: National Council of Teachers of Mathematics.

National Research Council. (1989). *Everybody counts: A report to the nation on the future of mathematics education*. Washington, DC: National Academy Press.

Skemp, R. (1989). *Mathematics in the primary school*. London: Routledge.

Sowell, E. (1989). Effects of manipulative materials in mathematics instruction. *Journal for Research in Mathematics Education, 26*, 498–505.

Stokes, J. (1994). Problem-solving and metacognition with computers. In M. Ryan (Ed), *Proceedings of the Asia Pacific Information Technology in Training and Education Conference* (pp. 107–113). Brisbane.

Sullivan, P. & Clarke, D. (1990). Calculators, mathematics and the early years of schooling. *Australian Journal of Early Childhood, 15*(1), 17–22.

Sullivan, P. & Clarke, D. (1991). *Communication in the classroom: The importance of good questioning*, Deakin: Deakin University Press.

Thompson, A. (1992). Teachers' beliefs and conceptions: A synthesis of the research. In D. Grouws (Ed), *Handbook of research on mathematics teaching and learning* (pp. 127–146). New York: Macmillan.

Williams, E. (1994). Metacognitive problem solving in primary school classrooms: A gentle introduction to technology. In M. Ryan (Ed), *Proceedings of the Asia Pacific Information Technology in Training and Education Conference* (pp. 67–72). Brisbane.

329

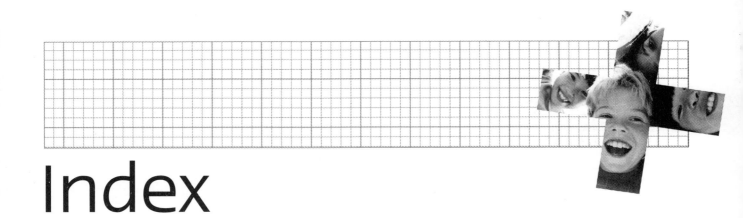

Index

2D plans   105–9
2D shapes   98–101
3D shapes   96–101
3D space   202–4

addition
  algorithm   170
  problems   138–40
  process   133
  strategies   161–62
air pollution index   79–80
air traffic investigations   180–81
Aldridge, S.   13
algorithms, written   157, 170–76
angles   109–11
animals, data   74–76
answers, reasonable   158–59
approximations   66, 158–59, 168, 181–82, 217
area   234, 235
arithmetical strategies   132–35
arrangement   88–89, 105–11
arrays   146–47, 165–66
assessment
  definition   274
  early number   137–38
  gathering evidence   274, 275
  individual interviews   287–89
  interpreting evidence   276
  linking with instruction   272, 275–76
  observation   277, 278, 279
  place value   131–32
  planning   275
  portfolios   285–87
  questioning   277–81
  at state level   283
  using evidence   276
  various strategies   276–77
  worksamples   282
  written tests   282–85
average   63, 64, 209–11

balance   231–33
Baroody, A.J.   41
base ten strategies   127–29, 130–31
Battista, M.   99, 112
bead string   206
benchmarks   see Numeracy benchmarks
billions   182–84

Bishop, A.J.   89
Bobis, J.   13
Boulton-Lewis, G.   157
Bowers, J.   171
bowling strike rates   212–13
box task   18–19
Bredekamp, S.   315, 316
Bruner, J.   7
budget billions   182–84
Burrill, G.   31

Cain, R.   13
calculator patterns   144
calculators
  computations, solving   160
  decimals, using with   197
  mathematical thinking, promoting   320
  number learning   143–44
  patterns, investigating   38
Callingham, R.   276
Campbell, K.J.   194
capacity   239–41
Carey, D.   312
Carpenter, T.   13
census, school   61–64
chance   245–68
chance of rain   253–55
Clarke, D.   318
classifying   123–24, 201
classroom layout   308–9
Clements, D.H.   112
Clements, M.   16
clock face   19–20
Clyne, M.   16
Cobb, P.   8, 64, 171
Cockcroft, W.   16
Collis, K.F.   194
communication modes   16
commutativity   166
comparisons   217, 218
computers
  effective use   317–18
  geometric reasoning, promoting   111–14
  graphing program   23–25, 61, 62
  software   319
  spatial awareness, promoting   111–14
  teacher's role   319
concrete materials   309–10

331

conjecturing 36
constructivism
    principles 7–12
    teacher education 13
cooperative skills 48, 322–23
coordinating units 192
Count Me In Too project 135–37
counting 65
counting patterns 178–79
cricket data 212–13
cubes 96–97

data
    categorising 66–68
    classifying 66–68
    collecting 68–69
    continuous 66
    discrete 66
    displaying 65
    handling 60–83
    interpreting 69–74
    organising 65
    real 60–64
    representing 69–74
    visualising 64–65
Davis, G. 192, 194
decimals
    classroom implications 213–14
    fractions, representing 206
    multiplication 21–23
    rational numbers 189
    understanding 196–200
decomposition 170, 171
Del Campo. G. 16
die, rolling 258–60
Dienes, Z. 6, 7, 15
discovery learning 12
displays 310
distance 229
distribution 63
division
    algorithm 174–77
    problems 140–43
    process 134–35
    semiformal routines 168–69
    strategies 163–64
    using decimals 207–9
dog growth, data 81–83
dot pattern cards 125
Duplo 202–4

Early Years Numeracy Program 137
Edwards, R. 63
Ellerton, N. 16
empty number line 130, 161, 169
English, L. 49
equal addends 170–72
equal grouping 127–29, 145
estimating 125, 168, 217
evaluation 274–75

fair shares 194
First Fleet convicts 83–84
Fischbein, E. 249

floor space 309
food fractions 204–5
Forster, M. 285
fractions 189–96, 213–14
frameworks, developmental 290–92
Franke, M. 312
furniture, classroom 309

games, for teaching mathematics 324–26
games of chance 255–57
Gardiner, H. 99
Gelistel, C. 13
Gelman, R. 13
geometrical understandings 87, 90–92, 96
Gervasconi, A. 132
graphs
    bar 70, 71, 75
    column 61–62, 71, 73, 79, 82, 83
    computer-generated 61, 62–63, 76
    informal 62, 69
    line 71, 73, 74
    picture 71, 73, 76, 77, 79, 81, 201
    pie 72
Gravemeijer, K. 64
Gray, E. 18
'Greedy pig' game 264–66
grids 65
Griffiths, R. 16
group work 320–24
grouping 65, 127–29, 130–31, 145
Groves, S. 143
growth chart 81–83

'Heads or tails' game 246–49, 250
hectares 236–39
height 34–36
Hill, S. and T. 322
home environment, mathematics in 311
'Horse race' game 262–64
hot and cold 226–27
house plans 98–101
Hughes, M. 13, 18
hundreds chart 119–21, 162–63
Hunting, R.P. 192, 194

independent events 250
Inhelder, B. 249
Internet
    access to real data 318
    names of large numbers 182, 184
    as starting point 34
interviews, student 287–89
inverse relationships 167
investigating 32–34

Jones, G. 249

Kieren, T. 18

Lamon, S. 194
language, role in learning mathematics 16–17
law of large numbers 250
learning
    constructivist principles 7–8

reflection 7
social process 8
theories 6–7
learning environment 303–27
 classroom implications 326
 computers and calculators 317–20
 determining factors 304–7
 inquiry-based 312–16
 outside the classroom 311
 physical elements 308–11
 teacher's role 315
Learning Framework in Number 135–37
Lego 202–4
length 228–31, 235
lesson plans 295–300
Liebeck, P. 12
likelihood 250
links, making 148–51, 202–4
literature, children's, time concepts 222–25
location 88–89, 105–11
Lovitt, C. 318

Mannigel, D. 324
maps, interpreting 32–34, 53–54
mass 34–36, 232
Masters, G. 285
matching 65, 123–24
materials to develop mathematical thinking 122
mathematics
 children's understandings 17–25
 conceptions 3–5
 definitions 4
 formal 14
 informal 13–15
 processes 29–30
mathematics learning
 children's 5–7
 teachers' 3–5
maths trails 311
McClain, K. 64, 171
McIntosh, A. 157
mean 63, 64
measurement 216–44
 classroom implications 243–44
 informal 218
 links to science, technology and mathematics 241–43
 standard units 228–33
median 63, 64
mental computation strategies 129–30, 157, 159, 160
Mitchelmore, M. 13, 109
mixed-up toys 251–53
mode 63, 64
Moser, J. 13
Mulligan, J. 13
multiplication
 algorithm 172–74
 derived facts 165
 problems 140–43
 process 134–35
 semiformal routines 168–69
 strategies 163–64
 using decimals 207–9

notating 123–24
number concepts 65, 117, 125–27
number learning, problem-based 137–43, 158
number learning programs 135–37
number learning research 121–23
number sense 155–56, 185–86
numeracy 5
Numeracy benchmarks 282–83
numerical relationships 177–78

observation 277, 278, 279
ordering 65, 123–24
outcomes-based education 276–77

partitioning
 addition and subtraction strategies 161
 base ten strategies 130–31
 fractions 194
 multiplication 169
 problems 134
 processes 65
patterns
 investigating 36–39
 recognising 125
 using calculators 144
Pegg, J. 91–92
'Pegs in a bag' activity 266–67
perimeter 234, 235
Piaget, J. 6–7, 15, 105, 249
pie charts 61, 63
'Pigs might fly' 261–62
Pirie, S. 18
place value 197
play 15–16
The playroom (computer software) 251
portfolios 285–87
Postle, D. 241
pre-number learning 123–24
prior knowledge 13
probability 245–68
 conditional 250
 theoretical 250
problem-based number learning 137–43, 158
problem solving 40–43
 affective factors 47–48
 co-operative tasks 48
 inquiry-based learning 312
 mathematical thinking 43–54
 representing problem 44–45
 strategies 45–47
problems
 open-ended 42
 posing 49
 real 41–42
 routine word 41–42
 types 41
processes, mathematical 29–30
program, mathematics, overcrowding 273–74
programming 293–98
proportion 189–90

quadrilaterals 93–95
questioning 277–81
 closed and open questions 278, 280, 313–15

333

quotion problems   134

random   250
range   63, 64
rate   190, 212–13
ratio   189, 193
rational numbers   189
real data   60–64
reasonableness of answers   158–59
reasoning, probabilistic   249
reflection on mathematical processes   7, 36–39
reflections (symmetry)   101, 103–5
regrouping   168–69
reporting   289–90
resources, physical   309–10
rolls, bags and boxes   147–48
Rosegrant, T.   315, 316
rotations   101, 103–5

sample space   250
Sandhill race   209–11
scales, numerical   10, 71
Schoenfeld, A.H.   48
see-saw, balancing   231–33
sequencing   161
'Set and match' activity   322–23
shape and structure   88, 96–101
shapes
    identifying   93–95
    manipulating   90–91
'Silence' activity   323
Silver, E.A.   39, 49
Smarties survey   23–25
social interaction   8, 12, 322
spatial understandings   87–114
'split and jump'   161–62
sprinkler system project   219–21
square metres   235–36
Stacey, K.   143
Stafford, A.   13
standardised tests   282–83
Steward, R.   13
structure   88, 96–101, 123
subitising   125
subtraction
    algorithm   171–72
    problems   138–40
    process   133
    strategies   161–62
surveys, Smarties   23–25
symbolising   39–40, 201
symmetry   20–21, 88, 101–5

Tall, D.   18
teachers
    memories of learning mathematics   3–5
    pedagogical knowledge   306
technology, using   34, 111–14, 317–20
temperature   8–12, 225–27
    and time   227–28
tessellations   102–3
tests, written
    standardised   282–83
    teacher-constructed   283–85
thermometers   8–12
'Think Board'   132
thinking, mathematical   31–40, 43–54, 55
thinking before computing   181–82
time   222–25
    literature-based activities   222–25
    and temperature   227–28
timetables, train, interpreting   36
toy collection, data   76–78, 201
transformation   88, 101–5

understanding, mathematical   17–25, 30
    classroom practice   26
    teacher's role   25
units, measurement   228–33

van Hiele, P.   91
visual thinking   64–65, 89, 98, 127
volume   49–52, 234, 239–41
Vygotsky, L.   7, 8, 15

Watanabe, T.   192
Watson, A.   280
Watson, J.M.   194
weather forecasting   253–55
websites
    large numbers   182, 184
    numeracy   311
    state education   285
Weir, M.   289
'what-if' situations   36
White, P.   109
Wood, T.   8, 278
word problems   41–42
worksamples   282
Wright, B.   13
written computation strategies   159–60
written tests   282–85

Yackel, E.   8
Young-Loveridge, J.   13

zone of proximal development   12–13

334